THE REVELATION:

A Reading of the Vision and Letter of John to the Churches

Mark A. McDonald, Ph. D

"The Revelation: A Reading of the Vision and Letter of John to the Churches," by Mark A. McDonald. ISBN 978-1-63868-013-0 (softcover).

Published 2021 by Virtualbookworm.com Publishing Company Inc., P.O. Box 9949, College Station, TX 77842. Copyright 2021 by Mark A. McDonald. All rights reserved. No part of this publication may be reproduced, stored in a retrieval system, or transmitted in any form or by any means, electronic, mechanical, recording or otherwise, without the prior permission of Mark A. McDonald.

Contents

Preface v
Part One: On the First Half of The Revelation 1
  i: Author, Introduction and Blessing: That it is John the Apostle Who Wrote the Revelation 1
  ii: *Tachus*, or "soon:" 31
    Were the Apostles Wrong About How Soon the End Would Come? 31
    The First Precondition 34
    The Second Reason that the Time Seems to be Quite Soon 36
    Parables of Delay 40
    The Calendar and the Six-Day Theory 40
    The Seventy Weeks of Years and The Seven Years of Years 43
    The Spread of Technology 46
    The Rapture and the Son of Lawlessness 54
    What it is That Will Occur "Soon" 57
    The Three or Four Different Readings of the Millennium 60
    Carl Jung: Antichrist and Symbol 68
    What Then Should We Do? 73
  iii: The Title, Greeting, and Introductory Vision of the Revelation 75
    Title: "The Apocalypse of John" and 1:1-4 75
  iv: The Seven Letters 87
    v: The Vision of the Throne 98
    And the Scroll 98
    The Throne 99
    Is the Rapture Portrayed Symbolically at 4:1 of the Revelation? 103
    The Scroll: Revelation Chapter Five 116
  vi: The Opening of the First Six Seals 123

The Sixth Seal	135
vii: The Seventh Seal and the Seven Trumpets	146
Chapter Nine	149
Chapter 10	154
Chapter Eleven	160
Part Two: The Second Half of the Revelation	175
i: The Woman Pursued by the Dragon (Revelation Chapter 12)	175
ii: The Beast that Arises from the Sea And the Beast that Rose Out of the Earth	197
iii: Chapter Fourteen	215
iv: The Seven Bowls of Wrath	227
Chapter 16	229
v: The Judgment of the Great Harlot	240
Digression: On the Meanings of *Babylon*	248
Digression: The Book of Daniel on the Beast	250
Revelation 17:15-18	275
Chapter 18	281
vi: Chapter 19	299
The Hallelujah Chorus	299
vii: Chapter 20: The Millennium	322
vii: The New Heaven and the New Earth	345
Chapter 21	345
Chapter 22: The River and Tree	356
The Bride	365
ix: Summary and Conclusion	372
Appendix A: The Three Secrets of Fatima	375
Appendix B: The Apocalyptic Texts	376
Index	378
Bibliography	391
Notes	397

Preface

Even more than other books, the reading of scripture unfolds with the reader, so that each time one takes up the work, it might appear anew. Commentary on ancient books is taken up in the cultivation of this unfolding. As a gardener works the yard where he finds himself to have been placed, we till the earth, bring water here and there, and work to keep up understanding. In what follows, the aim is to present a reading, and, by conversation, to enrich the reading of this book, for those who happen by. The commentary is intended for both the scholar and the layman. It is perhaps especially for the layman lured by the attraction of the mysteries to dabble in scholarship and study, or from one of this sort to another. Unlike the preachers, we will not aim to address the widest audience, but rather the most curious or perplexed. And rather than attempt a divine or theological reading, our work here is intended to be human and philosophical, and to converse with many sorts, both Christians and Jews, Romans and Greeks, Catholics and Protestants, and indeed anyone interested in what might be thought and said about these astonishing matters.

Yet unlike the scholars, I will also draw on the reading of the preachers, who with faith and inspired study make up for what may on occasion be lacking in the polish of scholarly objectivity. These do present a reading, where the scholars often seem too moderate to make an attempt. The perspective from which the work is written could be called "Half-Catholic," "Independent Christian," or perhaps just Christian. And most are neither pleased, nor too put out, by such a name. Roger Williams was this sort of churchless Christian when he founded Rhode Island, and began the first Baptist Church in America. His thought may have led to American religious liberty, as later Baptists persuaded Madison and Jefferson, in what became the separation of Church and State. However, as few agree on many points in the

Preface

interpretation of the Revelation, what follows is hopefully written so that, even where one should think or find the author mistaken, the work itself of commentary might help the reader to consider the text and the truth anew, growing in the faith.

It is very difficult to attain a consistent reading of the whole book of the Revelation. This may be part of the reason that the book had been neglected, at least until the past century or so. There are many contradictory readings, so that most must logically be in error, at least as complete understandings of the whole text. Often these readings are based on a hypothesis that one thing in the text is another thing in our world, taken as a principle or what would be a vision, which provides a comprehensive context into which other things are then fit. But, if one is to believe Aristotle, conclusions are no more certain than the premises on which they depend (*Ethics*, 1139b 33-34). It is possible to make these explicit, and to turn these hypotheses into "steppingstones and springboards" in attempting to ascend, as Socrates explains in Plato's *Republic* (511b, 510b). The premises are attained not by induction alone, nor by hearing them spoken, but by a *seeing*, a *gnosis* or intellection (Aristotle, *Ethics*, 1143a 35; 1139b 25-35). The word *gnosis* has been obscured by its relation to the title of certain heresies. But it is possible to restore the word to its pre-Christian and Biblical meaning. As shown in the person of Socrates, this emphasis on *gnosis* is somehow consistent with human ignorance, the *a-gnosis* of the agnostic. It is not in certainty, but rather in ignorance and humility, that genuine inquiry, especially into these things, proceeds. One suspects that in speaking of scripture, as in speaking of the Most High, the things said are somehow always wrong in *some* way, for what truth we manage to glean. I have sometimes been in error, and corrected, even as we may be corrected in reading things early in the text by things later in the text. And we may still wish to change some things in this commentary or, as is hoped, to see some new part or view of this, St. John's astonishing Revelation.

For some, the book placed last in the Bible is the beginning of their life as a thoughtful Christian, a gateway for entry into the study of the Bible, beginning with the end. And this is how it was for us, when Mr. Bustamante at the old Arcade 5 in Northville introduced a few of us—including an old friend, Keith Assenmacher—to *The Way*. Later Hal Lindsey, through his book *The Late Great Planet Earth*, impressed us with the question of the immanence of the end times or the end of the age. Again as a freshman in college, a few of us were astonished together when John Paul II became Pope, and then was nearly assassinated. We have grown up now, all of us, with a mixture of shock and numbness at the events that have occurred, and this is in a sense our entry into the reading of the Bible, and our leaning toward this *Way*. As an undergraduate studying psychology and philosophy, I was able to do the Bible in independent summer studies, with Stephen Rowe of Grand Valley State College here in Michigan, focusing on Proverbs and then Paul's Letter to the Romans. While my course of graduate study was political philosophy, questions of the Revelation continued to arise, especially in reading Shakespeare, and we have heard the teachings of Jack Van Impe and of Henry Schaeffer, pastor of the Baptist Church on the edge of Novi, Michigan. In this sense, we begin at the end, though this might turn out to be a proper beginning.

There are, of course, many errors in the attempt to understand *our* world in light of what is written in this book. One of the more famous in American history is called the Great Disappointment, when in 1843 and then again in 1844, many gathered, expecting to be taken away at the return of the Lord. A recent calculation set the date for the return of Jesus at May 21, 2011. While the prediction received media attention, none ever asked about the reading on which the prediction was based—a calculation that this date was 7000 years from Noah, and an assumption that something ought to then happen. Calculations and other predictions, always based on an assumption, are demonstrated false when the events thought to be foreseen fail to occur. Isaac Newton considered calculations based on an assumption and a reading of Daniel, and presented a conclusion of "not before 2060." Such calculations assume a beginning date and certain conversions of calendars and correlations of histories. And yet, when anything occurs according to any written time, or even

Preface

remotely resembling some feature, such as the roaring of wind and waves, or a bit of perplexity of nations, it then appears to some as the foretold universal calamity. "Rumors of war" may be the best example, for here the text clearly intends to say that there will be wars and rumors of wars from the time that Jesus is speaking until the time called the end of the age, although *"the end is not yet"* (Matthew 24:6). These are explicitly *not* especially signs of the end, except in the sense that the apocalyptic motion, or the latter days, began with the incarnation. So these things are called "but the birth pangs" (Matthew 24:8). The plague in fourteenth century Europe, when one third of all people then there died, appeared this way to those living through it. So did the American Civil War, as is evident in "The Battle Hymn of the Republic." Things vast and terrible have occurred, and can occur—and yet, as it appears, the end was "not yet." In hindsight, we wonder how those living through the Second World War could stand, in awe of the events.

These birth pangs, then, have now lasted over two millennia. Another common error appears to be when names, as "Nero Caesar," are plugged into a gematria-like formula without pausing to consider whether we even know the meaning of a "human number," or the "number of a man," but proceed again on an unexamined assumption. It is possible to make these assumptions explicit, and to consider how sure the assumption is. Even if we are given divine premises, *we* must still understand them, or the wrong conclusions will be drawn. Another error appears to occur when some course appears with all the power of persuasion of the Spirit itself, without even raising the question of the import of these things for human and political action, on occasion with disastrous consequences. It may be that we then forget that like Adam, our work is, at best, to till and keep the little plot of the garden of the Lord that has fallen to our lot to tend–a garden we do not own and did not plant. For the interpretation of this text is so uncertain, at least in any public way, that no orthodoxy is set on many matters. And here, we need not attain full knowledge of the text, but mere familiarity, in order to see that there is no necessity to many readings presented as clear, prophetic or certain.

On the Revelation

The excellence of Christians is belief. A kind of belief, however, fails us, or does not serve in matters of faith that have no clear or public interpretation. Here faith and belief are seen in their distinction. It is here especially that we see it is a fine thing to have the word of God, if only we could understand it! Often the mere thinking of other possibilities that cannot yet be eliminated is enough to restore human ignorance, from which a genuine inquiry might proceed. And so, it is here if anywhere in Christendom that a reading might truly attempt to begin in ignorance, and in a sense, aim to return there. Yet there is a true reading of the text, and we can make progress in this through the work of interpretation and commentary.

Meanwhile, when significant things do occur—such, as we think, are the beginnings of communism, the Holocaust, or the capture of Jerusalem—the contemporary prophets or students of prophecy seem not to notice except on rare occasion, and in hindsight. We too believe the book to have much to say about contemporary matters, if in a surprising way. And this is a good half of the reason for taking up this commentary. After all, these things, if they are to occur, must occur during *someone's* time, even if it were not quite yet ours. Even when the time *is* ripe, some may be correct by accident, for the same appearances as occurred to them when they were wrong, and the time was not yet. An important teaching of Pastor Schaeffer is that it is an angel, and not a man, who is to announce that the hour of his Judgment has come (Revelation 14:7). But for Christians, our work is to spread the gospel, live the life, and tell that He *is* coming.

After the introductory chapter on John, we will attempt to comment particularly on each thing from the beginning to the end. I have attempted to draw on the best commentaries to which I have access, the foremost appearing to be St. Victorinus (d. 304), St. Hippolytus (170?-235?), and St. Augustine (354-430) among the ancients; with Richard Bauckham, David Aune and Hal Lindsey, Jack Van Impe, C. I. Scofield, and others among contemporaries. With these as instructors, companions, interlocutors and conversants, I simply attempt to read the text, relating all the best thoughts that appear on each occasion, and

Preface

trying to see the whole, or how the parts might fit together. I have begun with the Revised Standard Version of the Oxford Annotated Bible of 1977. With this as a base, I have made some attempt to notice significant variants from the King James and occasionally the New American versions, and to follow along in the Greek text, using the Pocket Interlinear New Testament edited by Jay P. Green. My regrettable lack of Hebrew may soon be remedied by my friends. Shalom and Charis!

Part One:
On the First Half of The Revelation

i: Author,
Introduction and Blessing:
That it is John the Apostle
Who Wrote the Revelation

That John the Apostle is indeed our writer has been doubted, both in our time and in earlier times.[1] The text does not directly say that it is John the Apostle who is writing, so that it might be some other John, an "elder" though not an Apostle. Yet this John who receives the vision of the Revelation does seem to be the same as the Apostle John, the son of Zebedee. The ancient church assumes that John the Apostle is the author, from the earliest traditions, of those who knew firsthand, having seen and known him. The primary reason for the doubt, which arose in the fourth century, is the strange character of the Revelation. This strangeness is the first aspect to appear among those who read books in the present age. The strangeness is due not only to the animal imagery of the vision, but also to the shift of emphasis, from love and forgiveness to the divine wrath of the Day of the Lord. The word love barely occurs (1:5, 3:19), and the compassion of the statement that he will wipe away every tear (21:4) is the only alleviation of the theme of divine wrath throughout the vision. The familiar teachings of the love of the neighbor, mercy, and forgiveness are lacking, while the saints are shown to call for the avenging of the blood of the martyrs. This shift of emphasis, applied by Christians to more human vices and opponents, has resulted in grave misunderstanding. The depth of evil, in tyranny and in twentieth century totalitarianism, makes such wrath more understandable, if it remains difficult. This depth is usually beyond the limits of the human imagination, and so when more common things are understood in light of the things said about apocalyptic evil, these things are misunderstood.

As Aune relates, "Some ancient Christians regarded the theology of the Revelation as false, and for this reason they could not consider the book to be apostolic" (1997, p. liii). While twenty of the books of the New Testament were generally in use among the Christian Churches through the second century, seven were questioned but finally included in the canon. The Revelation was among the questionable books that were included, along with James, Hebrews, 2 Peter, and 2 and 3 John. Elaine Pagels notes that the Revelation was omitted from the lists of New Testament works drawn up by St. Cyril, a council of Bishops, Gregory of Nazianzus, and Amphilochius; and was included only in the 365 A.D. list of Athanasius (*Revelation*, p.161). By 376, the canon of scripture was settled, as we have in writing from the 39th Festal letter of Athanasius.[2] The book was not held to be canonical in the Armenian Church until the twelfth century, and is absent from the Syrian canon, though it was always a part of the Egyptian canon (Aune, 1997, p. cliv-clvi). It is assumed that if the work was written by John, it ought to be canonical, and if it was not written by John, it probably ought not to be canonical. That the book is especially strange, and that it does seem to have been written by John the Apostle, indicates the difficulty and wonder of the work of reading before us.

John is unique among the Apostles, and outstanding in a number of ways. He was the one loved by Jesus, as is mentioned in answer to the question posed by Jesus to Peter (John 21:7, 20). He is the author of the Gospel of John, and arguably the most authoritative of the Apostles, surely among those remaining in the later third of the first century. After collecting up the details of the story of his life, we will consider why he does appear to us, if only to a few remaining, to be the author of the Revelation.

On the Revelation

John was the only Apostle present at the crucifixion, one of the few who escaped being martyred to die a natural death, and the last survivor of all the Apostles.[3] It is surprising how little biographical material remains of John, though he may be the Apostle best known to history. Amid persecution, the early church did not have leisure to record much of its history, nor to preserve texts. Much is lost. The Apostles emphasized oral teaching, and some did not write, as Eusebius relates (*Church History*, III, xxiv.3). Matthew and John wrote their own gospels, while Mark and Luke recorded the teachings of Peter and Paul, respectively. Thomas seems to have recorded 114 sayings of Jesus without a gospel. There are works and teachings purported to have been written by Phillip and James which may contain authentic teachings. After the Acts of the Apostles written by Luke, early Church history is not chronicled in writings that have come down to us until Eusebius, writing in the early- and mid-fourth century. Eusebius cites a writer, Hegesippus, working in the third century, and we have stories of martyrs from the early second century.

Yet some of the life story of John can be pieced together. He was a fisherman with Zebedee his father, and James his brother (Mark 1:19-20). Jesus surnamed these two "sons of thunder" (Mk. 3:17). They were partners with Peter and Andrew, on the Sea of Galilee (Luke 5:10), just east and a bit north of Nazareth. According to tradition, Jesus worked in carpentry with Joseph in the city of Nazareth. Capernaum was the hometown of John. When John the Baptist was seized, Jesus left Nazareth and "dwelt in Capernaum by the sea, in the territory of Zebulun and Naphtali, that what was spoken by the prophet Isaiah might be fulfilled: The land of Zebulun and the land of Naphtali, toward the sea, across the Jordan, Galilee of the Gentiles–the people who sat in darkness have seen a great light, and for those who sat in the region of the shadow of death, a great light has dawned." (Matt. 4:14-16; Isaiah 9:1) In Galilee, Jesus first taught "repent, for the Kingdom of Heaven is at hand." (Matt. 4:17)

John may have been a cousin of Jesus if his mother Salome was, together with Elizabeth, a sister of Mary.[4] John was present at the wedding in Cana as a disciple or a relative, and was an

That John the Apostle Wrote the Revelation

eyewitness. This would mean that when Jesus was gathering the Apostles, he was not meeting all of them for the first time. Yet there is strangely no reference to their having known one another as relatives. Salome appears in the gospel of Matthew, asking that her sons sit at the right and left hands of Jesus in his kingdom (Matthew 20:20), just as a relative might, upon hearing that there might be political fortunes in the family. This scene also demonstrates the limitation of the imagination regarding the Kingdom. It was not then commonly thought to be a spiritual kingdom, but the restoration of Israel.

The early life of John is obscure. He was not at first especially educated or skilled in writing. Luke describes Peter and John as "uneducated, common men" (Acts 4:13). He did not marry because of a distinct calling. The *Acts of John* presents itself as having been written by an eye witness, one who knew John. This work cites John as saying that the Lord appeared to him and said he was in need of him, and a third time said to him, "John, if you were not mine, I would let thee marry."[5] With Andrew, he was a follower of John the Baptist (John 1:35-40), indicating a serious Jewish faith nearer to the Essenes or the Jews of the desert than to the temple.[6] He was there with Jesus from the beginning of his ministry, and may be the most complete witness, staying with Him until the end. With Andrew he began to follow Jesus when John the Baptist said "Behold, the Lamb of God!" (John 1:36). In the *Acts of John*, it is related that when he first called John and James, from their fishing boat, he appeared to James first as a child, then a beardless young man. But to John, he appeared as a beautiful and cheerful man, and then as an old man (88-89). John was present when the first miracle occurred at the wedding in Cana (John 2:1-11), and at the transfiguration.[7] With Peter and James, he was present when Jesus raised the daughter of Jairus, a principal of the synagogue (Luke 8:51). He is probably the "other disciple" known to the High Priest, the disciple who went in with Peter when Jesus was taken to the court of the High Priest (John 18:15-16). He was, again, the only Apostle present at the crucifixion, when the rest had scattered, and when Peter denied Jesus. He witnessed the blood and water flowing from the side of Jesus, as he writes: "He who saw it has borne witness–his testimony is true and he knows that he tells the truth that you may believe" (John 19:35). Mary Magdalene first reported the empty tomb to John and Peter. John refers to himself as the "other disciple, the one whom Jesus loved" (20:2). This is probably similar to best friend, as young people have, though they may not have known each other very well before Jesus was baptized. John describes outrunning Peter to the tomb, then going in after Peter had seen the shroud and the rolled napkin. The Apostles then went home, and Mary Magdalene stayed. She then spoke to the two angels, and then the one she thought at first to be the gardener. Mary Magdalene is the first to see the risen Messiah. She holds the place a wife would hold, were Jesus like other men, and it seems he loves her in a unique sense. He appeared to her first. It may be that as Mary represents the Church as Mother, Mary Magdalene represents the Church as Bride.

After the crucifixion and resurrection, John continued for a while in Jerusalem, probably with Mary the mother of Jesus, since from the cross he was entrusted with her care (John 19:26-27). They may have had a home in Galilee near Capernaum or Nazareth. John was present on three or four of the five or six recorded occasions of the appearances of the risen Christ. Over a period of forty days, He appeared, once on the road to some, including Peter, when he opened the scriptures regarding the Messiah and became evident to them in the breaking of the bread (Luke 24; Mark 16:12-14). He then appeared to eleven of the Apostles gathered (Luke, 24:33; John 20:19-23), and then eight days later to the Apostles including Thomas (John 20:26-29). Then he appeared to Peter, John and others in Galilee, on a mountain to the eleven gathered (Matthew 28:16-17), and to some seven while they were fishing (John 21).

In the Acts of the Apostles, John is not a prominent figure, as are Peter and Paul, and is nothing like a leader of the Apostles. He at first went around with Peter. He was going to the temple with Peter when Peter healed a lame man (Acts 3). He is present again when Peter is arrested and answers for his preaching and healing before the High Priest (Acts 4:13). Eusebius (*History*, II.1), citing Clement of Alexandria, writes that James was chosen first Bishop of Jerusalem, and then relates:

That John the Apostle Wrote the Revelation

> But Clement in the sixth book of his Hypotyposes writes thus: "For they say that Peter and James and John after the ascension of our Savior, as if also preferred by our Lord, strove not after honor, but chose James the Just bishop of Jerusalem." But the same writer, in the seventh book of the same work, relates also the following things concerning him: "The Lord after his resurrection imparted knowledge to James the Just and to John and Peter, and they imparted it to the rest of the Apostles, and the rest of the Apostles to the seventy, of whom Barnabas was one. But there were two James: one called the Just, who was thrown from the pinnacle of the temple and was beaten to death with a club by a fuller, and another who was beheaded."

The one beheaded is James, the brother of John. James the Just was not an Apostle while Jesus was alive, but was converted after the resurrection. This James may be the stepbrother of Jesus, a brother by law rather than blood, as we assume, a son of Joseph from a previous marriage, who like Paul was converted after seeing the resurrected Christ (I Corinthians 15:7). He was called the righteous because of some prominence among the Jews, which is not unusual for this family. In one story, the parents of Mary dedicated her to the temple, and Joseph was chosen by lot to be her husband in the same way as a legal guardian, and to look over her.[8] Joseph seems to have been older, and to be gone by the time Jesus is baptized and begins his ministry. So Joseph may have been the father of James the Just, or James may have been a cousin, called a brother in the sense of kinsman. There is another James, the son of Alpheus (Acts 1:13), who may be the father of Jude.

After the stoning of Stephen and the persecution that arose against the church in Jerusalem, John went with Peter to Samaria, and there met Simon Magus (Acts 8:14-24). His brother James was beheaded by Herod Antipas (Acts 12:2) in 44 A.D. Claudius was then Emperor.⁹ The troubles of the Church in Rome had barely begun under Caligula. Claudius expelled the Jews, including Apuleius, from Rome in 49 A.D. It is not clear how long John stayed in Jerusalem, but he did not move to Rome, so that he was not there when Peter and Paul were martyred under Nero in 62. John is apparently at Jerusalem about 54-55 A.D., when Peter, James and John gave Paul the hand of fellowship, and agreed that he should go to the Gentiles, and they to the Jews or the circumcised (Galatians 2:9). He went to Ephesus, apparently about 69 A.D., some years after the letter of Paul had been circulated from there (54 A.D.), and the Ephesian Church was established. The Ephesian Church began when Paul and Apollos gathered certain disciples of John the Baptist who were already at Ephesus (Acts 19:1), about 49 A.D. Mary may have come with John to Ephesus, though she would then have been at least 76, and perhaps into her eighties. There are separate traditions of her death in Jerusalem and Ephesus.

After the killing of James the brother of Jesus (son of Joseph), and the dispersion of the Christian church in Jerusalem, John is reported to have been assigned this Ionian area of the world in Asia to spread the gospel, when the Apostles were each sent to different places. This area of Asia Minor was colonized by the Greeks and called Ionia, after their war with Troy, which is just to the north. Homer was apparently from Smyrna. Paul went to churches from Jerusalem to Illyria; Peter to five Asian cities and the Jews of the dispersion; Andrew to Scythia; and Thomas to Parthia or India (Eusebius, III.1). It is thought that James, before 44, may have gone to Spain and even to Britain; Bartholomew to Armenia; Thaddeus to Edessa;[10] and Phillip to Hierapolis and Gaul. By the ninth and tenth decade, John seems to have functioned as a sort of Bishop over the seven Eastern Churches addressed in the Revelation. According to one apocryphal account, in the *Acts of John*,[11] he performed many miracles and converted many upon his arrival in Ephesus, curing Cleopatra the wife of Lycomedes and raising both from death; curing a whole theater of aged women; and demonstrating the truth of the Spirit in the temple of Artemis at Ephesus. While this account is not entirely trusted, there is apparently no other account of his

That John the Apostle Wrote the Revelation

activities upon his arrival in the East. He also visited Smyrna and Laodicea, establishing the churches there. His early associates at Ephesus were apparently Verus, Andronicus, and Drusiana, and the unnamed author of these Acts. Whether these stories have any basis in oral tradition, at the least they draw attention to the lack of any other historical account of the work of John in Ephesus prior to his banishment to Patmos. The letters of Paul to the churches around Ephesus are written from prison under Nero, in the early 60s. It does not seem that John is there in Ephesus yet, and he may then still have been in Jerusalem or Capernaum. This leaves questionable the story of these churches being established by John, and if John did establish the churches, it would seem to have been prior to the letters of Paul.

The letters of John included in the scriptures seem to have been written late in the first century, after a heresy had appeared in the churches which denied the divinity of Jesus. Their authorship is of course doubted by recent scholarship, though it is quite possible to read them as written by John, as Carl Jung does in his *Answer to Job*.[12] The second letter, from "the elder," and from one church or "elect sister" to another, "the Elect Lady," may be from John in Asia to another church in Asia, or it may be to the Church in Jerusalem, or even to Mary. The letter addresses some who denied "that Jesus Christ has come in the flesh." There is a suggestion that these were Pharisees who had converted to Christianity, but who had separated from the Jerusalem church, holding the Jewish teaching that the son of God could not possibly have come in the flesh. One wonders why the instruction is to not receive, rather than to try to teach and persuade, any who come to them and "do not bring this doctrine" (2 John 1:10). In the third letter, John blames another, Diotrephes, for not welcoming the brethren and not acknowledging the authority of John, called "the elder." In an Apocryphal story from Spanish legend, James defeated and converted two heretical magicians, before being beheaded by Herod Agrippa.[13] Philip converts the magician Simon, and Peter rebukes him, with some success (Acts 8:9-24). While it may be that these are two different sorts of heresy, it may be that James and Philip have a contrasting way with magicians. This contrast, and the question of the regard of

John for heresy and heretics, may be the only hint of any possible human imperfection in what is known of John. He did seem to go along with the plan of his mother for his advancement, but once cured of this ambition and wrong imagining of the Kingdom, he appears very near to perfection. He seems not to have held even an official position in the Asian Churches, setting an example of moderation, as the Apostles did when James the Just was chosen first Bishop of Jerusalem. He appears different, for example, from Peter and Thomas in this near perfection of man, and might be among the first of a few figures, such as John the Baptist, that Christendom could stand beside Socrates of the Greeks as showing the peak or fulfillment of man.

We have suggested that the regard of John for heretics may be an imperfection.[14] There is some question as to whether the appearance of heretical teachings *is* the Antichrist (2 John 7; Luke 9:50). Early in the history of the Church, it was important to keep the teaching pure, especially regarding the central more unbelievable aspects, such as the divinity of Jesus. It may be, for example, that John is right, that the heresy denying the divinity of Jesus *is* the crucial heresy, and that the Antichrist did emerge two millennia ago, in the same sense as that in which the end times began with the incarnation. It may characterize the apostasy of the end times. Yet when the anti-Christian things appear, the various slightly diverging doctrines, such as failed attempts to think out the trinity, then appear as having quite a bit more in common than appeared when the Antichrist was not yet on the horizon. When, for example, the Nazis appear, the Jehovah's Witnesses, Catholics, and Greek Orthodox suddenly appear nearer to being brothers and co-sufferers under the same persecution.[15] It is the same for Christians and Jews, who appear to be fundamental opponents until the genuine adversary appears. It is also the same for Islam, when the atheism of the antichristian becomes apparent, and they wish to follow the law from Moses and the monotheism of Abraham, and justice. Those who try to obey the commandments, or those who follow the teachings of Jesus but are skewed in theory—these are not the enemy in the same sense. John saw Nero, and so he had access to the differences indicated, and yet he still wrote what he wrote. Could

That John the Apostle Wrote the Revelation

he have written the letters *before* having seen Nero and the persecutions to follow? And would he have written the same things after seeing the Revelation? For we hold that the Antichrist is not someone whose name was forgotten two millennia ago, but the worst one of all time: not some local Pharisee or Gnostic competing with John for disciples, but one at least as bad as Antiochus, Herod, Caligula, and Nero. Could the Johannine regard for heretics have been imperfect, and could this error, in combination with the power of Rome three centuries later, have had a part in the disastrous consequences of the medieval persecution?

Is it not possible to grow in the faith from a small beginning, and must these intermediate places, like the Manichean phase of Augustine, be shunned or punished? Is it not possible to progress, as Augustine did from early Manichaeism? And would it not be absurd to not allow the student to receive the teaching in parts, ascending toward the full import of what is being said? Must not every thought then become the log in the eye of another? Soon all the faithful would be afraid to think, and thought itself might go uncultivated, even for centuries at a time. For, as is said of things astonishing, the Christian teaching *is* "incredible" or "unbelievable." This–that Jesus is the Messiah and the Messiah in some sense is God–*does* seem to be what is being said, the gospel or news, as is indicated by the instances in scripture where Jesus is worshiped (Matt 2:2; 9:18; 14:33; 15:25; 20:20; 28:9; Mark 3:31;5:6; 11:9; Luke 4:11; 5:8; 24:52; John 5:23; 9:38; Phil 2:10; Hebrews 1:6; 2 Peter 3:18; Revelation 5:8, 14). Further, what he says is blasphemy if it is wrong. He forgives sins (Luke 5:21). He says he is "the son of God," and when the Jews go to stone him, he says "I and the father are one" (John 10:30-32). He tries to explain this by referring to the psalm of David (82: 6; John 1:12-13; 3:7), "I said, you are gods ...," and the psalm continues "... sons of the Most High, all of you," yet we will die like men. These instances indicate that the Arian teaching denying the divinity of Jesus is not the teaching of scripture. When Peter answers Jesus that he is "the Christ, the son of the living God," Jesus tells him that he, Peter, is blessed because "flesh and blood has not revealed this to you, but my father who is in heaven." The

Church is built on this rock, but the hidden truth is revealed by the Father.

And so it seems that we cannot presume upon it, nor is it "proper to insist"[16] upon it: What if, in a particular instance, the revelation is coming but has not yet arrived? But do we truly know, for example, what it *means* to say he is the son of God, and how this is the same and different from saying he simply *is* the Father? Jesus himself also distinguishes himself from the Father, when he asks, "Why do you call me good?" How the "equal" or "same substance," when one is beyond substance, and *with* the logos (John 1:1)? "No one is good except one, God" (Matt. 19:17; Luke 18:19-20). From this, we call Him the Good One, or simply the Good. "Beyond being" is a Platonic formulation attributed to Socrates (Plato, *Republic*, 509b). We can see this directly, for example in the way that good man or good doctor is related to man and doctor. The good of things is what it *is* even without particular embodiments. Or is not the case with divine things that, just as Socrates tells the Athenians, we are ignorant regarding the most important things? He claims a sort of human wisdom that is "worth little or nothing" compared to the wisdom that is that of "the god" or divine wisdom. He might say that *we* do not have knowledge of this, our ignorance, and further that he, Socrates, is the only one who seems to know this (*Apology*, 23 a-c; 29b), that he does not know the first things. This ignorance, though, is at the beginning of philosophy, as it emerged out of the wisdom of nature of the pre-Socratics. Philosophy brings to Christianity the ability to transcend opinion, addressing the very problem that has led to the splintering of the churches.

Philosophy is often thought of as the championing of a particular metaphysics by reason, and these "philosophies" or "systems" indeed may be in conflict with revelation. Then philosophy and Christianity will be incompatible. Philosophy also appears as an attempt to know by reason "unaided," and to begin in the complete rejection of all images and stories, and hence of revelation. This is as though philosophy depended on the atheistic assumption unexamined, as an article of faith. But if philosophy begins in ignorance, and proceeds essentially by ceaseless inquiry, then the entire tradition of metaphysics, from Plotinus or even Aristotle on, might be something of an error, at least when thought of as the essence of philosophy, and surely of Socratic philosophy. The Socratic teaching is that we cannot know these things *directly* (*Phaedo* 99), so that when we say, for example, that being has a natural articulation or *logos,* or that He is the Good One, it is somewhat playful. Though these may be the best thoughts available to us, we really do not have full or certain knowledge of what we are saying. The name "Most High" points in a direction, but refrains from saying a *what*. Philosophy begins in the recognition that we do not have knowledge of the first things, and so it is of primary importance that we undertake the quest. Following the Socratic turn, *Being* is seen by its reflection in the human things, indirectly.[17] And this is just what we would expect if the soul or man is the image of God. In place of even our best thoughts on Being or God might be the study of man as the image of God. So the traditional contrast of the two ways of reason and revelation presupposes a certain understanding of *what* reason is, and what it means to receive revelation. It is fitting first to turn these two definitions into questions, asking what we mean by "revelation," and what we mean by "reason." Do we mean the way John saw the vision, or the way we have it through the work he has written, or the way Peter knew that Jesus is the Christ, the son of the living God? It may be that the highest faculty, called intellect or eye of the soul, is rarely opened, and its fulfillment extremely rare.

We should perhaps not forget what a thing this is to say, and not be surprised if some who like the teaching of Jesus do not receive this gospel. Thomas Jefferson, based firmly in the science of the Enlightenment, apparently did not believe the stories of anything miraculous, but recognized the superiority of the ethical teaching of Jesus. The word "supernatural" or super-nature does not occur in scripture, though there is reference to the "divine nature" (*Theos physis*, 2 Peter 1:4). But it is the one who has this ethical teaching, a teaching of astonishing philosophical consistency, who also does miraculous things and teaches things that are scientifically incredible, like the resurrection. Can we truly assume to understand the soul and physics of one who speaks such a teaching? What if these miracles *are* possible, and our scientific incredulity indicates that we do not truly understand the fundamental causes in nature? Time and time again, things once thought impossible or miraculous are shown to be natural, once the causes are shown. Or might there be some comprehensive causes that have escaped our instruments, especially regarding the human soul and how it fits in nature? Do we truly know ahead of time that it is impossible for him to heal? It is the teaching about the human things and man, as distinct from the natural and cosmic things, that indicates the truth of the Christian teaching, and this *is* directly accessible. We see for ourselves the *life*, for example in the healing of repentance, forgiveness and mercy, while we can only marvel at the cosmic implications of these truths. His words are the bread of life.

And is it possible that there *is* a diabolic influence in the schisms, sects and doctrines, since humans are involved? Watching the play *The Crucible*, about the Salem witch trials, the possibility appears that there *was* a satanic influence at Salem, even in the very madness that led to the persecution of some ignorant children, and of others completely innocent.[18] And here we can see a difference between what we will refer to as mythic and genuine diabolism. In Salem, the latter lacked visible horns, but had the more cruel effect. The early church lacked political power, and so did not punish heretics, but only sent them away or went away from them. But when joined with political power, this assumption would become the basis for the making of martyrs *by* the Church, and this development is astonishing. The early church, including John himself, never suspected the coming union of the church with the authority of the Roman Empire. Yet the problem is implicit: The churches are to be tested by holding political power, and the unregenerate character is to be revealed. What is made by man and the visible appearances are revealed to be just that. The whole question of the relation of the Christian teaching to law both religious and political is addressed not by Jesus, but by the Church, of necessity and by accident. The Church was not prepared for political office. There was no cultivation of the tradition of political philosophy, much of which was lost to the West with the burning of the library at Alexandria.

That John the Apostle Wrote the Revelation

The works of Plato were not accessible in the West for over one thousand years, translated into Latin only by the fifteenth century, from texts from Byzantium. Paul, most famously, speaks against Athenian philosophy (I Corinthians 1:18-2) and warns against being preyed upon by philosophy, according to human tradition and elemental spirits (Colossians 2:8). But Paul never mentions Socrates, and has not read Plato. Nor does John seem to have read Plato, despite the obvious similarity between the opening of his gospel and the things said by the Platonists. Socrates is not otherwise boastful, nor is Platonic philosophy a worldly wisdom based on elemental spirits, nor a wisdom of the present age, though what they do in Athens in the fifth and early fourth centuries (440-360) B.C. *is* different from witnessing or preaching Christ crucified (I Cor. 2:2). While there are teachings and inquiries that do fit the description of Paul, the pursuit of truth and the following out of the natural articulation of things is the following of the word, and will always be in tension with *convention*. Socrates and the philosophers generally are the only group outside of Abraham to think through the principles of the Greek and pre-Biblical poetic imagination regarding the gods, or to reject idolatry on the basis not of Abraham, but of reason. Justin Martyr seems to be the first Christian to encounter the works of Plato, and he is both a Platonist and a Christian. In his Apology, Justin writes:

> We have been taught that Christ is the first born of God, and we have declared above that He is the Word of whom every race of men were partakers; and those who lived reasonably (*meta logos* with, following, or after reason), are Christians, even though they have been thought atheists; as, among the Greeks, Socrates and Heraclitus, and men like them; among the barbarians, Abraham…Elias…

We hold that there is this great similarity between the teaching or way of Jesus and the teaching or way of Socrates, so that in the most important way, the Bible and Socratic philosophy are mutually confirming. Both Socrates and Jesus are in conflict with the city, in Athens and Jerusalem, and both are killed, though the death of Socrates is not for the salvation of all mankind, nor as horrible as Roman crucifixion. The Socratic philosophers are also especially like the Christians in their teaching of what can be called a *transcendent* metaphysics, of what is *always*, beyond and above the world of the changing and the visible things. The Most High is not within, but above and beyond the created or the changing things, and the cause of these. It is in the Bible and Socratic philosophy, and perhaps nowhere else, that the Highest is addressed as what *is*, so that in language, what was a verb, "to be," becomes like a noun. When Socrates teaches that astronomy is not for the sake of the "decorations in the heavens," but for the sake of seeing things that are intelligible, he points to what is always, and to an eternal logos. Hence Socrates, as in Book II of Plato's *Republic*, questions the idolatry of the Homeric Greeks even more than we do when we read Homer. We may be surprised to find that Socrates and Abraham have more in common with one another than with us and Homer. Socratic philosophy gives us a picture of inquiry independent of Christian custom, and so allows us to separate the two, and see what man is like without Christianity. It also allows the cultivation of certain crucial studies, the neglect of which has allowed for the great failures of the Christian churches. It is the service to the good one to cultivate the good of each thing in the world and in thought, as much or more than right doctrine. But the churches rarely help one another. There is a good of each thing, as in the good of education, of the nation, and of each person, and devotion to this is a work different from that of the promotion of right doctrine that happens to be our own, or the promotion of human institutions. The service to the Good is the service to the Father, and takes precedence over the service *to* the Church, being of greater dignity by nature. It is the service or work *of* the Church. It does not have a name, and so is better off to not appear in the world.

It is especially the Gospel of John that makes possible the teaching that Jesus is the Word of God (John 1:1; 14), and that others could have found this way. When we say that Jesus is the *only* way to the Father or the only way of salvation (John 16:9;

12:48; 20:29), it makes a great deal of difference whether we remember or forget that the way and the word are eternal, prior to our names for it. Some held to be atheists according to their visible appearances, rejecting the stories about the gods and turning to impersonal being, might in truth be nearer the Biblical God than those who believe in God in the same way that the pagans believed in the many gods, even if these are painted over with Christian images.[19] So, Enoch, Elijah, Abraham, or Moses might have found salvation through the savior while they lived, because He is always there, while those who have the appearance yet miss Him.

The beginning of Christianity occurs while Galilee and Judea are provinces of the Roman Empire, and the events, beginning with the promotion of those like Herod and Pontius Pilate, can be understood in their place within the Roman world, intersecting the Roman history of the first century. Judea was conquered by Pompey and subjected by Julius Caesar, given provincial governors and subjected to puppet kings like Herod. Josephus reports that Herod bought the Kingship of Judea from Antony and Caesar (*Antiquities*, xiv, xiv). Grateful Jews attended Caesar's funeral (Suetonius, I. 85). Elaine Pagels reports that Augustus allowed the Jews to revere the emperor without violating their religion, praying to their own God for the welfare of the emperor.[20] It is not usually noticed that the Church was not in obvious conflict with the Roman Empire very early, under the emperor Tiberius, and for the first few years after the crucifixion. Eusebius reports that there was even a proposal to make Jesus one of the Roman gods, but that the Senate declined because the religion had arisen without the approval of the Senate (Eusebius, *Church History*, II.2).[21] This is significant, because it shows that the conflict that later emerged between Rome and Christianity was not so necessary, when the emperors demanded to be worshiped as gods and were refused. Had Rome not gone mad, beginning late in the reign of Tiberius or with Caligula, the conflict may not have occurred at all. According to Josephus, Tiberius expelled the Jews from the city of Rome because of a particular fraud, and because they refused military service

(*Antiquities* XVIII, iii). According to Suetonius (*The Twelve Caesars*, III), Tiberius:

> ...abolished all foreign cults at Rome, particularly the Egyptian and the Jewish, forcing all citizens who had embraced these superstitious faiths to burn their religious vestments and other accessories. Jews of military age were removed to unhealthy regions, on the pretext of drafting them into the army; the others of the same race or of similar beliefs were expelled from the city and threatened with slavery if they defied the order. Tiberius also banished all astrologers...

Tacitus too reports this expulsion, about 19 A.D. (*Annals*, II. 84).

According to Suetonius, "Tiberius' first hostile action against his own family was when his brother Drusus the elder wrote to him privately suggesting that they should jointly persuade Augustus to restore the Republican constitution" (III, p. 138; Tacitus, I.33). Germanicus, his adopted son, the greatest hope for Rome, was poisoned by Piso. His son Drusus the younger was poisoned by Livilla and Sejanus, allowing for the succession of Caligula. After the deaths of Germanicus and Drusus, about 28 A.D., Tiberius retires into a world of private lust and cruelty, leaving Rome for the island of Capreae. The retirement of Tiberius to Capreae is a great turning point in the history of the Roman Empire, and nearly coincides with the ministry of Jesus and the crucifixion. Tiberius is overcome by fear of execution, destroys his whole family, and corrupts the succession, as Gaius or Caligula accompanied Tiberius into his world of lust. The future emperor Vitellius was even there, as one of the boys (Suetonius, ix, p. 269). This sets a pattern that would recur four times in the first century. Here the tyrannical soul crowns the Roman Empire, and four times, during the reigns of Tiberius, Caligula, Nero and Domitian, emperors who began as cruel but able generals and administrators would subject Rome to the worst tyrannies ever known. These emperors gave rise to the saying that it is absolute power that corrupts. The seizure of the law leaves a cesspool of bad appetites unrestrained, where lust and cruelty are joined. These tyrannies are the destruction of Rome, from which the city never recovered. It is argued that the Romans could no longer govern themselves as free political persons, having been corrupted through the civil wars that led to Caesar. The Republicans were killed when they lost with Pompey. Still, an attempt to restore the Republic could hardly have done more harm, and may have avoided the abuses caused by men unequal to the position of a prince.

As Josephus reports, Caligula caused a disturbance when he ordered his statue placed in the temple in Jerusalem, though he died before the issue came to battles (XVIII, vii). Caligula had deified himself and instituted his own cult, complete with priests and mysteries (Tacitus, *Annals,* xv. 41). Suetonius writes that Claudius expelled the Jews from Rome because "They caused continuous disturbances at the instigation of Crestus" (*The Twelve Caesars,* V). This is the first mention of Christians at Rome, about 49 A.D. They may have been there since the Day of Pentecost, as Christopher Drewes reasons from Acts 2:10.[22] It is to these that Paul writes his letter to the Romans, about 54-58 A.D. Nero, of course, had Peter and Paul killed around 62 A.D. The Acts of Luke goes silent at this point, as Paul has appealed to the Roman emperor and is in Rome awaiting a hearing. The scene is lost to history, but is likely to have been extraordinary–the meeting of Paul and Nero. Nero then blamed the Christians for the fire in Rome, beginning the very terrible persecutions by Rome, around 64 A.D. This is the first of ten persecutions of Christians through that of Diocletian, the tenth and most widespread. Suetonius, on the suppression of public abuses during the reign of Nero, writes: "Punishments were also inflicted on the Christians, a sect professing a new and mischievous religious belief." Tacitus writes:

> To suppress reports that the fire was deliberately set, Nero fabricated scapegoats–and punished with every refinement the notoriously depraved Christians (as they are popularly called). Their originator, Christ, had been executed in Tiberius' reign by the governor of Judea, Pontius Pilate. But

in spite of this temporary setback the deadly superstition had broken out afresh, not only in Judea (where the mischief had started) but even in Rome. All degraded and shameful practices collect and flourish in the capitol.

First Nero had self-acknowledged Christians arrested. Then, on their information, large numbers of others were condemned, not so much for incendiarism as for their anti-social tendencies. Their deaths were made farcical. Dressed in wild animal skins, they were torn to pieces by dogs, or crucified, or made into torches to be lighted after dark, as substitutes for daylight. Nero provided his gardens for the spectacle, and exhibited displays in the circus, at which he mingled with the crowd or stood in a chariot, dressed as a charioteer. Despite their guilt as Christians, and the ruthless punishment it deserved, the victims were pitied. For it was felt that they were being sacrificed to one man's brutality rather than to the national interest.

Annals, xv. 41

The report of the acts of Christians goes silent at this point, when the persecution under Nero begins. John barely refers indirectly to the martyrdom of Peter (John 21:19). It is the most common opinion among the scholars that John was intentionally commenting on Roman politics in his visions of the Beast, though none of the numbers correspond. Nero is either fifth or sixth, not seventh or eighth, etc, and there is every indication that John is being shown things in the future, from the reign of Domitian. Like the conflict of Rome with the Jews, the conflict of the Christians with Rome centers on the refusal to worship the emperor, though this is never mentioned by the Roman historians. The conflict between the Christians and the Jewish temple, though, seems to have been continuous, until James is thrown from its pinnacle in 66 A.D. The temple was then destroyed in 70 A.D. under Vespasian, by his general the future emperor Titus, and the Jews dispersed. Domitian himself promised to be a second Nero, and was nearly as terrible for a time, executing people and senators at whim. He was the first emperor to set up images of himself in places of worship throughout the Roman Empire, and the first to demand that the people address him as "Our Lord and God," as Jack Macarthur relates (1973, p. 18; Suetonius, xii, p. 309). This deification of humans began with Caesar and Augustus (Suetonius I.88; Tacitus, I.9). If it leads to Nero, the Romans do not seem to understand its significance. The custom very curiously coincides in history with the incarnation.

Early in the reign of Domitian (81-96), under a general order that Christians be put to death, John was called from Ephesus to answer for his rumored teaching that the empire of the Romans would be quickly rooted out, and the kingdom of the Romans given over to another. The soldiers sent to bring him in were impressed by his eating only a single date on the seven-day journey. In one version of the Acts of John,[23] he assured Domitian that his reign would continue "many years," with numerous successors, but that...

> when the times of the things upon earth have been fulfilled, out of heaven shall come a king, eternal, true, judge of the living and dead, to whom every nation and tribe shall confess, through whom every earthly power and dominion shall be brought to nothing, and every mouth speaking great things shall be shut. This is the mighty Lord and king of everything that hath breath and flesh, the Word and son of the living one, who is Jesus Christ.

As a sign, John drinks poison and is not harmed. The poison is then tested on a criminal, who dies from it and is then raised by John. Domitian is impressed and so removes the decree of death to all Christians. He does not kill John, but banishes him to Patmos. How John escaped being killed by Domitian is indeed an enigma. Domitian killed many for accidental reasons, as Suetonius reports (xii, p. 306). In another story, John is set in a vat of burning oil, but is unharmed, and Domitian, giving up trying to kill him, banishes John to Patmos.[24] Before he leaves, John raises a servant girl of the house of Domitian who had died.

Another story confirms the character of the persecution under Domitian. According to Hegesippus, Domitian commanded that the descendants of David be slain, fearing the second coming of Christ, as Herod had feared the first. An inconvenience of hereditary monarchy is the extreme interest given to some in the deaths of others, and it is this that representative democracy replaces with the principle of popular election. In the first century, political assassination was so common, it was nearly assumed, for example, that Tiberius would begin by murdering Posthumus, and stepmothers conspire to kill the offspring of their rivals. The heavenly kingdom being misunderstood, political kings find the teaching about it to be a challenge to their sovereignty. When the grandchildren of Jude, called a "brother" of Jesus, were brought before Domitian, and questioned about the coming of the kingdom…

> …they answered that it was not a temporal nor an earthly kingdom but a heavenly and evangelic one, which would appear at the end of the world, when he should come in glory to judge the quick and the dead, and to give to everyone according to their works.

And so we know, if Hegesippus and Eusebius are trustworthy, that the teaching that the second coming is real and is future-relative to Domitian are not teachings peculiar to John or the Revelation. The Revelation is not about Nero. Domitian then dismissed the grandchildren of Jude, and at this time stopped the persecution of the Christians, just before Nerva succeeded as emperor.

John was, then, exiled to the island of Patmos by Domitian. Victorinus, in his *Commentary on the Apocalypse of the Blessed John*, writes that John worked in the emperor's mines there on

That John the Apostle Wrote the Revelation

Patmos, and did not expect to survive, but when Domitian died and he was freed, he then delivered the writing.[25] This would be about the year 96 A.D. He may have been on Patmos for as long as twelve years, and probably did not receive visitors or smuggle out instructions to the churches from 83 or so until 96 A.D. He returned to Ephesus after the death of Domitian, when Nerva reversed the decrees of the previous emperor. On the writing of the Gospel of John, it is written in *The Muratorian Canon*[26]:

> When his fellow-disciples and bishops exhorted him he said, 'Fast with me for three days from today, and then let us relate to each other whatever may be revealed to each of us.' On the same night it was revealed to Andrew, one of the Apostles, that John should narrate all things in his own name as they remembered them...

This story could also have described the writing of the *Didache,* if the gospel is written later. Andrew is thought to have been martyred in Patrae in Achaia in 69 A.D. (McBirnie, p. 83). It is also said that John wrote his Gospel late in his life, after his return from exile. According to St. Jerome, John was asked by the churches in Asia to write a gospel "against Cerinthus and other heretics and especially against the then growing dogma of the Ebionites, who assert that Christ did not exist before Mary." From Polycarp it was heard that John, the disciple of the Lord, going to bathe in Ephesus and seeing Cerinthus within, ran out of the bathhouse without bathing, crying, "Let us flee, lest even the bath fall, because Cerinthus, the enemy of the truth, is within." (Eusebius, IV, xiv.6). Victorinus writes: "...for when Valentinus, and Cerinthus, and Ebion, and others of the school of Satan, were scattered abroad throughout the world, there assembled together to him from the neighboring provinces all the bishops, and compelled him himself also to draw up his testimony" (p. 353-354). One wonders if he could not be involved in the writing of the work called the *Didache,* or even the earlier *Epistula Apostolorum.*[27] The latter presents itself as a letter from the council of the Apostles, shares a number of elements in common

On the Revelation

with the Gospel of John, and lists John first among the Apostles by whom the letter claims to have been written.[28] John may have had the luxury of being able to review the other gospels when he wrote his, though he seems to have drawn even the sayings and teachings of Jesus from his own memory, rather than from the previous writings. It is not even obvious that he had letters of Paul, though one would assume he had seen the letter to the Ephesians.

It is difficult to find any direct evidence of the other three gospels in the Gospel of John or the Revelation. Eight instances have been collected by Louis Vos, as cited by Aune (Revelation, p. cxxvi), such as the saying that all who take up the sword will perish by the sword (Matt. 26:52; Rev. 13:10). All eight are fragments of sayings that might have been collected by any of the Apostles directly from Jesus. They do not demonstrate that he used any of these texts in composing either his gospel or the Revelation. It is said that he read and approved of Matthew, Mark and Luke, yet noted that these treated only one year, from the beheading of John to the crucifixion. John relates earlier events, accounting for the apparent discrepancy between the Gospel of John and the others.[29] He sometimes corrects the others regarding the sequence of events, like the overturning of the moneychangers in the temple. This occurs one year earlier in John (2:13-20), rather than after the entry of Jesus into Jerusalem the year of the crucifixion. He has the last word among the writers, and might have corrected anything that seemed a significant error.

His gospel is known for its distinction, among the four gospels, of addressing the hidden nature of the Christ as the *logos* or word of God (John 1:1-4; Revelation 19:13), synonymous with the light that is the light that enlightens men (1:9). As John Burnet writes, "There is no Greek word for a word," *onoma* or name and *rhema*, or a speaking, being used instead (Plato, p.50). This is very nearly the same as that described in the sixth and seventh books of Plato's *Republic* (507e-509c), and the word for *word* is Greek. The thought may be implied in Genesis, as at creation God *speaks*. He speaks at least once on each of the first six days—and so the orders of being, as distinct from the beings that inhabit them, each come to be by a word of God. Here, rather than in the genealogy that opens Matthew, is the new beginning of the New Testament, implicit in the old. His thought is the only significant counterweight to the teaching of Paul, verifying Paul on points sometimes thought to be peculiarly Pauline inventions, such as the mission to the Gentiles and the divinity of Jesus. The Apocalyptic thought or prophecy of Paul, as for example concerning the rapture (1 Thess. 4:17) and the mystery of lawlessness (2 Thessalonians 2), may be in agreement with the Revelation of John, and a supplement which allows the picture to appear more clearly, though these elements are not explicit in the writings of John.

The life of John is easily the most important part of church history from the fall of Jerusalem in 70 A.D. throughout the end of the first century. By 70 A.D., Paul, Peter, James and others had already been martyred, though Matthew may have remained. It is likely that Thomas has already died in India.[30] Eusebius cites Irenaeus, who writes that John lived among the elders at Ephesus into the reign of Trajan (98-117), presiding over the selection of bishops. As the famous A.D. 112 letter of Pliny to Trajan indicates, persecution under Rome continued even under less despotic emperors. Torture and execution were routine, while the faith continued to spread, in Bithynia, "in cities, and villages and rural districts as well," while "the temples...have been almost deserted."[31]

Some of those known to history who knew and heard John were Polycarp, the Bishop of Smyrna martyred in about 155 A.D.; Papias, whose five-volume work on the sayings of Jesus survives only in fragments; and St. Ignatius. Eusebius includes a story about John's stealing back a man who had become a robber. An aged and vigorous Apostle John gets himself captured by thieves in order to shame their leader, a former student of the priesthood, into returning.[32] The story occurs when John was quite old, after his return from Patmos. It is interesting as the action of an Apostle, and would be an interesting subject for drama, showing the Apostle as the robber of robbers. Jerome relates the story that when John was very old, and carried into church each time, he would say only, "Little children, love one another!" When finally asked why he always said only this, he answered: "It is the Lord's command. And if this be done, it is enough."

The account in the *Acts of John* concludes with the possibility that John ascended, as did Enoch. This would also fit the saying of Jesus to Peter: "What is it to you if he remain until I come." McBirnie notes that unlike the other Apostles, no bones of John have ever been found. Eusebius cites an epistle of Polycrates, Bishop of Ephesus, which identifies the burial place of John at Ephesus.[33] There it also says that "being a priest, he wore the sacerdotal plate," though it does not seem that he was a Levite. The tribes of the Apostles are, interestingly, not mentioned, though it is clear that John the Baptist was a Levite, and related to Mary through Elizabeth. But the tribe of Zebedee and the tribe of Simon bar Jonah are not emphasized. Most of those that return from Babylon are of the tribes of Judah, Benjamin and Levi (Ezra 1:5).

Our writer, then, would seem to be John the Apostle—first because the thought of John in his gospel is arguably the highest thought of any of the Apostles to which we have access through writing, and may well be the highest Christian thought. Paul would be the other of these two peaks, of which none can see the top. According to Maimonides, prophecy presupposes an intellectual perfection (*Guide*, II. 36-38), and it would seem sensible that the vision of the Revelation should come to the most perfect, the most constant, the most intelligent among the Apostles. He is not formally educated, but as Jesus was born in a manger, this perfection arises from simplicity. To receive the Revelation would also provide a purpose that he should remain, rather than be martyred (John 21:23).

The text of the Revelation seems to identify which servant John is its author by saying it is the John "who bore witness to the word of God, and to the testimony of Jesus Christ, even to all that he saw." This could be read as referring to all that he saw on Patmos. Yet it may mean that this John is an eyewitness of the teaching and passion of Jesus. There seems to be no reason that this could not refer to the things told in the Gospel of John, and to all that he saw while he went about with Jesus through his life, death, and resurrection. As the one Apostle present at the Crucifixion, he is the fullest witness. The same statement, "the word of God and the testimony of Jesus," occurs at 1:9, referring to the reason John was sent to Patmos to begin with—that is, prior to the vision. And again the phrase occurs referring to the reason that the martyrs are beheaded (20:4), as was his brother James. The Apostles are the eye witnesses of the Gospel. John is the last of the Apostles, the only one alive in the last decade of the first century, and the only John sent to Patmos. So the end of the Gospel of John ("this is the disciple who is bearing witness to these things...") seems to lead into the beginning of the Revelation ("...John, who bore witness to the word of God and to the testimony of Jesus Christ, even to all that he saw").

One reason that the Gospel of John and the Revelation seem to have been written by the same author is that while the other three gospels have an apocalyptic section, recalling the teaching of Jesus on the coming of the Kingdom, the Gospel of John does not, so that the two fit together quite nicely. For unlike Matthew in Chapter 24, Mark in Chapter 13, and Luke in Chapter 21, the Gospel of John does not contain a late section of the words of Jesus regarding the end times. It is just as if the author left these things to be discussed elsewhere, or was content with that discussion. *His* apocalypse will be that of the risen Christ.

The Apocalypse section in the Gospel of John is very brief, occurs early, and describes the resurrection of the dead (5:28-29), as in the twentieth chapter of the Revelation. It begins:

> "The one who hears my word and believes him who sent me has eternal life; he does not come into judgment, but has passed from death into life...
> Truly, truly, I say to you, the hour is coming, *and now is*, when the dead will hear the voice of the son of God, and those who hear will live...Do not marvel at this; for the hour is coming when all who are in the tombs will hear his voice and come forth, those who have done good to the

resurrection of life, and those who have done evil,
to the resurrection of judgment."

Together with the passage in Luke (17:20), the kingdom is not coming with signs to be observed, the kingdom *is present*. And so these passages are the basis of the reading that these things are *entirely* spiritual, and not coming at all, in the sense in which we read it "with signs to be observed." "…But if it is by the Spirit of God that I cast out demons, then the Kingdom of God *has come* upon you" (Matthew 12:28). The things of the Revelation, like the incarnation, describe how being *is*, always, and what is always true: The Kingdom of heaven is accessible now, and in the most fundamental sense, is present, though *we* do not come into it. The hour *is now* when the dead will hear his voice and rise. This is the sense in which the coming of the Kingdom *begins* with the incarnation, like a mustard seed. It may be because being *is* this way that human history and the world in time unfold in this way; and this would be the most fundamental source of prophecy: It is because things are the way they are that their unfolding in time can be foreseen. The resurrection is both present *and* future, though in John it is emphatically also future: "And I will raise him up at the last day" (John 6:40; 44; 12:48). The future kingdom is assumed but not addressed in the Gospel of John. Though the statement is an attempt to write what Jesus said and not what John said, still, it is very interesting to wonder whether the Apocalypse could have been seen and written yet when John wrote his gospel. The above passage reminds of those in Chapter 20 of the Revelation, those over whom the second death has no power (20:6). The Revelation, then, seems to fit together with the Gospel of John as the missing apocalypse section obviously authored by the Apostle.

Of John, Jesus said to Peter, "If it is my will that he remain until I come, what is that to you?" (John 21:22). Some then said, wrongly, that this meant John does not die (21:23), and would remain until the second coming. John seems to suggest that he simply meant that it is not his concern, and no more. In the *Acts of John*, at the end of the days of John he is presented as disappearing, like Enoch and Elijah, possibly to remain in this

That John the Apostle Wrote the Revelation

way until the second coming. There is another possibility. In the text, Jesus has just told Peter what is taken, in hindsight, as a prediction of the martyrdom of Peter (John 21:18-19). If the statement to Peter is serious, the remaining may be John's not being martyred, and the arrival, when Jesus comes to John on Patmos. In this sense, it is clearly true that John was to remain "until I come," in order to receive and transmit the vision of the Revelation.

William Smith (Holy Bible, 1881, p. 28) gives a fine summary of the reasons it is obvious that John wrote the Revelation:

> ...The evidence in favor of St. John's authorship consists of the assertions of the author and historical tradition... The author's description of himself in the first and [last] chapters is certainly equivalent to an assertion that he is himself the apostle. He names himself simply John...He is also described as a servant of Christ, one that had borne testimony as an eyewitness of the word of God and of the testimony of Christ–terms which were surely designed to identify him with the writer of the verses John 19:35; 1:14, and 1 John 1:2. He is in Patmos for the word of God and the testimony of Jesus Christ. It may be easy to suppose that other Christians of the same name were banished thither, but the Apostle is the only John who is directly named in early history as an exile at Patmos. He is also a fellow sufferer with those whom he addresses, and the authorized channel of the most direct and important communication that was ever made to the seven churches of Asia, of which churches John the Apostle was at that time the spiritual governor and teacher. Lastly, the writer was a fellow servant of angels and a brother of prophets, titles which are far more suitable to one of the chief Apostles, and far more likely to have been assigned to him than to any other man of less distinction. All these remarks are found united together in the Apostle John, and in him alone of all historical persons.

On the Revelation

The theory that John was *not* the author may require that the text is lying or misrepresenting itself. While this is possible, and not unheard of, there is no reason to think that is what is occurring here. Similarly, in the face of the admonition not to alter the text (22:19), it seems unlikely that followers of John did much editing, let alone writing on it, though it would not be surprising if John himself did some work on it.

The same reason as that which shows why the Revelation would come to John is involved in the blessing to the one reading the words of the prophecy (1:3). An alternate reading of the third sentence is: "Blessed is the one (singular) *recognizing*," since the word for reading (*anagignoskon*) is also the word for recognizing, with *nous* in the root.[34] And "keeping" can also be "watching" for that written in it. Line 1:3 might then read: "Blessed is the one recognizing, and those hearing the words of the prophecy and watching for that written in it, for the time is near." The blessing here is the first of seven blessings in the work. Those too are blessed (2) who die in the Lord prior to the reaping, after the call of the third additional angel (14:13). Also blessed are (3) he who is awake and keeps his garments so that he is not exposed (16:15); (4) those who are invited to the marriage supper of the Lamb (19:9); (5) he who shares in the first resurrection, over whom the second death has no power (20:6); (6) the one keeping the words of the prophecy of this book (22:7); and (7) those who wash their robes, that they might "eat from the tree of life and enter the city by the gates" (22:14). The alternation of singular and plural references, combined in the first and reversed in the final two, is noteworthy. The singular are those who read or recognize, who are awake and clothed, who share in the first resurrection, and who keep the words of the prophecy. Those who hear, who die after the call for endurance, and who are invited to the marriage supper, who wash their robes to prepare to eat from the tree of life and enter the city, are plural or many.

The reading of the Revelation may not be for everyone, not even all those who are saved, though it is not unimportant, nor is it important only for the fascination with the time and imminence

That John the Apostle Wrote the Revelation

of the end. The reading of the Revelation is a cultivation of the highest perfection of the intellect and imagination together, and so a cultivation or an invitation to the highest blessing. In this blessing, we who consider and comment on it hope to share.

ii: *Tachus*, or "soon:"

Were the Apostles Wrong About How Soon the End Would Come?

God has given the revelation to Jesus in order to show to his servants what must "soon" occur. *What it is* that must soon occur is the coming of Jesus, as he says, "Surely, I am coming soon" (3:11). Yet what the second coming entails, and how to picture *what* it is that is said will occur, is of course very difficult. This difficulty of *what* is to occur is related to the ambiguity about how soon the end would come, as will be shown.

The nearness of the time is emphasized repeatedly in the opening and closing messages that frame the text (1:1; 22:6, 7, 12, 20). It is not said *how* soon, but only that "the time is near." From the beginning, readers throughout the ages think of the coming of the kingdom as *very* imminent—in their own lifetimes, or shortly thereafter—before the present generation passes away (Matthew 24:34, Luke 21:32; 1 Peter 4:7). The Apostles "supposed that the Kingdom of God was to appear immediately" (Luke 19:11). Paul in the first letter to the Corinthians advises a different way of dealing with the world, because "the appointed time has grown very short" (7:29). Peter identifies the outpouring of the Spirit on the day of Pentecost, with that said to describe "the last days" (Acts 2:17; Joel 2:28-32). John himself, in the first letter, writes "it is the last hour" and "now many antichrists have come" (2:18). And it is something of a question whether Jesus himself did not expect *the great* tribulation, the time of the worst trouble *ever* for mankind, to coincide with the fall of Jerusalem and the desolation of the temple, which occurred as foreseen, in 70 A.D.

Although he teaches that first the gospel must be preached throughout the world, it is not clear that Jesus did not share the expectation of the Apostles that the second coming was *very* imminent. Jesus himself taught that he did not know the day and the hour, apparently, of his own return, when he says: "But of that day and hour no one knows, not even the angels of heaven, nor the son, but only the Father..." (Matthew 24:36). One possible meaning of this is that the day and hour depend in part on human choice and action, and the day is not prophesied because it is genuinely free, though it can be foreknown, if only by the Father (Matt. 24:36). Are some things set when Daniel receives his vision, but other things dependent on what mankind does when the Messiah arrives? Or was it set that, coming among sinful humanity, he would be killed like the sacrificial lamb? And do end time events depend upon human actions at all, such as the allied response during World War II and the saying "Never again?"

We are told that it will come by surprise, at an hour we do not expect, "like a thief in the night," as when one is especially not looking. Unless the difference of two thousand years is negligible, the Apostles do seem to be wrong, to a man, about *how* imminent the judgment of the world is (Acts 2:16; 1:7). The scholars teach that when the end did not come as the Christians expected, the theory had to be altered to adjust for the delay.[35] Those who disbelieve the promise of the second coming cite as reason for doubt the truth that it has apparently not happened yet. Peter writes that there will be scoffers in the last days who say: "Where is the promise of his coming? For ever since the fathers fell asleep, all things have continued as they were from the beginning of creation" (2 Peter 3:3-4). We may see in hindsight that this is all just as it would be were the Revelation true, for "soon" to us may be a bit different from "soon" to eternity. The end times or the last days, in one sense, begin with the crucifixion, and continue as they have for two millennia. In this sense, it is now occurring, and has been, beginning with the mustard seed of the incarnation. The culmination of it is, however, "soon."

Yet it can be argued that in the apocalyptic sections of Matthew (24), Mark (13), and Luke (21), Jesus does *not* assume that it will be *very* imminent, or literally within the present "generation," because he knows that the gospel must first be preached throughout the whole world. "And this gospel of the Kingdom will be preached throughout the whole world as a testimony to all the nations, and *then* the end will come" (Matt. 24:14). The parable of the talents in Luke is in answer to the expectation that the Kingdom was to "appear immediately." In all three gospels, he tells them that they, the Apostles, will be hated and persecuted for the sake of his name. It is not clear in these chapters when he stops speaking to the apostles then alive, and of the events surrounding the fall of Jerusalem, and when he begins to speak of those into the future. Unless the event refers only to the destruction of the temple, it is simply wrong that "this generation will not pass away," in both Luke and Matthew. The second coming has not yet occurred, nor have the sun and moon been darkened, and that generation *has* passed away.

Hal Lindsey reads the line as meaning the generation that sees these signs, the fig tree sprouting, or Israel returned as a nation (1998, p. 27-28, 98). The word *genea* can also mean race or tribe. Henry Schaeffer reads *genea* as the generation of the spirit, which of course will continue to the end. He could also refer to Israel, to race or nation in that sense, including those without a land. Van Impe reads that *generation* refers to those born of the spirit in the church age, and this has not yet passed away. The next sentence, "heaven and earth will pass away, but my words will not pass away" suggests that he speaks also of the generation of the word. The generation of the Apostles has not in this sense passed away, but, as foreseen, has spread the gospel toward the ends of the earth. Yet he does speak to the present generation, and the fall of Jerusalem did occur to that generation, as well as the foretold persecution of the Apostles and the Church. The persecution he describes, where family members turn one another in before kings and governors for being Apostles of the gospel, is like what had occurred and would occur in the Roman persecutions—but it is also like what occurred in the Inquisition, and again in what occurs under modern tyrannies such as that in the Soviet Union prior to 1989,[36] not to mention the German tyranny.

Tachus, or *"Soon"*

The First Precondition

The three apocalyptic sections do give a sense of the vast time that might be involved. In Matthew, Jesus says: "And this gospel of the Kingdom will be preached throughout the whole world, as a testimony to all nations; and then the end will come" (24:14). Jesus tells the Apostles of how they will be delivered up and persecuted in palaces and synagogues, and be hated for the sake of his name. They are specifically told *not* to be alarmed that nations rise against one another, and that there will be earthquakes, famines, and pestilences, but that "the end is not *yet* (*outo*)" (Mt 24:6), and "...the end will not be *at once* (*eutheos*)" (Luke 21:9). These various events would take some time to occur. In all three, Jesus teaches that when false ones come in his name, or they hear rumors of wars and disturbances, they are *not* to go after these, nor fear, because "the end" is not signaled by these things. These together describe events prior to the destruction of the temple, and it is not clear just when the account slides into events indicating the end times as distinct from the destruction of the temple. When they see Jerusalem surrounded, they are to know that its ruin or desolation has come. The imperative to flee Judea, also in Matthew (24:16), refers in Luke explicitly to the time of the destruction of the Jerusalem Temple (21:20-21). In Matthew, they are told to flee when they see the desolating sacrilege spoken of by Daniel, "standing in the holy place (let the reader understand)" or in Mark, "where it ought not to be (let the reader understand)." They avoid saying "in the temple." In Matthew, and Luke, the time of the desolating sacrilege set up in the temple seems to refer to this time of the fall of the temple in 70 A.D. In Mark, the tribulation *follows* the time when those on housetops are not to go down or look back, while in Luke, the time when Jerusalem will be trodden by the Gentiles intervenes between the desolation and the darkening of the sun and moon. As Josephus reports, such a sacrilege did occur under Antiochus, though he does not report a desolating sacrilege at the time of the destruction of Jerusalem. Jerusalem and the surrounding area did become desolate, like a cottage in a vineyard or hovel in a cucumber garden; a besieged city (Isaiah

1:8), as Hippolytus notes (p. 210). But this, the fall of Jerusalem, is also the time of the "great tribulation," "such as has not been from the beginning of the world until now, nor ever shall be," a one-time event. The text, with a leap that is like a lacuna or gap of a missing section, jumps immediately from the fall of Jerusalem in 70 A.D. to the darkening of sun and moon and the coming of the son of man on a cloud. This has not yet occurred, though two millennia have passed. There may be a repetition of these events in the end times: the surrounding of Jerusalem and the flight of Jews from Judea, and the desolating sacrilege, so that it is true both that that literal generation would not pass away (24:34) before the destruction of Jerusalem, and that the end was not yet.

Jesus foretold the destruction of the temple (Matthew 24:1-2; Mk. 13:1-3; Luke 21:5-7). It is said in his accusation that he said he could destroy the temple and rebuild it in three days (Matthew 26:61; 27:40). John reports that, after overturning the tables of the moneychangers, the Jews asked him, "What sign have you to show us for doing this?" and Jesus answered: "Destroy this temple, and in three days I will raise it up" (John 2:19). He did not say that *he* would destroy it, as in the accusation. The Apostle, writing after the fall of the temple, says, "But he spoke of the temple of his body." Hence, when he was raised, the disciples remembered this saying. One wonders what they would have thought of these things when the temple was indeed destroyed by Titus in 70 A.D, and of the eruption of Vesuvius in 79 A.D. The three gospels record this prophecy, as is likely, just *before* the temple falls. Josephus writes of a prophet also named Jesus who foretold the destruction in Jerusalem from 66 on, until he was killed prophesying (*Antiquities*, VI. v).

The time of tribulation in one sense begins with the crucifixion, is suffered by the Apostles and the church throughout history, and still this is different from the great tribulation to come in the end of days. While Jerusalem suffered to the extreme during the siege, the Jews suffered even worse under the Nazis. The tribulation in one sense would seem to coincide with the time of the Church from the fall of the temple until the persecution of the Jews by Hitler, as the time of the Gentiles, when the nations will overrun Jerusalem. It is also possible that the tribulation *began* there, with Hitler or Lenin, is not yet completed, and the time of the greatest trouble for all mankind is yet to come.

The statement in Luke reads: "And Jerusalem will be trodden down by the nations (*ethnon*) until the time of the nations is fulfilled" (Luke 21: 25-27). The angel tells John that the outer court of the temple is to be trampled by the nations for 42 months (Revelation 11:2), and this seems to refer to the same thing as when the time of the nations is fulfilled. This is one of the few recognitions in the New Testament of the prophecy of the return of the Jews to Jerusalem. While the prophecy of the return of the Jews is prominent in the Old Testament, it is very strangely not mentioned directly in the New Testament, though it often seems to be assumed, as when the 144,000 are sealed. This, then, is a second thing said to occur before the end. The first two things that are fulfilled before the end–the preaching of the gospel throughout the world, and the return of the Jews to Israel–may coincide. The time may be a short and a long period. The short period may in some way encapsulate the long, and also contain a repetition of things that occurred at the fall of Jerusalem, if Jerusalem is to be surrounded and fled and trampled yet another time.

The Second Reason that the Time Seems to be Quite Soon

Strangely, then, the New Testament does not otherwise mention the fulfillment of the prophecy of the return of the Jews to Israel from worldwide dispersion (Ezekiel 36, especially: 24; Jeremiah 3:18; Isaiah 11:11-12; Deuteronomy 30). When he asks how long, Daniel hears the man clothed in linen say: "a time, two times and a half a time…when the scattering of the power of the holy people comes to an end, all these things would be accomplished" (12:7; Revelation 10:6; 12:6). Conversely, the prophets do not directly foretell the preaching of the gospel of the Messiah throughout the world, though Isaiah (29:18-19) prophesies:

> In that day the deaf shall hear the words of a book, and out of their gloom and darkness, the eyes of the blind shall see. The meek shall obtain fresh joy in the Lord, and the poor among men shall exult in the Holy one of Israel.

Isaiah also prophesies (42:6-7; 49:6) that salvation is to come to the world through Israel:

> I have given you as a covenant to the people, a light to the nations,
> To open the eyes that are blind,
> To bring out the prisoners from the dungeon,
> From the prison those who sit in darkness...
>
> I will give you as a light to the world, that my salvation may reach to the end of the earth.

Zechariah (8:23) writes:

> Thus says the Lord of hosts: In those days ten men from the nations of every tongue shall take hold of the robe of a Jew, saying, 'Let us go with you, for we have heard that God is with you.'

With the popularity of the Kabbalah and the recovery of Maimonides, this has in a sense become so in our age, in a rediscovery of the wisdom of the Jews neglected through the Christian centuries. Daniel and Revelation together, or the story of the Jews and Christians together, makes possible a reading of the apocalyptic prophecy that has not otherwise been available.

The nations are to be saved through the salvation of the Jews (Is. 55:5; 56:7):

> You shall call nations that you know not,
> And nations that knew you not shall run to you.

Tachus, or "Soon"

> ...for my house shall be called a house of prayer
> for all peoples.

The Old Testament does not say that it is *the Messiah* that, in a first epiphany, will start a universal religion that will bring the Hebrew God to the recognition of the whole world. So it may not be surprising that those remaining non-messianic Jews did not believe that Jesus is the Messiah. Some believe that his death demonstrated that he was *not* the Messiah, since the reign of the Messiah was to be forever. It is difficult in prophecy to separate or distinguish the First from the Second Advent. Yet Maimonides recognized that both Christianity and Islam have brought the world to recognize the God of Abraham.[37]

When Daniel asked the angel "How long," he was answered that, paradoxically, these things would be accomplished when the power of the holy people was restored. Beginning with Moses: when the blessing and curse come upon them, and they recall these things among all the nations among which the Lord has driven them, and they return and obey the Lord, then...

> ...the Lord your God will restore your fortunes,
> and have compassion upon you, and he will gather
> you again from all the peoples from where the
> Lord your God has scattered you, if your outcasts
> are in the uttermost parts of heaven, from there the
> Lord your God will fetch you, and the Lord your
> God will bring you into the land which your
> fathers possessed, that you may possess it; and he
> will make you more prosperous and numerous
> than your fathers. And the Lord thy God will
> circumcise your heart...
>
> Deuteronomy 30: 3-6

The prophecy is repeated frequently (Ezekiel 36-37; Amos 9:14-15). It is explicit, as in Ezekiel, that it is a return from a *second* worldwide dispersion, apparently following the return from the

Babylonian conquest. Isaiah writes: "In that day the Lord will extend his hand a second time to recover the remnant which is left of his people..." (Is. 11:11). The return of the Jews to Israel from a *second* worldwide dispersion is the most clear and amazing sign or indication that the time may indeed be for us quite soon. To repeat, it is strange that this prophecy, central to the vision of the end times in Isaiah, Ezekiel and Zechariah, is not directly mentioned but is implied in the Revelation.

As Van Impe notes, the restoration of the temple seems to be assumed in certain scenes of the visions of John, as when the temple is measured (11:1), or the portent seen in heaven of the seven angels with seven bowls coming out of the temple (15:6). The restoration of Israel as a nation is probably assumed in the sealing of the 144,000 in Chapter 7 and their gathering on Mount Zion in Chapter 14, and in the gathering of the nations of the world at Armageddon. The desolating sacrilege seems to assume the rebuilding of the temple—though, like the rapture, the sacrilege is also not mentioned directly in the Revelation. But the statements in the three gospels are consistent with the temple not being rebuilt until after the millennium.

The restoration of Israel is a truly amazing twentieth century occurrence–all the more because, though the process began in 1917, or even in the 1880's, the mass immigration and restoration of the nation in 1947 were the result of persecution under the sort of tyranny peculiar to the twentieth century.[38] The return of the Jews also results in conflict with the Arab or Islamic world– reminiscent of the conflict between the sons of Abraham, Isaac and Ishmael. Mohammed teaches a descent from Abraham through Ishmael, and so the conflict central to our world is a return to the conflict of these sons of Abraham, both inheritors of the belief in one God. While it is said that no one knows the day and hour, we are, as Van Impe and others indicate, told in the parable of the fig tree (Luke 21:29-31; Mark 13:28) to know when the Kingdom of God is near. "As soon as they come out in leaf, you see for yourselves and know that the summer is near" (Luke 21:30). Van Impe explains that the fig tree is Israel.

Tachus, or "Soon"

Parables of Delay

The period between the expectation of imminent return and the actual fulfillment of the prophecy is directly addressed as a recognizable period of delay. There are parables of delay (Matthew 24:48; 25:5), and warnings such as that against a wicked servant who, when the master is *delayed*, begins to beat his fellow servants (Matthew 24:49). Have the servants of Jesus done any such thing throughout history? In the Revelation, there is delay, as that of the four winds, until the sealing of the 144,000, when the multitudes too are shown having come out of the tribulation. Maimonides cites Habakkuk (2:3): "If he tarries, wait for him."[39] In 2 Esdras (4:36), the angel explains that the delay is "until the number of those like yourself is completed." When in the fifth trumpet, those under the throne ask impatiently "How long," the answer is "until the number of their fellow servants is complete…" (6:11). With the sixth trumpet, the angel announces that "there will be no more delay," but that in the days of the seventh trumpet of the seventh angel, the mystery of God will be fulfilled. The reason for the delay seems to be that the time must wait upon the sealing of the full number of the servants of God. This, then, is the reason that the time is not yet.

The foretold time is thought now to be quite soon; first, then, because the Gospel has been "preached throughout the whole world, as a testimony to all nations…" The second reason is the restoration of Israel as nation. Maimonides writes: "The days of the Messiah will occur when rule returns to Israel and they return to Palestine. This king who arises will have the seat of his rule in Zion."[40]

The Calendar and the Six-Day Theory

A third reason that the time seems to be quite soon is the calendar, though it is amusing to note that we do not know what day it is. This is something like the recognition in astronomy that we do not know which way is "up." In calendaration, the trouble is that the earth goes round the sun while spinning 365 ¼ times or so, while the moon goes round the earth by months that are not rationally divisible into solar years, with just over twelve months in each solar year. So, a day or month does not end at the same time when each annual revolution round the sun is completed. The early Hebrews and the Sadducees use the lunar calendar, while Enoch and the Pharisees followed the solar calendar. Months are a lunar measure, while weeks and days are solar. In addition to the difficulty of converting solar and lunar calculations, our dating, from the birth of Jesus, was not adopted until centuries later. According to the Byzantine calendar, Augustine thought that the latter part of the sixth millennium was then passing (XX.7). The Christian calendar was not set until Dionysius Exiguus, or "Dennis the small," calculated the dates of Easter for the Pope and called the year from which he began 376. This calculation has no year zero and is thought to be off by about four years.

Herod, king of the Jews when Jesus was born, who persecuted him at his birth and slaughtered the innocents in Jerusalem, is thought to have died in 4 B.C. The original calculation is thought to have mistaken the date of the birth by three to five years. The birth of Jesus is sometimes dated prior to 4 B.C. There was a supernova around 6 or 7 B.C. This supernova is a candidate for the Star of David, though it would not hover over the cave in Bethlehem. Another candidate is a conjunction of planets in 6 B.C., as the Babylonian magi may have known from astronomy to follow the star (Matt. 2:2).[41] That would seem to mean that Jesus lived from about what we call 6 or 7 B.C. until 23 or 26 A.D. The death of Jesus is thought to have occurred at about 32 A.D., when he was 32 or 33 years old, with the anniversary of the crucifixion to occur some time between 2026 and 2033, the usual date being 2031-32. Our time is then the bi-millennium of his lifetime, and the date approaching is that of the bi-millennium of the crucifixion, the point of victory over death. The dating from the birth of Jesus was not common or popularized until the historian Bede, writing in the eighth century. Under Pope Gregory, a correction was needed to account for a buildup of the quarter days, which are the cause of leap years. The Jewish calendar, adopted in the tenth century A.D., takes over our dating from the birth of Jesus, calling this the "Common era," and setting the creation of the world at 3756 B.C.E. The Hebrew calendar posts a difference of about 240 years, so that the year 2000 is equal to 5761 of the world, and 2239-40 would be equal to 6000. It has been argued very convincingly that the Hebrew calendar is in error, including too few years in the Persian period.[42] It is also suggested that the error was inserted intentionally to obscure the time of the true Messiah. According to the famous calculation of Bishop Usher from the generations in the whole Bible, the birth of the Messiah occurred in the year 4004 of the world. If the birth were actually in 4 B.C., as some suggest, the year from the Usher calculation would be perfect, with the Messiah arriving in the year of the world 4000. The seventh day would have begun with the year 6000, in about our 1996. This need not be what has been imagined of the beginning of the world in order to be the beginning of the present "world," and of our calculation, but it suffices that humanity from Adam began there.

There is what is called the six-day theory. This teaching of the early church was apparently buried by the commentary of Augustine (*City of God*, XX.7). Augustine wrote that because the first resurrection is mistakenly thought to be future and bodily, rather than spiritual and in this life, this passage of the Revelation regarding the millennial reign of these is construed into "ridiculous fancies." Some of the Chiliasts or millennialists imagined a thousand years of carnal pleasures. Augustine himself once held the opinion of the better sort of Chiliasts believing in a thousand-year reign of the saints, with spiritual joys consequent on the presence of God. The six-day theory states that as the Lord created the world in six days, and a day is to the Lord as a thousand years (2 Peter 3:8; Psalm 90:4), so the world will endure six thousand years, with the thousand-year reign of the saints or the millennium occurring in the seventh thousand (Irenaeus *Against Heresies,* III. 28). Van Impe (1998, p. 59-60) cites Barnabas (*Epistle*, XV):

> For with him one day is as a thousand years...Therefore, children, in six thousand years

shall all things be accomplished. And what is that he saith, and he rested on the seventh day, he meaneth this; that when his son shall come, and abolish the season of the wicked one, and judge the ungodly; and shall change the sun and the moon and the stars; then he shall gloriously rest on that seventh day.

Yet a day in the Bible is sometimes a day, so that none ever suggested that the forty days and nights were forty thousand years, etc. His raising of the temple in three days may be a prophecy of the millennium. Van Impe also cites the Talmud: "The world is to stand 6000 years, vis, 2000 confusion and void, 2000 with the law, and 2000 the time of the Messiah" (1983, p. 59-60). Dr. Van Impe relates that the two thousand years of the scattering of the Jews till their return seems to be prophesied by Hosea, writing: "After two days he will revive us; on the third day he will raise us up, that we may live before him" (6:2). "Us" refers to the Jews, from whom the Lord has withdrawn until they "acknowledge their guilt and seek my face" (Hosea 5:15).

The Seventy Weeks of Years and The Seven Years of Years

According to the prophecy of the seventy weeks of years in Daniel (Daniel 9:24-27; Nehemiah 2:1-8) there were to be "seven weeks" from the going forth of the word to rebuild Jerusalem to the coming of "an anointed one, a prince" (9:25). Then it was to be rebuilt for "62 weeks," or 434 years. Then after the sixty-two weeks, "an anointed one shall be cut off, and shall have nothing, and the people of the prince who is to come shall destroy the city and the sanctuary" (9:26). In the conversion of lunar into solar years, it is difficult to transfer, for example, a prediction of 490 years from the rebuilding of the temple after the Babylonian conquest. Transferring lunar and solar years to their common denominator of days, Van Impe (1998, p. 167-168) conjectures that Jesus rode into Jerusalem on the donkey 483 years, or 69 weeks of years, after the call to rebuild the temple. Van Impe calculates that 1 Nisan 445 B.C. was March 14, the Ides of March, according to our calendar. The entry into Jerusalem is said to be on April 6, 32 A.D. (Ibid, p. 167-168). Here, some 477 solar years are equal to 483 lunar years. There are *fewer* solar years than lunar in the same period, but if the years referred to by the weeks of years *are* solar rather than lunar, the period itself is longer. Enoch too is concerned with this calculation (Enoch 74, 75, 82). The final week is then divided into half, and for half a week this one "shall cause sacrifice and offering to cease," before the desolation. This final week is treated separately and will be considered later, in place below.

In both Daniel and the Revelation, there is a period of three and one-half years, or 42 months, 1260 days, and this recurs in various contexts. It is the "time two times and a half a time" the saints will be given into his hand (Daniel 7:25), the time, two times and a half a time till "the end of these wonders," "when the shattering of the power of the holy people comes to an end" (Daniel 12:7). Then in the Revelation, this is the amount of time the two witnesses are granted power to prophesy clothed in sackcloth (11:3). Then after they are killed, their bodies remain unburied for "three and a half days" before they are raised (11:9; 11). "A time, two times and a half a time" is also the amount of time that the woman is nourished in the wilderness (12:14), and forty-two months the time that the Beast is given authority (Revelation 13:5). And in Daniel, the continual burnt offering is taken away and the sanctuary trampled underfoot for "two thousand three hundred evenings and mornings" (8:11-14), and there are 1,290 days from the time sacrifice is abolished to the time of the abomination, and 1,335 days through which the blessed persevere (12:11-12). This seven years of years–2,520 days divided into two periods of 1,260 days, or three and one-half years–has been the basis of all the calculations of the American Protestants from the Disappointment through the Witnesses; to the contemporary Baptists; and apparently even of Isaac Newton, and we will have occasion throughout to consider these things.

According to Van Impe, when Israel took Jerusalem in 1967, 2,553 years of foreign rule ended. The capture of Jerusalem in 1967 ended some 2,553 years of foreign control over that city, excepting the brief period under Antiochus when the Jews rebelled successfully and purified the temple. This number reminds of the seven years of days, and the two periods of three and one-half years which are in the lunar calendar 2,520 (7x 360) and in the solar 2,555 (7x 365). It is 2,553 solar years from 586 B.C., when the temple fell, to 1967, and the year zero may throw off the calculation by a year or two. The attempt to calculate from the first destruction of Jerusalem by Babylon is complicated by disagreement as to what date this occurred, though 586 B.C. is often agreed upon. The Witnesses, beginning from 607 B.C., calculated to 1914, the year World War I began, and teach that a mystical kingdom was then established, following the reading of Mr. Russell (1988, p. 19).[43] 607 B.C. is the date given for the fall of the Northern Kingdom of Israel, the ten tribes scattered by the Assyrians. 607 is also the approximate beginning of the seventy years of the Babylonian captivity prophesied by Jeremiah (Jeremiah 25:12; Daniel 9:2). 607 – 2,520 = 1913. 2,520 – 586 = 1934, the year Hitler took power. The calculations are further complicated by the difference between the lunar and solar calendars, and the question of how to convert these. Again, the Pharisees and Sadducees are said to have had a disagreement about the lunar and solar calendars.[44] If the years are converted to solar years, 1,277.5 is half of 2,555 and fits the time from the fall of Jerusalem in 586 (if that is the correct date) to the building of the Dome of the Rock on the Temple Mount in 691. That the number of days in seven years be taken as years seems to be suggested from seventy weeks of Daniel Chapter 9, and the two thousand some days of Chapters 8 and 12. The 2,520 lunar years are equal to 2,555 solar years, which is very near to the period from the fall of the temple in 586 B.C. to the retaking of Jerusalem in 1967. The dates must be adjusted for the seasons and the year zero. If lunar years are originally intended, the number would be about 35 years less per bi-millennium, equal to our solar 1933 instead of 1967, etc.

But it is some distance from the mere statement of a time two times and a half a time to two three and one-half year periods amounting to seven years, suggesting seven years of years, and we may look further into these things in place below. It is, though, amazing that the seven years of years comes so near to convergence with the millennium and the end of the sixth day. This, then, is the fourth reason that the time seems to be soon.

The Spread of Technology

A fifth reason is that, as Daniel was told, "Knowledge will increase" (Daniel 12: 4).[45] The fruition of technology in the present century surprisingly makes many of the prophesied destructions and events seem rationally possible. The locusts (Revelation 9) are a bit like specialized drone planes, just now beginning to be used, while the horses are like the remote land vehicles sure to accompany the drones in any future war. It is just now possible for a two hundred million man army to cross the Euphrates, or for the waters to be made wormwood, or for there to be a need to stop those destroying the world (11:18). It is also now possible to join genetic engineering with tyranny. Computers too, just now, make it possible to collect multiple pieces of information regarding every person on the planet. The need for security and the danger of terrorism make such imitations of omniscience seem necessary.

Two terms—the development of nuclear, chemical and biological warfare and the spread of technology to many nations, coupled with the apparent inevitability of war among the nations in the human condition—seem plenty enough to lead us to the conclusion that there is cause for grave concern about the present time. The danger of imminent catastrophe is evident. Twice near the conclusion of the past century, in 1983 and again in 1995, there were near accidents in which computer defense systems seemed to indicate that a nuclear attack had begun. A man named Stanislaw Petrov may have saved more lives than anyone in history through a single action. Petrov was substituting at the Soviet post of firing a nuclear missile when there was an error in monitoring, due to the test of a missile from Norway. His instruments told him there was a missile coming from the United States, and his job was to fire one that would have hit the East Coast. On a hunch, he proceeded as though his instruments were in error and did not fire. Though his hunch was correct, his career was destroyed for disobeying an order. When these events were made public in the news,[46] people hardly noticed. We continue under the proverbial sword of Damocles with hardly a shrug, since there is little we can do about it. The threat, if not the logical necessity, of chemical, nuclear and biological warfare are visible. These are possibilities in the created nature, unlocked by one of its creatures. The unseen hope is that the Savior will return before the earth and humanity are simply destroyed. It is just now possible that wars may be as cataclysmic as those described in the Revelation, and science has just now become convinced of the vulnerability of the earth to asteroids and pole shifts, etc. This, the cataclysmic change of the earth in the past, was not previously known before the geology of Sir Charles Lyell, and seemed miraculous. Stones do not fall from the sky.

Francis Bacon seems to have seen that the project of modern science is related to the increase in knowledge that was to precede the coming of the kingdom. In Chapter 93 of his *New Atlantis*, he writes:

> "The Kingdom of God cometh not with observation," so it is in all the greater works of Divine Providence; everything glides on smoothly and noiselessly, and the work is fairly going on before men are aware that it has begun. Nor should the prophecy of Daniel be forgotten, touching the last ages of the world:–"many shall go to and fro and knowledge shall be increased;" clearly intimating that the thorough passage of the world (which now by so many distant voyages seems to be accomplished, or in course of accomplishment), and the advancement of the sciences, are destined by fate, that is, by Providence, to meet in the same age."

The special increase in knowledge that results from the project of modern science may be the specific increase foretold in the Book of Daniel, as it would seem on hindsight to be. It is often thought that there was a direct line of the development of technology from the wheel, through Archimedes and da Vinci, to engines and computers. But the great growth of technology in our world beginning in the nineteenth century was very much the result of a deliberate project begun in Renaissance Italy, and continued among the French and English, to investigate and pool knowledge in a dedication to truth through science that rivaled the dedication of the religious of the past. To them we owe much of both our medicine and free government, expanding the Greek traditions. This development, specific to the West, was introduced very much as a response to the superstitious understanding of the causes, as the strength and authority of medieval custom crumbled and religious violence seized Europe.

Something else, though, also occurred in the development of the imagination of the West, as ideologies emerged from the ashes of the old regime joined to violent political movements. A void in the imagination was filled with new utopian theories, based on the vision of nature characterizing modern natural science. Alexis de Tocqueville discusses this occurrence in his book *On the French Revolution* (III.1). These ideologies begin in the rejection of the tradition of faith, though they share surprising features in their envisioning of the future with the images of the Kingdom. Communism, or the extreme "left," and Nazism, its opposite extreme, emerged from the German philosophy of the nineteenth century to spawn political movements covering a quarter of the globe, leaving a wake of some seventy to one hundred million dead *in addition* to those killed in war. Only the astonishing victory of liberty in the Second World War prevented these things from then becoming global. While Communism seemed, in 1990, to be ready to dissolve like the witch of the West, it yet persists, if in a less noxious form.

The success of modern technology results in the extreme importance of the preservation of liberty and the prevention of tyranny. Under free government, the powers of technology are both useful and annoying, but the people can prevent the more obvious abuses. The nightmare of modern man is if these powers, developed in liberty, should fall into the hands of unchecked tyrannies. Yet liberty is rare, and fragile.

On the Revelation

The place of modern science in making possible the things foreseen in the Revelation reminds us of the account of Enoch, of the cause of the depravity of mankind before the flood. The angels that then fell to earth and had intercourse with human women also gave mankind the forbidden knowledge and arts that led to drugs, cosmetics, and the metal weapons of war (Enoch VII-VIII). Azazel...

> ...taught all unrighteousness on earth and revealed the eternal secrets which were in heaven, which men were striving to learn (IX.6).

And the flood occurs...

> ...that all the children of men may not perish through all the secret things that the watchers have disclosed and have taught their sons (X.3).

What occurred, then, is that men were killed, and their blood cried up to the heavens as Abel's did when Cain committed the first murder:

> And as men perished, they cried, and their cry went up to heaven... (IX.10).

Rousseau would have called Enoch as a witness to the thesis of his Second Discourse, on the harm to man due to the arts and sciences. A copy of the Book was found in a cave in Ethiopia in 1773, translated into English by Richard Lawrence in 1821, and then by R.H. Charles in 1912. What is especially intriguing for us is the repetition of the pattern of the days of Noah. The revealing of the secrets of electronics, biology, chemistry, and nuclear physics has led to a circumstance where the potential for both destructiveness and tyranny have reached Biblical proportions, many times worse than that unleashed by the metals and the weapons of war in the ages of bronze and iron. If at any time in human history, one were to say "there will soon be war" or "soon a tyranny," they would have been correct. Yet now, with the powers of technology, tyranny and war cannot happen without great catastrophe. This may be part of the reason that there is less war per capita now than at any time previous in human history.

The topic of the Apocalypse sometimes incites terror. Our fear need not be that he *is* coming, or that the apocalyptic things are true. Due to technology, the human population has just now exploded to cover the globe like mould on a piece of bread, also indicating the ripening of the time. Given human nature and nuclear, chemical, and biological technology, the destruction would seem almost assured. What we have to fear is that He is *not* coming to destroy those destroying the world (11:18). The impending doom is visible; the spiritual truth invisible.

Plato is notorious for considering mechanics to be a corruption of the "one good" of geometry, which is to turn our minds away from matter, as Plutarch reports in his *Life of Marcellus*. Technology makes reason a servant of ends not its own, usually the ends of wealth and power, which are the ends of the body. Were technology to serve reason, there might be much helpful and little wrong with it as an occupation for mechanical types, bringing some relief to the pain and toil of the human condition. Nor does modern psychology attempt an understanding of the hierarchy of ends based on the right ordering of the parts of the soul, which provides the basis for an objective ethics at the root of classical psychology. *Our* psychology is a set of techniques or instruments, to be used toward unexamined ends to which the science claims indifference. The very success of modern science led to a depravity of the human studies, the very studies which could address the question not of how to gain power over nature and man, but how to use these abilities *well*. There is nothing in modern science–no scientific knowledge–that suggests we use technology *for* the relief of the human condition. Science gives us medicine, but the Church gave us hospitals, and humanity the intention to heal. The instrumental character of scientific knowledge means that it can be used for either good or evil, increasing powers toward ends which are most common by nature, such as wealth and power.

Usually, the current scientific understanding of the causes of things is thought to preclude the Biblical understanding, so that miracles are thought impossible, and the coming of the son of man nonsensical. Faith in our age may require an obscuring of certain truths that seem to argue against faith. Yet, while science refutes and replaces much of the mythic or superstitious understanding of the causes, it does not claim to understand the first or most important things any better than religion did—things like the purpose or the shapes of things, why is there order, how, and what each thing is, and each kind of thing, etc.

There is a very interesting study of the exodus by Jacobovich, a recent archeologist from Jerusalem, shown on a program of the History Channel, *Exodus Decoded*. He unravels the plagues inflicted on Egypt by considering these as natural consequences of the huge volcano that occurred about 1470 B.C. at Santorini. Each plague—how frogs would come from red water, which would kill their predators, up through the killing of the first born on the main floor of the Egyptian houses by a release of methane gas, and the exposure of the shoal across the Reed Sea—is understood quite well, and for the most part truly. One would expect some of the swords, shields, and bodies of the Egyptian soldiers to be found there at the Reed Sea (Ex 14:28, 30). The marvel is that these things *coincided* with the exodus, so that each consequence was helpful in the escape. What is amazing is that their exodus *coincided* with the natural events. There is no "super nature" or "supernatural" in the Bible, but, we might say, also a nature that is divine, and a nature that we do not understand. If one had perfect geological knowledge so as to predict Santorini, as geological and astronomical science may allow the prediction of a cataclysm by fire, still one could not from this predict the events of the apocalypse, any more than one could have predicted the exodus from the prediction of Santorini. These, the exodus and the apocalypse, concern the human and spiritual world.

In the same way as Jacobovich has presented the exodus, the judgments, especially the first four trumpets and bowls, may be considered as part of a single event. It is said, for example, that when an asteroid hit the Yucatan Peninsula 65 million years ago, debris was thrown back up into space, only to then rain back down, igniting the atmosphere with the heat of the friction and burning about half of the forests on the earth. In the second

Tachus, or "Soon"

trumpet, something like a great mountain is thrown into the sea. In the first, fire, hail and blood rain down, and in the third a meteor seems to fall, poisoning one-third of the waters and destroying one-third of all ships. Then in the fourth trumpet, the sun and moon are darkened, as may also result from a meteor. The increase in knowledge has allowed us for the first time to see into the vastness of the galaxies and the age and motions of the earth, and to see how the things described by John are quite possible, and not in the least incredible.

The fruition of modern science and technology, political and philosophic modernity, the persecution and return of the Jews, and the Arab-Israeli conflict: these are, then, the principal constellations whose conjunction seems–far more than any astrological conjunction–to suggest that the time may indeed be quite soon.

A sixth reason that the time seems near is that Catholic prophesies converge to indicate the present time. The prophecy of Malachy,[47] in which he lists the Popes from his time until the end, seems to conclude with the one to follow Pope Benedict XVI, Pope Francis I, though Malachy calls him Peter of Rome. The convergence of the three secrets of Fatima (see Appendix A) with the other five reasons is very ominous.

A seventh reason that the time seems to be near is the convergence of many other prophesies, from the Mayan calendar and Hopi prophecy[48] to those of Merlin and Mother Shipton and Edgar Casey. The end of the Mayan calendar was of course 2012, though it was not said by the Maya just what this means. The Hopi, from a tradition that may be related, speak truly of the "gourd of ashes" and the end of the fourth world, looking forward to the beginning of the fifth world. They may also draw the prophecy out to describe a pole shift, as though the crossing of the galactic equator would result in a reversal of the cosmic polarity. The description in Luke following the signs in the sun and moon (21:25 ff) sounds much like what might be seen from earth if the poles were to gracefully shift: The surface would be disturbed, leading to roaring waves and universal panic, as described by Luke (21:26-28):

...upon the earth distress of nations in perplexity at the roaring of the sea and the waves, men fainting with fear and with foreboding of what is coming on the world; for the powers of the heavens will be shaken. And they will see the Son of Man coming in a cloud with power and great glory. Now when these things begin to take place, look up and raise your heads, because your redemption is drawing near."

As will be discussed in place below, there are other descriptions from the prophets that sound like a pole shift and the ruffling of the old crust that is not itself the end, but sets the end times in motion, or allows these things to occur. If a natural disaster, such as the eruption of the super volcano at Yellowstone, were to remove the U.S. from world politics, the events foretold might be allowed to occur.

Still, there are convergences in other ages, and it is amusing to think that, had we lived and wondered in the days of the Second World War and known what was occurring around us (as most did not), we might similarly think that the time appeared to be at hand, though for different reasons. It is good, especially when we think something in the text to have been made clear, to think of and try to eliminate other possibilities. A good exercise might be to consider "why so" and "why not" on the question of whether Hitler is the Antichrist, for we hold that while this is not it, it is *like* it. He is defeated much as the tyrant of Isaiah 14, his body burned. His holocaust resulted in the return of Israel as a nation. This might appear to be a New Jerusalem, were it not for the ominous unresolved circumstances of world politics. Hitler indeed thought or planned "to change the times and the law" (Daniel 8:25), as did many modern revolutions, beginning with the French. The similarity of Hitler to the one described in Daniel would have appeared prominent, going forth to persecute many, and even putting down three kings, while the prophecy regarding the return of the Jews to Israel would have appeared less prominent. Yet Hitler never took Jerusalem, which remained under British and Palestinian control. Mussolini took and lost

Tachus, or "Soon"

Rome for the Axis powers, so that Rome was quarantined, but spared. It is also possible that World War II is the destruction of one-third of the world, which seems to be what is described in the trumpets, and that this precedes a third world war which will be an even more universal conflagration. Above all, no Christian reader, to my knowledge, ever predicted that the Nazis would be a cause of the restoration of Israel. And there may then have been something to the thought, though we often miss large historical motions due to our excessive concern with our own little lifespan. "The end is not at once" (Luke 21:9). The unfolding could easily cover two millennia, and it is not clear that what is prophesied is not a third millennium. The present Jewish calendar marks the end of the sixth day at what would be 2239. The present tensions among the nations could conceivably continue without resolution until then, and yet the prophecy be fulfilled. It does *not* seem that a large-scale persecution aiming particularly at Christendom has occurred, as it has with the Holocaust of the Jews–though many Christians were caught up in that, as our Pope John Paul II knows at first hand. While the martyrs under Communism are considerable in number, this seems only to foreshadow what is seen in the vision. Nor does it seem that the Antichrist has yet appeared.

The Rapture and the Son of Lawlessness

The three apocalyptic sections of the gospels contain the best description of the rapture (Matthew 24:30-31; 39-43; Mark 13:26-27; Luke 21:27; and 17:20-37). In Matthew: "And then they will see the son of man coming in a cloud with power and much glory." The sun and moon are darkened *after* the time of the "great tribulation" is spoke of, and just before the sign of the son of man appears in the heavens (24:29-30). As will be discussed in more detail below, it is sometimes taught that the rapture is distinct from this "coming of the son of man," but this coming of the son of man is just what is said to be like the days of Noah in its suddenness. Then, it is written: "two men will be in the field, one is taken and one is left..." (Matthew 24: 32). This is especially explicit in Luke's Gospel, as "the day the son of man is revealed" (17:30). The other great text on the rapture is from the letter of Paul to the 1 Thessalonians 4:15-18:

> ...For this we declare to you by the word of God, that we who are alive shall not precede those who have fallen asleep. For the Lord himself shall descend from heaven with a cry of command, and with the archangel's call, and with the sound of the trumpet of God. And the dead in Christ will rise first; then we who are alive, who are left, shall be caught up together with them in the clouds to meet the Lord in the air; and so shall we always be with the Lord.

Paul leaves record of an understanding of the time scope involved, when he writes to the Thessalonians (2 Thess. 2:1-12) that they should not become excited by reports that the day of the Lord has come, and it is time to gather:

> Let no one deceive you in any way, for that day will not come unless the rebellion comes first, and the man of lawlessness is revealed, the son of perdition, who opposes and exalts himself against every so called god or object of worship, so that he takes his seat in the temple of God, proclaiming himself to be God.

It seems here that the manifestation of the lawless one must *precede* the rapture (though it is still logically possible that "that day" refers not to the rapture, but to the separate Revelation to all the world at the second coming, described in Chapter 19 of the Revelation, and that the rapture addressed in the first letter to the Thessalonians precede the revelation addressed in the second letter to the Thessalonians). But in Matthew, it is very clearly written: "And when *you* see the desolating sacrilege..." (Mt. 24:15). This seating of the lawless one is not something that there will be mistaking about, though those who do not receive the truth are left to be deluded by the lie (2 Thess. 2:10-11). Paul, continuing, writes that "he who now restrains the mystery of lawlessness will do so until he (or it) is out of the way" (2 Thess. 2:7). Some teach that this "he" or it who now restrains is the church, whose presence in the world as the vessel of the Spirit prevents the manifestation of the lawless one, so that the whole church will be raptured *before* the man of lawlessness is revealed.

We, though, would then wonder for whom it is that the Revelation is written. It is addressed to his servants, to show them what will happen soon (1:1). The whole work is written for the church, about the church. It is about *martyrdom,* and the avenging of the blood of the martyrs. Those teaching the pre-tribulation rapture teach that the church will not be present on earth for any of 21 successive judgments described from chapters 6-18 of the Revelation. But if the man of lawlessness is seated at the middle of the seven-year tribulation period, the gathering of the dead in Christ and then the rapture may occur just after. Hence there are pre-, mid- and post-tribulation teachings about the rapture. These things will be discussed in place throughout, as in the sections on Chapters 4 and 11 below. But this is a third precondition, together with the preaching of the gospel throughout the whole world and the end of the time of the nations or Gentiles. This third does *not* seem yet to have occurred. The thirteenth chapter is especially about the revealing of this lawless one, and what the church is to do when he appears, namely: do not take the mark of the Beast. We, then, are presently in the time between the return of Israel and the appearance of the one called Antichrist.

When Jesus appeared to the Apostles at Jerusalem, in the forty days after the resurrection as described in the Acts (1:4), he told them to remain at Jerusalem to "wait for the promise of the father," and that "before many days you shall be baptized with the Holy Spirit." When asked if he would restore the kingdom to Israel at that time, he answers:

> It is not for you to know times or seasons which the father has fixed by his own authority. But you shall receive power

when the Holy Spirit has come upon you; and you shall be my witnesses in Jerusalem and Samaria and to the end of the earth.

(Acts 1:7-9)

The times and seasons are not for them to know, but theirs is to preach the gospel to the ends of the earth, after which, as is said in Matthew and Luke, the end will come. In contrast with the apparent expectation of all the Apostles prior to the destruction of the temple in 70 A.D., John seems by the ninth or tenth decade to have an idea of the course of what is now to occur. In the *Acts of John,* as cited above (p. 20), in response to the rumor that John was teaching that the empire of the Romans would quickly be rooted out and given to another, John himself told Domitian, "Thou also shalt reign for many years given thee by God, and after thee, very many others; and when the times of the things upon earth have been fulfilled, out of heaven shall come a King,...

What it is That Will Occur "Soon"

What it is that is said to be coming soon turns out in some ways to be a very difficult question. It is the latter days or the end times that is said to be coming soon, though there is some question as to just what this is. It is the subject of the Revelation, and in these terms it is in a word the revealing of Jesus as Christ or Messiah upon the defeat of the Beast and false prophet, after the great tribulation, the worst time in the history of mankind. First, it is questioned whether the prophecy refers to anything temporal and future at all. Second is whether what is foreseen is the end of the world, or rather only the end of the age. And third, will the end of the age then be the end of the world, with time and eternity somehow joined, or rather the beginning of the millennial rule of the saints from Jerusalem, with the truly final end to come one thousand years later? An additional question is whether the rapture, for which we hope and wait, is not distinct from the second coming of Jesus, and whether the followers of the Lamb will not be taken out of the tribulation, the worst time in all human history. The question of the millennium, in both the punning and direct senses, is whether this will be a literal thousand-year period. And will the Messiah himself reign in that thousand years? Further, what does it mean to say that the Beast and false prophet are now to be defeated, and the Dragon bound—that is, prevented from deceiving the nations—only to be loosed a while at the end of the millennium before being finally defeated, as in Chapter 20?

From the teaching of Jack Van Impe, *what* is said to be coming soon is not the end of the earth, nor even the end of humanity, but what is better termed the end of "the age," or of the world as we know it—the inhabitable human cosmos of nations as it has come to be. The question becomes very difficult because of the millennium and the question of how this event, the coming of the Beast and the second coming of Jesus, is related to the resurrection, final judgment, New Jerusalem, new heaven, and new earth. Are these one and the same, or two different things—perhaps two different events that happen one thousand years apart?

The change of ages does appear to be accompanied by great destruction and tribulations that are very literal, appearing now to most readers as foreseeing the result of nuclear war, astronomical cataclysm, or both. Peter is the most graphic, writing that "the heavens will be kindled and dissolved, and the elements will melt with fire" (2 Peter 3: 12). This destruction of fire may occur after the millennium, rather than at the defeat of the sea and land beasts. But it is not the end of the world or earth that is foreseen, and this is encouraging. It is the end of the *aeon* or age, as Paul writes to the Ephesians, of "not only in this age but in the age to come" (1:21); (Matthew 14:39, 49; 24:3; 28:20; Hebrews 9:26). There is to be a fundamental change in the human condition, a millennial kingdom; and then a New Jerusalem, in which the divine is present on earth and reigns. It is possible that this change is so fundamental that it can be considered an undoing of the fall of man, or of the banishment of Adam and Eve from the garden of the Lord and the Tree of Life.

But this–that the revelation teaches the end of the world–is one of the first of the common opinions that are dispelled when one begins the study of these things. As Van Impe relates, "the earth endures forever" (Ecclesiastes 1:4). The Catholic mass includes the Trinitarian prayer of "World without end," and the credo concludes "...of his kingdom there will be no end." The reign of the Messiah is forever (Daniel 7:14; Revelation 11:15). It is good to have this said, that the earth will endure forever, because it is also said that the heavens and earth will pass away (Matthew 24:35; Revelation 21:1). The throne of the Lord is forever, while the earth and heaven will perish, growing old like a piece of clothing. "Like a mantle thou wilt roll them up, and they will be changed, But thou art the same... (Ps. 102:26-27). As Peter writes:

> ...according to his promise, we wait for a new heaven and a new earth in which righteousness dwells (2:13)... The day of the Lord will come like a thief, and then the heavens will pass away with a loud noise, and the elements will be dissolved with fire, and the earth and the works that are upon it will be burned up (2 Peter 3: 10).

There is a distinction, then, between the world or the present order of things that makes up an age, and the world or the planet earth, just as there is another distinction between the planet earth and the material world. The former may perish while the latter remains. We now believe the material world to be some eight or ten billions of years older than the planet earth. It is not quite said that *all* the world or *all* the elements are burned—and in the Revelation, in the trumpets, one third is afflicted or burned; while in the bowls, no portion is specified, so that the destruction may well be total. The change may be similar to the destruction of the world through the flood. Here, the Lord said that the rainbow is to be a sign of the covenant "between me and the earth" "that never again shall all flesh be cut off by the waters of a flood, and never again shall there be flood to destroy all earth." (Genesis 9:11-13). From this we say He has promised not to destroy the world again ...by water! Yet it is not clear that the fire is not *man*-made. The change, including that after the millennium, is to be even more fundamental than that of the flood of Noah, when the earth was cleansed of violence and the Law of Noah given to all mankind. The world is to be changed, and there may be an analogy with the change said to occur in the resurrection of the body (1 Thess. 4). So this is what is *not* said to be coming soon: the end of the world or earth, though it is a very fundamental change, even more so than the end of the world by water in the time of Noah. The end of the present world is not an end of the earth, or of men on the earth, but an end of the present age. This appears to lead, in one thousand years, to a condition where, if descendants of the present nations continue, the fall of man has been undone. And is the eternal life of angels then mingled with that of men? The city of God, the New Jerusalem, is on the new earth (Revelation 21:24).

The Three or Four Different Readings of the Millennium

Finally, to unite the themes of "*what it is* that is said to occur soon" with the theme of the delay and the teaching that "the end is not at once," the time sequence presented in the Revelation is strange, especially in the nineteenth and twentieth chapters, giving rise to at least three very different readings. The Beast and the false prophet are thrown into the lake of fire (19:20), **and then,** apparently "one thousand years" later, the Devil or Satan is bound and thrown into the pit (20:1-3). It is not explicit when the scene described in the opening chapter, when He comes on a cloud (1:7) occurs, the Second Advent of the Messiah, or where his feet touch the Mount of Olives (Zechariah 14:4). In Chapter 14, he simply appears with the 144,000 standing on Mount Zion, and then the earth is reaped, and the winepress trodden outside the city. In Chapter 19, heaven is opened and John sees the King of Kings and Lord of Lords, and the Beast and his armies gathered to make war against him. The millennial reign of Chapter 20 is that of the saints beheaded by the Beast and raised in the first resurrection. Yet he is to be loosed *after* a thousand years, deceiving the nations. It is *after* the thousand years that Satan will gather the nations that are at the four corners of the earth for battle. This battle occurs *one thousand years after* the battle through which the Beast and the false prophet were thrown into the lake of fire, the battle of Armageddon. The Devil is then thrown into the lake of fire where the Beast and false prophet *were already* (20:10). This is followed by the last judgment, and then the new heaven, new earth, and New Jerusalem. The visions of Chapter 13, then, and the gathering at Armageddon of 16:16, would seem to pertain to a time one thousand years ***prior to*** the final battle and the last Judgment. If so, then what it is that is to occur "soon" is not the last judgment nor the New Jerusalem, but rather the defeat of the Beast and the millennial kingdom.

Difficulties in scripture may be there for a reason, even in order to prevent our resting with a certain reading. This device of intentional difficulty appears to be the case with the two accounts of the creation of man in the first three chapters of Genesis. Were birds created before or after man? Were the animals given to man for food? Who is it that Cain feared would kill him? How long is a day prior to the creation of the sun? For Christians, this section is at the opposite end of the Bible, even in a place corresponding to the last three chapters, so that one suspects the two difficulties, at the beginning and the end, are related. Any interpretation identifying the present time with the end of days as a last judgment would seem to have to get around this thousand years, or to choose *which* end time is said to be at hand. If it is the time of the Beast, it would seem to be also one thousand years prior to the final world war and the last judgment, which would come after the seventh day. If it is the latter, after the millennium, that is at hand, then the images of Chapter 13 and elsewhere may indeed have already occurred, as is said by those who think these things are about Roman emperors such as "Nero Caesar."

A literal millennium of the rule of the saints and the Messiah from Jerusalem would allow for the understanding of this post-millennial loosing of the dragon to be given during this time, after the defeat of the Beast and false prophet. A thousand years might also allow for the recovery and development of medicine and technology, so that a city of this sort might literally descend from heaven: Who knows? It is difficult to tell in what way prophecy will be literally fulfilled, sometimes even after the events occur. Regarding the Messiah, this was not even clear to all after it occurred. While it was occurring, the Roman world barely noticed. The Jews who paid the most attention to the prophecies of the Messiah, and were most accurate about the *time* of his arrival, the Essenes, seem to have been the most mistaken about the deliverance of their nation. Might it be so, regarding the events of the Revelation, that what has occurred is not clear to all, even when it has just occurred? Could Hitler have been the foretold Beast and Jerusalem be now re-founded? Yet it is especially said of the second coming, "every eye shall see him."

There are three or four distinct ways that these things have been understood. In an 1881 edition of the Bible, William Smith outlines these three according to three periods of interpretation. 1) The Chiliastic reading of Irenaeus and Barnabas, introduced above, so called from the Greek word for one thousand. This understanding is said to characterize the first two centuries, from Jesus to Constantine. The expectation is for the second coming of Christ and a literal millennium. The best example of the chiliast reading may be that of Justin, about 155 A.D, in his *Dialogue with Trypho*, Chapter 81. This is also the first reference to the Revelation in other writing:

> ...there was a certain man with us, whose name was John, one of the Apostles of Christ, who prophesied by a revelation that was made to him, that those who believed in our Christ would dwell a thousand years in Jerusalem; that thereafter the general, and, in short, the eternal resurrection and judgment of all men would likewise take place...

But 2) when Rome was no longer adversarial, Christians "...began to look on the temporal supremacy of Christianity as a fulfillment of the promised reign of Christ on earth" (Smith, p. 29). The world became Christian, when the Roman Empire under Constantine and his father Constantius ceased to persecute Christians, with the Edict of Toleration, and then Rome herself was made Christian. This is the great change that occurred with Augustine, and buried chiliastic or millennial interpretation for centuries. Augustine himself taught that no earthly kingdom can claim to represent the kingdom of God.[49] Yet this needed then to be stated. A third reading that developed later is called 3) the figurative reading, of the millennium as "the reign of Christ in the heart of all true believers" (Ibid, p. 29). This reading of the presence of the kingdom is based on the sense in which what unfolds in the end times is a revelation of what is always so, and the eternal is more fundamental than even these horrors. Some would read the Revelation as being *entirely* symbolic, or as not in any way at all describing things that are to actually occur in the outside world. Often the images in the judgments, such as the smoke-filled air of the fifth trumpet, suggest spiritual circumstances of the human soul, perhaps, rather than a literal physical catastrophe. Sometimes there is hope that the violence of the scenes might be symbolic only, as appears plainly to be the case when the dragon pursues the woman with a stream of water from its mouth (12:15), or where the sword with which the one on the white horse will slay them is his word (19:15, 21). Similarly, Augustine teaches that the "first resurrection" of the twentieth chapter is spiritual, and not a literal resurrection after a literal beheading. And so the millennial reign, in which the Saints rule for 1000 years before a truly final battle and the last Judgment, need not be literally one thousand years (*City of God*, XX.7). He conjectures that by a thousand years, the writer meant either the last part of the millennium then passing, or the completion of time, since 1000 is the cube of 10.

Luke writes directly enough that Jesus said, "The Kingdom of heaven is not coming with signs to be observed; nor will they say, 'Lo here it is' or 'there!' for behold, the Kingdom of God is in the midst of you" (17:20-21). Otherwise, the events are shockingly prophetic and literal. If it is to occur, it must occur in *someone's* time. And so some, most notably Jack Van Impe, believe it to be clear that it is for *our* time, for reasons that will be discussed throughout. The fourth kind of reading, called the "futuristic" by Walvoord (p. 520), coincides with a recovery of the pre-Augustinian millennialism or Chiliasm. It looks to events

Tachus, or "Soon"

in the future and the literal emergence of a very terrible tyrant, the worst of all time, preceding the coming of Jesus on a cloud to defeat him, as was written. We sometimes wonder whether the readings called figurative, and that which assumes these events have already occurred, are not calming delusions. These are perhaps better for children, and we are all in some sense children. The same might be said for the teaching that we will not see it for the snatching away, and the teaching that the work was not written by John, so that its strange theology need not be taken so seriously, or that the Beast refers to the emperors of John's time. The most plausible reading appears to be that the end of days and the things described in the Revelation are yet to come or future. These things occur not at once, but over a period of more than one thousand years, beginning from the time of the incarnation. The long period culminates in a short period of seven years. There will be certain cataclysmic events, like the plague of the fourteenth century in Europe, or the American Civil War, or the Second World War, which will lead many to think that this must be the prophesied day, and still "the end is not yet." These things are, though, but the birth pangs (Matt 24:8).

The fourth kind of reading is called by Smith a "regular chronological interpretation," and is traced to a Bereguard of the ninth century, preceding Joachim of Fiore. Joachim influenced the later Protestants by reading Rome as the Beast and Babylon, and devised a three-part division of history into ages of the Father, Son, and Holy Spirit, the later of which was to begin in the year 1260. It is following Joachim that Luther and Wycliffe thought of the Pope as the Antichrist (Ibid., p. 29). The thought of Joachim is interesting because it is at about this time that Christian Rome, together with the power of the kings of the nations, begins with new vigor to inflict the death penalty for heresy—and to make martyrs—with the persecution of the heretical sects of the Waldenses and Albigensian in France. The whole issue is difficult, because from the time that Christianity became the religion of Rome, it almost appears as though it had never occurred to anyone that it was possible to *not* kill heretics, until Luther. The popularity of the events makes us, in hindsight, embarrassed of our species, or its general representatives, and reminds us of the fragile blessing of civilization, won by peaceful reflection and the promotion of the liberal arts. The Protestant sects, with rare exceptions, also persecuted others on the basis of doctrine, and participated in persecutions of witchcraft and fringe sects. The people are much to blame, and the kings of nations participated in what became a persecution unrivaled until the twentieth century. To Calvin, Moore, and others, the problem with persecution was not obvious. Luther and Calvin both deemphasize the Revelation.

It is somehow especially the Americans, the Baptists, Witnesses and Adventists, who have tended to read and emphasize the book. Yet it is possible to step back and wonder whether this whole period—beginning about 1215, nearly 1260 years after the end of the Roman Republic and the beginning of the empire of Julius Caesar, fraught with heresy and barbaric punishments, the end of the Middle Ages and the beginning of modernity—could not be seen as the beginning of the motion of the ascent of the Antichristian, over now nearly 800 years, leading up to the actual appearance of such a figure. The mission was to spread the gospel to the ends of the earth, teach repentance for the forgiveness of sins, to be baptized, and to warn mankind: "repent, for the kingdom of God is near." There is little else the church is told by Jesus to do. He tells us to do the bread and wine in remembrance of him (Luke 22:19), and to love one another (John 13:11). We are surely not told to establish opinion by law, nor punish unbelievers. The mission resulted in a rather vast persecution from about 1215 until sometime in the seventeenth century, the persecution of heretics and witches resulting also in many errors and the making of some martyrs. The disruption to the soul of the Western world, required to set aright the resulting confusion, is staggering. The appearance of the holy things was joined to cruelty, resulting in rebellion and the reaction against the Christian as such–the anti-Christian ire that would inspire modernity. Everywhere men seek to be free, it has been against the power and authority of Christian convention. The reaction against the light may even be caused by the reaction against its reflection in convention, opinion, and the earthly city.

Tachus, or "*Soon*"

Eric Voegelin, in the *New Science of Politics*, traces what he calls a "Gnostic" theory at the root of modernity to this development in Joachim, which he identifies as the "immanentization of the *eschaton*," an error of seeing the end of history in the literal temporal fulfillment of the kingdom (119-121). This results in attributing meaning to history, which by itself is not intelligible. He uses the word "Gnostic" to refer to the supposed insight of these movements into a course of history and its end, and means also to relate the contemporary ideologies to heretical Gnosticism. Heretical Gnosticism, as written against by Irenaeus, is a system of myth with more to do with the imagination than the intellect. Yet we are left with a question: do John and Jesus avoid this "immanentization" of the "*eschaton*?" Or is not the Revelation, if not the Catholic Creed, the Gnostic immanentization par excellence? The Creed concludes: "He is coming again in glory to judge the living and the dead, and of his Kingdom there shall be no end." History *has* a meaning, not in human but divine terms that extend from Adam through Noah, the chosen people, the incarnation, and the Revelation. We lose, then, the distinction of these modern movements, which, because they are materialist, *invert* the *eschaton*, which may as a matter of fact be imminent. The word Gnostic is derived from *nous*, the Greek word for intellect, the eye of the soul and light of the mind. John 1:4 and 9 read: "In him was life, and the life was the light of men...the true light that enlightens every man was coming into the world..." We hold that this is somehow the very thing in man, or what we truly are, that is born out of the earth, by which Jesus said "you are gods, sons of the Most High" (John 10:34; 1:12-13; 3:6; Ps. 82:6). There is a sort of Johannine Gnosticism. *Nous* somehow implies its revelation in the end times.

To restate the matter: one way of attempting to understand these things would be to explain the millennial reign as having already occurred, for example in the rule of the saints and martyrs in the Middle Ages, which took over from the rule of Rome after Constantine, and in a sense lasted just about or a little over one thousand years. None can doubt that it is Christendom that set up hospitals all over the world and caused humanity to become a bit more peaceful toward one another, mitigating the brutality of the ancient world, still with us, where the enterprise often seems to be conquest. It is sometimes read that the binding of Satan is what occurred at the resurrection, and so the gathering of the nations and the time when he is "loosed awhile" is indeed our time, and the end times. The difficulty here is that the beasts and the mark of the Beast would have already occurred. Augustine writes: "Now the devil was thus bound not only when the Church began to be more and more widely extended among the nations beyond Judea, but *is now and shall be bound till the end of the world, when he is to be loosed*" (*City of God*, XX.8). It is true that the persecution of Christians ceased, from the early fourth to the thirteenth centuries, and so in this sense *something* was bound. To be clear, we think Augustine here confuses the casting out from heaven with the binding. From the time of the incarnation, for the earth, he has in a sense been loosed, making the martyrs that appear beneath the altar in the fifth seal (Revelation 6:9). At the same time, we are intrigued by the possibility that the millennial reign has been occurring, through the rule of his saints since the incarnation. The Beast with the number 666 might then indeed have been Nero Caesar, as many commentators try to read this. Peter and Paul are two witnesses killed, and Jerusalem fell with the temple that was destroyed eight years later. But Nero is not seventh or eighth, and he never caused everyone to be marked, nor did all the nations gather to attack Jerusalem, but only the armies of Rome, and under a different emperor. Although the siege of Jerusalem was extreme, Hitler was far worse. The sun was not then darkened with the moon turned to blood, nor was there a worldwide earthquake.

One difficulty with the Augustinian account is that the devil is said to be active, as though "unbound," in the letters to the churches (2:9; 13). The binding might seem to coincide with the end of the making of martyrs by Rome, but to be inconsistent with the unbound activities, such as the pursuit of the woman who gave birth to the male child of Chapter 12, when he is described as having been cast down to earth.

The leading opinion of the scholars through the latter half of the twentieth century has been that John is referring primarily to the Roman Empire, and to Nero as the Beast, apparently referring backwards to events thirty years prior to his banishment to Patmos. Richard Bauckham has presented a reading based on this assumption, and the notes to the Oxford Bible of 1973 are written on the same basis. Richard Gunther, meanwhile, has posted a reading common to Protestants, from Joachim of Fiore through Wycliffe and Luther, which assumes that the Pope is the Antichrist and the events are those of what are now called the Middle Ages and the Reformation. Contrary to both these, it seems that the prerequisites above were not then fulfilled, and neither a millennial nor a messianic reign has yet come to be. The gospel had not yet been preached throughout the whole world, nor has there yet been a time of trouble such as never was "since there were men on earth," unless this time referred to the circumstances of the Jews in the Holocaust. The literal restoration of Israel shows the way in which certain images of prophecy may be quite literal, and the question is always *what* to read literally and what symbolically. The resurrection can be understood symbolically to refer to the soul that is its image, to a passage of the soul that corresponds, as baptism corresponds to the Flood of Noah. Because of this, some say there is no literal resurrection, or that the teaching of resurrection was the voluntary or involuntary invention of the Apostles. Some, too, thought there was no literal Flood of Noah. Yet the teaching of Jesus to Thomas is that the resurrection is quite literal (John 20:24-29). The cosmos can be read by reading the soul, which in its mysteries might be evidence of the greater mysteries. That man is the image of God implies that the study of man is the key, for us, to the contemplation of the whole.

Carl Jung: Antichrist and Symbol.

The thought of Carl Jung on this point is very interesting. In the context of a discussion of the image of God in the soul and the doctrine that evil is only a privation of *being* and good, he writes (1978, p. 42):

On the Revelation

> For anyone who has a positive attitude towards Christianity the problem of the Antichrist is a hard nut to crack. It is nothing less than the counter stroke of the devil, provoked by God's incarnation. For the devil attains his true stature as the adversary of Christ, and hence of God, only after the rise of Christianity, while as late as the Book of Job he was still one of God's sons and on familiar terms with Yahweh...The coming of the Antichrist is not just a prophetic prediction–it is an inexorable psychological law...The ideal of spirituality striving for the heights was doomed to clash with the materialistic earth-bound passion to conquer matter and master the world. The Renaissance [as a] spirit of the renewal of the antique spirit...was chiefly a mask... The subsequent developments that led to the enlightenment and the French Revolution have produced a worldwide situation today which can only be called "anti-Christian," in the sense that confirms the early Christian anticipation of the "end of time." It is as if, with the coming of Christ, opposites that were latent till then had become manifest, or as if a pendulum had swung violently to one side and were now carrying out the complementary movement in the opposite direction...

The psychological law to which Jung refers is called enantiodromia, an opposite development that attends things good in the world, where the balance of opposites is the rule. The shadow of the God-image Christ is the Antichrist, and Jung understands the astrological age of the fishes or Pisces to portend a shift from one to the opposite. The Antichrist–as counter stroke of the devil provoked by the incarnation–may help us to understand Chapter 12 of the Revelation, in which the birth of the Messiah coincides with the defeat of the devil in heaven and his casting out onto the earth. Coincident with this astrological age is the balancing of two fishes, Christ and Antichrist. Jung considers

St. Francis and Bernard, and the stirring that led to the struggle with heresies that characterized the second millennium of Christianity, Joachim and "the Holy Ghost movement, which some have rightly seen as the forerunner of the Reformation" (*Aion*, p. 87). The second half of the age of Pisces would then contain the development of the anti-Christian, culminating in the beginning of the new age of Aquarius, when the procession of the equinoxes enters into the next constellation, dated roughly as between 2000 and 2200 A.D. (Ibid., p.92; 94 n. 84).

Jung will be revisited on various points throughout. On the eve of World War II, in 1936, when Heidegger was delivering speeches for the Nazis, Jung wrote an article called "Wotan" in which he considered what was then arising in Germany. He had begun to call attention to the rising problem as early as 1919. After the Second World War, in his essay "After the Catastrophe," he recognizes the events that have occurred as "apocalyptic," though he does not from here enter into a reading of the Revelation. Jung wrote: "It is above all the Germans who have an opportunity, perhaps unique in history, to look into their own hearts and to learn what the perils of the soul were from which Christianity tried to rescue mankind" (p. 187).[50] He was one of very few then alive who saw the diabolical aspect of the new German nationalism.

In *Aion*, Jung considers the connection between the motion toward the coming of the Antichrist and the development of the Western world:

> ...until 1933 only lunatics would have been found in possession of living fragments of myth...After this date, the world of heroes and monsters spread like a devastating fire over whole nations, proving that the strange world of myth had suffered no loss of vitality during the centuries of reason and enlightenment...(1978, p. 35).
>
> The dechristianization of our world, the Luciferian development of science and technology, and the frightful material and moral destruction left behind by the second world war

have been compared more than once with the eschatological events foretold in the New Testament.

Jung then cites John in the second letter (4:3) regarding "the spirit of Antichrist ... of whom you have heard he cometh" (Ibid, p. 36). He continues:

> The antichristian era is to blame that the spirit became non-spiritual and that the visualizing archetype gradually degenerated into rationalism, intellectualism and doctrinarism, all of which leads straight to the tragedy of modern times now hanging over our heads like a sword of Damocles...[51] Fortunately for us, the threat of his coming had already been foretold in the New Testament–for the less he is recognized, the more dangerous he is (Ibid, p. 86).

When a symbol is seen, as in a dream, the meaning is above our minds, and so unknown.[52] This is different from seeing snapshots of visible scenes from the future, though this may also occur. An example can be seen in the fact that John writes of a world with horses and chariots, if strange ones, and locusts that look like futuristic fighter planes. *Cavalry* are arrayed for battle rather than tanks, etc. (9:17). Even the most literal of literalists has not considered a teaching that there will literally be horses and chariots in the battle. And so it seems we are not being shown something that is like a snapshot or photograph.

On the difference between a symbol and a sign, Carl Jung writes that a symbol refers to something *unknown*. *Sign* here means not a prognostication or indication, but like a stop sign, one image that refers to something easily apparent to common sense, where one must for safety perform a certain action here; i.e., stop. When symbols are explained as though they were signs, such as saying that seven represents perfection, and this or that represents this or that, the explanation may be useful as a beginning, as are lists of dream symbols and their meanings. But as a replacement for knowledge, these interpretations are ridiculous. The symbols come from and lead to knowledge that is apparently *in* the soul, and can be recollected, as Plato's Socrates explains regarding geometry (*Meno* 81b-e). While the knowledge is not *ours*, the access can be cultivated. The symbols help to awaken this knowledge in us, which in turn makes the images become intelligible. There is a faculty that is awakened, though, as we think; it is a mistake to call this knowledge. We can be mistaken in our relation to it, but it is like gaining access to a realm through a door. It may result from our participation in the death and resurrection. Al Farabi writes of the difference between madness and gnosis: the mad receive the "first intelligibles," but "not as they really are."[53] Some are not equipped to receive them, but happiness is possible, he says, only when the "Active intellect first gives the first intelligibles." Cults and fascist movements may be possessed by the "archetypes," using images like swastikas and thousand-year reigns as instruments in the pursuit of power, yet this is only possible because the archetypes or something like this *is* there, and *can* be found in the *right* way. There are things involved in the Revelation that most readers do not know about: We see the cities, like Rome, but do we see what Augustine calls the City of Man, contrasted with the City of God? We see the woman and the particular churches. But do we see the mystical bride? We see the particular persons or nations, which readers try to identify with the referents of the symbols in the Revelation. But do we see the movement of history and church history over the course of centuries and ages, and the fundamental questions involved? Do we see what must have occurred within humanity in order for the political movements of Nazism and communism to emerge?

In contemplating an image or symbol, there is some question as to what to see "literally" and what "symbolically," or allegorically. As Al Farabi writes, in a story regarding the works of Plato:[54] A certain ascetic was forbidden from leaving the city of a tyrant, so he pretended to be a reveling drunk. When the gatekeeper asked who he was, he said "I am so and so, the ascetic." He was thought to be joking, and so was able to pass without having lied in what he said. Farabi says that the writings

On the Revelation

of Plato are like this. If the Revelation too is like this, it would mean something like the following: The images we are shown are symbols of high things that are real but unknown. Every once in a while, though, things are said that are shockingly literal, and in a way that would be impossible without prophecy. Scripture too is like this, and sometimes slips a truth past the gatekeeper of a tyrant.

What Then Should We Do?

It is often said that *it* will come as did the flood, while people are going about their usual human business (Mt. 24:37; Luke 17:26-27). "Watch, therefore…" (Mt. 24:42). Humans are of course terrified by the natural disaster foretold. Yet to each, it is no more terrifying than one's own death. A secret truth may be that the body itself is not really afraid of death. Humans are always shocked by sudden deaths, as though surprised to learn that we are mortal. This may be because we never knew a time when we *were not*. The wonder, though, is that we are here at all, not that the gift is limited. It is very amazing when we consider that we—I now and you the reader—are here now and then. The miraculous opportunity of created life is more amazing than its limitations. Though we cannot but live our lives oblivious to the necessity of our own death, the terror of death itself is said to come from the imagination. Yet birth and death are ordinary, and not astonishing, like the apocalypse. And while measures that take into account certain possibilities are prudent, the most important things to be done in preparation are the same as any other time: "Repent, for the Kingdom of heaven is at hand" (Mt. 3:2; Acts 2:38), and turn toward the Lord (Mt. 18:3; Acts 4:19). Love one another (John 12-14), for he who seeks to save his life will lose it (Matthew 10:39), but the one who lays down their life for their friend will gain life in the highest sense. Forgive, or we will not be forgiven (Mt. 6:14). Do not waste time, but live for what lasts! The moments we are alive are as if recorded in the book. We are to be watchful, pray that we be counted worthy to escape all the things about to happen, and to prepare to stand before the son of man (Luke 21:29-34). As in all times of catastrophe, it would be difficult for humans to retain the human character rather than turn on one another, and so we would be tested, and can prepare, by cultivating the human character and strengthening this against the animal.

When reading the Revelation, an obscuring of the purpose can occur, and this tendency is countered by a reading of the parable of Matthew (25:34-36). When the *nations* gather before the son of man, and he is separating sheep from goats, he will say to those on his right hand:

> "Come, oh blessed of my Father, inherit the kingdom prepared for you from the foundation of the world; for I was hungry and you gave me food, I was thirsty and you gave me drink, I was a stranger, and you welcomed me, I was naked and you clothed me, I was sick and you visited me, I was in prison and you came to me…"

Another way of saying this same thing appears in the Gospel of Thomas (59[55]):

> Jesus said, "Take heed of the Living One while you are alive, lest you die and seek to see him and be unable to do so."

iii The Title, Greeting, and Introductory Vision of the Revelation

Title: "The Apocalypse of John" and 1:1-4

The most ancient form of the title is simply *Apokalupsis Ioannou*, "Apocalypse of John." This is said to be most likely a title placed on the outside of ancient papyrus rolls generally, and probably not given to the work by the author. The first sentence probably functioned as the title given by the author.[56] This reads: "The revelation of Jesus Christ, which God gave him to show to his servants what must soon take place (1:1)." Since we have discussed, in the preceding chapters, the author John and the saying that these things will occur "soon," and gathered much of what is said in the rest of scripture regarding these things, we will continue reading and commenting on the text.

In reading, it is important to consider to whom a work is addressed. The addressee of the Revelation is "the servants of God." It is a private or select audience, of those already committed to the service of God. Unlike the gospels, the purpose is not, for example, to witness the story of Jesus to all mankind. It does not contain an apology arguing that Christianity ought to be allowed, or even a presentation of the gospel, the story of the death and resurrection, aiming to show or persuade the reader that Jesus is the Christ. This select audience and purpose may account for the strange absence of usual Christian themes in the text. It is addressed to the churches or the servants of God, and assumes certain things common to this audience or group of hearers. It is written to all the servants, rather than, like the seven letters, to particular churches.

The revelation is given by God to Jesus Christ, then to John by means of the angel, then to the churches or the servants, by way of writing, in order to show his servants what must soon occur. According to Aune, the genitive in Greek, "revelation of Jesus

Christ" might mean *either* that he is the object of the uncovering or that the revelation, given by God, is his or belongs to him. The genitive of possession is consistent with the rest of the sentence, though the objective genitive is a possible reading, a possibility preserved by the English 'of' rather than 'from.' The revelation of Jesus is the second coming or presence, the *"parousia"* by which he destroys the Beast and the false prophet. As nearly every recent commentary notes, the word *apo-calypse* more literally means "un-covering." It means un-eclipsed, a double negative which does not mean the same thing as open. "Open" includes what has never been hidden. The word occurs only in the title and in the first line of the text. It is used elsewhere in scripture, by Paul (as at 2 Thess. 2:8), and once by Peter, sometimes to refer to high mysteries (I Cor. 12:1, 7; Galatians 1:13), though not in the sense of the second coming or the last judgment. Macarthur notes that the word occurs 18 times in scripture, "and always indicates that something has become visible to the eye" (1973, p. 4). Luke uses the word as it would be used here in the objective genitive: "on the day when the son of man is revealed." The word might have been used at 11:19, where the temple in heaven is opened and the Ark of the Covenant seen, though it was not. Jesus made the uncovering known by sending his angel to John. John now addresses the book to the seven churches in Asia, as he was told in the vision to do.

Asia is the Roman province around the city of Ephesus where John lived after leaving Jerusalem, and before Domitian exiled him to Patmos. It is not said why the revelation is sent to these seven churches and not explicitly to all the churches, or to the whole Church. It seems likely that John would be the leading elder or Bishop in the Church of Ephesus, and that he sends this letter to these seven churches to prepare them for what is soon to occur because these are under his care. Victorinus notes that Paul too wrote letters to seven churches, and taught that the churches are arranged by sevens (*Commentary on the Apocalypse*, 1.16). It is strange that the churches of Rome, Alexandria, and Syria are not addressed. The church at Jerusalem had been destroyed, when James was thrown from the pinnacle of the temple, just prior to

70 A.D.[57] The people of the church had been commanded by a revelation before the war to leave the city.[58] The seven letters address the seven churches under the care of John regarding the things which are, but then the great future revelation is no longer a part of the seven letters. It is addressed to these seven, but also to all, or to all the servants. Victorinus writes that seven is the typical number of the Church, or all the churches, and cites Isaiah 4:1 "In that day seven women will take hold of one man…" (p. 345). In this way it becomes clear that the seven stars or the seven lamps before the throne may not be simply the seven churches of Asia, but the whole church.

[1:4] John delivers a greeting of grace and peace from God, here referred to as "the one who is and was and is to come." As Richard Bauckham relates, this is a name of God that is unique to the book of Revelation. It is said to be an interpretation of the three tenses of the divine eternity implicit in the name of God given in Exodus (3:14). A part of each of the tenses of the verb to be; for past, present, and future are combined in Hebrew to form the name.[59] The name occurs four other times in the book (1:8; 4:8, 11:17, and 16:5).[60] The form of the sentence occurs also in a line of Hesiod's *Theogony*, where the muses are said to reveal, "What is and what will be and what was before" (38). Hesiod, famously, prophesies the sixth age of man (*Works and Days*, 180 ff.), and the apocalyptic ending of the fifth age. Aune cites Plato's *Laws* (715 e) and *Timeaus* (37 e) "For we say being was and is and will be." The appellation is contrasted with that of the Beast who "was, and *is not*, and is about to ascend from the abyss and go to perdition" (17:8). This is a very strange contrast, based on what looks like Greek thought, where being and non-being are first written about (Plato *Republic 477a- 478d, etc.*). The use of the verbs of being as nouns occurs first not in Greek philosophy but in the book of Exodus, at 3:14. Aune (*Revelation*, p. 31) gives examples of the use of '*o on*' as a divine name in the Septuagint and among the Greek-speaking Jews, and notes that John is the first Christian author to use this name, here in the Revelation. While the phrase does not occur in the Gospel or Letters of John, it is especially John who is able to receive an account in these terms. The Lord *is*, was "in the beginning" (John 1:1), and is to

The Introductory Vision

come, as it seems, when the son and the Kingdom of God comes. In the sense that the Lord *is*, the Beast who is the Antichrist[61] and incarnates the dragon *is not* (Revelation 17:8). The contrast of good and evil is somehow fundamentally related to the contrast of being and non-being. What *is*, or the natural articulation of things, may be *the good* of each thing, rather than only an essence abstracted from the imperfect things. That the good of things exists, and is more real than the changing things, is the proof of the existence of the divine. This proof is related to what is called the ontological argument presented by St. Anselm. When things become better, where does the good come from? Hence there surely is the divine, though we do not know what it is like. Let every city be unjust,[62] still there is justice, by which these are measured.[63] The imperfect shapes we draw in geometry are measured by the perfect, which hence exists "in" space, and time, since these exist in it.

The primary meaning of the Kingdom includes a sense in which it is actual always, and so can be present now, "in the midst of you" (Luke 17:20-21), "spread out upon the earth, and men do not see it" (#113; #2).[64] The eternal Kingdom is now, yet not in the sense that it would be if men *were* seeing it or living in it.[65] It may be man that changes, to reenter the harmony of all things that we somehow left, through what is pictured as the fall.

[1:4b] The Trinity is apparent in the greeting of the book of Revelation, which is from God, from the seven spirits before his throne, and from Jesus Christ. Bauckham writes: "Revelation always avoids referring to God and Christ as a plurality," with plural verbs and pronouns (cf. 11:15; 22:3-4). The singular shows the Johannine unity of the son and father. The seven spirits, sometimes identified with the sevenfold nature of the spirit (Isaiah 11:2-3), are not the same as, but are related to, the angels of the seven churches, who appear as seven stars (3:1), and the churches, which appear as seven lamp stands The seven spirits appear as "seven lamps of fire, which are the seven spirits of God" (4:5). Aune (P. 34) identifies these with the seven archangels, "the seven angels who stand before God" (8:2). Moses is told on Mount Sinai to make a lamp stand with seven lamps (Exodus 25: 31-40). The seven spirits are later said to be seven eyes on the seven horns of the Lamb, seen standing as though it had been slain, between the throne and the four living creatures (5:6). In the book of Zechariah (4:10), prior to the beginning of the Christian churches, the seven lamp stands are "the eyes of the Lord which range through the whole earth." It is possible that the churches are vessels of the spirit, horns being like kings (as at 13:1) or ruling powers or organizations. The distinction and relation of these two, spirits and lamp stands, is important for the question of the understanding of the churches in the Revelation. There is a sense in which the churches are authoritative, as vessels of the Holy Spirit; and a sense in which the churches are under a higher authority, and mortal, worthy of either praise or blame. The one like a son of man addresses the angels of the seven churches, and these are both praised and blamed, and they are told to hear "what the Spirit says to the churches." Aune comments: "Since each of the proclamations is presented as the word of the exalted Christ, a close relationship between Christ and the Spirit is presupposed, one that is theologically similar to the fourth gospel, though not expressed in the same language" (John 14:25-26; 15:26; 16:13-14). The son of man appears to John "in the midst" of the seven lamp stands, leading us to think of his presence in our midst, "Whenever two or more are gathered in his name" (Matthew 18:20).

The Holy Spirit in the singular is present in the Revelation only as the one who addresses the churches, in the signing off at the end (22:17), and when John enters into the spirit (1:10, 17:3, 21:10). The Holy Spirit is not present as a character in the vision, except as the seven spirits before his throne, and in the speaking of Jesus to the churches, said to be "what the spirit says to the churches."

[1:5-6] The greeting from God is followed by a greeting from John, or a dedication to Jesus. Jesus here is called faithful witness, first born of the dead, and the ruler of kings on earth. The second three show some relation to the first three: was, is, and is to come. In what sense is Jesus called the ruler or king of kings? He is not the king of all the kings in the book of Revelation. It may be that Jesus is king of spiritual kings, or priests, or that he ought to be king of kings, or is the king of good

The Introductory Vision

kings. John then wishes glory and dominion "into the ages of the ages (*eis tous aionas ton aionon*) to him who loves us, freed us from our sins by his blood, and made us a kingdom of priests to the Father." The Revelation is addressed especially to the priests (14:4-5).

[1:7] That "He is coming in the clouds," or in the same way in which he was seen to go (Acts 1:11; Daniel 7:13), is important also because in this way we might know that it is no man born of woman who will appear as the Messiah. It seems from this that we can know that anyone who enters the world in the usual way, as a child, and claims to be the Messiah, is a false Messiah. It is said that there will be many of these (Matthew 24:5; 24-27). And if someone says he is here or there, we are not to follow them, as his arrival will be unmistakable: "as the lightening comes from east and shines as far as the west, so will the coming of the son of man be" (Matthew 24:27; Luke 17:24), coming on all who dwell on earth (Luke 21:35). All the tribes will see "the son of man coming on the clouds of heaven with power and with great glory" (24:30). Daniel sees a night vision in which "with the clouds of heaven there came one like a son of man" (7:13).[66] That every eye will see him, too, means that he will not be here for a while and then be revealed, or gradually become known. One suggestion is that television, or some similar worldwide media, might fulfill the prophecy.[67] That they will look on him whom they have pierced is prophesied by Zechariah (12:10-11), when the Lord pours out a spirit of compassion and supplication on the inhabitants of Jerusalem. Here, all the tribes of the earth will wail because of him, the Messiah we rejected.

[1:8] Bauckham notes that the eighth verse is one of only two places in the Revelation (with 21:5-6) where God speaks directly:

> I am the Alpha and the Omega, the beginning and the end, says the Lord God, who is, and who was and who is to come, the Almighty.
> [*Ego eimi to A kai to O, archen kai telos, legei o kurios, o ov kai o en kai o erchomenos, o pantokratour*]

He also says in Chapter 21 that He is "the Alpha and Omega, the beginning and the end." Other possible places are the unidentified voices, as at 16:13 and 18:3-24. John doesn't say when the Lord said this, and it may indicate the divine presence as he is writing. Isaiah (44:6) had similarly written:

> Thus says the Lord, the king of Israel
> And his Redeemer, the Lord of hosts:
> I am the first and I am the Last;
> Besides me there is no god.
> Who is like me? Let him proclaim it.
> Who has announced from of old the things to come?
> Let them tell us the things to be.

And again (48:12-13):

> Harken to me, O Jacob,
> And Israel, whom I called!
> I am He, I am the first
> And I am the last.
> My hand laid the foundation of the earth,
> And my right hand spread out the heavens.
> When I call them,
> They stand forth together.

As in the opening chapter of the Revelation, it is the Lord and his Redeemer who say they are the first and last. In Isaiah, the name "the first and last" occurs in saying that the Lord announces the things to come, and calls the earth and the heavens to stand forth together.

The divisions of the first chapter that appear are A) verses 1-3, which might have been prefaced to John's letter; B) 4-7, which is the greeting to the churches from John and the Lord; C) verse 8, then, stands by itself, following the greeting and preceding the story of the initial vision on Patmos (verses 9-20).

The Introductory Vision

[1:9-11] John was on Patmos in the Spirit on the Lord's Day when he heard a trumpet-like voice behind him. Without saying who is speaking, John is told to write what he sees in a book, and send it to the seven churches, which the one speaking names. From what is said later (4:1), it appears that the voice is distinct from the one like a son of man, who speaks the messages to the seven churches. John then turned (*epistrephe*) to see the voice, or to see who it is that he hears. Aune cites Exodus 20:18 and Daniel 7:11, where, as commented by Philo, the Voice is paradoxically visible, and the prophets write the word that they "saw" (Isaiah 2:1; Aune, pp. 87-88).

It is first significant that John is seeing a vision rather than a dream. In light of Maimonides' discussion of the eleven or twelve degrees of prophecy: John *hears* a voice and then turns to *see*, going from the ninth to the tenth degree of prophecy. When he sees Him, the one like a son of man, he falls at his feet *as though dead*, and is then addressed by the one who is "first and last, the living one who died and is alive for evermore, who has the keys of Death and Hades." Maimonides writes that only Moses spoke to God without the mediation of the imagination, or in a *vision* rather than a dream, seeing that it is God who spoke to him. This may have occurred at line 8. Ezekiel sees in a vision, then like John falls on his face and is lifted up (1; 3:23; 8:3; 11:24; Isaiah 6:1). Maimonides writes that the other prophets do not hear the speech of God in a vision, but after a state of submersion, from vision into dream (*Guide*, II.46; Numbers 12:6-7). It is at this point of submersion, after hearing and prior to seeing Him, that John falls not into a sleep, as did Daniel (10:9), but "as though dead." He is then touched by the right hand of the one like the son of man and told to write.

[1:12-16] John sees there seven lamp stands, and "one like a son of man" in the midst of the lamp stands. The one like a son of man does not say "I am Jesus," nor does he address John in a familiar way, as one who he knew so well in life. He identifies himself by saying "I am the first and last, and the living one; I died, and behold, I am alive evermore." John describes the appearance of each of eight parts of the one he sees: his clothes–robe and girdle; his head and hair; his eyes, his feet, his voice, what he held in his right hand, what issued from his mouth, and his face. The sharp two-edged sword that issues from his mouth is the only thing that is not a part of him or his clothing, and one might guess that it is the "sword of the spirit, that is the word of God" (Ephesians 6:17), two-edged because it both kills and makes live (Hebrews 4:12).[68] The vision is similar to the one seen by Daniel (Daniel 10:5-6), of a man clothed in linen with a golden girdle, eyes of fire, and feet like burnished bronze.

[1:17-8] The churches are addressed by the one like a son of man who is the living one who died and is alive for evermore, who has the keys of Death and Hades. We do not usually think of this emphatic teaching of our faith, that Jesus is alive *right now*. "For evermore" is literally "into the ages of the ages," something like millennia of millennia. The keys of Death and Hades are a mystery. These two are mentioned again together at 20:13, when Death and Hades, along with the sea, give up the dead in them. The key is the power, then exercised, of opening them for that purpose. Death is the name of the rider on the fourth horse, and Hades followed him, and these come forth when the Lamb opens the fourth seal (6:7). Together these are given power over one-quarter of the earth, somewhat as occurred in the twentieth century. And at the fifth trumpet, the angel is given the keys to the shaft of the bottomless pit (9:1), apparently by Him who has those keys.

[1:19] John is to write what he sees, that is, "what is and what is to take place hereafter." The following section of letters to the seven churches describes things that, for John, presently *are*. The seven Churches of Asia are addressed, as Bauckham notes, in the order in which a messenger landing near Ephesus would visit them. Paul visited Ephesus twice, though apparently none of the other of the seven churches. His letter to the Colossians is to be read at Laodicea, nearby, in the early sixties. John addresses a much later church, with different persons and problems, as would be if he wrote nearer to 90 A.D.

[1:20] The word mystery (*mustarion*) occurs four times in the Revelation (Aune, 106; 569-70); here, at 10:7, where the final event is called "the mystery of God," at 17:5 and 7, where "mystery" is either part of the title of, or an adjective modifying

The Introductory Vision

Babylon. Then the word is used immediately to refer to the image of the "mystery of the woman and the Beast with seven heads and ten horns that carries her." The mystery of the Revelation is about the church, Babylon, the Beast, and the end times, when the time of delay is finished.

He explains only the seven stars in his right hand and the seven lamp stands. These are the angels of the seven churches and the seven churches. In the midst of them is where Jesus said he is whenever two or more are gathered in his name (Mathew 18:20). He stands in their midst, speaking this message to the churches–i.e., the vision presents an image which reveals the true or intelligible nature of what is actually occurring at this moment, even as some dreams present a picture in symbols of the present circumstances and condition of the soul of the dreamer.[69] There is an explanation of the vision by one seen in the vision, one of the examples in scripture in which a symbol in vision is explained in the vision itself. A sort of algebra is set up on the occasions on which the text or vision is self-interpreting. In reading the Revelation, certain things are explained in the text itself, so that it is possible to begin from these, and stray as little as possible from coherence with them. More examples occur in the Revelation (7:14-17; 17:7-18), in Daniel (7:16-27; 8:17-26; 9:22-27), and to some extent in Zechariah (4:5). Daniel receives the explanation of the vision of the fourth beast, the last world empire, which makes war on the saints. It is from these internal explanations that solid interpretation might begin. We are told what the stars and the lamp stands are (the angels of the seven churches and the seven churches). The seven torches are the seven spirits (4:5). The smoke of the incense is the prayers of the saints (5:8). We are told that the multitudes seen with white robes are those that have come out of the tribulation, and we are told what their white robes are (7:14). We are told what the two witnesses are: the two olive trees and lamp stands (11:4); what the heads and horns of the Beast are: seven kings and ten kings (17:9, 12); what the woman Babylon is: "The great city which has dominion over the kings of the earth" (17:18). We are also told what the waters on which she is seated are: the peoples and multitudes (not tribes) and nations and tongues (17:15). This algebra is the most solid basis from which to begin to read the Revelation. As in algebra, one might fill out the terms of an equation by beginning from the variables that are identified–the numbers that are given–so in the reading of the prophecy, the terms uncovered should cohere with the scriptural angelic explanations. The angelic explanation is also in symbolic terms, so that we are not relieved of the opportunity to try to see the meaning for ourselves. Yet from the beginning, the first term in the interpretation of the Revelation is that it concerns the churches.

The lamp stand in the temple treasures commissioned through Moses in the wilderness is made of gold, with six branches, three on one side and three on the other side (Ex. 31-32). It has seven lamps, indicating that the stand is one of the lamps. It is to be lit with pure olive oil, and set up to burn continuously (Ex. 27:20) "as a sign of God's presence" (Oxford note to Ex. 27:20). Zechariah sees a lamp stand with a bowl on it, and seven lamps, with two olive trees by it, one on the left and one on the right. Zechariah asks what these are, and it is explained there that these "are the seven eyes of the Lord which range through the whole earth," and the two olive trees are "the two anointed who stand by the Lord of the whole earth" (Zechariah 4:10, 14). In the work called the *Gospel of Phillip*, it is written:

> It is from the olive tree that we get the chrism, and from the chrism the resurrection...The chrism is superior to baptism, for it is from the word 'chrism' that we are called Christians, certainly not because of the word 'baptism.' And it is because of the chrism that 'The Christ' has his name. For the Father anointed the Son, and the Son anointed the apostles, and the apostles anointed us. He who has been anointed possesses everything. He possesses the resurrection, the light, the cross, the Holy Spirit. The Father gave him this in the bridal chamber; he merely accepted the gift. The Father was in the Son and the son in the Father. This is the kingdom of heaven (*Nag Hammadi Library*, p. 144).

The Introductory Vision

The churches are the presence of the Lord lighting the world, and are in a sense the eyes of God in the world, among things in one strange sense not otherwise known by him. These two olive trees may be connected to the two witnesses who are two olive trees and two lamp stands (11:4), and the seven eyes to the seven eyes of the seven horns of the Lamb (5:6) –that is, the two witnesses are not individuals but churches (or something like churches), and the horns of the Lamb are to the Lamb as the horns of the Beast are to the Beast–the ten horns then being like diabolical churches or regimes. This too will be considered in place below.

Regarding the sense in which the churches are the eyes of the Lord in the world, I recall a certain sunrise at which I wondered if there were not a sense in which, were I not viewing it, the cosmos itself would not see this sunrise from this particular perspective, at least in one sense–that the perception would not have been. I had just spent the whole night up talking with the girlfriend of a friend, while my own was away. The presence of the Lord lighting the world is through the church, and while in the fundamental sense, He is never not there, there is a sense in which He would not be right there in this way, were we not there.

iv: The Seven Letters

[2:1-7] Each letter is addressed to the angel of each church; that is, to the stars rather than the lamp stands. That the angel of each church is addressed in human language, praised and blamed, encouraged to endure, and told of a reward, seems to suggest that the angel of each church is something like the soul, opinion, or mind of each of the churches. Though this might be strange, it is also strange that Jesus would address the angels *through* John. The messengers of each church may be mortal humans, not angels. Or, the addressing of the angels in mortal terms and through John may be the first hint or example of the closeness of the angels and men which is suggested later in the Revelation (19:10; 21:17).

Each of the first six churches or angels are addressed by him from one part of the introductory vision: some from an essential aspect or what he is, some from what he has, and some from what he does. Beginning with Ephesus, the address is: "The words of him who holds the seven stars in his right hand, who walks among the seven gold lamp stands." The seventh, Laodicea, is addressed from Jesus in part as described in the greeting (1:5). It is possible that a complete reading would demonstrate a particular connection between each church, and the aspect from which each is addressed. In two instances, regarding Ephesus and Laodicea, the church is threatened from the aspect from which it was addressed. Ephesus might be addressed first and from this aspect because it is the leading church among the seven. The other aspects are 2) "the first and last, who died and came to life;" 3) "him who has the two-edged sword;" 4) "the son of God, who has eyes like a flame of fire, and whose feet are like burnished bronze;" 5) "him who has the seven spirits of God and the seven stars;" 6) "the holy one, the true one, who has the key of David, who opens and no one shuts, who shuts and no one opens;" and 7) "the Amen, the true and faithful witness, the beginning of God's creation." The fifth address is like the first, almost but not quite identical. Only in the case of the third is the connection between the aspect and the particular message evident: if those of Pergamum who hold the teaching of Balaam and of the Nicolaitans do not repent, he will come soon and "war against them with the sword of my mouth." Following the aspect from which each is addressed, five of the seven are praised and then blamed. Two are not praised (Sardis and Laodicea), while two are not blamed (Smyrna and Philadelphia). The Ephesian Church is praised for patience, for testing and discovering false apostles, and for rejecting the teaching of the Nicolaitans. The Ephesians are blamed for backsliding, or having fallen from the love and works which they had and did at first, and threatened with the removal of their lamp stand if they do not repent and return to their earlier works. For those blamed, a remedy is suggested, and also a threat of what will occur if the prescription is not followed. Next, in the address to each of the churches, there is the statement familiar from the gospels: "He who has an ear, let him hear what *the spirit* says to the churches." The one seen in the vision is speaking to the churches *and* the spirit is speaking to the churches. The statement occurs in the first three prior to the promise that concludes each address, and in the last four just after the promise. The statement itself occurs in the gospels after parables, as after the parable of the sower (Mark 4:9), or after the parable of the lamp put on a stand (4:22). This sort of hearing is a "spiritual discernment," an ability to perceive an esoteric meaning, apparently by the activity of knowledge or understanding of the hidden spiritual nature of things within each. The saying is not "he who has eyes, let him see," in the analogy of sight which goes with the uncovering of the *apo-kalypse*. Rather, the analogy is of hearing, which goes with the authoritative communication of an account, or of the word. Famously, the Gospel of Thomas, the 114 sayings of Jesus, opens with the saying that "whoever finds the interpretation of these sayings will not experience death."[70] Salvation involves the opening of the spiritual perception that allows for the discernment of the parables, or the ability to hear, and see. Mark explains: "With many such parables he spoke the word to them, as they were able to hear it; he did not speak to them without a parable, but privately to his own disciples, he explained everything" (4:33).

This knowledge and faculty appears, according to the Socratic or Platonic account, to be in the soul or nascent mind of each, waiting to unfold (*Meno*, 81-86c), and to be related to rebirth and immortality (81c-d). One in whom the knowledge is awakened is able to discern, to the extent that it is awakened. And even while the knowledge is asleep, images based on the knowledge attract the mind, through the shimmering of the images of the imagination. Even while awake, it is not said that we know, but that we have access to or serve a knowledge that is the preserve of mankind. Hence it is possible to be at once both a Gnostic and an Agnostic. Indeed, we wonder how anyone who tells the truth could be otherwise.

Each of the seven letters concludes with a promise to the victors or to him who conquers (*To nikon* or *'o nikon*). The seven promises all relate to the coming kingdom. Four of the seven contain images or statements that recur later, in Chapters 19-22 where the kingdom is described. There is an eighth "He who conquers" (21:7). What is meant by conquest or victory is related to that which allows the Lamb to open the seven seals (5:5; 3:21), and this allows the victors access to the Kingdom or to an aspect of the Kingdom. The first of the seven promises is:

> To him who conquers, I will grant to eat of
> the tree of life, which is in the paradise of
> God.

This is, of course, the tree which, along with the tree of the knowledge of good and evil, was in the midst of the garden (Genesis 2:9), "the paradise of God" (2:7). In the Kingdom, the leaves of the tree of life are given for the healing of the nations (22:2). The way to the garden or paradise of God is guarded with a flaming sword that turns in every way, and there is a Cherubim there. This is to prevent man, who has become "like one of us, knowing good and evil," from living forever in his imperfect condition. Immortal life is the effect of eating from the tree of life. By following the Christ through death, the saints go as if through the eastern gate of the Garden of Eden, and are allowed then to eat from the tree of life. That is what the passage of rebirth or baptism is like, analogous to but not the same as death and resurrection (Romans 6). Wisdom, according to the Book of Proverbs, is "a tree of life to those who lay hold of her, and those who hold her fast are called happy" (3:18). The tree of life seems to have something to do with the pursuit of wisdom–which according to the Greeks is the cause of happiness–and to have something to do with political philosophy, or with the healing of the nations.

[2:8-11] Polycarp was head of the second Church at Smyrna, probably until his martyrdom in 155 A.D. Smyrna was chosen by the Roman Senate as the site for a temple to Tiberius, in about A.D. 26, and a temple of Rome was built there in 195 B.C. (Tacitus, *Annals*, IV. 56, Grant ed., pp.185-186). Like the sixth, Philadelphia, the church at Smyrna is not blamed. Rather, it is praised when it is told that he knows their tribulation or affliction and their poverty, and the slander of the Jews who oppose them. These are called a "synagogue of Satan." It is said that the Christians at Smyrna were Jews uprooted from Jerusalem, and were poor for this reason.[71] They are told of a coming affliction, when "the devil" will throw some of them in prison. They are told to be faithful even "unto death," and he will give them the crown of life. The second "He who conquers" is that they will not be hurt by the second death (cp. 20:6).

Once, at a coffee shop counter, an anti-Semite cited this line in support of his teaching. The response was to gather every scripture of the New Testament regarding the Jews. The list was presented to him the following day, and he kept it. We remember the "race" of Jesus, his family, and the Twelve Apostles. Anti-Semitism, or anti-Jewish anti-Semitism (since the offspring of Ishmael, too are Shem-ites), is a like a strange delusion that came upon the Christian world. Salvation, and Christianity itself, enters the world through the Jews. Christian or European anti-Semitism begins in the early Jewish persecution of the Christians as a heretical sect. One also wonders about the reluctance of the Christian texts to blame or confront the Romans regarding the persecution of Christians. In first-century Rome, nothing of the sort could be suggested in writing, nor is there any objection to the deification of the Emperor in any of the writings.

[2:12-17] The angel of the church of Pergamum is addressed from he who has the sharp two-edged sword. It may be that this address is because he will, with his word, war against the Nicolaitans and those who hold their teaching. Those at Pergamum are said to dwell "where Satan's throne is," and are praised for fidelity even when one witness, Antipas, was killed among them. Pergamum is blamed, though, for some "who hold the teaching of Balaam, who taught Balak to put a stumbling block before the sons of Israel, that they might eat food sacrificed to idols and practice immorality."[72] The teaching of Jezabel to the fourth church, Thyatria, is the same (2:20). One wonders what the connection between these would be, in some lost significance regarding idolatry and temple or cult prostitution. These are the minimal laws or necessary things, beyond which no further burden is placed by the early church on gentile Christians (Acts 15:28-29). In explanation of why it is said that Satan dwells there and that his throne is there, Pergamum is said to have been "a noted center of idolatrous worship."[73] Later, the fifth angel pours his bowl of wrath on the "throne of the beast" (16:10). The character of the teaching of the Nicolaitans is also obscure. Eusebius writes that Nicolaitius was a deacon, one of the seven appointed with Stephen. Accused by the apostles of jealousy over his beautiful wife, he offered her to the apostles, in order to overcome the passion that is the cause of jealousy. The Nicolaitans, following his teaching that one ought to "abuse the flesh," apparently practiced free love, on the basis of this interesting and questionable understanding of the passion and its conquest. Victorinus writes that these held a heretical opinion according to which "food that had been offered to idols might be exorcised and eaten, and that whoever should have committed fornication might receive peace on the eighth day."[74] Irenaeus writes that in the opening of his gospel, John seeks "to remove that error which by Cerinthus had been disseminated among men, and a long time previously by those termed Nicolaitans, who are an offset of that 'knowledge' falsely so called, that he might confound them, and persuade them that there is but one God who made all things by his word; and not, as they allege, that the Creator was one but the Father of the Lord another" (*Against Heresies* III, xi).

The third "to him who conquers" is more mysterious, and contains elements not mentioned later in the text:

> To him who conquers, I will give some of the hidden manna, and I will give him a white stone, with a new name written on the stone which no one knows except him who receives it.

The new name on the white stone is like the name inscribed on the rider of the white horse which no one knows but himself (19:11). This rider is called "Word of God," and on his robe and thigh are inscribed the name King of kings and Lord of lords. The unknown name may likewise be a capacity or attribute of the Messiah, and so of the servants. The stone reminds of other symbols of the image of God in man, such as the philosopher's stone or the "coping stone" of dialectic set at the top of studies by Socrates in the education described in Plato's *Republic* (VII, 534e). It might be a pure image for thinking on the knowledge of the divine in man, or the image of God in man. The stone (*lithos*) elsewhere in scripture is the stone rejected by the builders (Acts 4:11; Psalm 118:22), and the stone that smites the statue seen by Daniel. The manna that came down from heaven in the wilderness did not give eternal life, but was provided by God to feed Israel in the wilderness (Exodus 16:13-36). A jar of this manna was kept in the ark, so that the generations would see the bread with which the Lord fed them in the wilderness. The hidden manna is the body of Christ that is the bread from heaven (John 6:51, 57-58).

[2:18-29] The angel of the Church at Thyatira is addressed from the one who has eyes like flames and feet like burnished bronze, here explicitly called the son of God. Thyatira is blamed for those who tolerate Jezebel, a self-proclaimed prophetess who teaches idolatry and adultery, like Jezebel the wife of Ahab (1 Kings 16:31-32). She has been given time to repent, but refuses.

She will be made ill, and her adulterers thrown into great tribulation unless they repent, and her children will be stricken dead. It would be interesting to hear if this actually occurred. It is said to be so that "all the churches know that I am he who searches mind (literally "kidneys") and heart."

[3:1-6] The angel of the church at Sardis is addressed from him who has the seven spirits of God and the seven stars. Sardis is admonished as having the name of being alive, but being dead. They are encouraged to awaken and strengthen what remains. There are a few in Sardis who have not soiled their garments, who will walk with him in white. The fifth "he who conquers" is that he "Shall be clad thus in white garments, and I will not blot his name out of the book of life; I will confess his name before my father." The book of life is another element of the kingdom, in the promises to those who conquer, as appears explicitly later in the Revelation, surrounding the description of the heavenly city (20:11-15).

[3:7-13] Philadelphia is addressed from outside the visual image of 1:12-16, from the holy and true one who has the key of David, who opens and shuts definitively (Isaiah 22:22). The key of David opens the Kingdom, as Jesus continues the Kingship of the line of David, interrupted in 607 B.C. He knows their works, and has set before them an open door. Philadelphia is the second church, after Smyrna, that is not blamed. And like Smyrna, Philadelphia is harassed by a Jewish or Judaizing group called a "Synagogue of Satan."[75] Beyond what is told to Smyrna, the church at Philadelphia is told that the false Jews will be made to bow at their feet, and will learn that he has loved them. Also unlike those of Smyrna, the Philadelphians are told:

> I will keep you from the hour of trial which is coming on the whole world, to try those who dwell upon the earth. I am coming soon; hold fast what you have, so that no one may seize your crown.

Does he here refer to the tribulation hour, or to some more brief and imminent period of tribulation, as the ten-day period foretold to the Smyrna? Are the persecutions of the Philadelphian church not counted as part of the great tribulation? Does the Philadelphian Church in particular still exist? Or is the trial coming on the whole world one which pertains to a more general church? Or does the vision not present the universal tribulation hour as coming within the lifetimes of the persons who then made up the Philadelphian church? Is it possible that the vision itself, too, expected the tribulation hour to come *very* soon? The persecution of Christians continued through the time of Justin and Ignatius, until the time just before Constantine, early in the fourth century.

The sixth promise reads as follows:

> He who conquers, I will make him a pillar in the temple of my God; never shall he go out of it, and I will write on him the name of my God, and the name of the city of my God, the new Jerusalem which comes down from my God out of heaven, and my own new name. He who has an ear...

Bauckham reads the promise of becoming a pillar in the temple in light of the exclusion of the Christians from the temple of the Jews. The new name written on a white stone, in the promise to those of the church of Pergamum who conquer (2:17), may be the same as his own new name, here written on the victorious ones themselves.

[3:14-22] The seventh church, at Laodicea, is addressed from "the Amen, the faithful and true witness, the beginning of God's creation." Following the parts of the introductory vision in each address, the Amen is from 1:18 of the introductory vision. The faithful witness is from 1:5 of the salutation, and the beginning from the Alpha, so that the statement proceeds in reverse from what is like a conclusion, through a middle, to the beginning. Laodicea is only blamed and in no way praised. The Laodiceans are told they will be spewed out of his mouth for being neither hot nor cold. Laodicea apparently considers itself to be rich and in need of nothing, while being "wretched, pitiable, poor, blind, and naked." The city, now in ruins, was a center of commerce, selling a well-known eye salve, and had water from a hot spring that flowed lukewarm.[76] The illusory fullness is similar to what is said by Babylon, when she denies that she is a widow (18:7). They are given the most elaborate counsel of any of the seven churches:

> Therefore I counsel you to buy from me gold refined by fire, that you may be rich, and white garments to clothe you and to keep the shame of your nakedness from being seen, and salve to anoint your eyes, that you may see.

The apparent wealth and actual poverty of Laodicea is to be remedied with refined gold, or the true wealth of knowledge or wisdom. White garments, which Laodicea thinks it has but truly needs, are the chastity and good actions (19:8) which are the best condition of the body, and cover for the nakedness or vulnerability of man that comes from having a body. Their blindness or need of sight would be remedied by an anointing salve which would bring spiritual sight; the sight of the eye of the soul (Matt 7:22). According to one ancient text, it is the word that is applied to the eyes of the soul as a medicine, because matter "strikes blows at her eyes, wishing to make her blind."[77]

Though Laodicea is blamed and in no way praised, the way is open for them to take this counsel and repent. Those he loves, he reproves and chastens. The precedent to the seventh 'to him who conquers' shows how open the way is for Laodicea:

> Behold, I stand at the door and knock; if any one hears my voice, and opens the door, I will

> come in to him and eat with him, and he with me. He who conquers, I will grant him to sit with me on my throne, as I myself conquered and sat down with my father on his throne. He who has an ear, let him hear what the spirit says to the churches.

This line is one of two places (with 22:1-3; cp. 11:15) where the son and Father are both enthroned, and those who conquer also share in the throne. This is astonishing and demonstrates that the Bride is a completion of the throne.

The seven letters are framed by the seven attributes of the sender and the seven promises to him who conquers. He who conquers will eat from the tree of life, not be hurt by the second death, receive the hidden manna and the white stone with a new and secret name. He will be given power over the nations and be given the morning star, be clad in white garments with his name in the book of life, confessed before the Father and his angels, be made a pillar in the temple of his God, with the name of his God, of the city of God the new Jerusalem, and have the new name of Jesus written on him, and he will sit with him on his throne. The seven things described separately as seven may be one, pertaining to the victors in all the churches in the New Jerusalem. In this way, the introductory vision and the letters to the seven churches set the topic and provide a base for the interpretation of the vision of the whole of the Revelation.

There is a common reading attempting to relate the seven letters to seven ages of the church. There seems to be not a line to support this: none of the descriptions correspond at all to one period any more than another. The attempts to relate the particulars are awkward, and again one suspects that a wrong turn in the argument has been carried over from a common source. Scofield explicates that the fore view of the church period *must* be in the seven letters, because "the church does not appear on earth after 3:22." But this again involves assumptions, to be addressed in the following chapter. For the present, we note that the attempt produces a weak understanding of church history and ignores the fundamental point: There *is* no church singular in the

Revelation, and the seven churches are not authoritative in any final sense.

What is the relation of the seven churches, their angels, and their seven sealed letters to the sets of things that occur in sevens throughout the remainder of the text? After the seven letters, there follow five or six sets of things that occur in sevens. After the seven angels of the seven churches are addressed, there is (2) the scroll with seven seals, (3) seven trumpets blown by seven angels, apparently within the seventh seal. Then (4) there is a statement of the seven thunders, during the sixth trumpet, which is "sealed up." Then, (5) apparently as part of the third woe or seventh trumpet, prior to the new heaven and earth, there occurs a series of visions (are there seven?) in the second half of the book, from Chapter 12 on, introduced and demarcated by a phrase such as "then I looked" or "then I saw." These include (6) seven angels with statements or messages (Chapter 14), before (7) seven angels with seven plagues or seven bowls of wrath (Chapter 16).

v: The Vision of the Throne
And the Scroll

In the previous section of the seven letters, Jesus is the speaker, and John writes what he is told to write. The remainder of the text, regarding what must take place "after this," is narrated by John himself, each vision or sight often introduced with the statement "I looked" or "I saw…" In the fourth chapter, John sees a vision of the Lord on the throne, and twenty-four elders and four living creatures around the throne. The Lord has a scroll, and in the fifth chapter, the twenty-four elders and the four living creatures say that the Lamb is worthy to open the scroll. In the sixth chapter, each of the four seals is opened, revealing one of the Four Horsemen of the Apocalypse. The fifth seal reveals the martyrs under the throne, who are told to wait for the avenging of their blood until the number of their fellow martyrs is completed. With the opening of the sixth seal, the sun becomes black and the moon like blood, and everyone hides in the mountains from the wrath of the Lamb. Chapter 7, still within the sixth seal, then shows the devastation held back while the servants of God are sealed, and then the multitudes who come out of the tribulation. Finally in the eighth chapter, the seven seals are opened, showing seven angels with seven trumpet blasts that accompany another series of seven occurrences, patterned similarly with four catastrophes introducing three events. The events and visions that accompany the blowing of the trumpets take up the remainder of the first half of the book, through the eleventh chapter. The seventh trumpet is not blown until 11:15, and the first half of the book is completed with a vision of the Ark of the Covenant seen within the temple. As it seems, the seventh seal is to contain the third woe, and so must be understood to continue into the second half of the book, or even to make up the content or focus of the second half of the book.

On the Revelation

The Throne

[4:1] John looks and sees an open door in heaven. Jesus had just mentioned an open door to Laodicea. This was the door of the home of one who would let him in, to his house as to his soul, rather than, as now, an open door in heaven. Jesus describes himself as the door of the sheep in John's gospel (10:7). Victorinus suggests that the door is the New Testament, and that since it is shown as being opened, it must have been previously closed to man. One wonders if it is the same way as the ascent of Paul, and if similar visions did not occur. Ezekiel describes his vision by the river among the exiles as occurring when "the heavens were opened" (Ezekiel 1:1, as at 11:19 of the Revelation). There are at least four major images in common between the visions of John and Ezekiel, which may be in one sense the highest of all recorded visions. Here, John is returned to the presence of the first voice, which he hears speaking to him like a trumpet (1:10). This voice is now clearly distinguished from the one whose voice is like the sound of many waters (1:15), though when John heard the former and turned to see, he saw the latter. The voice tells him "Come up hither,[78] and I will show you what must take place after this." The question is "after what?" The voice would seem to mean, after "what *is*," as was described in the letters to the seven churches, "what is to take place hereafter" (1:19). "What must take place after this" is described from Chapter 4 on, through the opening of the seven seals in Chapters 6-11, and the seventh trumpet. The vision is to describe what is to take place after the current trials of the seven churches, into the future of the churches, and the world. Because the Lamb has conquered, the scroll can be opened, revealing— and in one sense causing the events about to occur—events which lead to the coming of the kingdom.

[4:2] The text does not say that John went through the door, but that at once he was in the spirit seeing a throne in heaven, and one seated on the throne. The vision described in Chapter 4 is of what *is*: not of things that are future, but what is always. So, technically, it may belong among the things that *are*, as well as things that were and will be. The present tense is used. Even the twenty-four elders, the part that seems as though it could at some time be otherwise, is described in the present tense, as by the word "whenever" (4:9).

The vision of the Lord on the throne occurs in four other places in scripture. The prophet Micah sees the throne when prophesying to Ahab that the other prophets were lying, and that he would die in a battle with Syria (1 Kings 22:19-23). Isaiah sees the throne, and then prophesies the desolation of Israel (Is. 6). Ezekiel, most famously, sees the throne when he is sent to prophesy to Israel (Ezekiel 1:26-28; 10:1). And Daniel sees the throne of flames with fiery wheels, with other thrones placed (Daniel 7:9-10). Enoch too saw the throne, as crystal with wheels like the sun, when he ascended to intercede for the watchers (I Enoch 16.18). Paul, in the only other New Testament account of an ascent, does not say he saw the throne. Maimonides comments on the meaning of the terms "throne" and "seated" in his guide for the Perplexed (I. 9, 11). The vision of the throne is, as Aune relates, "…frequently associated with prophecy…for prophets were thought able to join the assembly, to hear the deliberation of the council, and then to announce God's word;" according to Jeremiah (23:18), "For who has stood in the council of the Lord so as to see and hear his word?" (Aune, *Revelation*, p. 277).

The fourth chapter is the description of this vision of John, when he is taken as if into the heavens in the spirit. The one seated on the throne does not say or do anything, but appears like Jasper and Carnelian, like jewels, which are stones. Ezekiel calls the object of his vision "the appearance of the likeness of the glory of the Lord (Ezekiel 1:28). Ezekiel saw "the likeness of a throne, in appearance like sapphire" (1:26), and "something like a sapphire, in form resembling a throne" (10:1). Ezekiel saw "a likeness as it were of a human form" above the throne, appearing like gleaming bronze and enclosed fire above the loins, and fire below. Ezekiel too sees a rainbow around the throne. Isaiah saw a train of followers that filled the temple. Ezekiel saw the four living creatures under the throne, which is above a firmament that shines like crystal. The four living creatures are later identified as Cherubim (Ez. 10:20-22). Isaiah sees the Seraphim above the throne. John sees twenty-four thrones, and twenty-four elders crowned with gold crowns seated around the throne, and four living creatures around the throne. That they are seated is significant, since, as Aune reports, "There was a widespread Jewish tradition that no one is permitted to *sit* in the presence of God" (Revelation, p. 291). They may be the same as those seen seated on thrones, to whom judgment was committed. It would be strange if these included the Twelve Apostles, as is sometimes suggested, if John was one and he was seeing himself. He is addressed by one of the elders at 7:13. This seeing of the twelve occurs in Chapter 21, and is cited as a reason the work could not have been written by John–though this does not seem necessary. The twenty-four, though, are related to the twelve gates and twelve foundations (21:12-14) on which are inscribed the names of the Twelve Tribes of Israel and the Twelve Apostles. Victorinus, citing Matthew 19:27-28, identifies these as "the twenty-four fathers–twelve apostles and twelve *patriarchs*" (p. 348), such as Moses and Abraham. He also says these are the twenty-four books of the Old Testament, and in another place, at the end of his essay *On the Creation of the World*, he writes that these are the twenty-four witnesses of the days and nights, the angels of each hour, and are "older both than the other angels and than men." Lightning, voices, and thunder issue from the throne. Before it are seven torches burning, and a sea of glass like crystal. Again, giving the interpretation on this point, the text says that the seven torches are the seven spirits of God. These are the same as those "seven spirits before his throne" which greeted John in the opening (1:4). Torches are also seen by Ezekiel moving to and fro among the living creatures (Ez. 1:13). There are also seven angels of the seven churches, seven angels with seven bowls in Chapter 16, and seven messengers in Chapter 14.

In the vision of John, around the throne, on each side, are four *Zoa*, or "living creatures." Here the King James translation seems deficient in using the same word, "beast," for the Greek *zoa* and *Therion*, the word for the beasts of Chapter 13. *Zoa* is "animal" or "living" (being). The *Zoa* are "full of eyes in front and behind," "full of eyes all around and within." The first is like a lion, the second like an ox, the third "with the face of a man," and the fourth "like a flying eagle." In the vision of Ezekiel, the four "had the form of men, but each had four faces" (1:5-6), with the face of a man in front, of a lion on the right side, an ox on the left and an eagle at the back (1:10). Each of the Zoa has six wings, as do the Seraphim seen by Isaiah (Is. 6:2). Ezekiel's Cherubim have four wings, with the form of human hands under two of the wings.

Our word "animal" could be used to translate *zoa* if our word would recover some of the original meaning of the Latin word *anima*, or soul, related to *animate* and *animation*, describing self-moving or ensouled creatures, in contrast with vegetables and other creatures which do not move themselves, though they are alive. In Hebrew, the equivalent is the "breath of life," which includes all animals but no plants, and one wonders what the Hebrew equivalent in the vision of Ezekiel is that is translated as *zoa* in the Greek. The Greek word is connected to the higher sense of the word "life," higher than the meaning "ensouled," the life of the light of the mind. These four animals are alive in this highest sense. So in the ninth line, the one sitting on the throne is "the one living to the ages of the ages." Divine life, as that of the Cherubim, is apparently symbolized through animal forms, or thuriomorphically. This curious aspect of the image leads some to reflect on the subhuman, and wonder why it should be involved in the image. The image itself is thought questionable on this account.[79] Yet there may be some connection to the thuriomorphic images of the Beast, both in Daniel and to come in the thirteenth chapter of the Revelation.

The mixture of the animal and the human, as well as the particular animals that appear—lion, calf, man and eagle—and the order in which they appear, all require explanation. Why are these four the appearances or embodiments of the Cherubim, as seen by both John and Ezekiel? Does it make any difference that the four animals pertain to each cherubim alike as seen by Ezekiel, while each of the four appears to John as one of the animals? That the carnivorous appears before the vegetarian, and the upright land animal before the eagle, may indicate the unseen thing being shown. And what does it mean that they are full of eyes, "before and behind," or all over? Could they be all-seeing, and could they be the same as the four angels at the corners of the world? These are alike four, though the cherubim are higher. We will see if another explanation emerges that will account for the reason that the animal is involved here in the appearance of the highest things. Victorinus relates each to a writer of the four gospels, in a traditional reading that is well known, though no reason for it appears. As a rule, we ought to refrain from settling on a certain explanation of an image for no more reason than a similarity of number or a suitable meaning.

The four *Zoa* sing day and night: "Holy holy, holy is the Lord God Almighty, who was and is and is to come!" and whenever they sing this, and give glory, honor, and thanks to the Creator, the twenty-four elders fall down before the one seated on the throne, and cast their crowns before the throne. The rule or participation in the throne of the twenty-four elders is based on their sacrifice of rule in the recognition that the Lord is Creator, and the *Zoa* lead this worship around the throne. They sing that the Lord is worthy to receive glory and honor and power because He created all things, which are and were created through his will. The four *Zoa* will reappear in Chapter 14, where the new song is sung before them and the twenty-four elders, and again when one of the four gives the seven bowls of wrath to the seven angels (15:7).

Is the Rapture Portrayed Symbolically at 4:1 of the Revelation?

Is 4:1 a depiction of the rapture? From a common source within the American Baptist tradition, C. I. Scofield, Jack Van Impe, Jack Macarthur, Hal Lindsey, and others contend that the ascent of John here at 4:1 is synonymous with the rapture. The rapture is to occur before the time called the tribulation, the time of the worst trouble ever for mankind. By this pre-tribulation rapture, the church is preserved "out of the time of trouble." The "tribulation" is taken to mean the series of 21 judgments described from Chapter 6 through 18 of the Revelation. The assumption is that the tribulation refers to all 21 judgments of the seals, trumpets, and bowls, and that the Church is raptured prior

The Vision of the Throne and the Scroll

to the tribulation, or all events from Chapter 6-18 of the Revelation. Their picture is of a book describing the troubles Christians will avoid, and their message one of hope because the church will be taken up out of all these things. Hence the images of piles of empty clothing, and buses left driverless, when the rapture occurs. The hope suggested by this teaching is both comforting and one basis for the very lucrative market in end times books and teachings. The elect are raptured, and the hundreds of thousands are brought to Christ by the preaching of 12,000 from each of the twelve tribes. No reason is given for this teaching, but it is based on the promise and the hope that we will be taken out of the tribulation. In this section, we will show that this version of the pre-tribulation rapture is not the teaching of the Revelation.

The rapture is not explicitly included in the Revelation at all, and this is surprising. Convinced that it must be there, the attempt is then made to place it where it may fit. Sardis, the third church addressed, was told that if they did not stay awake "I will come like a thief, and you will not know at what hour I will come upon you" (3:3). But the Revelation is also consistent with there being no rapture at all. The closest the text comes to including the rapture is the interjected statement of the Christ: "Behold, I come as a thief in the night," very strangely at 16:15, amid the seven bowls of wrath, after the sixth, which gathers the nations for the battle at Armageddon. It is granted that when he comes like a thief, it is for the rapture, and there would be no reason for this to be inserted here if the church had been raptured already. He may come like a thief in that it is by surprise, rather than by stealth. It is argued that 4:1 is the only place that the rapture could fit. Our question is whether the text is quite that clear or quite that hopeful. Are these readers, usually committed to a literal reading and the authority of the scripture, not inadvertently adding something to the message that is not in the text? But, as the reader will see, the taking up of this question is very helpful in reading the text, and taking these preachers as a basis, the critical view of their teaching may lead us toward the heart of the Revelation.

On the Revelation

The rapture is so called from the Latin word *rapio,* used by Jerome to translate the Greek *arpazo-*, a "snatching away," (Van Impe, 1983, p. 12) to translate 1 Thessalonians 4:17: "And the dead in Christ will rise first; then we who are alive, who are left, shall be caught up together with them in the clouds to meet the Lord in the air." The word occurs in Revelation at 12:5-6, where the offspring of the woman is caught up to God and to his throne, and the woman escapes into the wilderness. Rapture is also the word for being taken up in the apprehension of beauty, in transcendent musings, as to be "rapt in secret study," and this is what happens to John when he sees a door opened in heaven. He himself continued on Patmos, and what these readers mean is not that John is here raptured, but that the rapture is symbolically or allegorically included in the Revelation at this point. There is a similarity to the call to the dead witnesses in Chapter 11, and the same words, "Come up hither," are used when these are called up in what, in the literal aspect, looks much more like the rapture than the call to John to ascend. We will argue that if the rapture is shown cryptically in the Revelation, it is here at 11:12, rather than at 4:1.

We must first see what is being said, and then we can answer each point in the argument. The attempt to show that the rapture of the church occurs at 4:1 begins **(1)** with a reading that the time of the churches is addressed in the seven letters, and then the things shown from 4:1 on are what must occur "after this." The reading is that this refers to after the age of the churches, and all things shown after this are assumed to be after the rapture. **(2)** The church does not seem to these readers to appear from Chapters 6-18 of the Revelation. None of the characteristics of the Church appear, while many characteristics of the Jews appear. Lindsey cites the difference between the statement of the letters, "hear what the spirit says to the churches" and the statement in Chapter 13, "He who has ears let him hear" (13:9). The Church seems to be gone. But **(3)** it seems that the twenty-four elders, shown crowned, could not appear this way prior to the rapture, and that they are or symbolize the church (Van Impe, 1982, pp. 53, 61-62). **(4)** The church of Philadelphia is told: "Because you have kept my word of patience, I also will keep you from the hour (*ek tas horas*) of trial about to come..." (3:10). Henry Schaeffer writes: "In Luke 21: 34-36 we have the promise of Jesus that the saved will be accounted worthy to escape all these things, and to stand before the son of man." Similarly, the statement: "For God has not destined us for wrath, but to obtain salvation" seems to suggest that those saved will be saved also out of the wrath of the day of the Lord. (**5**) It is the removal of the people of Christ that allows for the terrible events described in the visions to occur, so that the rapture at the very start of the tribulation seems to fit or to cohere with the picture of the whole. Paul seems to refer to this when he writes: "For the mystery of lawlessness is already at work; only he who now restrains it will do so until he is out of the way" (2 Thessalonians 2:6-8). Similarly, (**6**) the best argument for the pre-tribulation rapture at 4:1 seems to be that of Hal Lindsey (1973, pp. 78-79):

> If Jesus' historical illustrations refer to his coming for his people at the end of the tribulation, as some teach, then believers as well as unbelievers would pass through its horrors while doing their business as usual–...but none can live a normal life in the chaos of the tribulation...

When he comes *by surprise,* people will be going about their usual business, as in the days of Noah. This hardly seems possible if the tribulation were occurring around them. Lindsey also cites the pattern both in the stories of Noah and of Sodom and Gomorrah, where there was first a prophetic warning, then God helped his people to escape, and then destruction as judgment occurred.

The answers to these arguments should be considered, because there is no suggestion that the rapture occurs at 4:1 of the text, or that the church is not on earth for *any* of the things described in Chapters 6-19 of the Revelation. That the Church is raptured when John is called up to see his vision is simply not what is said in the text. It is thought that it must be implied, but rather the pre-tribulation rapture is contradicted by numerous considerations.

So, (**1**) *Meta Tauta*, or "after this," is entirely consistent with either mid- or post-tribulation rapture, since it need imply no more than that what is to be shown occur after the present condition of the churches, at the close of the first century. In the letters, he does describe things that will happen in the near future for these churches, such as the ten-day ordeal coming for Sardis. But he does not describe the complete future even of the seven churches, nor end the description with their rapture. Nor is there any suggestion that these seven are the whole church to the exclusion of Rome, Antioch, Jerusalem, and Alexandria. Does the church in Jerusalem even still exist as John is writing? The looming question is what of the Church in Rome, and what is the relation of these seven to the others, Alexandria and Antioch, etc. Some of these seven no longer exist, and yet the rapture was not yet. "After this" could easily mean the two millennia to follow, including the end of the end times.

(**2**) While the word "church" may not appear from Chapter 6 to 18, the word "Church" in the singular *does not appear at all* in the Revelation. The churches plural are not mentioned again until the closing of the letter (22:16), and the other churches are never mentioned unless it is here. The Church singular is the bride, and is never called the Church or identified as a "Church" in the Revelation. It is the New Jerusalem, and her bridal garment is the righteous deeds of the saints. The churches are lamp stands, and there is no need of lamps in the New Jerusalem (22:5; 21:22) When Paul tells of the union, he reveals a mystery (Ephesians 5:28-32). As has been said, a symbol refers to something unknown.

While the word church does not occur, the 144,000 and the multitudes *are* a part of the church, even if they were converts after the rapture, so that the church *is* of course present. These are followers of the Lamb, those with his name on their foreheads, as are those who refuse the mark of the Beast, and some are slain. If this were to occur literally, the ten lost tribes would have to be found. The sealed are explicitly said to be from the twelve tribes, while those who refuse the mark of the Beast would seem to be from all nations. Isaiah (27:13) prophecies:

The Vision of the Throne and the Scroll

> ...And in that day a great trumpet will be blown, and those who were lost in the land of Assyria and those who were driven out to the land of Egypt will come and worship the Lord on the holy mountain at Jerusalem.

These may be any one of us, especially since the ten northern tribes were disbursed. No other nation or group is referred to either in these chapters, except symbolically. The "Great city," thought to be Rome, and the city "allegorically called Sodom and Egypt" are examples. Mount Zion may be an exception. The characteristics of the church are the worship and witnessing of Jesus, the singing of the new song, literal and/or figurative celibacy, and these are exactly those targeted. What is not said is that this is the post-rapture church, as Van Impe reads it, and given that no reference is made one way or another in the Revelation, there is no reason to assume it. That the 144,000 were faithless, then left behind, and then suddenly especially saints all before Chapter 7, seems unlikely. There is surely no reason to introduce the rapture in the text at 4:1. The text of course simply does not say that. No humans are seen in heaven around the throne in Chapters 4 and 5 except the twenty-four elders. So (**3**) an attempt must be made by these readers to identify the church symbolically with something that *does* appear, like the sea of glass (Lindsey) or the twenty-four elders, whom no one would otherwise argue are to be identified with the raptured part of the church. It is not said how the elders or anyone else in the scene arrived there. The enthroned elders may include the Apostles, or, strangely, John himself, if these are twenty-four, because they are the twelve gates and foundations. They are the only men present, though they seem to have always been there, rather than to have recently arrived.

What is *not* seen in heaven around the throne is man, or general humanity. Many angels are seen, but no men, until the fifth seal is opened, and the martyrs are seen *under the altar* asking "how long?" Then in the sixth seal, the 144,000 are sealed, and then the multitudes "from every nation..." are said to be those who "have come out of the tribulation" (7:1-9). These are like the people of Jerusalem on the first Palm Day, and sing the Christian song. Is the number of the martyrs now completed? As this is said in the fifth seal to be the cause of the delay, and there need be no more delay (6:9-11), and it is sworn by the angel that there will be "no longer time" (10:6). The throne scene does not stop at Chapter 5, but continues through the opening of the seventh seal. What we are shown then is the completion of the throne scene by the addition of mankind. Chapters 4-7 show the entrance of man into heaven. While these come "out of the tribulation," the *whole point* of the scene is that they are *not* there yet in 4:1.

(**4**) The Philadelphia church, the sixth addressed, is told that he will keep them from the time of trouble. While the promise is delivered particularly to the Philadelphia church, it may, like other things in the seven letters, be addressed to the whole church. But this was for Philadelphia consistent with their suffering persecution from those who are not truly Jews, and may be consistent with a mid-tribulation rapture, since they, or rather some future church, will be kept out of the worst of the tribulation, if only because they have been martyred. The things escaped may be the seventh bowl and trumpet. The things pertaining to the Christians that are taken up all occur in the sixth, whether seal or trumpet, and attention is drawn to the sixth seal, trumpet, and bowl

It is said that in Luke 21:34-36, we have the promise of Jesus that the saved will be accounted worthy to escape *all these things*, and to stand before the son of man. The things they will escape are those of Matthew 24:4-26, Luke 21:4-19, and Revelation 6-19. But in the text of Luke (21:34-36), Jesus tells the Apostles to watch at all times, and not to be distracted by cares of the world, to have that day come upon them suddenly like a snare, "for it will come upon all who dwell upon the face of the whole earth." The Apostles are told to pray "that you may have strength to escape all these things that will take place, and to stand before the son of man." He does not promise that all those saved will be accounted worthy to escape all these things, but rather that that day will come upon all who dwell on the face of the earth.

The Vision of the Throne and the Scroll

Do Peter and Paul fail to escape the wrath of God? I think they do escape the wrath, and yet they were martyred. To be martyred for refusing the name and number may be a supreme blessing, and it is these and no others who are said to come alive to reign with him in the millennium (20:4). It is not clear whether others martyred, as those in the fifth seal, are included here. He will make war on the saints and perhaps conquer some (Daniel 7:21. Revelation 13:7). I Thessalonians is entirely consistent with a mid-tribulation rapture. It may be required, as will be shown, because the dead in Christ will rise first, then "we who are alive" with the sound of the trumpet," "the last trumpet," which would seem to be that blown at 11:15 of the Revelation. Paul implies, or rather explicitly states, that the transformation of physical into spiritual bodies occurs at the seventh or "last trumpet" (1 Corinthians 16: 52) "...in a moment, in the twinkling of an eye, *at the last trumpet. For the trumpet will sound, and the dead will be raised imperishable, and we shall be changed." And not all will sleep, but some be raised alive, though this will not, unless Paul is wrong, occur before the seventh trumpet. The Church is on earth for the sixth seal, trumpet, and perhaps bowl, and their martyrdom and divine vengeance for their martyrdom is the theme of the Revelation. The suggestion is that they are not present for the seventh trumpet and the seventh bowl because some have been martyred for being Christians, while others might be taken up alive at this time.

The seventh trumpet is blown *before* the Beast and false prophet are thrown into the lake of fire. But the raising of the dead, first of the martyrs in the twentieth chapter, appears to occur after, and the general resurrection after Satan is bound and cast into the pit where the Beast and the false prophet *were*. Unless the trumpet blast was understood to continue through the millennium, all the way through Chapter 20 to the Last Judgment, there would seem to be a contradiction in scripture between the account of John and that of Paul. The Church is on earth for the sixth seal, trumpet, and perhaps bowl, and their martyrdom is the theme of the Revelation. The suggestion is that they are not present for the seventh trumpet and the seventh bowl because some have been martyred for being Christians, while we hold hope that others might here be taken up alive.

The dead rise before the rapture (I Thess. 4-17), but not until after the millennial reign (Rev.20:5; 12-13). Unless the dead that are raised are the martyred witnesses, this contradicts both the pre- and mid-tribulation readings. One way around this difficulty of the rapture and the millennium is to say that there are multiple resurrections, and the dead raised at the last trumpet are different from the dead raised after the millennium. The dead rise when Jesus rises, in 31-33 A.D. So, some of the dead may also rise when the martyred witnesses rise at the end of the sixth trumpet, and even more rise at the general resurrection at the end of the millennium. In this way, Paul might yet be consistent with the twentieth chapter of the Revelation. Similarly, there are dead raised at the crucifixion (Matthew 27:52), dead raised before the millennium (20:4), and dead raised after the millennium (20:12), in addition to the spiritually dead who hear his voice and rise (John 5:26), making four or five resurrections, not including those like Lazarus and the one raised by Elijah, and those like Enoch and Jesus, who were taken bodily into heaven.

And not all will sleep, but some will be raised alive, though this will not, unless Paul is wrong, occur before the seventh trumpet. What undermines the hope of a pre-tribulation rapture is the teaching that the dead will be raised before the rapture, though the dead are not raised until the last trumpet.

So, (**5**) 2 Thessalonians 2:6-8 cannot refer to the spirit present in the church restraining the diabolical elements *from emerging* until taken out of the way in the rapture, though these might prevent world government and the worst of the evils to come. The presence of the United States seems to be all that now prevents these things from occurring. If it were removed, or if the Christians were removed from it, the unresolved elements in the development of Europe that once led to fascism might reemerge. Yet the presence of the spirit in the Churches did not prevent the emergence of Hitler or the holocaust of the Jews. It did, however, prevent the Nazis from taking over the whole world, or achieving world dominion, at least for a while. But, as the rise of the Nazi movement in America and even more in Europe has demonstrated, the trouble in the soul of the West has not yet been purged or overcome.

And this is consistent with the rest of the passage in the Letter to Thessalonica, which contradicts the thought that the Antichrist cannot appear until after the rapture. The Thessalonians are awaiting the Messiah, and are told not to be deceived "for that day will not come, unless the rebellion comes first, and the man of lawlessness is revealed...so that he takes his seat in the temple of God..." They seem, like those in Matthew (24:15), to be told that *they* will see the desolating sacrilege. The rapture seems to be what is shown in Matthew 24, after the desolating sacrilege spoken of by the prophet Daniel is seen standing in the holy place (24:15), and those in Judea are to flee without going down from the housetop to get his things, nor him in the field to turn back to get his mantle. But this *is* the great tribulation, and it is not clear that even those fleeing are unaffected by it. The time of trouble describes the conditions under which they flee Jerusalem, and in Luke, a part of the prophecy is: "When you see Jerusalem surrounded by armies, know that its desolation has come near." That generation did not pass away before they saw the destruction of Jerusalem. But it has just been said that *after* the sun and moon are darkened, the sign of the son of man will appear in the heavens, the tribes will mourn, "and they will see the son of man coming on the clouds of heaven with power and great glory; and he will send out his angels, and gather his elect from the four winds, from one end of heaven to the other." Those shown restraining in the Revelation are the four winds, in the sixth trumpet, restraining the four angels that are bound at the Euphrates, Kings of the East—or, all the armies of the world—from advancing to gather at Armageddon. These are restrained until the full number of the martyrs has been reached.

The Church is on earth for the sixth seal, trumpet, and perhaps bowl, and their martyrdom and divine vengeance for their martyrdom is the theme of the Revelation. The Revelation is not about how God will keep the Christians from suffering. To repeat: the Revelation is, from start to finish, about the martyrs. It is written to the Churches, and if there is one teaching, even the last Biblical commandment, it is not to take the mark of the Beast

On the Revelation

(14: 9-12). Its teaching is not to believe in order to avoid punishment. The pre-tribulation rapture applied to the Revelation requires that none of the Church will have to make this decision, to have loved their witnessing more than their own lives. It requires that the church is being told of events that do not really concern them, and that might have been known after the rapture. We, however, think that the Revelation is a warning to the Church of the last great persecution, this time of both Christians and Jews. But the mid-tribulation rapture, after the sixth or at the seventh trumpet, makes sense of why the Churches and servants (1:1, 4) are addressed in this to begin with. The Jews were warned in Daniel, and the Christians in the Revelation, of an attack on the Biblical God through an attack on His people. The suggestion is that they are not present for the seventh trumpet and the seventh bowl because some have been martyred for being Christians, and the hope is that others might be taken up alive at this time, in a mid-tribulation rapture of sorts, in a tribulation beginning with the sixth trumpet or sooner, for it occurs between the sixth and seventh trumpets. He will make war on the saints and perhaps conquer some (Daniel 7:21; Revelation 13:7). When the Churches are told the blessings for him who conquers, it was implied though not stated that some, even of the saints or the elect (Mark 13:22), might be misled and conquered.

In any case, it is in a way ridiculous to say that the Church is not there, since the 144,000 and the multitudes of Chapter 7 *are* a part of the church and the number of martyrs to be completed. The 144,000 are explicitly said to be followers of the Lamb. Van Impe means the pre-tribulation church, so that all the martyrs shown have been converted after the rapture, possibly from having seen the rapture occur and finding themselves left behind. But there is no distinction in the text between the raptured and the martyred church, unless those sealed are those raptured. In the fifth trumpet when the locusts are seen ascending from the bottomless pit, it is assumed that those with the seal of God on their foreheads are still on the earth, and are not to suffer from this (9:4), the fifth trumpet and bowl, which effect the kingdom of the Beast. These are the same that appeared before the throne in Chapter 7. The church as the body of believing Christians *is* there, then, in the seventh, eleventh, twelfth, thirteenth, fourteenth, and fifteenth chapters, as well as in the millennial reign of the saints beheaded for not taking the number, and then especially in the description of the New Jerusalem. What is not present in the Revelation is a picture of the raptured church as distinct from those that are martyred. Nor is there an explicit rapture, nor any effect of the example of persons having suddenly disappeared, other than those murdered.

Our conclusion must be that the Revelation is much darker than Van Impe and Lindsey assume, and its warning is not only for those other people, but for the Christians or for the Church. The preaching of the message of hope that we may not have to die or face death and martyrdom, should the end times come upon us, may then be a bit of a false hope, at least as far as the text of the Revelation goes. It is sometimes said that the Lord would not leave his church to suffer, but this was not the case for the Apostles and martyrs of other ages. Hippolytus writes that one reason the prophecy is obscured is to avoid disquieting the minds of men (p. 210, #29).

The pre-tribulation rapture teaching, though, is very instructive regarding the probable distinction between the rapture and the revelation proper, the second coming, since those making this argument require the distinction. Hal Lindsey writes:

> One passage of scripture speaks of Christ's coming in the air and in secret, like a thief coming in the night. Another part of scripture describes Christ's coming in power and majesty to the earth, with every eye seeing him...Both of these can be true only if there are two separate appearances.

The reading of Lindsey and others, Van Impe and Scofield, requires that the second coming is what is described at Matthew 24:30-31, when the son of man is seen coming on the clouds with glory, and the angels are sent out with a loud trumpet call to gather his elect from the four winds, or from one end of heaven to another–but that this is different from the rapture which comes like the flood of Noah, when "two men will be in the field; one is taken and one is left" (24:40). And when he comes, on a cloud and with glory, all his saints, or "ten thousand of his saints" are said to be or come with him (Jude 14-15; Enoch 1:9). Van Impe notes that it does not seem that the two would coincide, with the raptured ascending only to return at nearly the same time, or simply to be then gathered.

It is not clear, though, that Peter follows this division, as he has Jesus coming as a thief when the elements are dissolved and the earth burned (2 Peter 3:10). Yet he may write of the "Day of the Lord" as containing both, beginning with one and ending with another, all in the same day.

The same words, though, as those said to indicate the rapture at 4:1, "Come up hither," are spoken in what does seem like the rapture, except that those who ascend have died. The two witnesses, having preached three and one-half days and then lain dead and unburied three and one-half days, ascend to heaven in a cloud. We will present an argument that these two witnesses are two large groups. It is not clear how these are related to the 144,000, or to those who complete the number of the martyrs, which was the cause for the delay at the fifth seal. The 144,000 appear again with the Messiah on Mount Zion, after the witnesses are raised.

So, rather than say that the key to the Revelation is the distinction between the things that are and the things that will be, and then requiring that *everything* described after Chapter 4 be future and after the rapture, the key seems rather to be this: The Revelation is about the martyrs, the completion of their number, and divine vengeance for the making of the martyrs. It foretells the most horrible persecution of all time, and warns the church not to take the mark of the Beast. The Beast is "allowed to make war upon the Saints and to conquer them" (13:7; Daniel 7:21). This is a warning to the church, a call for endurance, and pertains most directly to us believers as we approach the end times. While we do pray to be found worthy to escape these things, we ought to pray to endure the trial or test that would come upon all mankind if a worldwide earthquake revealed that most, when put to the test, are ravenous, like starving animals. And we pray especially for the strength and grace to refuse the mark.

It may be that the point in the prophesied end times at which the rapture occurs is not revealed, since "if the householder knew in what part of the night the thief was coming, he would have watched..." (24:43-44; Revelation 3:3). It may be that we may have three accounts of the rapture—pre, mid, and post—because it is not revealed "in what part of the night the thief is coming," and we are simply told to be watchful. We, though, should be watchful at all times, and prepare. We should prepare to be tested and to overcome the fear of death, and to not take the mark.

The Scroll: Revelation Chapter Five

The scene of the throne is the setting of a drama that unfolds though the fifth chapter. First the scene is presented, in Chapter 4, and then in the fifth chapter, something is shown to occur. The one seated on the throne has a scroll, which none are found worthy to open. Then the son of man is found worthy by his having been slain, and ransoming mankind by his blood. The scroll can then be opened, and the body of the text from Chapter 6 onward is contained within this scroll.

[5:1-5] John saw the book or scroll in the right hand of the one seated on the throne. It was written on the front and on the back, as is the scroll given to Ezekiel (2:9), and sealed with seven seals. He saw a strong angel with a loud voice proclaiming, "Who is worthy to open the scroll and break its seals?" However, no one in heaven or on earth was able to "open the scroll or look into it," because none were worthy. What this means, the sealing and opening of a writing, is not immediately clear, but John weeps because no one is found worthy. Daniel is told to seal up his writing until the time of the end (Daniel 12:9). Then one of the elders says to him, John, "Weep not; lo, the lion of the tribe of Judah, the root of David, has conquered, so that he can open the scroll and its seven seals." Judah is described as a lion. The Judah oracle (Genesis 49:10) is that the scepter and rod or staff would remain with this tribe until the Messiah comes, to whom the

On the Revelation

scepter belongs. Israel was not then a kingship, and so Judah remained the leading tribe until the Messiah, as is still the case, all Israelites now being called Jews. The Messiah is called the root of Jesse, as well as a shoot from the stump or branch from the root of Jesse, the father of the father of David. He is called this by Isaiah in one of the clearest prophesies of the Messiah (11:1-11). Mathew traces the genetic line of Jesus to David through Joseph (1:16), and this would be by adoption or by law, though Mary is also of this line. No one has traced the lineage of Mary, though her parents Joachim and Anna are known, apparently of the tribes of David and Levi.[80] But to return, to have conquered, is what makes him able and worthy to open the scroll and its seven seals. It is possible that the scroll is the following vision, and that it is baptism or rebirth, following the Christ through death, that makes it possible to follow the opening and unsealing the text of the revelation. It is also possible that the opening of the seals is an unfolding of historical events that occur as a result of the incarnation and the conquest of the crucifixion– we shall have to see when we consider the seals.

Victorinus writes that the book is the Old Testament, the Torah scroll, and "to open the book is to overcome death for man" (p. 349). He writes:

> The unsealing of the seals is, as we have said, the opening of the Old Testament, and the foretelling of the preachers of things to come in the last times, which, although the prophetic scripture speaks by single seals, yet by all the seals opened at once, prophecy takes its rank.
> (Ibid., p. 350)

That the scroll is written on front and back means that there is a hidden meaning. There is a fold in the text, so that the parts of the second half are behind certain parts of the first half. Chapters 7 and 14 go together, as do chapters 1 and 21-22. The seven trumpets and seven bowls also go together. The fold seems to occur at about Chapter 11, where a distinct break occurs between

The Vision of the Throne and the Scroll

two halves of the text (11:19 / 12:1). We will see if other indications of this ordering emerge.

[5:6-10] John sees a Lamb with seven horns and seven eyes, standing among the elders between the four *Zoa* and the throne, as though it had been slain. As John explains, the seven are the "seven spirits of God sent out (*apestalmena*) to all the earth." The seven horns are seven churches, and the churches are the spirits and the eyes of God, in a sense. Here we have an important clue to the meaning of horns and eyes related to the horns, and the image will reappear in the explanation of the Beast below. "Behold, the Lamb of God, who takes away the sins of the world" is what is said by John the Baptist in the Gospel of John when Jesus approaches (John 1:29; 36). Jesus is called the Lamb 28 times in the Revelation.

The slain Lamb went and took the scroll from the right hand of the one on the throne, and when he does this, the living creatures and the elders fall down before him, with bowls of incense that "are the prayers of the saints." Here we have another important translation of an image in the text itself, incense being prayers. To fall down would not be proper before a man or an angel (19:10), and it is right to worship the Lamb along with the Father. These sing a "new song" (5:9), like the 144,000 (14:3). They are apparently not there yet before the throne, here in Chapter 5. This song is related, though that song can only be learned by the 144,000. This song sings that the Lamb is worthy to take the scroll and open its seals because he was slain and ransomed men for God, making them a kingdom of priests that shall reign on the earth. This is the gospel in essence, preached after the life of Jesus and before the end time. If the new song of the 144,000 is not the same, it may be what priests or those like these sing regarding the gospel after the seventh angel blows his trumpet.

[5:11] John then looks and hears the voices of many angels, "numbering myriads of myriads and thousands of thousands," who also sing that the Lamb is worthy, here worthy to receive seven goods: power, wealth, wisdom, might, honor, glory, and blessing. John also hears every creature (*Ktasma*)—those in heaven, on *and under* the earth, and in the sea—say that four of these: blessing, honor, glory, and might, should be to "Him who sits upon the throne and to the Lamb." This conspicuous absence and later presence of the humans in the vision of heaven may be central to the point of what is shown unfolding in the chapters to come: the entrance of men into heaven. The stage is set, and then through the seven seals and seven trumpets, the number of the martyrs is completed before the seventh seal, the revelation of the Messiah at the Second Advent, and the last judgment leads to the New Jerusalem. The martyrs are a completion of the throne scene, when before the seventh trumpet John is shown those that have come out of the tribulation. They are thousands and myriads, like the angels (5:11). This reminds one of the teaching that each has a guardian angel in heaven, and that we somehow, in our true self, are that angel.

This too seems to be at the root of a mystery of the account of the seven days in Genesis. According to an old account, which we heard from George Anastaplo: following each day of the creation, it is written that the Lord "saw that it was good," with the exception of the second day–the creation of the dome or sky separating the waters above from those below–and the sixth, the day of the creation of man. He does find that the whole is "very good." (Genesis 1:31). The two, the heavens and man, are not yet complete, but are to be completed with one another. The suggestion is that what we are shown in Chapters 4-7 of the Revelation is the completion of these two, or the entry of man into heaven.

[5:13] "And I heard every creature in heaven and on earth and under the earth and in the sea, and all therein, saying, "To him who sits on the throne and to the Lamb, blessing and honor and glory and might for ever and ever..." These four or five realms—heaven, earth, sea, and under the earth—were introduced at 5:3, when no one "in heaven or on earth or under the earth" was able to open the scroll or look into it. The five realms appear in the passage about the last Judgment. Earth and sky fled away from his presence. The sea then gave up the dead in it, and "Death and Hades gave up the dead in them" (20:11-13). Death and Hades were then thrown into the Lake of Fire. From this, we say that purgatory may exist, though it is not eternal.

The following out of the five realms allows us to try to see the arithmetic of the analogy at the root of the vision of the Revelation. The picture is wholly allegorical, describing spiritual realms in images moved down one level, or one octave on the scale, in order to enter visible terms. This dropping of things down one level may be why Cherubim, a high kind of angel, are here presented as three animals and a man. The Catholic Bible tries to explain: "these symbolize what is noblest and strongest, wisest and swiftest in the creation." Heaven becomes the sky; the place of those whose principle aims are worldly, the earth; and the place of the imagination the sea; or, as Jung might have it, the realm of the human collective unconscious. The father of Hamlet speaks to him from *under* the earth, that is, from purgatory (Shakespeare, *Hamlet*, Act I, Scene V). The mind, then, can ascend through the visible images to the being that is their referent and source. This is a spiritual sight, a natural thing, but like natural plants such as the mustard seed, it can also be cultivated. Its attainment may be the reason that the reading of the Revelation leads to a blessing, even while we humans cannot see much consistently or bring back much of a clear, communicable account of these things. We may care too much about the effects of these things on our bodies and the visible world to read the Revelation.

A literalization or confusion of the realms seems to occur when the spiritual beings, angels and demons, etc., are presented as literally in the air, as drivers of UFOs inhabiting a heaven directly up above, a seventh layer beyond our known cosmos. While there are striking similarities, for example of Ezekiel's Chariot to an interplanetary spaceship, or of the New Jerusalem to a space station, the suggestion is that we do not look for the spiritual beings among these, the "decorations in the heavens" (*Republic*, 529d). It is found amusing, to those who consider the presence of animals in the images of the Kingdom (Isaiah 11:6-9), that all creatures are here heard chiming in with the angels in their praise and blessing of the Lamb. Every creature in heaven, on earth, and in the sea is seen praising the Lamb. Some hold out hope for the immortality of the animal souls from this passage, though the animals are not in heaven but on earth. It is sometimes said that all living remains in his presence, but only man has gone out from it with the fall, because our self-motion includes ethical self-motion, called "free will," so that we might choose voluntarily to follow the Lord.

The scroll might be the unfolding of the Revelation or the events themselves, and the opening of the scroll is only possible for one who is worthy. It is only Jesus, through his death and conquest of death, who is worthy to open the scroll. If it is possible for us to see it opened at all, it is through our participation in the death and resurrection. This seems to be the primary meaning of sealed and unsealed. Through our own penance and sacrifice, the way of the cross, the meaning of this and all things can become accessible. This is not *certainty*, but *access*, to the wonders of contemplation, elsewhere known as philosophy. If Socrates is here to be taken seriously, the knowledge we contemplate is not our own, but belongs to "the God." But further, it is the death and resurrection that makes possible not only the reading, but the actual events themselves.

Daniel is told to seal up the vision, because it pertains to the time of the end (Daniel 12:9). So the scroll might be the book of Daniel. There is a certain sense in which the vision of the end times does not make sense, even to Daniel himself, until certain events, and the incarnation, occur. For Dr. Van Impe, this is the primary meaning of "unsealed:" the vision begins to make sense, for example, when Israel is restored, the Jews return from worldwide dispersion, and Israel takes Jerusalem.[81] Hal Lindsey cites Dr. Scofield: "The book is so written that as the actual time of these events approach, the current events will unlock the meaning of the book."[82] Yet the primary meaning in the text is that the death and resurrection unseal what was sealed up by Daniel. It may also be that by our participation in his death and resurrection, we are enabled to read what prior to Jesus was sealed or unreadable. Both of these would be so at once if the historical event of the Messiah unsealed what was yet sealed, even for Daniel. It may be too that the events of the end times begin to occur with the incarnation, setting in motion what will be consummated over the course of millennia. It would then be the events themselves, rather than the prophecy of the events, that unfold when the seals are broken. If the two meanings of "sealed" are combined, it is going through death with the Christ that allows for the seeing of the events as they unfold.

When asked why the third secret of Fatima (Appendix A) might be released after 1960, Sr. Lucy is reported to have said that its meaning would be clearer after that time. At this time, the third secret was read, but not released until the year 2000. Now it is not clear whether the worst of times have just passed or are about to come. The vision is of many martyred, though the faithful continue. The conquest of death by Jesus allowed for the seals to be opened, or for the consequent events of the now two thousand years since the Incarnation and crucifixion.

I. vi The Opening of the First Six Seals

The opening of the first six seals leads up to the sealing of the 144,000 and the appearance of the multitudes that come out of the tribulation. The Four Horsemen *lead up to* the appearance of the martyrs under the throne in the fifth seal, who are told that they must wait for the avenging of their martyrdom until the number of their fellow martyrs is fulfilled. This seems to be the best clue or foothold in reading the horsemen. The first four seals, the Four Horsemen of the Apocalypse, seem to refer to things between the crucifixion and the tribulation, and to be related to the slaying of the martyrs shown in the fifth seal. The horsemen are each introduced by one of the four living creatures, who each speak in turn as the seal is opened. At the opening of the three remaining seals, no one speaks, but something is seen without intermediary.

[6:1-2] When the Lamb opens the first seal, the first living creature, the one like a lion, says "come." John sees a white horse, "...and its rider had a bow; and a crown was given to him, and he went out conquering and to conquer." Lindsey (1973, p. 103), Van Impe and others assume without cause that this is the Antichrist, apparently because they assume that the tribulation begins when this one rides out, and because he conquers. Van Impe considers this rider on the white horse to be a counterfeit Christ, and begins his reading of the signs in Matthew at 24:3 and the seals in the Revelation, with the warning that false Christs will come (1982, p. 77). But this is one of the very uncertain things in the Revelation which are often treated as though they were clear. For the first appearance of the Antichrist, the description is rather sparse and devoid of any identifying characteristics, and such a reading is corroborated by nothing else in scripture. Elsewhere in the book, the one who conquers and rides on a white horse is Jesus (19:11), and those who conquer are members of the churches. It is sometimes suggested, as by Victorinus, that the first horse is the first Advent. Yet this one has a bow, and when the crown is given to him, he rides out to conquer for its own sake, making him seem like an earthly conqueror, or like the Roman Empire in the period following the crucifixion. And this was, in a word, the aim of mankind during the late Roman Republic and early empire, until only very recently. Every King after the fall of Rome seems to aim at enlarging their kingdom through conquest, as though every kingdom must by nature seek to become the empire over kingdoms in a contest for the first place, or survival of the fittest, sort of war of all against all, leading by necessity to empire. The first is the only horseman given a crown.

One wonders how these four horsemen might compare with the four beasts seen by Daniel (Daniel 7), which "are four kings which shall arise out of the earth." The horsemen may be four successive world rulers *beginning* with Rome, from the time following the events foretold to the seven churches. The beasts in Daniel's vision also could be the same as the last four of the five world empires addressed in the statue in the Dream of Nebuchadnezzar (Daniel 2). The bow may indicate the Medes or Parthian empire. But the Four Horsemen of the Apocalypse may, like the four beasts, represent successive large periods or movements among humanity, from the crucifixion over the next two millennia, and so the story from the churches of the second century and leading up to the appearance of the Antichrist begins with the nations riding out under the principle of conquest.

What appears, then, is the possibility that the Four Horsemen, and indeed the seven seals, cover larger time periods leading up to the seven trumpets contained in the seventh seal. The seven trumpets would then not *coincide* with the seven seals, but might occur according to the same pattern as the larger time scale, though in a smaller time scale. Later we will be considering a long and a short period of 1,260 years and 1,260 days, and the suggestion is to look for the same relation of large and short time periods. The Four Horsemen seem to coincide with the now two-millennium long time period, and this long period, *prior to* the rapture and Van Impe's 21 Judgments, seems to be what Jesus addressed when he told the Apostles:

On the Revelation

> And you will hear of wars and rumors of wars; see that you are not alarmed; for this must take place, but the end is not yet. For nation will rise against nation, and kingdom against kingdom, and there will be famines and earthquakes in various places; all this is but the beginning of the birth pangs.

Again, Lindsey appears to err in reading the seals:

> The first seal releases a dictator, the Antichrist, who ultimately succeeds in subduing the whole world. The second seal takes peace from the earth. Russia and her Arab confederates attack the young state of Israel, resulting in a wide-ranging war that lasts three and one-half years. The third seal results in a worldwide economic collapse. The fourth seal precipitates a tremendous outbreak of death through famines, epidemics and civil violence. The fifth seal marks the beginning of the greatest persecution of all time–a period when believers will be slaughtered in the streets.

We say this only because Lindsey did so well with the book, and is so well respected. But there is no reason to think that the first horseman is the Antichrist, nor that the red horse is communist Russia, nor that their advance results in a three and one-half year war under the seal, nor that the rationing is a resulting famine. Nor can the pale horse be placed in this scheme, if the first horse is the Antichrist and has passed, to be followed by three other horses. This is so much so that some readers have thought the opposite: that the rider is the one who later appears on the white horse in Chapter 19. For "to conquer" might mean that the church rides out to spread the gospel after the incarnation. And this would fit with the description of him who conquered as the Lion of the tribe of Judah (5:5). There is especially no reason to think the martyrs that appear under the throne were killed in the coming worst persecution of all time. They appear, ask how long, and are told until their fellow martyrs

The Opening of the First Six Seals

complete their numbers. Lindsey's reading requires that this scene be a pause in the great tribulation, distinguishing these few killed at its beginning from the bulk to be killed throughout. He has simply misread the seals, from the old assumption that the horsemen are the beginning of the great tribulation. Much can be said for sticking to what is actually said in the text, and none of this is said. The rider on the white horse of Chapter 19 is not called forth by one of the living beings, but is seen in heaven when the heavens are opened. All that is said here is that he had a bow, was given a crown, went out to conquer and did so. We do not know what this means.

[6:3] The second horse is introduced explicitly by the second Zoa, which would be the one like an ox. The relation of the four living creatures to the four horses and riders seems important, and not at all clear. The horses are described before their riders, and are the primary subject of the vision. When the Lamb opens the second seal, "out came another horse, bright red…" He does not say "I saw, and behold" but only "out came…" Then, unlike the first horse, it is not said that he actually did go out, leaving open the possibility that at the time of John, he had not gone out yet. The rider of the second horse is allowed to take peace from the earth, so that men slay one another, and he was given a great sword, as the first had a bow. And why are these not reversed? One pictures this bow like one in cave paintings, or as a similar sign, and there is a bow in the vision of Fatima, though we do not know what it means. Is it the bow of the Medes, and then the sword that of Mohammed? If the horsemen lead up to the martyrs, these may be understood by looking in hindsight for the makers of martyrs.

[6:5-6] When the Lamb opens the third seal, the third Zoa, the one with the face of a man, says "come." He then saw a black horse, and its rider had a balance in his hand, and a voice from amid the four living creatures says "a quart of wheat for a denarius, and three quarts of barley for a denarius, but do not harm wine or oil." All three—grain, wine, and oil—are used in sacraments, though the riddle of the phrase is not clear. Why grain but not wine and oil? It does seem that if we understood the third horse, we would understand this riddle. The announcement is of subsistence for the price of one day's wage. The high price of grain reminds one of food shortage, and the scene is one of rationing, as though there were famine, or as though something had happened to the U.S. Midwest. If what occurred in the dust bowl of the thirties were to occur today, the result would be worldwide famine. The third horse, then, is famine, striking food in particular and not other commodities like oil and wine. The balance may be for rationing, or it may mean that this is retribution, as in the scales of justice.

[6:7-8] When the Lamb opens the fourth seal, and the fourth living creature, the one like an eagle, says "come," he sees a pale or pale green horse. "Its rider's name was Death, and Hades followed him..." Death and Hades, of which Jesus has the keys (1:18), are later thrown into the lake of fire after giving up the souls these contain (20:13). Here, Death and Hades are "given power over one-quarter of the earth, to kill with sword, famine and pestilence, and by wild beasts of the earth." The famine caused, as well as their control over one-quarter of the earth, remind us of something like the old Soviet empire, or the extent of twentieth century tyranny. Rome used wild beasts as a means of killing, and Genghis Khan at the outbreak of the plague used pestilence, when bodies were catapulted into besieged cities. These sorts of means seem to fit what is here described. While one expects the fourth horse to be *pestilence*, as the second and third were *war* and *famine*, the pestilence of the fourth horse, Death, is also accompanied by war and famine. As in the vision of Daniel, the fourth is the most terrible. It is possible, then, that the popular picture of the Four Horsemen of the Apocalypse, bringing war, famine and pestilence just before the end times, is a myth and an oversimplification; another of those things like "wars and rumors of war" which not even the text says are signs of the end times. Roman conquest would fit the first, the second the wars following the decline of Rome, the third indeed seems like a shortage of food that is unlike anything that has yet occurred, except in certain regions of Africa. Yet even here, food is scarce, but wine and oil are not affected? In pattern, the third is like the Depression that preceded World War Two. The fourth beast is exceedingly terrible, and not unlike the German ideologies that came to cover one fourth of the earth. Since the Nazis were apparently defeated, Marxist communism, which also arose from German philosophy, is what continues. The upshot, then, of the first four seals is the making of the martyrs seen in the fifth seal; and still the Beast has not yet appeared and the tribulation proper, the great tribulation, not yet begun. The long-term and the short-term readings approach one another if the pale horse pertains to the tyrannies of the twentieth century, and culminates in the pre-tribulation martyrs, those martyred before the great tribulation even begins, whose number is to be completed by the persecution of the Beast.

The Four Horsemen, then, may *result* in the deaths of the martyrs whose souls are seen under the altar when the Lamb opens the fifth seal. The text seems chronological in this sense. Bauckham suggests that because the blood sacrifices on the altar of burnt offering was poured out under the altar, these martyrs are here seen as sacrifices (p. 1294). These ask the Lord how long it will be before their blood is avenged. They are given white robes and told to rest a while longer," until the number of their fellow servants and their brethren should be complete." This number is then completed through the tribulation, so we can see that the Four Horsemen are distinct from the tribulation, or at least from the three woes of the tribulation. The sixth seal is then an avenging of the souls of the martyrs seen at the opening of the fifth seal. It seems difficult to underestimate how much the events in the Revelation are about martyrdom and the avenging of the martyrs. It is difficult to believe that the prophecy would not strike peril into the inquisitors who sentenced women and heretics to burn. The theme of the first seven letters, regarding persecution, is continued in the vision of the future of the church.

If the Four Horsemen occur *before* the tribulation, then the usual understanding of these–as being unleashed at the start of the crisis that is the end times–is mistaken. War, famine and pestilence are foretold, but these things are not especially signs of the imminence of the second coming. Rather, these are things that will occur at various times between the crucifixion and the second coming. Or rather, it could be said that the end times *begin* with the coming of the Messiah and continue for over two thousand years. The end times in this sense refers to the time between the first and second appearance of the Messiah. We see something like the succession of four empires seen by Daniel, only *after* the incarnation, and these have led to the making of martyrs through their preaching of the word and their witnessing. But the wrath of the Lamb is for the making of the martyrs. Wheat, oil and wine (18:13) are used in the holy service, though not barley, and the sale of these could have something to do with the merchants of the mysterious Babylon (18:23). Indulgences sold forgiveness, a kind of simony (Acts 8:18-24), though not especially for a day's wages.

Wine and oil are parts of the sacraments excluded by Protestants. The Eucharist, and then the whole chrism, is no longer held to be a sacrament, though it is not clear how this would relate to the obscure request to not harm wine and oil. If the famine of the third horse is symbolic of a spiritual condition, it may be that of modernity which precedes the pale horse of twentieth-century totalitarianism. In the vision of Fatima, it is as though the underworld was opened in 1917, and this was prepared by a great spiritual famine. The Four Horsemen are how the first group of martyrs were slain, and so might consider for the first horse the conquering Roman Empire, followed by three other makers of martyrs leading up to the pale green horse. The breakdown of the Roman Empire was followed by war between nations, and Islam brought the sword and some martyrdom. The Crusades, the plague and the famine of the Middle Ages led to the famine of modernity, and to the fourth: twentieth-century totalitarianism.

The famine of the third horse would then be symbolic of spiritual famine. He may be introduced by the Zoa with the face of a man because this epoch appears to have a human face, being ostensibly Christian. The sale of wheat and barely might represent simony, the giving of sacraments for a price, even the price of obedience.

We must admit that the reading here is not sufficient, and return to the solid point that the Four Horsemen lead up to the martyrs shown in the fifth seal. Cohering with the assumption that the things in the Revelation refer to Rome from the time of

The Opening of the First Six Seals

John forward, the Four Horsemen are how the martyrs of the fifth seal were made. The second possibility might be that the Four Horsemen are the same as the four world empires leading *up to* Rome. A third possibility is that much broader time scales are referenced, so that we cannot yet see, as would be the case if six more thousand years were involved, and we were still somewhere in the first or second horseman.

[6:9-11] The fifth seal presents a theoretical difficulty in that the martyrs desire that their blood be avenged on the earth. This does not seem to fit with the Biblical reservation of vengeance for the Lord (Deuteronomy 32:35) nor with the forgiveness of the Messiah even for those conducting the crucifixion, and the teaching to pray for those who persecute us. Before the seven trumpets are blown, an angel is shown taking a golden censer of incense mingled with the prayers of the saints, and throwing it onto the earth. It is the avenging of the blood of the martyrs that brings about the seven trumpets, and apparently the end of the age and the destruction of the old earth. Ought we not rather repent this desire for vengeance, and could these terrible things be avoided if we would forgive?

After a parable about a widow who annoyed an unjust judge until she was avenged on her adversary, Jesus, as recorded at Luke 18:7, taught:

> "And shall not God avenge his own elect, which cry day and night onto him, though he bear long with them? I tell you that he will avenge them speedily. Nevertheless, when the son of man comes, will he find faith on the earth?"

The *elect* are those chosen by God, or called, and refers to Israel as the chosen people (Is. 44:1), the Messiah as the elect of God (Is. 42:1), and to the 144,000 as well (7:4), though the elect would seem also to include the Apostles and all the saints. The 144,000 may, though, be a very specific group of Israeli end time Christian martyrs.[83]

This question of the mystery of divine vengeance is very difficult. But one might begin to unravel this complexity with the suggestion that such a teaching might be to misunderstand a metaphor, or a symbol. After Cain slew Abel, it is said that the voice of his blood cried to the Lord from the ground (Genesis 4:10). Enoch too writes of the call of the martyrs for vengeance, and shows how the martyrs and the avenging of their blood is central to the plot of what is occurring in the apocalypse or Revelation, leading to the new heaven and new earth (Enoch, 47):

> And in those days shall have ascended the prayer of the righteous,
> And the blood of the righteous from the earth before the Lord of Spirits.
> In those days the holy ones who dwell above in the heavens
> Shall unite with one voice, and supplicate and pray...
> On behalf of the blood of the righteous which has been shed...
> And the hearts of the holy were filled with joy;
> Because the number of the righteous had been offered,
> And the prayer of the righteous had been heard,
> And the blood of the righteous been required
> Before the Lord of Spirits.

There is a truth noted in murder mysteries that bodies tend to rise. It is possible that the scene of the martyrs calling for vengeance is symbolic of the natural reaction of the human world to the murder of saints. After something like the Holocaust, even the Quaker or the most principled pacifist becomes reconciled to the necessity of violence or force–the rod of iron–to prevent some from harming others by force. While we might try to forgive the Nazis, the avenging of the holocaust involves bringing Nazi Germany down with force, and even holding them accountable in courts. Similarly, the alternative to nuclear war may be to simply allow the nations to devour Israel in a nuclear attack—and there is no good reason, when the destruction is weighed, to allow this to occur. So it is that we might find the world heading toward

Armageddon like a train that "won't stop going," and circumstances might lead us even to find ourselves among the armies of the nations gathering at Armageddon. It is easy to think, from outside, that "well, we just won't do that," but the necessity of the circumstance is evident in the particular. That is, when the computer is invented, the economy collapses, and terrorism threatens, we begin to see how some of the particulars described might be not only possible, but indeed occur of necessity. We often think that it was fortunate that the West chose to use the *economic* reductionists, or the communists, against the *biological* reductionists, or the Nazis, because, while taken as economic science, Marxism is not serious but imaginary. Things held in common get less care, and an economy is ruined. But it is biologically possible to harm the tree of life even at the branch of humanity, and bring about a world that it might be better had not existed at all. And things in this direction are what we would have seen, had the Nazis rather than the Communists been given seventy years, as Russia saw under her Communist tyrants.

But to return, this vengeance is noted by some, such as Jung, who appeals to the peculiar psychology of John and the repression of the image of the evil side of God. The popularization of Jung's teaching wishes to say that He is really both good and evil. The Satanists too have some such reasoning, that the Devil is only a manifestation of God, and evil therefore a part of his will. One is reminded of what is said about Judas—that while it was set that one such would come, still, woe to him by whom it comes. This theoretical difficulty appears blatantly in the text when it is said that God put it into the minds of the ten kings to enact the diabolical schemes of the Beast (17:17). This is extremely difficult, but calls for us to step back from the metaphor of God willing everything that occurs, to look at how humans and whole societies can store up wrath for themselves by their own injustice. A man commits a murder, then is killed in an unavoidable accident: this, the argument wants to say, may not be divine vengeance, but accident, though it must have the appearance of divine vengeance. America imports slaves and allows cruel slavery. This built up a national guilt and judgment that led to the Civil War. It is not that God willed all those innocents to die unjustly for the sins of their grandfathers, nor that the killing of innocents is by this justified, but that a nation cannot have the injustice of slavery without building up wrath or provoking the reaction that, in the nature of the soul, is as if necessary. Justice turns out to be more important by nature than modern science imagines. As Colonel Mason said in the Constitutional Convention: Since nations cannot be rewarded or punished in the "next world," they must be punished in this world. "By an inevitable chain of causes and effects Providence punishes national sins, by national calamities." (Madison, *Notes of Debates*, August 22, 1787). America aborts millions of fetuses, but then must suffer not only the lack of soldiers and citizens that would otherwise have been born, but also a decreased awareness of why murder is wrong. Whether one who aborted a fetus should find that they lack social security or an heir, or be killed by one who does not know why murder is wrong, is likely to be a matter of chance. A man in a tragedy kills, or is angry with his brother, as Achilles was with Agamemnon for his insult, and it costs him the life of his friend or brother by the necessary connection of human events. The same was shown in the recent movie *American History X*. For the murder he committed, the lead character lost his own friend, his younger brother. This is like divine vengeance, because it is based on the nature of the soul and right, which in the beginning was tragically violated. In this way, the persecution of the church in the end times may be because we have participated in the making of martyrs, and this crime has led to the growth of the anti-Christian reaction, which in turn unleashes twentieth-century totalitarianism. It is not that God punishes the women and children who had nothing to do with it, unjustly willing that they be killed for the sins of previous generations. What did Anastasia have to do with the burning of Huss? It is that men cannot kill one another, let alone the saints of God, without the most grievous consequences for the *ecumenae*, the human or the inhabitable world in the future, because of the nature of things, or because the soul is the way it is and things are the way they are, and we disregarded this.

The Opening of the First Six Seals

Similarly, and finally, the secret truth is that what we do to one another is done to our true selves. This is just, as we cannot be forgiven unless we forgive, as is explained after the Lord's Prayer. If the soul is immortal and our deeds written in the book of life, how will the cruel avoid eternal torment? They will, in the presence of God, see their actions in their true light, and hence be tormented with what they have done to themselves. What is done is done, and they have extinguished by choice the part of man that repents, seeing itself in the light of the divination of the good. It would be better if they had gone out of being, and the saints may plead for them. It is not accurate to take literally the image that God then hates these souls and makes the saints view their eternal torment, extending the metaphor beyond the bounds of its meaning. We plead for their souls, though there is a natural satisfaction in the destruction of every sort of tyranny, ancient or modern, and judicial punishment of its deeds.

There is a scene at the conclusion of the *Epistula Apostolorum* (40-45), purported to be a teaching of the Twelve Apostles, very important for this argument. Here the Apostles petition for the damned, and Jesus answers regarding the difficulty of this request. Stephen, when he is stoned, prays that the sin of his persecutors not be held against them, as Jesus does his own persecutors. As has been noted, a difficulty of the Revelation is that the whole theme is that of divine vengeance for the murder of the martyrs. That vengeance belongs to the Lord, but not to man, is along the lines of the same point: the martyrs in history pray for their persecutors, while the martyrs in the Revelation ask how long it will be before their murders are avenged. One suggestion, then, to resolve this paradox of the Revelation is that the forgiveness is literal, and the request for vengeance symbolic. It is not Abel, but his blood that cries from the ground. Humans cannot murder the saints of God without the gravest of consequences, as the Nazi assault on the people of God and its aftermath reveal. Look at what has occurred to the German nation, how this was the result of the abomination, and how the nation has begun to heal, and yet remains near to danger. The Apostles ask that their sin not be held against them, but the vengeance of the Father—not upon human ethical failings, but upon inhuman cruelty—is what occurs. What we do to others is, especially, what occurs to our true selves. If we do not forgive others, we will not be forgiven.

In the vision of Fatima, Mary looks down into Hell, saying to the children, "this is hell, where the poor sinners go..." This was 1917, when in a political sense Hell opened, and unlimited means of modern politics were made possible the ideological tyranny that covered one-quarter of the globe. Ideas, those of ideological tyranny, opened the way for millions to partake in unprecedented cruelties. This might be described as a possession by a diabolic spirit, and the days of the Antichrist will be similar, though worse.

The Sixth Seal

[6:12-17] The opening of the sixth seal results in the blackening of the sun and reddening of the moon in an earthquake accompanied by meteors or shooting stars. This, rather than the darkening of one-third of the sun and moon at the fourth trumpet, seems to be the event foretold by the prophet Joel (2:10-12; 3:4; 4:15; Is. 13:10; 24:23). Jesus describes this in Matthew (24:29-31) and Luke (21:25-6). In Matthew, it occurs "immediately *after* the tribulation of those days" described in 24:5-28. *After* the wars of kingdoms and nations, famines and earthquakes, the martyrdom of Christians, and the preaching of the gospel throughout the whole world, the end will come. Those in Judea are told to flee when they see the desolating sacrilege spoken of by Daniel, and then the worst tribulation ever occurs, the one shortened for the sake of the elect (24:21-22). Jesus emphasizes false Christs, and the assurance that his return will be obvious, "as the lightening comes from the east and shines as far as the west, so will be the coming of the son of man" (24:27). After the tribulation, the sun will be darkened, the moon will not give its light, stars will fall from heaven, and the powers of heaven are shaken. Then the sign of the son of man appears in heaven, all the tribes of the earth mourn and see the son of man coming on the clouds of heaven, and he sends out his angels with a trumpet call to gather his elect from the four winds, or from one end of heaven to the other. In Matthew, there follows the teaching that we do not know the time, and then the warning against the example of the bad servants when the master was delayed. One began to beat his fellow servants (25:48). In Luke, Jesus also begins from his prophecy of the fall of the temple, when asked for a sign of when these things would occur (21:6-7). He tells the Apostles of their persecution to come even before the wars, famines, pestilences, earthquakes, terrors and great signs from heavens. When they see Jerusalem surrounded, they are to know that its desolation has come near, and those in Judea are told to flee. "Jerusalem will then be trodden down by the Gentiles, until the times of the Gentiles are fulfilled." In Luke, the desolating sacrilege and even the tribulation seem to occur surrounding the fall of Jerusalem, which happened in 70 A.D. The strange statement "until the times of the Gentiles are fulfilled" appears to us to be a gap in history of more than two thousand years. There appears the possibility that, as with the desolating sacrilege of Antiochus, the fall of Jerusalem in 70 A.D. may be a pre-figuration of the later end time event of the surrounding of Jerusalem, after the times of the Gentiles are fulfilled. This would make some sense of why the prophecy of the fall of Jerusalem in the account leads directly to the description of the Second Advent. After this strange statement, there occurs what appears to coincide with the opening of the sixth seal in the Revelation:

> And there will be signs in the sun and moon and stars, and upon the earth distress of nations in perplexity at the roaring of the sea and the waves, men fainting with fear and with foreboding of what is coming on the world; for the powers of the heavens will be shaken. And they will see the son of man coming in a cloud with power and great glory. Now when you see these things, look up and raise your heads, because your redemption is drawing near.
>
> Luke 21: 25-28

On the Revelation

In the Revelation, following the signs in the sun and moon, the sky is rolled up like a scroll, as would occur in a large earthquake. Isaiah too saw the stars falling from the sky, and "the skies roll up like a scroll" (Isaiah 34:4). Victorinus writes: "And the heaven withdrew as a scroll that is rolled up. For the heaven to be rolled away, that is, that the Church shall be taken away" (loc. cit., p. 351). By this he means either that the church and hence the current access to heaven will be gone, or else he means the rapture, and this is then another place where the rapture may occur, as when earth and sky flee before the judgment (20:11).

Everyone—or rather, the kings, the great, generals and the rich, the strong, and "every one, slave and free"—who is able hides in caves and rocks amid the leveled mountains, calling to the mountains and the rocks to fall on them and hide them from the face of "him who is seated on the throne, and from the wrath of the Lamb." Are those hiding open to the wrath of the Lamb because of the martyrs seen when the fifth seal was opened? Victorinus writes: "Mountains and islands removed from their places intimate that in the last persecution all men departed from their places; that is, that the good will be removed, seeking to avoid the persecution" (Ibid., p. 351).

The notes to the Oxford (1977, p. 1499) text assure the reader: "The great earthquake and cosmic catastrophe are not to be understood literally, but represent social upheavals and divine judgment in the Day of the Lord." We are not at all to fear that we will literally be unable to stand before the great day of the wrath of the Lamb (6:17). To say the least, there is nothing in the text to suggest this, and it can appear as little more than another addition to the account based on wishful thinking. The Day of the Lord is what is prophesied, whether one believes it or not. It is prophesied in part because it is unbelievable. Isaiah (2:10-21) wrote:

> Enter into a rock, and hide in the dust from before the terror of the Lord and the glory of his majesty...and the pride of men shall be brought low...In that day men will cast forth their idols of

> silver and gold...to enter the caverns of the rocks and the clefts of the cliffs, from before the terror of the Lord...

One wonders whether something like this scene might occur in a pole shift. Amos (8:8-9) writes:

> Shall not the land tremble on this account
> And everyone mourn who dwells in it,
> And all of it rise like the Nile,
> And be tossed about and sink
> Again, like the Nile of Egypt?
>
> And on that day, says the Lord God,
> I will make the sun go down at noon,
> And darken the earth in broad daylight.
> I will turn your feasts into mourning,
> And all your songs into lamentation;

We can try to translate the prophetic vision into our Copernican universe, and see that this is what would appear if the poles were to shift at noon Jerusalem time, or just before dawn in Central America. Modern geology understands both plate tectonics and meteor impacts, as were not previously understood. Again, until the twentieth century it was not thought that meteors impacted earth, and stones that fell from heaven were generally revered, as at Mecca and Ephesus (Acts 19:35). Isaiah writes:

> Therefore I will make the heavens tremble, and the earth will be shaken *out of its place*, at the wrath of the Lord of Hosts in the day of his fierce anger (13:13).
>
> Behold, the Lord will lay waste the earth and make it desolate,
> And he will *twist its surface* and scatter its inhabitants (24:1).

> ...the earth staggers like a drunken man, it sways like a hut (24:19).

In the second and third chapters of Joel, this time is also described after telling how the Lord will pour out his spirit on all flesh, so that many prophesy, dream, and see visions. He writes:

> And I will give portents in the heavens and on the earth, blood and fire and columns of smoke. The sun shall be turned to darkness, and the moon to blood, before the great and terrible day of the Lord comes.

Amos (5:18-20) writes:

> Woe to you who desire the day of the Lord!
> Why would you have the day of the Lord?
> It is darkness, and not light;
> As if a man fled from a lion,
> And a bear met him;[84]
> Or went into the house and leaned with his hand against the wall
> And a serpent bit him.
> Is not the day of the Lord darkness and not light,
> And gloom with no brightness in it?

The earthquake is apparently of worldwide though limited consequences, different from the great earthquake to come with the seventh trumpet (11:19), and the greatest earthquake of all, in the seventh bowl (16:18). That later cataclysms are possible indicate the limited extent of this one, and the skies must clear if they are to be darkened yet again. The darkening of sun and moon, and the falling of stars from the sky, indicate a volcano coinciding with a meteor shower, or possibly a volcano producing volcanic hail. Here everyone on earth seeks to hide in the mountains, though the mountains have all been removed from their places, as might occur if the geological plates were to shift about, even just a little. This in turn might occur should the poles shift, even gracefully. After the great earthquake, John sees an angel who ascends from the rising of the sun tell the four angels standing at the four corners of the earth *not* to harm "the earth or the sea or the trees" *until* the 144,000 servants of God have been sealed on their foreheads. Strangely, the four winds are similar to the four horses in the first chapter of Zechariah, sent out to patrol the earth. But these especially seem related to the nations at the four corners of the earth, who are as if held back from the cataclysmic war until the 144,000 are sealed.

And so the drama that is the focus of the Revelation begins with a worldwide earthquake. The resulting disturbance of the human world might then allow for the events to occur: the ascent to power of the Beast, as though into the voided office or the void of power that results from the earthquake. There follows then the persecution of the martyrs, and then the gathering of the nations at the four corners of the world for the battle of Armageddon. This makes possible the clarification of what amounts to another precondition, and an emerging *logos*: Before the wars of the end times begin and the persecutor emerges, the present order is shaken by the earthquake, though the technology and nations of our world persist through the confusion. The earthquake is followed by a long profound silence, during which the 144,000 are sealed, and then silence for one half hour when the seventh seal is opened, the censer with the prayers of the saints cast onto the earth, and the seven trumpets begin with the destruction of one-third of the world. So, it seems, we need not worry about these things emerging from our world, at least before the earthquake.

[7:1-8] He did not see, but heard the sealing of the 144,000 (Aune, p. 466). Those having been sealed are then listed, 12,000 from each of the twelve tribes. The anomalies of the list are the inclusion of Manasseh and Joseph, which may be another name for Ephriam. The tribe of Dan is omitted, and the tribes of both Manasseh and Joseph included. Hippolytus famously suggests that this is because the Antichrist is of the tribe of Dan.

These tribes have been scattered, the first ten in the seventh century B.C., so that only two or three are known any longer. This means that the ten tribes are scattered among the nations–

some hidden amid the Christian world after the holocaust. Ten of these were disbursed among the nations, and as a result of the persecutions of Jews, many hid their heritage, as for example in Poland. Genetic ancestry studies might allow for the re-identification of the twelve lost tribes, as was foretold (Isaiah 27:13), and so the picture may in this way be literal. The high place accorded the Jews in the Revelation reminds of the warning at the end of Paul's saying about the grafted olive tree, that the Gentiles too might be cut off, when they do not bear fruit, and Israel grafted back in again (Romans 11:24). And what are these two branches by the olive trees (Romans 11:19; Zechariah 4:12)?

The word seal in Greek is *sphragis*, and the verb to seal, *sphragisdzo*. It is the same word in Greek as that used for the seven seals that keep closed the book that is being unsealed. The word has three related meanings: the seal on a letter, to mark, and to confirm. Something that is secret or not revealed is yet sealed, from the first meaning, as in Daniel (12:4) and here, "seal up what the seven thunders have said" (Rev. 10:4). The same word is used for those sealed with the Holy Spirit, as Paul writes: "…and do not grieve the Holy Spirit of God, in whom you were *sealed* for the day of Redemption." (Ephesians 4:30; 1:11). Confirmation, the Catholic sacrament of the anointing or the Chrism, receiving the Holy Spirit, is called a sealing from the third meaning. It also means the authentication of one sent (John 6:27, I Cor. 1:22). The mark as a visible sign, on the followers of the Beast, is rather called a *charagma*, which is very close in meaning, also used for the imprint on a coin. But this sealing is like that achieved in the vision of Ezekiel by the mark placed by the man dressed in linen on the foreheads of those who sigh and groan at the abominations committed in Jerusalem (Ezekiel 9:4). The forehead indicates the purpose toward which one's mind is set, one's true intention, or the direction of his forethought. The three meanings are related, as the sealed secret is revealed in the Holy Spirit, when those sealed see the events unfold, and those sealed with the spirit are those marked. The difference between the 144,000 and the multitudes may correspond or be identical to the difference between those baptized and those also confirmed, receiving the anointing of the oil called the Chrism in the mystery of receiving the Spirit.

The reader expects that the 144,000 complete the number of the martyrs, as those seen under the throne were told, but these are rather marked for protection from the locusts of the fifth trumpet (9:4). This is like the marking seen by Ezekiel. Ezekiel saw the scribe in his vision given fire by the Cherubim, from between the whirling wheels of the Cherubim at the foot of the throne (Ezekiel 10:2, 7). This one is a man clothed in linen, who put the mark on the foreheads of the men who sigh and groan over the abominations committed in Jerusalem, so that they are passed over when the executioners go through the city in the vision (Ezekiel 9:4-11). This mark is said to have been a Tao, a letter that looks like an X, or a sideways cross. This marking, in turn, is like the marking of the posts at Passover in Egypt, so that death passes by (Exodus 12:7). So these are also contrasted with the multitude in that they are not martyrs. Aune surveys three opinions regarding the identity of the 144,000—whether Jews or Christians, martyrs or survivors—and concludes:

> In my view, the 144,000 of Revelation 7:4-8 represent that particular group of Christians (including all ages and genders) who have been specially protected by God from both divine plagues and human persecution, just before the final eschatological tribulation begins, and who consequently survive that tribulation and the great eschatological battle that is the culmination of that tribulation. The preservation of this group of survivors ensures that the number of the elect will not be cut off (Mark 13:20) and guarantees the continued witness to Jesus during the unfolding end time events.

If the persecution was this time against Christians, and Jews by race were protected by nationality or Israeli citizenship, the sealing too would make sense. Aune refers to 4 and 5 Ezra and 2 Apocalypse Baruch for a teaching regarding the survivors that gather on Mount Zion. Esdras writes not of 144,000, but of a multitude from the ten lost tribes (2 Es. 13:39-40), and of "those who have been saved throughout my borders" (12:34). "Every one who has been saved...will survive the dangers...and will see salvation in my land...which I have sanctified for myself from the beginning."[85] And in the second chapter, a great multitude are seen on Mount Zion, where a man of great stature gives them crowns and palm branches (Esdras 2:42). In Chapter 14 of the Revelation, the 144,000 are described a bit more as chaste, and as followers of the Lamb wherever he goes (14:4-5). The literal text requires that they are virgins, which is interesting historically because of the Protestant teaching against the celibacy of the priesthood and simultaneous insistence on the literal text. They may literally be celibate Jewish Christians like John, though of the age of the completion of the martyrs.

A clue to the symbolic meaning of the sealing of the 144,000 may be in the promise to Philadelphia that he who conquers will be kept out of the time of trial coming on the whole world, and that he, Jesus, will inscribe on him the name of God and the New Jerusalem, and his own new name (3:11-12). The Church at Philadelphia no longer exists, and still the time of trouble has not yet been.

[7:9] After this, John sees a great, innumerable multitude, of every nation, tribe, people and tongue, as contrasted with the 144,000 from the twelve tribes. The contrasted multitude is seen "standing before the throne and before the Lamb clothed in white robes, with palm branches," as was done when Jesus entered Jerusalem, and as is done by the Christian churches on Palm Sunday to this day. One of the elders asks who these are, and John answers, "Sir, you know." The elder tells him, "These are they who come out of the great tribulation." They *are* before the throne through the whitening of their robes in the blood of the Lamb, and are sheltered because the one on the throne is spread out like a tent, or entabernacled over them. The Lamb will guide them to living water, and God wipe away every tear. Their presence before the throne, together with those seen under the throne in the fifth seal, completes the throne scene with the representatives of humanity, otherwise absent. Are these multitudes then the completion of the number of those seen under the throne? And are the 144,000 not like them, though they are not martyred?

As Aune indicates, it is not clear *when* the multitudes appear before the throne (p. 447). The scene does not seem to be the New Jerusalem of the final chapters, but rather to occur in heaven before the throne, and after the opening of the sixth seal. They are before the throne, which seems to be how things *are*, day and night, which would also be in the New Jerusalem. The present tense is changed for the translations. The line reads "those who *are coming* out of the tribulation" as though this were occurring as they looked on.

As Aune reads, these represent:

> ...all Christians who have died, whether naturally or by martyrdom, before the completion of eschatological events, which conclude with the victory of the Lamb and his followers. However, this group cannot represent all Christians for the simple reason that the 144,000 are still living on the earth under divine protection.

If the rapture is depicted in the Revelation, it occurs after the events of the sixth seal, and may surround events described in the sixth trumpet. It either is or coincides with mass martyrdom. The mass martyrdom seems simultaneous with the invasion of the kings of the East. This again is described or addressed in the sixth, whether seal or trumpet or bowl, and possibly even in the sixth angel of Chapter 14. After the martyrdom there occurs, in the seventh place, there is the judgment of Babylon and the defeat of the Beast and false prophet, when the kingdom of the world becomes the Kingdom of the Lord, and He begins to reign. The visions following the eating of the little scroll seem to elaborate different aspects of this mass martyrdom just before the seventh trumpet, which is the wrath of God for the making of the martyrs.

In sum then, through the seventh chapter, what has been shown is that after the martyrs made throughout the centuries, in the Four Horsemen there is a great cataclysm, such as a moving of the whole crust of the earth, and this cataclysm unleashes the martyrdom of the Christians, as may be elaborated in the sixth trumpet and bowl. The number of the fellow servants of the martyrs is then completed, and the blood of the martyrs can be avenged.

vii: The Seventh Seal and the Seven Trumpets

[8:1-5] Bauckham writes: "The events which accompany the opening of the seals are not the content of the scroll, which cannot be read until all the seals are opened" (p. 1293). At the opening of the seventh seal, the scroll is opened. Yet strangely, the vision continues as it has, with John seeing the seven angels given seven trumpets. It is not said that now what is seen will be the content of the scroll, though nothing else is ever said to be the content. The content of the scroll is either the seven trumpets or both the seals and trumpets. It cannot be the throne and the throne scene, and one can distinguish between the vision that began in 4:1 and the visions within the vision that are apparently the content of the scroll.

When the seventh seal is opened, there is silence in heaven for "about half an hour." This silence is especially fitting if the prophecy is the literal destruction of one-third of the earth and the death of one-third of mankind. John sees the seven angels who stand before God, "and seven trumpets were given to them." As a prelude to the blowing of the trumpets, another angel comes and stands at the altar with a golden censer. This one is given incense to mingle with the prayers of the saints, "and the smoke of the incense rose with the prayers of the saints from the hand of the angel before God." This event is similar to the image in the third secret of Fatima, where

> …Beneath the two arms of the cross there were two angels each with a crystal aspersorium in his hand, in which they gathered up the blood of the martyrs and with it sprinkled the souls that were making their way to God.

On the Revelation

Yet here, the angel fills the censer with fire from the altar and throws it on the earth, and there is thunder, lightning, and an earthquake, in a contrasting meaning. The scene is similar to that after the rebellion of Korah, when Eleazar is told to take the censers of the rebels out of the fire and scatter the coals far and wide (Numbers 16:37). But it is especially similar to the scribe who Ezekiel saw in his vision given fire by the Cherubim, from between the whirling wheels of the Cherubim at the foot of the throne (Ezekiel 10:2, 7). It appears that the censer of fire thrown onto the earth is the result of the martyrdom. The same container is used to take up fire from the altar as that which was used to mingle incense with the prayers of the saints.

The seven trumpets of the seventh seal are *patterned* like the opening of the seven seals, where the first four go together and introduce the last three. The Four Horsemen introduce the story of the avenging of the martyrs in the seals. Here in the trumpets, the first four introduce the three woes, which occur with the blasts of the last three trumpets. The pattern is similar, though the content is different, so that it is surely not as though the trumpets were an elaboration of the seals. In the four trumpets, one-third of the earth, sea, freshwater and then the heavens are affected, with the blowing of each successive trumpet. The third of the earth is burned when hail mixed with fire falls on it. The third of the sea becomes blood when something like a great mountain burning with fire is thrown into the sea. The third of the freshwater is struck when a great star, blazing like a lamp, falls from heaven onto a third of the rivers, which then become "wormwood." It is often said that the word wormwood in the Ukrainian language is Chernobyl. All four trumpets are consistent with a super-volcano or meteor shower, or a nuclear war which destroys one-third of the planet. It is not clear which third. At the fourth trumpet, a third of the sun, moon and stars are struck "so that a third of their light was darkened." This dimming seems to occur across the whole planet. The striking of the sun and moon, and the earthquake that occurred when the censer of fire was thrown onto the earth, are similar to what occurred at the opening of the sixth seal. This similarity raises the possibility that these two series overlap, with each trumpet blast an unfolding of what is contained in each of the seals. But it is most likely that there are two separate occurrences regarding the sun and moon, becoming black and red in the sixth seal and then dimmed by one-third at the fourth trumpet. There seems to be no recognition of cumulative damage in the Revelation. So these are either simultaneous or simply successive occurrences in the same pattern; successive although the seven trumpets occur *within* the seventh seal, rather than after the seventh seal.

We will look for and consider different ordering principles for the seals, trumpets, and bowls. Victorinus writes: "The unsealing of the seals …is the opening of the old testament, and the foretelling of the preachers of things to come in the last times, which, although the prophetic scripture speaks by single seals, yet by all the seals opened at once, prophecy takes its rank" (p. 350). It may be wisely that Victorinus (p. 352; 354) writes:

> We must not regard the order of what is said, because frequently the Holy Spirit, when he has traversed even to the end of the last times, returns again to the same times, and fills up what he had before failed to say. Nor must we look for order in the Apocalypse; but we must follow the meaning of those things that are prophesied.

And, after addressing the two witnesses and the events of Chapter 11, he writes:

> When he has gone forward to the last times, he again repeats the former ones. And now, what he will do once for all, he sometimes sets forth as if it were done; and unless you understand this as sometimes done, and sometimes about to be done, you will fall into a great confusion.

The first four trumpets might be a single event, a geological and astronomical or man-made catastrophe covering one-third of the earth. The catastrophes of the four trumpets may go with the earthquake of the sixth seal, even resulting from it. These catastrophes prepare the ground for the catastrophe in the human world of the first two woes, the fifth and sixth trumpets.

Chapter Nine

[9:1-11] There is no division between Chapters 8 and 9, so that here, as between Chapters 2 and 3, and Chapters 20 and 21, a new chapter begins in the course of an account, without a natural chapter break. Without these divisions, there might be 19 chapters, and what is now Chapter 12 would be Chapter 10 and central. The place of the division between Chapters 8 and 9 is between the first four and the last three trumpets. When the fifth angel blows his trumpet, John sees a star fallen from heaven to earth. "He," who is apparently the angel, was given "the key to the shaft of the bottomless pit," which he then opens. Smoke rises up, darkening "the sun and the air." If the sun and air were already darkened from the first four trumpets, this would seem repetitious. Similarly, if one-third of the earth were already burned, one-third of mankind would already be gone, and the number to be killed by the kings of the East one-third of the remaining two-thirds. But from this smoke arises locusts given the power of scorpions. These are told not to harm grass, trees, or green growing things, as literal locusts would do, but only those of mankind who do *not* have the seal of God on their foreheads. This suggests that the locusts are symbolic of an affliction not of the bodies, but of the souls of the humans not sealed. The mark of the Beast does not seem yet to be imposed, and later in the bowls, those with the mark of the Beast are struck with evil sores (16:2). But the sting like that of the scorpions comes on all those not sealed. Like the mark placed on the forehead of those who sigh over the abominations committed in Jerusalem, and like the blood on the doorpost at Passover (Exodus 12:12-14), the seal here prevents those wearing it from being afflicted. Strangely, for the fierce appearance and scorpion sting of the locusts, they are here not particularly on the side of the enemies of God, but afflict mankind in general with the exception of those sealed. The fallen star and opening of the pit seem as much an affliction of the enemies of God as a releasing of them.

The prohibition of harming vegetation is like the prohibition from harming earth or sea or trees until the 144,000 are sealed (7:3), in the opening of the sixth seal. It is strange because it has no meaning in one-third of the world, where one-third of all the trees and grass have been burned. The locusts were allowed to torture, though not to kill, the unsealed of mankind for five months, with a torture like a scorpion sting. It is these who will wish to die but will not be able to. The description of the locusts is very similar to the description of the horses of the two hundred million man army, with certain differences in the heads (man, lion) and tails (scorpion, serpent, etc.), and the locust too might be some sort of air weapon, a helicopter or drone plane, seen either as in a snapshot or as in a symbol. War may be conducted by automated instruments in our own very near future. Armies on the move are like locusts, devouring the land they pass through in search of provisions. The visible appearance of the locusts is described in detail. They look something like the lead singer of a modern heavy metal rock band. The noise of their wings is like the sound of many chariots entering battle. Their noise may be contrasted with the new song of the 144,000 (14:3). The effects seem consistent with the moral effects of cultural deterioration; and the detailed description of 9:7-9 would fit the foreseeing of the album cover of a heavy metal band, with hair like the hair of women and all sorts of warrior attire. These things are like things we are beginning to see in our world, that were previously unimaginable, and the things described may come from these things in our world, but the locusts occur after the earthquake and the great catastrophe of the first four trumpets, and so belong to a world unlike anything we know, except from futuristic fiction. It may be, too, that the worldwide earthquake of the sixth trumpet is another precondition, necessary before the political upheaval that leads to the Beast. This would mean that prior to the earthquake, we need not worry about the emergence of these things, as most have worried about them, as imminent.[86] The affliction is not like the physical *result* of the first four trumpets, and is not said to be confined to one- or two-thirds of the earth. The sting of the scorpion is not like a bomb, but more like the spread of an especially nasty STD. Another possibility is that it is some spiritual torture, as that despair that makes so many today suicidal, wishing to die. These locusts "have as king over them the angel of the bottomless pit, whose name is destruction or destroyer, in Hebrew *Abaddon* and in Greek *Apollyon*." So the first woe is a punishment of the unsealed by agents or subjects of the angel of the bottomless pit. This seems to occur before the Beast has appeared, but after the 144,000 have been sealed. Why these would especially punish the unsealed, or how it would come about that they would do so, is not clear. And the multitudes, that are distinct from the 144,000 that are sealed—are these not then alike subjected to the locusts, unless they had been raptured, coming out of the tribulation after the earthquake of the sixth seal, but before the grave destruction of the first four trumpets?

The sixth trumpet blast seems to have three distinct parts. There is first the battle which kills one-third of mankind (9:13-21); then there is the vision of the mighty angel and the eating of the scroll (10:1-11), and finally the martyrdom of the two witnesses (11:1-13). It is also possible that the sixth trumpet ends before Chapter 10, where a new vision begins: "Then I saw..." But at 11:14, after the story of the witnesses, it is said that the second woe has then passed, with the third to follow soon, and then the seventh angel blows his trumpet. The better reading, then, seems to include the interlude of Chapter 10 within the sixth trumpet.

[9:12-21] When the sixth angel blows his trumpet, John hears a voice "from the four horns of the golden altar before God." The voice tells the angel with the trumpet to release the four angels who are "bound at the great river Euphrates," and these are released. These four are like the four angels at the four corners of the earth, who were held back during the sixth seal, while the servants of God were sealed (7:1). These four angels had been "held ready for the hour, the day, the month and the year" to kill one-third of mankind. The number of the troops of cavalry is given as two hundred million. There is no necessity that these all be the army of the kings of the East, as is often assumed. These may be the total of all the armies. It is usually assumed that the two hundred million man army is that belonging to the kings of the East, for whose passage the Euphrates is to be dried up (16:12). But the troops may be all those belonging to the kings of the whole world (16:14) that are assembled together by the three frogs when the Euphrates is dried for the passage toward Armageddon, elaborated in the sixth bowl (16:12-14). If two-thirds of the world are fighting one another undiminished, the third destroyed would seem to be the remaining third, and that might be the western hemisphere. Victorinus writes that by these four are meant four nations, because to every nation is sent an angel (p. 353). The nations at the four corners of the earth are again to be gathered after the millennium (20:8). These presently would be, most literally, the U.S., Russia, Brazil, and Australia. It is more likely, though, that the phrase is like an idiom for all the nations, or the Biblical equivalent of our "World War."

John describes the horses of these cavalry in detail, as he described the locusts of the first woe. The detail fits a futuristic tank force armed with tactical nuclear weapons, engaged in a battle which inflicts nuclear destruction on one-third of the planet. If the events of the first four trumpets are simultaneous rather than successive, this may be the same third of the planet that is destroyed.

Again, strangely, if the seven trumpets are read as unfolding chronologically, one-third of mankind was not yet killed when one-third of the earth was burned up; one-third of the sea turned to blood, with one-third of the ships destroyed; one-third of the rivers poisoned; and one-third of the sky darkened. Nor, if the events are seen as chronological, unfolding one after another, do these events affect the ability of the four angels to wield such an army, nor does the one-third global catastrophe affect the strength of their opponent, and hence their need to wield such an army. A more coherent reading may be that the event of the trumpets, at least the first six, is a single occurrence, in which one-third of mankind and one-third of the globe is destroyed. This may be

On the Revelation

caused by a world war unleashed by the dissolution of society and government that would result from a worldwide earthquake in our computer-dependent world. If the earthquake is not caused by human action, such as fracturing the crust in search of oil or testing bombs underground, the sixth seal may be due to nature. The seventh, then, would be due to mankind, when we are tested by the world that results from the sixth seal. Only the fifth trumpet does not fit under the single occurrence hypothesis—but this, the locusts and their sting, could be occurring elsewhere while the two hundred million troops are gathered to destroy one-third of the earth and mankind. It is not said that the two hundred million man army are followers of the Beast, nor even that they are all from the same nation, and it is as consistent to imagine the armies of the world gathering to fight the Antichrist who has taken over the world from Jerusalem, in imitation of the Messianic kingdom.

After the battle which kills one-third of mankind, those remaining still did not repent the works of their hands: They continued worshiping demons and idols made of five materials. These five are nearly identical to the metals of the vision of Daniel, except that iron and clay are replaced with stone and wood. Nor did they repent "of their murders or their sorceries or their immorality or their thefts." The word for sorceries is *pharmakia*, which is also the word for drugs, pharmaceutical things. There may be a connection between the two meanings: drugs may affect the relation between consciousness and the unconscious, similar to involvement with spirits in the old understanding. Marijuana is not a pharmaceutical drug, and may, like wine, be a spiritual benefit, allowed under the First Amendment. But the reliance on drugs is an offshoot of modern science, both those *rightly* illegal or *pro*scribed, and those prescribed as supposed cures for supposedly chemical maladies. There may be a connection, for example, between school and workplace shootings and our use of psychiatric drugs, especially anti-depressants. We literally do not know what we are doing when we prescribe these, and it is not science but the hit-and-miss of folk medicine behind these prescriptions, without the benefit of a long tradition behind the remedies. Literal idolatry—

worshiping sculptures, etc. as gods—is nearly nonexistent in the modern world, and it is difficult to see a return of this way, so strange to us that we can barely understand it. One is reminded of the formula of Paul Tillich, defining idolatry, to paraphrase, as taking anything less than the Most High to be for us the first thing, be it money or whatever, and in this sense few avoid idolatry. The worshiping of demons might be literal, or it might be no more literal than the use of horses and chariots in the battle. It might be a way of stating the cultural catastrophe that seems to occur with the fifth trumpet, showing its logical connection to the sixth. The vice of mankind leads to world war, either following the destruction of one-third of the world or causing this. It is a world we cannot imagine, like a new age following the destruction of our familiar world, though emerging out of elements, such as computers, that are already present for us. One-third of the earth and mankind are destroyed, and the punishment is not yet complete. The remaining two-thirds of mankind, over two-thirds of the earth, do not repent. Literally, this means that one-third of mankind and the earth could be destroyed, and the time of the last Judgment *still* not have arrived. The sixth trumpet is not even yet finished.

Chapter 10

[10:1-11] Apparently still within the sixth trumpet, John sees "another mighty angel coming down from heaven, wrapped in a cloud, with a rainbow over his head," whose face was like the sun, and whose legs like pillars of fire. Bauckham identifies this angel with that mentioned in the opening line as the intermediary sent from Jesus to John, and the little scroll he identifies with the scroll or book in Chapter 5, unsealed by the conquest of the Lamb. The earlier vision of the one like a son of man and the letter to the seven churches is not made known to John through an intermediary angel. The other angel who enters into the vision is that one who comes from the rising of the sun to seal the servants of God, at the opening of the sixth seal. This one is identified by Victorinus as "Elias the prophet, who is precursor to the times of the Antichrist" (p. 351). Here, at the sixth trumpet, the angel has a rainbow over or around him, encircling his head (Lindsey, 1973, p. 84), and what are like legs of fire. Sometimes a rainbow is seen to encircle the sun, when it shines through fog. I myself first saw a "sundog" when I began reading the Gospel of John, back at Grand Valley. The one on the throne also appeared to Ezekiel to have what are like legs of fire (Ezekiel 1:27). This one (10:2-3):

> ...had a little scroll open in his hand. And he set his right foot on the sea and his left foot on the land, and called out with a loud voice, like a lion roaring; when he called out, the seven thunders sounded.

This scene described in the vision of the Revelation is very similar to the scene at the end of Daniel (12:5-12), when the man clothed in linen–who may be either Gabriel or Jesus–is seen above the waters of the stream, while two others stand on either bank of the stream. The angel connects the two realms, whether sea and land as in the vision of John or the two sides of a river, like a bridge, as in the vision of Daniel. Daniel asks, "How long shall it be till the end of these wonders?" At this:

> ...the man clothed in linen, who was above the waters of the stream, raised his right hand and his left hand toward heaven, and I heard him swear by him who lives forever and ever that it would be for a time, two times, and a half a time; and that when the scattering of the power of God's people comes to an end all these things shall be accomplished.

Again, *we* would be in the time between the return of Israel and the earthquake, and the emergence of the Beast.

Sea and land are connected by the angel over them. Sea and land here seem to introduce the things said about sea and land in the following two chapters, where one stands on the boundary between them, the shore, (13:1); and then the beasts emerge from the sea and land, after the dragon was cast from heaven portending woe to sea and land. Earthly or political things are connected with or invaded by spiritual things. An example would be the use of symbols and the imagination in the earthly power of the Nazis.

Are the seven thunders to the little scroll as the seven trumpets are to the other scroll, or to the seventh seal? John hears a voice from heaven tell him to seal up what is said, though he has heard it and would himself have known. As Bauckham indicates, in the twenty-ninth Psalm, the thunder of God's voice is mentioned seven times. The seven thunders, occurring in the sixth trumpet, is the central of five series of sevens; surrounded by the opening of the seals, the seven trumpets, the messages of the seven angels (14), and the seven bowls of wrath (16). Because what is said by the seven thunders is sealed, a part of the Revelation is permanently mysterious, or perhaps not to be unsealed until the events occur. This is sealed and not opened, but in the place of unsealing, John ingests the open scroll, and by this is enabled to prophesy. The series of visions that follow may be the content of that scroll, the little scroll, though these overlap, and one contains the start of the seventh trumpet.

The little scroll, though it is open and is seen after the seven seals are opened, seems to be a different scroll from the one which only the Lamb was found worthy to open. The little scroll might be the Revelation itself, as distinct from the great scroll that is the unfolding of the events of the end times. John would ingest this scroll by writing it down, in contrast with the unwritten sayings of the seven thunders.

The angel then swears by "him who lives forever," who created the heavens, earth and sea, that there would be no more delay (*oti xponos ouk estai eti*–the time should be not until, or no longer–it almost reads that "time should be no more"), but in the seventh trumpet, the mystery of God should be fulfilled (10: 6-7). The delay was mentioned prior to the opening of the sixth seal, and here again in the sixth trumpet. The seven thunders would seem to say something related to this delay, and something that occurs before the third woe or seventh trumpet. The delay is until the number of the martyrs is completed. This, something related to the martyrdom, may be what leads the angel to say in stern response to the final persecution that there would be no more delay, but that when the mystery to be announced by the seventh trumpet, the mystery of God that he announced to his servants the prophets should be fulfilled. The things said by Paul about the rapture and the sacrilege are candidates for two of the seven thunders. When the narrative resumes, what we see occurring, still within the sixth trumpet, is the martyrdom of the two witnesses. When these are raised, the seventh trumpet is blown.

[10:8-11] The seventh trumpet is not sounded until 11:15. Still, apparently, between the sixth trumpet and the seventh trumpet, John digests the little scroll in the hand of the angel, and is told he must "again prophesy about many peoples, and nations, and tongues and kings." Next the voice that he heard from heaven, telling him to seal up what the thunders have said, spoke again. It told him to take the scroll open in the hand of the angel standing on the land and sea. When John goes to the angel, the angel tells him, "Take it and eat; it will be bitter to your stomach, but sweet as honey in your mouth." Like Ezekiel, he eats the scroll, which is sweet to taste, but unlike Ezekiel's scroll, with which he is told to fill his stomach, John's is bitter in his stomach. Victorinus writes that this ingestion means to commit the scroll to memory. That it is bitter to the stomach may mean that it is like the scroll that has just been opened, a very sad scene, and the digesting of this makes the following series of visions possible. These are visions *within* the vision which began at the throne seen through the open door in heaven. I do not recall another example of a vision seen within a vision. One suggestion is that the throne scene is not a vision, but an occurrence and visitation.

Eating this scroll, John is to prophesy regarding many peoples, nations, tongues *and kings*, in the visions of the sixth and seventh trumpets, the second and third woes to follow. This form of referring to world humanity occurred describing the ransom of men for God from every "tribe and tongue and people and nation," and describing those who will gaze on the bodies of the two witnesses. As Bauckham notes, "The fourfold formula for all the nations occurs seven times" (5:9; 7:9; 10:11; 11: 9; 13:7; 14:6; 17:15). The order is altered in every instance, so that it is not once the same. Here in the tenth chapter, "kings" are the topic added to the four items, replacing "tribes." The only other topic added, in the seventeenth chapter, is "multitudes." In Daniel, the formula is "peoples, nations and languages." The redeemed come from every sort of person in the world. But the added topic here is "kings," and so the visions that follow have especially to do with the sovereignties of the world at the end of the age.

The ascent of those called to "come up here," which occurs in the sixth trumpet, may be the same as the coming out of the tribulation at the opening of the sixth seal. The earthquake again raises the possibility that these are synonymous, or that the seven seals and trumpets overlap–each describing the same occurrence from a different part, or aspect, of the same time period. To repeat, the same event could be described in each of the series of sevens from a slightly different perspective. The sun and moon are struck in the sixth seal and the fourth trumpet, and if these are not different strikes, then the time would seem shifted. Has the air cleared from the worldwide earthquake to be dimmed again? The dimming of the sun may be a separate instance, similar to the fifth trumpet, when smoke from the abyss clouds the sun and air. The seals describe the martyrs who are sealed, while the trumpets describe what occurs to the *unsealed*—and if these seals are the same, the striking of the unsealed in the fifth trumpet does occur *after* the sealing of the martyrs in the sixth seal. The plague of locusts passes over or does not harm them *after* they are sealed.

Here is an amazing detail that seems obvious once it is considered. The tenth and the first part of the eleventh chapter of the Revelation, like the fourth and fifth chapters of the Gospel of John, may have been accidentally reversed. This could easily occur if John handed over one manuscript written on both sides of individual pages without numbers, instead of a scroll. Something is strange about the order of what is presented. The account of the sixth and seventh trumpets apparently continues in Chapter 11, after being interrupted by the vision of the eating of the scroll in Chapter 10. If the two witnesses were to follow Chapter 9, the account of the trumpets would be more continuous. Chapter 10 would be a more fitting introduction to Chapter 12 than it is to Chapter 11. The angel says there will be no more delay, and then there occurs the martyrdom of the two witnesses, and 42 months longer delay? Or are the witnesses the fulfillment of the mystery of God? The problem with the hypothesis that Chapter Ten has been misplaced is that the seventh trumpet seems to be spoken of as future in Chapter 10 (10:7), and is blown at 11:15. Chapter 10 might still be inserted at 11:14, after the measuring of the temple and the two witnesses, though Chapter 11 would be as discontinuous with the end of Chapter 9 as is Chapter 10. If Chapter 10 were placed just before the seventh trumpet, after 11:14, the seven thunders would be between the seventh trumpet and the sixth. The sixth trumpet seems to end at the conclusion of Chapter 9, so that the text must explicitly say, or we would not know, that the second woe is passed *after* the witnesses are raised, making Chapters 10 and 11 a part of the sixth trumpet. Then the seventh trumpet is blown, at 11:15. The seven thunders and the little scroll might then be contained in the seventh trumpet, as are the seven bowls, or might come between the sixth and seventh trumpet.

Or does the conclusion of the story of the witnesses describe a seventh trumpet event, as though their witnessing spanned the sixth and seventh trumpets, and their martyrdom were the very same event as that described through a different image in Chapter 13? The Beast must arise before they are killed by him, but is not shown coming out of the sea until Chapter 13. Are the witnesses unaffected by the mark of the Beast? Yet the Beast may be the same as the angel of the bottomless pit, called *Apollyon*, who is king over the locusts who came out when the pit was opened, at the fifth trumpet. Is the ascent from the bottomless pit the same as the rising out of the sea seen in the seventh trumpet? If not, when does this ascent occur? Is he not overcome until after the millennium, leading to the possible reading that this ascent, spoke of as future, occurs during the millennium?

Finally, 11:1-11:14 might be placed after 11:19, so that the temple in heaven appears *before* John is told to measure the temple that will be trampled. Chapter 10 might then follow 11:14, the angel seen coming down from heaven just *after* the witnesses ascend.

Chapter 10 does seem to have been misplaced, and one wonders if it is not part of the introduction of the seventh trumpet. "In the days of the trumpet call to be sounded..." might then still be future, even while following 11:15. The appearance that it must speak of these days before, rather than during, the blowing of the seventh trumpet may have caused the leaves to be misplaced. Chapter 10, too, coheres with the sort of visions that turn out to be seen regarding the seventh trumpet, and it would be the seventh trumpet that is especially about kings, and requires the ingesting of the little scroll. We may settle for the present ordering, retaining its difficulties and anomalies. But the exercise is helpful, if only for the attempt to read these chapters and see how they *do* fit together. From this exercise, we note that the opening of Chapter 11 is at Mount Mariah, where the temple was built, while the opening of Chapter 14 is on Mount Zion, where the 144,000 are assembled.

Chapter Eleven

[11:1-2] According to the present ordering, Chapter 11 does not introduce a new vision, but continues the vision of the little scroll, in which John is to prophesy on many peoples, tongues, nations and kings. The chapter begins and ends with the temple—first the measuring apparently of the temple in Jerusalem, and then the opening of God's temple in heaven, where the Ark of the Covenant is seen. In the first lines, John is given a measuring rod or yardstick and told to measure "the temple of God, the altar, and those who worship there." Victorinus reads that this reed "itself is the Apocalypse which he subsequently exhibited to the churches' (p. 353). He is told not to measure the court outside the temple, but to "leave that out, for it is given over to the nations, and they will trample over the holy city for forty-two months," or "...until the time of the Gentiles is fulfilled" (Luke 21:24). This is the same as the amount of time He will give his two witnesses: 1,260 days, clothed in sackcloth because, as the Oxford note relates, their prophecy was of repentance. Their time is the same amount as, and possibly simultaneous with, the time the Gentiles will trample over the holy city. It is assumed that this trampling refers to that which began in 70 A.D., and so throughout Chapter 11 we sense a long period in a symbol that is not a snapshot, but an allegory. We will also consider the possibility that there is simultaneously a short period, perhaps of literally seven years, but that the snapshot view of the short period is hidden. The history of the Church, which is the history of martyrdom as a witness to Jesus, will culminate in the short period of the martyrdom of these latter-day saints, even at the center of the seven-year period of his ascent and reign, the time of the worst persecution of all time. The visions hedge about its horrors, but these can be imagined by combining the intent of a Hitler directed at the Christians as well as the Jews, at a *belief* rather than a race, with modern technology at the disposal of his tyranny.

The presence of the temple is cited as evidence that the Revelation was written before its destruction in 70 A.D. (Aune, p. lx). This is, of course, not the only possible implication of John being told to measure the temple. Yet this point draws attention to the strangeness of the vision. That John is told to measure the temple, altar, and those who worship there in the inner court, in contrast with the outer court, is strange in a Christian work. Jesus is supposed to have overcome the difference between Jew and Gentile, which divided those allowed to enter the inner court from those permitted to go only into the outer court of the temple. The temple seen in Chapter 11 stands in contrast with the vision of the new heaven, earth, and New Jerusalem in the twenty-first chapter, in which John sees no temple. The temple in heaven, and the Ark of the Covenant within, are seen at the conclusion of Chapter 11, which is also near the present center of the work.

The body of the chapter does not mention the temple at all, but rather tells the story of the two witnesses. The destruction of one-tenth of "the city," apparently Jerusalem, with seven thousand killed, occurs when these are raised and taken up (11:12-13). Again there is no account of cumulative damage from the earthquake of the sixth seal, from which the world seems to have recovered. Does the author know Jerusalem to have been destroyed, and write of the measuring of a heavenly temple? Or is he to measure the restored temple? He does not measure here, and when he does measure, it is the measuring of the city, the New Jerusalem, in which there is no temple or altar seen. The reason that these two, the order to measure the temple and the account of the two witnesses, occur in the same chapter is that they are related. It may be that the two witnesses somehow *are* the temple, even as the saints *are* the New Jerusalem. When the city *is* measured, at 12,000 furlongs, its wall is 144,000 cubits "according to the measure of a man, that is, an angel" (21:17). It may be these that are the saints with whom the Beast will make war, and conquer them, until the ancient of days arrives (11:7; 13:7; Daniel 7:21). There may be two separate groups of 144,000, or these may be the same as the 144,000 that are sealed.

There is a traditional reading that these two witnesses are Elijah and Enoch, or Elijah and Moses.[87] Malachi writes: "Behold, I will send you Elijah the prophet before the great and terrible day of the Lord comes" (4:5). The Hebrew tradition is that there will be one, Elijah, who precedes the Messiah (Aune, p. 598). It is thought that these two are Enoch and Elijah, because it is thought that these did not die (Genesis 5:24; 2 Kings 2:11). Lindsay notes that Elijah and Moses left their missions incomplete (1973, p. 163). Van Impe notes that Elijah performed the same miracle as that these prophets are said to perform, when he prayed that it not rain, and rain was withheld for three and one-half years (1982, p. 151). John the Baptist was thought to *be* Elijah, as Jesus seems to say (Matthew 17:11-13); and Enoch may, like Melchizedek, be a type or incarnation like the Messiah.[88] John the Baptist may return, though he was beheaded, but the statement of Jesus may contradict the thought that one of the witnesses is Elijah. The vision may be more like a dream than a snapshot, symbolizing things unknown in images produced by nature, from the soul and for the soul. The two witnesses may not be two individual prophets at all.

[11:3] The only indication of the subject matter of these prophets or witnesses is that they are clothed in sackcloth, indicating repentance. They may call the people to repent, as at 9:21. They may call the church to repent the sins of the church, as the Antichrist that is to martyr the Christians and punish Babylon arises. Their message may also be deduced from the description of their ministry and the fact that they draw the attention of the Beast. Lindsay writes that the witnesses will preach that the reconstructed temple is a sham, because everything in it was already fulfilled by Christ, and the new ruler is the Antichrist, and so the Beast murders them (1973, p. 162). He also interprets the prophecy of Malachi, continuing from 4:6: "He will turn the hearts of fathers to their children and the hearts of children to their fathers," considering Israel: "…the presently apostate 'younger generation' would now find mutual harmony in their true messiah, the Lord Jesus Christ." The fathers are the patriarchs or Jews, and the children the Christians (Ibid., p. 163).

[11:4] "These are the two olive trees and the two lamp stands which stand before the Lord of the earth." As Bauckham reads: like the seven lamp stands of Chapters 2-3, the two lamp stands (also called olive trees, following Zechariah 4:1-4), here represent the church. The passage from Zechariah seems to be quite decisive. The prophet persistently asks the angel about the two olive trees, and is answered cryptically: "These are the two anointed who stand by the Lord of the whole earth" (4:14). These are the two olive trees seen near the seven lamp stands (Zechariah 4:2-3). There is no precedent for identifying olive trees with individuals. In Romans (10:12; 18-21; 11:17-32), Paul discusses the Jews and Christians as an olive tree from which a branch was broken off, and another, a wild olive shoot, grafted on. Paul warns that those engrafted might be broken off, and those broken off re-grafted. He explains: "a hardening has come upon part of Israel until the full number of Gentiles come in" (11:25). It may be that they are two because, like the two legs of Daniel's vision, they are the eastern and western churches, as Van Impe indicates regarding the two legs in Daniel's vision (*Final Mysteries Unsealed*, p. 35). Another possibility is that they are Rome and Jerusalem, or that the time of their witness is the same as the time during which Jerusalem was trampled by the Gentiles, as over the past two millennia. The two might also be Israel and the Christian churches, and the olive tree the union of these represented in those who a) obey the commandments, and

b) worship Jesus; or, the Jews and Christians. The two may be united in martyrdom and opposition to the Beast, or it may be that these are united in 144,000 Jewish Christians. It is not impossible that these be both literally Jewish and a body of members, or the angels of these two churches, since if the Jews were converted, they might be members either in the East or in the West. A key to reading the Revelation may be the re-grafting in of the Jews.

[11:5-6] The powers of the witnesses during the days of their prophecy are described in detail. They have amazing and violent powers, apparently of self-defense, for if anyone would harm them, fire pours out of their mouths. They also have the power to stop the rain during their prophesying, turn waters to blood, and strike the earth with plagues. These powers are to inflict drought and death and plague, like the fourth horseman, and to turn the sea to blood, as in the second trumpet (8:8). These things were done by Elijah and Moses (Exodus 7-10; 1 Kings 17:1; 18:1). Could these judgments in the horsemen and trumpets refer to the torments inflicted, or symbolically to spiritual conditions caused by, or in part by, the churches? The two prophets had tormented those dwelling on earth, and so these rejoice over their death, celebrating and giving gifts as though it were a holiday. Could this be the burden of the yoke of the law and the prophets from which Christ, celebrated in Christmas, freed people? Or is it not some futuristic Nazi-like holiday celebrated over the defeat of the Christians or the people of God? Or, why then is it so like this? Van Impe reads this as though the teachers of purity are disliked for spoiling the party of earthly pleasures of those on earth (*Revelation Revealed*, p. 153). Piety may prevent our reading the text as critical of the witnesses, but is the text, in speaking of the churches, limited in this way? This may be a strangely honest prophetic portrayal of the fallible Christian church throughout history, assuming that the witnesses ought not to have tormented anyone. Or why, by their preaching, do they not bring happiness? But this may not be the right question either. Why did Elijah bring drought (1 Kings 16)?

The possibility that it is the witnesses that are a torment to the people of the world is interesting in light of the teaching that it is the reflection of Christianity in the law, custom, and the human world that makes it possible for the anti-Christian to develop. Because human things are both good and evil, or at least bad; at the same time, human institutions of every kind require constant cleansing by the integrity of those who uphold the honor of each institution. The American Constitution is one way, as Madison writes, to oblige the government to control itself. Non-Christians believe, from the example of persecution and the inept attempt of Christians to govern and apply Christianity as a law onto the people, that these things are implied by Jesus and his teaching. Jesus is not a legislator, but the savior, and these are different: Legislators are notoriously violent without exception. Moses and Mohammed are examples. This is as though violence is done to nature in cultivating the higher nature. Christianity is not a law, but salvation. To make a law out of the light is to inform the rejection of the law (Romans 7:8-12), or to inflame the opposite of the law in the attempt to be free of the law. The suppression of philosophy and political philosophy, the pursuit of wisdom, has left Christians with unwise government and artless shepherding.

[11:7-12] When they finish their testimony, the Beast that ascends from the bottomless pit will make war on them and kill them. This phrase is nearly repeated at 13:7, which also addresses a 1,260 day period, as forty-two months (13:7). If this is the same 1,260 days, then the story of the two witnesses might be inserted by the chronological reader at 13:7, and the two sections are elaborations of one another. Their bodies will lie "three and one-half days" in the street of the city where their Lord was crucified, which would be Jerusalem. The three and a half days may be days after three and a half years, or even, if the witnesses are the churches, 1,260 years and then three and a half years. The city where this occurs is referred to symbolically as Sodom or Egypt, cities that represent the corruption of the world or the imprisonment in the things of the body. It is not allegorically called Babylon, though that is the other name in the text that might be used allegorically to refer to what Augustine wrote of as the earthly city. Babylon may be Rome, while the scene here is Israel. Then, after three and one-half days, they stand up on their feet, terrifying those who saw them. Then these hear a voice from heaven saying "Come up hither!" and in the sight of their foes, they went up into heaven in a cloud. Here something like the rapture occurs, though it is for these after being raised from martyrdom. Victorinus writes, "Therefore their preaching is three years and six months, and the Kingdom of the Antichrist *is as much again*." If so, these two are killed, resurrected, raptured, and in this way escape the three and one-half year period of the worst tribulation, though they are not taken up until after the three and one-half days. There are *two* three and one-half year periods that pertain to the tribulation and the seven year reign. It may be that the rapture of the church occurs just before the latter three and a half years or "days" of the seven-year tribulation, at the outbreak of the worst of all times. The description just prior to the pouring of the bowls may be the same, as the 144,000 appear on Mount Zion, and then in heaven by the fiery sea of glass, with harps, singing the song of Moses and of the Lamb.

The number 1,260, which is the number of days in three and a half lunar years, appears for the first time in the Revelation here. The number appears for the first time in scripture in Daniel (7:26), as a "time, two times and a half a time," thought to be three and a half years in Chapters 11 and 13, and is here first the period that the outer court of the temple is to be trampled by the Gentiles. When one asks "For how long"? is the vision of the burnt offering, the abomination, and the giving over of the sanctuary to be trampled underfoot, he is told, "For two thousand and three hundred evenings and mornings," either 2,300 or 1,150 days. "Then the sanctuary shall be restored to its rightful state." This is said to refer to the 164 B.C. desolation of Antiochus (Scofield, p. 1078). The cessation of offering and the abomination are again described as half of the week for which he will make a "strong covenant with many" (Daniel 9:27). In the context of weeks of years (Daniel 9:24), this is thought to be a period of three and one-half years, half of one week of years. "A time two times and a half a time" is how long before the end of the "shattering of the power of the holy people," and "the accomplishment of all these things" (Daniel 12:7), and 1,290 from the time the continual burnt offering is taken away and the abomination set up (Daniel 12:11).

On the Revelation

As discussed above (p. 45), seven years of 360 days would be 2,520 days; of 365-day years, 2,555. As Van Impe indicates, in 1967, on June 5-10, when the Jewish army won the six-day war, "the holy city was in Jewish hands for the first time in 2,553 years." Strangely, 1,260 years from 586 B.C. is also very close to the date of the building of the Dome of the Rock on the site of the temple (691 A.D.), figuring half of the solar years (1,277.5). The Witnesses count from 607 B.C. to 1914, and the lunar calculation of seven years of years from 586 B.C. lands on 1934. This may be the long period that ended when the time of the rule of the Gentiles over Jerusalem ended. The conclusion of Daniel refers cryptically to an additional period of thirty, and then forty-five more days (Daniel 12:11-12). It is possible that the days refer to both a large period of years and / or a small period of days, in which the same pattern is encapsulated. The large would be seven years of years, or 2,520 years; and the small, literally seven years, or 2,520 or so days. It may be possible to reason from one to another—that is, from the large to the small period—by analogy, so that for example there will be a time when Jerusalem is occupied, as by the United Nations, and a brief but severe martyrdom that equals that of the previous centuries, an abomination of desolation set up in the middle of the week, in a rebuilt temple, and so on.

The time referred to as 1,260 days, or forty-two months, or a time two times and a half a time, occurs twice more after chapter 11 of the Revelation: as the time the woman is nourished in the wilderness (12:14) and the time that the Beast is allowed to exercise authority (13:5; 12:17; 13:7-10).

Amid a fine history of the city of Jerusalem, Hal Lindsey joins the description of the temple with the witnesses and Daniel 9:27. The temple is a future rebuilt temple, and the Antichrist is thought by the Jews to be the messiah because he rebuilds it. Lindsey prophesies:

> Antichrist will make and later break a covenant with the Jewish people of the tribulation period, allowing them to reinstitute

animal sacrifices...The only place a God-fearing Jew would venture to offer sacrifice.

If the seven trumpets are to be read as describing the same time period, or times simultaneous with the visions seen with the opening of each of the seven seals, then the rapture of the church, symbolized in the slaying and rapture of the two witnesses, may be *the same* as the multitudes who have come out of the great tribulation, or their martyrdom. The literal suggestion would be a holocaust of the Christians, or Jews and Christians. It is possible or consistent to read that the 144,000 who appear with him on Mount Zion in Chapter 14 have survived, and gather on Mount Zion in hope of the return. The three groups would then be the Jewish Christians, the Eastern Christians, and the Western Christians.

The "Come up hither" of 11:12 might describe the rapture, consistent with the reading that the two lamp stands are the churches rather than two particular prophets. If the seventh trumpet were the great tribulation, the worst time in the history of mankind, the martyrs and those raptured between the sixth and the seventh would escape the tribulation.

According to the teaching of Victorinus, cited also above (p. 148), the Revelation is to be read by looking not to simple chronology but to the meaning of parts gone over repeatedly: The chronological reading, though, is not consistent, so the fact that an element is described in the text later than another does not imply that it literally comes afterward in time, though it *is* a temporal event that is foretold. The text goes over different aspects of seven parts at different times. As Jack Van Impe notes, 6-11 is in some sense repeated in 12-18 (*Revelation Revealed*, p. 154-155). The rapture appears to occur between the sixth and seventh parts, at 11:15, between the sixth and seventh trumpet, and again between the sixth and seventh bowl, just after the kings of the East march toward a dried-up Euphrates, right where he says "Lo! I am coming like a thief! ...blessed..." (16:15). The three sixes, though, may each concern a great martyrdom.

The *Epistula Apostolorum* or *Letter of the Apostles* is astonishingly consistent with the mid-tribulation rapture that

On the Revelation

appears from the text of the Revelation. Again, this letter claims to be from the Twelve Apostles, and the Ethiopian translation contains a preface listing John first among the authors. We wonder if it was not transcribed and in part written by John. In the section numbered 16, Jesus is asked, "O Lord, is it perhaps necessary again that we take the cup and drink?" He said to us, "Yes, it is necessary until the day when I come with those who were killed for my sake." Then, after the description of the beginning of the tribulation period in sections 34-35, in the section numbered 36, the letter reads:

> And we said to him again, "O Lord, will the Gentiles then not say, 'Where is their God?'" He answered and said to us, "Thus will the elect be revealed, in that they go out after they have been afflicted by such a distress," And we said to him, "Will their exit from the world (take place) through a plague that has tormented them?" And he said to us, "No, but if they suffer torment, such suffering will be a test for them, whether they have faith and whether they keep in mind these words of mine and obey my commandment. They will rise up, and their waiting will last (only a) few days, that he who sent me may be glorified, and I with him…

Jesus then told them also to tell the Gentiles, who are also to be saved, to believe in him and escape "the plague." He then addresses some who escape the distress of death, but are then taken to prison under torture. Asked if these will suffer as do unbelievers, he answers: "Believing in my name they have done the work of sinners; they have acted like unbelievers." So it appears that some are martyred, but others remain, only to be tortured —the true and false or partial Christians, who may avoid martyrdom because they are willing to compromise their faith and do not hold to the warning, but then suffer anyway in the persecution of everything related to the Biblical God. It may be worse for us to balk at martyrdom, since it may be even physically worse for those who do not suffer martyrdom. The mark of the Beast may be accompanied by various torments worse than a simple death, so that to take it is no earthly advantage in any case.

[11:14-19] When the third woe is announced, the seventh angel blows his trumpet, introducing the scenes that conclude Chapter 11. Voices in heaven are heard proclaiming: "The kingdom of the world has become the kingdom of our Lord and of his Christ, and he shall reign for ever and ever." There is a sense in which, prior to the seventh trumpet, the Lord did *not* reign, and the return of the fullness of Providence is what occurs. This may sometimes occur when humans invite the Lord to come and reign. But what occurs at the seventh trumpet is a fundamental change. The twenty-four elders give thanks to the Lord God Almighty, who is and was–omitting the future, because it has now come to be. The thanksgiving is because "thou hast taken thy great power and begun to reign." The name "Almighty" may be the only Biblical teaching of the Providence of God, which is otherwise described mysteriously. The Bible does not teach that God is the cause of all things by willing them to occur, as nearly all believers assume. This may even be a pagan idea, an imagination that attends the image of a corporeal God, rejected by some of the philosophers. Socrates, in Plato's *Republic*, rejects that the divine is the cause of anything but the good, changes shape, lies, or takes on various forms (*Republic*, II, 377c-383c). This section of Book III of Plato's *Republic* is called a theology, and this is the first use of the word *theology*, or the coining of the term, which is of course not used by Jesus. Jesus seems to teach this point about Providence in Luke (13:1-5) regarding the fall of the tower: "were these the 21 most unjust men in Israel?" This is as if to imply that had it been the will of God, he would not have missed. The Lord's Prayer can be read as implying that it is *a prayer* if the will of God is ever done on earth as it is in heaven. This is more often read as a submission to whatever misfortune does occur (Matthew 6:9-10). But the imagination of Providence as the intentional cause of all that occurs may be natural to man, and so present in all human societies in some way, evident in Christians sometimes to an extreme. We attempt to use God to bring about our own good fortune, rather than to serve God, in a sense regardless of fortune. What of when we pray for others, rather than ourselves, and for both say only the Lord's Prayer? It is written that He knows what we truly need before we ask, and the Spirit intercedes. This fact, though, about common humanity, led Machiavelli to teach that for mankind, God is fortune. The teaching of the non-Socratic philosophers, as in the poem of Epicurus *On the Nature of Things*, was that men devise religion because they are in fear, not knowing the causes of things. As there is a sense in which the Lord is not provident, as a puppeteer of the universe, so too there is regarding omniscience, a sense in which the Lord might say to us "I have not known you," and of sins forgiven that they are "forgotten," etc., contradicting omniscience. The common opinion of Providence does not account for how it could be that the Lord at one time in human history would *begin* to reign. Our suggestion is that the evil done by humans to one another would not occur if the Lord did reign directly in this way, and that it is prophesied that in the future, the Lord will reign in a way that will prevent the sort of evils that now occur, if not also the misfortunes that mar the human condition. If the Lord reigned in this sense, the evil would be punished, and this is the first thing that happens when the Lord begins to reign: the kingdom of the Antichrist is destroyed, and the Beast and false prophet thrown into the pit. This reign is in contrast to the rule of the nations, as at 11:17-18, the saying of the twenty-four elders at the blowing of the seventh trumpet is:

> We give thanks to thee Lord God almighty,
> who art and who wast,
> That thou hast taken thy great power and begun to reign.
> The nations raged but thy wrath came,
> And the time for the dead to be judged,
> For rewarding thy servants, the prophets and the saints,
> And those who fear thy name, both small and great

The Seventh Seal and the Seven Trumpets

> And for destroying the destroyers of the earth.

The first half concludes with the revealing of the Ark of the Covenant[89] in the temple when God's temple in heaven was opened. The section concludes as it began, with the opening of heaven. There is thunder and lightning, and an earthquake, as at the opening of the seventh seal, with the addition of hail.

There is a special prayer when we pray that the Lord come to reign, given the sense in which, because of man, He does not reign, and so the terrible things that have occurred could occur. His reign begins after the martyrdom, and is the beginning of the end for the world ruler who caused, or will cause, the martyrdom.

In explaining why, in his reading, the king returns both in Chapter 11:15 and in 19:16, Van Impe (1982, p. 154-155) writes:

> ...Chapters 6 through 11 and 12 through 19:15 run concurrently, or side by side during the tribulation hour. Chapters 12 through 19 are but a repeat of the events described in Chapters 6 through 11.

This seems to conflict with the chronological reading, but to be on the right track of the principle of the ordering, evident in what appears to be a fold in the text, when the account of the trumpets breaks into the series of visions that begins with the ingesting of the little scroll. It is in a way natural for the introduction of the seventh seal to encapsulate the whole of the seventh seal, including the trumpets and bowls, and so for the end to appear here in the middle, as the introduction to the seventh trumpet encapsulates the seventh trumpet. But that is not what the text means by the coming of the kingdom. The temple and the ark are seen rather than the city of God coming down from heaven. What we are shown here is not the end but rather the introduction of the seven trumpets. The seven bowls of wrath *come out* of the temple in heaven, as do the fifth through seventh angels, so that these are contained in the temple shown in heaven here, when the seventh trumpet is blown. The section from 11:15-11:19 is then only the introduction to the seventh trumpet, as is clear if one considers that no woe is yet involved in this section.

The seals and trumpets have little in common except the important pattern of 4/3. They do not seem at all to describe the same time periods. They may describe different time *scales*. The seven trumpets occur temporally within the seventh seal, and therefore *following* the first six seals. The seven bowls, though, are much more obviously related to the seven trumpets, not only in pattern but also in content: The first four of each consider the striking of roughly the same realms: earth, sea, fresh water and sky. The last three of each concern the throne of the Beast, the Euphrates and then, sky.

There is some clue to the pattern 4/3 within the seven seals, trumpets and bowls if one considers the seven days of the creation and the six day theory. The sections 5-7 are a set as are the two millennia after the incarnation together with the seventh day. The Seventh millennium would be very bad if not for the defeat of the Beast and the false prophet, even as would have been a thousand year Nazi reign. Those who think, with Hobbes, that tyranny is only monarchy misliked (*Leviathan* XIX), or with Machiavelli that the difference is only that history is written by the victors, so that whatever is done will be praised for those who win and maintain the state (*The Prince* XVIII) – these might rather go live in such an age as that they nearly helped to bring about with their shocking as well as their more moderate and mundane teachings about kingship and tyranny. We, rather, think that there is a soul, and that its nature is the principle of the regimes in political science. Hence kingship and tyranny are understood with reference to the nature of the soul. But there will be a millennial reign instead. The pattern 4/3 then is also like the pattern of the first four thousands of years, before the Messiah, and the last three, after the Messiah has come. The sixth concerns the creation of man, and concludes with the fulfillment of the number of the martyrs and the entrance of man into heaven, making good the second and sixth days.

Of twenty-two chapters, 11 is the central number, though the numbering is not in the original text. There are chapter breaks where there are not section breaks, at 2-3 and possibly 8-9, 15-16

The Seventh Seal and the Seven Trumpets

and 21-22, and some chapters contain multiple visions introduced separately with "then I saw." A certain symmetry is apparent in that Chapters 7 and 14 both concern the 144,000. Chapter eight is the seven trumpets of the seventh seal; Chapter 16, the seven bowls of the seventh trumpet. A fold in the text indicates a tight internal structure. This structure in turn suggests certain comparisons of the images. The bulk center, dividing my Greek text in half, is at 12:10, and the numerical line center is at 12:8.

Part Two:
The Second Half of the Revelation

i: The Woman Pursued by the Dragon (Revelation Chapter 12)

The second half of the book, at least through Chapter 19, then, is to be included in the seventh trumpet. This appears from considering that the last three trumpets were to introduce three woes, the third of which is only introduced, rather than completed, by the opening of the heavens which concludes Chapter 11.

[12:1] The following section is separated from the previous vision by the introductory phrase: "A great sign then appeared in heaven," instead of "then I saw," which separates and introduces most of the previous visions. "Portent" and "wonder," in the Revised and the King James versions respectively, are interpretations, in addition to translations, though they may be correct interpretations. This phrase "a sign in heaven" occurs one other time, when the seven angels with seven bowls of wrath are introduced opening Chapter 15, and here it is explicitly called "great and wonderful" (15:1). Here at the center of the work the great sign is:

> ...a woman clothed with the sun, with the moon under her feet, and on her head a crown of twelve stars; she was with child, and she cried out in the pangs of her delivery.

The center of a great writing is worthy of special attention, often showing the principle around which the text is constructed. The

The Woman Pursued by the Dragon

center of the Revelation is a symbol, and so, a mystery that *we* have to ascend in order to see. It is not clear what we are being shown, and first, even whether it is an event to occur in the end times. Is the Messiah to again become incarnate after the seventh trumpet is blown (11:15)? Or is it some other offspring that is to rule humanity with a rod of iron (12:5)? The leading readings of what the woman is are 1) Mary; 2) Israel, 3) the true Church, and 4) the Bride (Aune, 1998, p. 680). The bride is of course a mystery, but to have somewhere to begin we say she is somehow both the body of the redeemed and *wisdom* or knowledge (Luke 7:35, Matt. 11:19; Proverbs 3:17-18). Her offspring is thought either to be the Messiah or a future group of sons of Israel. The principal different readings depend on whether what we are being shown refers a) to the incarnation and crucifixion that occurred in the first century or (b) to something that is to occur near the Second Advent. A third possibility is that 12:1-6 refers to the incarnation, while 12:7-17 refers to the subsequent apocalyptic appearance of the dragon upon the earth, when he is cast down from heaven onto the earth, and sees that his time is short. This might be the time between the crucifixion and the end times, or it might be *at* the end times.

Chapter 12 is pivotal in the structure of the Revelation, because it connects the Beast and dragon, and presents the woman that is contrasted with the mystery whore of Babylon in Chapters 17 and 18. Like the face of the vision of Jesus 1:16, she is clothed with radiance like the sun. The 66th chapter of Isaiah opens with the statement of the Lord: Heaven is my throne, and the earth is my footstool" (66:1). So the moon is beneath the feet of the woman, as a footstool, indicating her supremacy to it and rule over it. We have an old statue of Mary in the yard, and she is standing with the moon under her feet. This has something to do with the three aspects of the feminine symbolized by the moon. These are a) the chaste moon, or Diana, b) the moon of love, like the moon in *A Midsummer Night's Dream*, and c) the Halloween moon, of Hecate and the things of night. The moon may indicate the realm of spirits as distinct from the angels of light. That the moon is under her feet is the same as the supremacy of man, through Christ, to the realm of the spirits (Luke 10:20). As the moon is illumined by the sun, and not the cause of its own light, so is this watery world of the night sky. Through Christ, the spirits are subject to the Apostles, and so the moon is beneath her feet in the vision.

[12:2] This very Chapter 66 of Isaiah presents the example from the prophets of Zion giving birth (66: 7-8).

> Before she was in labor, she gave birth;
> Before her pain came upon her, she was delivered of a son...
> Shall a land be born in one day?
> Shall a nation be brought forth in one moment?
> For as soon as Zion was in labor
> She brought forth her sons.

Here it is also alike ambiguous whether the birth refers to those born after the incarnation, in the first century, or rather to the new Israel of the twentieth century, approaching the second coming (Compare 66:18-20). Scofield also cites Micah (4:10), of Israel in travail when she went into Babylon:

> Writhe and groan (or: be in pain), o daughter of Zion,
> Like a woman in travail;
> For now you shall go forth from the city and dwell in the open country;
> You shall go to Babylon.
> There you shall be rescued,
> There the Lord will redeem you from the hand of your enemies.

If "open country" is like "wilderness," the daughter of Zion goes into Babylonian exile as into the wilderness. It is again difficult to separate out the first and Second Advent in some of the prophecies, as noted above regarding the distinction of the fall of Jerusalem in 70 A.D. and the things to occur to Jerusalem in the end of the end times. Y. Collins, in *Combat Myth*, as cited by Aune (1998, p. 689), brings up reasons that the child here is *not* like the Messiah: The snatching away of the child occurs immediately after birth; 2) The ascension of Jesus is never described as a supernatural rescue from Satan; and 3) references to the cross and crucifixion are strikingly absent from the vision. The same word *arpadzo-* is used by Paul to describe the rapture (4:17 *arpadzometha*), suggesting that the snatching away of the offspring here might symbolize the rapture. But the story reminds of Herod awaiting the birth of the Messiah, his snatching away to Egypt, or rather, in the resurrection of Jesus, and the consequent persecution of the Christians.

The Baptist reading takes the image as describing something that is to occur in the end times, again referring to the "after this" or "what is to take place hereafter" as a principle that requires that no background or context be given, even if it is necessary to understand the martyrdom. Van Impe directs us to the dream of Joseph, in which he saw "the sun, moon and eleven stars were bowing down to me." The sun and moon here are thought to be his father, Jacob, and his mother, Rachael, though in the vision of the woman, these are of course different. Scofield too, in a brilliant note, identifies the twelve stars with the twelve tribes, from which twelve thousand are sealed (p. 1341; Rev. 7:4-8). The other things that are twelve in the Revelation are the gates, which are the twelve tribes, and the foundations, which are the Twelve Apostles (21:13-14). The two sets of twelve seem to converge into a single set, as they would if the reference were literally to 12,000 Christian Jews from each of the twelve tribes. Elsewhere, stars are the seven stars that are the angels of the seven churches, and shortly, in the same vision, stars are fallen angels, swept from heaven by the tail of the dragon. But Van Impe reads the image as Israel, and the dragon's pursuit of her offspring as a pursuit of the *Jews* yet to occur, worse than that in the twentieth century (1982, p. 163). This is difficult because of verse 17, which says that he then went off to make war on "the rest of her offspring, who are those who obey the commandments *and* testify to Jesus." There is no reference to nationality. But this is either the Christians or both the Jews and Christians. While the construction does not require that the first of her offspring, the male child, be Christian if not the Christ, this reading seems most likely.

Van Impe predicts in this a future persecution of Jews (1982, p. 163). Schaeffer presents a reading of the woman as the nation of Israel, as distinct from the spiritual Israel, and identifies the male child with the 144,000, as Jews converted after the rapture. However, it does not seem that the Messiah is to be born again in the end times. Rather He was born already, and will be coming with the clouds (1:7; Acts 1:9), in the same way that he left (Acts 1:11). Hence, if the image is read as referring to the end of the end times, the reading that the child is not the Messiah is preferable, and it may be these 144,000 of the modern nation of Israel that are born in the end of the end times, or baptized Christian.

The most fundamental reason that Chapter 12 seems to refer to the early church and the birth of Jesus comes from the reading of what it *means* that the dragon was cast down from heaven to earth. By contrast, the Beast of the following chapter *ascends* from the sea or the abyss (17:8). The casting down from heaven, so that the dwellers there rejoice, onto earth, so that the time has come for those who dwell there, seems to be a symbolic representation of what it is that occurs in the spiritual cosmos when the incarnation occurs. It is the Beast that emerges from the sea that pursues the church in the end times, taking up where the dragon leaves off at the end of the chapter, or continuing this pursuit.

Our reading follows the more traditional, according to which the woman is Israel / Mary / true Church / Bride. The Messiah is born from the nation of Israel, and born to Mary as a representative of Israel. Yet this Israel, or the betrothed, comes to include Gentiles, and so is not the literal political nation of Israel, but the true church of God. This is the same as the Bride or New Jerusalem, seen coming down from heaven like a bride adorned for her husband (21:2) and it is this woman that is *contrasted* with the whore of Babylon. The ten horns and the Beast will *also* hate the harlot, i.e., the Beast will also persecute the whore of Babylon as well as the true church. Her offspring here are identified as "those who keep the commandments of God and bear testimony to Jesus" (12:17). This seems to identify her as much as the text is willing to do, and so we have settled on Israel / Church. It seems that the vision in Chapter 12 describes the *setting* of the Revelation, by reaching back to give a symbolic description encapsulating what it is that occurred at the incarnation. So she is Israel, crowned with the twelve tribes, and she is the Church: not the visible, but rather the invisible Church that is mystically identified with mankind or the redeemed of mankind, and the womb of which those reborn are born. Hence she is the bride, and her offspring the Messiah. This seems consistent with, rather than opposite to, what Jesus said at John 12:37: "Now is the ruler of this world cast out." This might mean "out of heaven," though he is then loosed onto sea and earth.

It is interesting in this connection that the extreme cruelty, madness and degradation of the Roman emperors began at just about this time, when Tiberius retired to Caprae, nearly coincident with the crucifixion and resurrection. Tyranny to an extent never before seen enters the world right here, in a reign of terror unleashed because Tiberius fears assassination. The Romans were always brutal, and Augustus did not stop the slaughter of the innocents by Herod at the birth of Jesus. But a new line is crossed when Tiberius descends into lust and cruelty. This extreme would re-emerge and deepen, with brief respites, throughout the first century in Caligula, Nero and Domitian.

The difficulty with the interpretation that the woman is the nation of Israel is that her offspring are the Christians (12:17). This would not be so difficult if, after the rapture of the Christians, many in the nation of Israel became Christian, though it does not seem likely that the nation as a whole would become Christian, so that her sons would especially be the Christians. Israel weeps to look on him who they have pierced, and it is at this time that Israel is persuaded, at the second coming, when his feet touch the Mount of Olives.

[12:3-6]

> And another sign was seen in heaven: behold, a great red dragon, with seven heads and ten horns, and seven diadems upon his heads. His tail swept

down a third of the stars of heaven, and cast them to the earth.

The dragon, with its seven heads and ten horns, is almost the same as the Beast in the following chapter with its seven heads and ten horns, except that it has *seven* diadems on its *heads*, while the Beast has *ten* diadems on its *horns*. Details like this can become crucial clues. A diadem is the band as that around the Tierra of the Persian King. Alexander wore this as emblem of his universal empire. When the Beast is explained in Chapter 17, the explanation of this detail, that the diadems are on its heads, is left out. A diadem is different from a crown or *stephanos*, though not as a victory wreath is to a crown, but sometimes as a royal or sovereign crown is to a lesser piece of headgear, like a ducal coronet. It is sometimes a crown that is not sovereign, like the diadem worn in the kingship of Herod, granted by the Roman emperor (Josephus, *Ant.* Book XVIII c. ix). And here the diadem refers especially to what remains of kingships or nations under an empire. Isaiah writes (28:5-6): "In that day, the Lord of hosts will be a crown of glory, and a diadem of beauty, to the remnant of his people; and a spirit of justice to those who sit in judgment, and strength to those who turn back the battle at the gate." Caesar is offered a diadem rather than a crown by Antony, in order to thinly veil his assumption of royal authority, at the root of empire (Plutarch, *Life of Caesar*). Following Alexander and Caesar, the diadem becomes the symbol of the emperor. Gibbon writes:

> ...The pride or rather the policy of Diocletian engaged that artful prince to assume the diadem, an ornament detested by the Romans as the odious ensign of royalty, and the use of which had been considered as the most desperate act of the madness of Caligula. It was no more than a broad white fillet set with pearls, which encircled the emperor's head...
>
> *The Decline and Fall of the Roman Empire*, XIII

Empire is of course different from kingship, each occurring at opposite ends of the cycle of regimes, one at the dawn, and the other at the dusk of civilization. Kingships are a paternal rule over a tribe, city or nation. Empire, though, is transnational, a rule over many kings. The crown symbolizes the wisdom or knowledge of one who would be worthy of royal office, similar to the halo that encircles the head of saints and angels. It is not clear what the diadem symbolizes. The title "King of kings" is derived for the Jews from the Babylonian or Persian king and reserved by the Christians for Jesus, for whom alone it may be fitting. When the one on the white horse comes in Chapter 19, he has many diadems on his head (19:12).

The dragon is different from the Beast and false prophet, but the defeat of the later two leads to the binding and final defeat of the former, described as occurring surrounding the millennium, before the beginning and at the end. The dragon vision is of a different time scale than the Beast and false prophet visions, covering millennia, and seven empires. It is the more fundamental political order of the worldly city or the principle of empire, finally defeated with the defeat of the seventh that is an eighth but belongs to the seven (17:11). Where chapters 11 and 13 focus on the short period of the end, in their dramatic action, Chapter 12, depicting the incarnation and early persecution rather than the end times, addresses this more fundamental level of political being, again, something like the principle of empire itself, or how such a thing could come to be among men. The seven heads of the dragon seem to represent the seven empires, the last five of which are shown in the statue in the dream of Nebuchadnezzar. There is an obvious, if rare, reference to things outside the "what is to be hereafter" framework of the Revelation, and it is somehow this one thing that was manifested in all these empires that is the dragon and sought to devour the Messiah.

[12:4] This dragon stood before the woman who was about to give birth, in order to devour the child when it was born. He was born, the "one who is to rule all the nations with a rod of iron" (19:15). While the saints will share in the rule of the rod of iron, the one who is to rule with a rod of iron can only be the Christ.

On the Revelation

The child is the Christ, and the woman is or is like Mary, the representative of Israel and the symbol of Church. Mary is the representative of Israel, a "type" of the church, if the Messiah is Jesus, and she represents the maternal Church. Not she herself, of course, but the Church fled into the wilderness, pursued by the dragon as the Christians were pursued by both Israel and Rome, in the early monastic movement. The attempt to devour her child also reminds of Herod, and Mary is said to have fled from Herod into Egypt or to the Jewish colony in Ethiopia. But here, "… her child was caught up to God and to his throne, and the woman fled into the wilderness, where she has a place prepared by God, in which to be nourished for one thousand two hundred and sixty days." The crucifixion and resurrection are what is described, as the child is caught up to God. Here again, as is characteristic of the Revelation, a thing like the rapture or snatching away is the spiritual truth behind what appears in the world as persecution and martyrdom: the crucifixion. The image, speaking as does a dream, in spontaneous images, is able to present this historical event in this symbolic form. The woman in the wilderness is the Church as the widowed bride, in the period between the first and Second Advent. The 1,260 days are also 42 months or three and one-half years. The scene covers many centuries, rather than describing something that occurs *after* the events of Chapter 11. It is the prelude to Chapter 13, and so to Chapter 11, since the two witnesses are killed by the Beast after it ascends. The 1260 days may indicate that the nourishing of the woman in the wilderness and the preaching of the two witnesses is simultaneous. One wonders if this might not describe 1260 years through which the church continued before the burning of heretics and witches, and the corruption of the church which seems to have characterized the following four or five hundred years. In any case, because of the incarnation in the image, the time scale or scope appears vastly different from the previous visions. We are not being shown a simple temporal progression of what occurs after the events of the sixth trumpet blast at all. The vision of Chapter 12 appears not even to address the end times, since the incarnation will not occur in the end, but has occurred already. Again, since he is to return in the same way

The Woman Pursued by the Dragon

that he left, or is coming on a cloud, there will not be a birth of the Messiah in the end times. And so, the false Christs can be known because they were or will have been born.

What appears to occur in the text, then, is that the seventh trumpet contains the series of visions described from Chapter 12 on, and this first vision sets the context for what is to be shown: the dragon pursues the offspring of the woman. These visions are an unfolding of what has been shown already in outline in the seventh seal, as the trumpets unfold what is contained in the seventh seal. After the killing of one third of mankind in the second woe or sixth trumpet, the third woe or seventh trumpet is described and explained by a series of visions which may be numbered in various ways, but amount to somewhere between seven and ten. These are **1)** the woman and the dragon, in Chapter 12; **2)** the beasts that arise from the sea and land, in Chapter 13; **3)** the six angels and the seven bowls, in Chapters 14-16; **4)** the judgment of the great harlot, in Chapters 17-18; **5)** the coming of the Word on a white horse and the binding of Satan, in Chapters 19-20; **6)** And in Chapters 21-22, the new heaven, new earth and New Jerusalem. In our reading, it appears that Chapter 12, like the first five seals, sets the scene and provides the background or context for what is to occur with the sixth and seventh seals, the seventh containing the seven trumpets. The sixth and seventh seem to pertain to the last *shabua*, each describing 3 and one-half years of the last seven year period.

[12:6] Again, a number of things are described as being of the duration 1260 days or three and one-half years. The 1260 days in which the woman will be nourished in the wilderness is the same number of days as the 1,260 days that the two witnesses of Chapter 11 prophesy. It is also nearly the same as the time told to Daniel, the time, two times and a half a time that is the 1,290 days, the period from the time that the continual burnt offering is taken away and the abomination that makes desolate is set up (Daniel 12:11). In English, it is almost ambiguous whether these two, the taking away of the offering and the abomination, occur at one end as a terminus to an unnamed event 1260 days later, or whether there are 1,260 days *between* these two. It is also the

On the Revelation

same number of days as the "time two times and a half a time" that the saints of the Most High will be given into his hand, and the "42 months" in which the Beast is given authority, when it is allowed to make war on the saints and to conquer them. It is also nearly one half the two thousand three hundred evenings and mornings concerning the question of how long the sanctuary will be given over to be trampled, before it is restored to its rightful state (Daniel 8:15), 1,150 days if the evenings and mornings are counted together, but double if they are taken separately. It is the other calculation in Daniel, of the seventy weeks of years or 490 years, that contains the most explicit suggestion that the 1260 days may be one half of a seven year period, or that there are two successive 1260 day periods, so that all these 1260 day events need not be understood as occurring simultaneously. The suggestion is as follows: The woman is nourished in the wilderness at the same period of time as the Gentiles trample the outer court of the temple. The witnesses preach at the same time, as is consistent with the reading that the two are the lamp stands or churches rather than literally two individuals. A second possibility is that the 1260 days of the woman are years, while that of the two witnesses is days, the long and short periods.

It is in the following 1260 days that the Beast will make war on the saints and conquer some, and this second half will begin with the desolating sacrilege and the martyrdom of the Christians from the churches of the East and West that preach in Jerusalem as the Beast arises.

This period might refer either 1) to a period of years for days, some 1,260 from the time of some ancient event like the conquest of Jerusalem in 586 B.C. or the destruction of the temple in 70 A.D. to the beginning of the persecution of heretics in medieval Europe, considered as a corruption of the Western church; Or 2) to a period of days, literally three and one-half, from the time that a modern abomination occurs; or 3) to a period of years, such as the seven years in which Hitler committed the holocaust of the Jews; or 4) somehow to both the long period during the history of the Church and the short period during the seven year tribulation. The triangulation of the three images of this period of time given in days and months and years suggests the possibility that this is the period of the Christian Churches, from the fall of the temple to the end times. The difficulty is that 1,260 does not describe the number of years, as it would if the events of 1947-48 were to have occurred on the year numbered 1260, or perhaps 1310. Isaac Newton presented a calculation of 1260 years from the conjunction of Christianity and politics in the first anointed Christian sovereign.[90] This is also about the time that the British took the Holy land from the Turks, accidentally fulfilling the goal of the crusades a thousand years previous. And for the most part, no one noticed the significance of the event in this way. Our dating of the fall of the temple twenty years later, when Judah fell to Babylon in 586, plus 1260 x 2 = 2520 would bring one to the significant date of 1934. The seven worst years were 1938-1945, when the persecution of the Jews was unleashed. The persecution of heretics began about 1215, almost 1260 years after the death of Caesar, or the beginning of the Roman Empire in 44 B.C. Now if there were a modern abomination, and the Gentiles in some present sense were to trample the outer court of the temple for a literal three and one-half years of 360 days, it would also appear that the prophecy were fulfilled. Again we are returned to the suggestion that we look for both a long and a short period, the long in which days are years, and the short, which is literally seven years of 2,520 days. Finally, the seven seals might cover seven 360 or 365 year periods, the trumpets seven years within the seventh period, and the bowls seven days within the seven year period.

Victorinus writes, regarding the 42 months or 1260 days that the Gentiles will trample the holy city: "Therefore their preaching is three years and six months, and the kingdom of the Antichrist is as much again" (p. 354). This amounts to a seven year period, which is also discussed in the book of Daniel (9:27). Hippolytus[91] cites Daniel:

> And one week will make a covenant with many, and it shall be that in the midst (half) of the week my sacrifice and oblation shall cease. By one week, therefore, he meant the last, which is to be at the end of the whole world; of which week the

two prophets Enoch and Elias will take up the half. For they will preach 1,260 days clothed in sackcloth, proclaiming repentance to the people and to all the nations.

The Baptist teaching is that the three and one-half days is one-half of the seven year period that concludes the interrupted seventy weeks. The communication of time by angels is sometimes shockingly accurate and sometimes simply strange, apparently because angels do not always speak in terms of human conventions regarding time, according to which we mark off years and think of significances in terms of a number system based on tens, and different calendars. The revolution of the earth around the sun, or the annual cycle of the seasons, would seem to provide a solid or common basis for noting time. By presenting the time period in both days and times, is possible to double check, to see that "times" are years and days are literally days. The addition of 42 months further underlines the literal and lunar meaning of the period intended. What are literal days in the vision, though, may translate differently in our terms and what to us actually occurs.

The reading that the woman is Israel / Church and the male child the incarnation that has already occurred implies a symbolic reading of the seven years as also something like two periods of 1260 years, in which first the church is nourished in the wilderness, then at and after midweek, subjected to persecution. At the end of the long period might come the short period, of the most extreme persecution. And it is here that we hope that the rapture might occur, perhaps to be barely noticed amid the turmoil of the earthquake and people going off to captivity and war.

[12:7-17] War arose then in heaven, and Michael defeated the dragon, who with some of his angels was thrown down to earth. This is like the event described in the first half, at 9:1, when at the fifth trumpet a star fell to earth and was given the key to the shaft of the bottomless pit. It may be the same or a similar event. It is extremely difficult to see what this means, and we are reminded that symbols refer especially to the unknown. Is this the same as the event symbolized by the dragon sweeping down one third of the stars of heaven (12:4)? He was not then cast down himself? When the dragon pursues the woman, he would seem to be *on* earth. Yet this is not said, nor is it clear when the woman seen in the sign about to give birth came to be on the earth. There is a confusion in Chapter 12 between the vision seen as a sign in heaven and the vision that shows what is occurring in heaven and on earth. Does the war in heaven, the defeat of Satan and the throwing down, *precede* his attempt to devour the child, and does the text not go back and reveal some of the depth of this occurrence? If so, then the casting of Satan out of heaven is what has occurred with the incarnation, crucifixion, resurrection and martyrdom. Hence, when the seventy return, Jesus says "I saw Satan fall like lightening from heaven" (Luke 10:18), and this is when the teaching is given that the spirits are subject to them (10:20). This is somehow related to the subjection of the spirits to his name. As Jesus prepares to go to be crucified, he says: "Now shall the ruler of this world be cast out…" (John 12:32). In the Revelation, a voice in heaven comments that now salvation and the authority of Christ have come, since the accuser of our brethren has been thrown down. They have conquered him by the blood of the Lamb and the word of his testimony, and by their martyrdom (12:10-11). This event is then *after* the crucifixion from the time that Christians are first martyred. The Antichrist presupposes the Christ, and arises as a reaction to the incarnation, a sort of opposite reaction or shadow cast by the incarnation, to use a Jungian turn of phrase. Heaven and those who dwell therein are to rejoice, but "woe to you, O earth and sea, for the devil has come down to you in great wrath, for he knows that his time is short" (12:12). The war in heaven would be a sort of spiritual warfare in which, for those who dwell there, the Devil is defeated. The consequence of this is that there is no longer a place for these in heaven, and their effect is on those who dwell in the middle and lower regions of sea and land, in contrast with heaven. This throwing down is said to be done not only through the crucifixion, but the martyrdom, when "they loved not their own lives even onto death" (12:11). In the spiritual world of mankind, the gospel has defeated the alternate account, based on the primacy of worldly goods, self-interest and power. It is interesting that Satanism, or diabolism, did not really exist among men at all until the incarnation. It arises as if provoked, and depends on what it hates, rather than its own principles, for its existence. The Lords prayer is reversed, rather than opposed by an alternative, etc. The account however of worldly goods, self-interest and power has always existed, as have magic and witchcraft-like things, nearly as long as man remembers. Like incitement to reproduction, the love of worldly goods is in some sense natural, and does not usually need the support of cultivation, which generally tries to moderate these. The worldly teaching is advocated by some of the Sophists before Socrates, but comes back with a vengeance in Machiavelli and Nietzsche. It seems that the resurrection, by showing the way through death, has made salvation accessible to the people who inhabit the realm of air, a realm of spiritual things that are higher either than the things of sea or the things of land. The image of angels expelled from heaven is very difficult, but the result is that these affect the sea and land, that is, the middle realm of the soul and poetry, and the earthly realm of mundane matters of economics, politics, and the body. These realms are as though unaffected by the victory that occurred with the resurrection, but then impacted by the opposite reaction, when it becomes possible to consciously reject the things of light. Innocent paganism is different from post-Christian paganism. Pre-Christian atheistic philosophy, too, is different, as evident in the contrast between Thrasymachus and Machiavelli.

The basis of the interpretation of the meaning of air, sea and earth does seem to be this three part division of the places people dwell, or which part of the soul leads in our lives. Those who dwell in heaven set the things of the intellect highest, or the life of the spirit. Those who dwell in the sea follow first principles based on the heart, in the middle sense, the things of love and the things of honor. And those who dwell on earth set the enjoyments of the bodily comforts and pleasures first, in the end sacrificing love and honor to these things. In some sense, then, the Devil and his angels were cast out of the higher realm through the incarnation and the martyrdom of the saints. The saints in some sense did reign, even for over one thousand years. The persecutions of the empire against Christians, which had occurred from Nero to Diocletian, ceased. The saints came to set the fundamental opinion of the East and West, and their way of life came to be honored as highest, for at least one thousand years following. So it is not impossible that this was the millennial reign of the saints. But the leading possibility is that such a thing is to come even more in the succeeding age.

The casting down of Satan seems to mean something like this: The example of the resurrection and the martyrdom, like the wisdom of Socrates in the face of death, is the example that demonstrates the virtue of the highest men, or that the high things are the things of virtue and not the things of power. While it may be said that Christ laid down his life from the beginning, and always dies for man, the example of the incarnation provides the particular, so that the argument, always true, is demonstrated in the occurrence. Salvation becomes available through the visible, as the image of God that we are is attracted to the son, his death and resurrection, something like a magnet, as Jung writes (*Aion*, p. 185). This is the gospel, the story of the incarnation, life, teaching, death and resurrection which as an example is like a magnet, drawing out the image of God in man, so that in bearing our own cross we follow him. It is also a theoretical demonstration. As a result of this defeat, a third of the stars of heaven enter into the earth and sea. By their rejection of the appearance of the Christ, the imagination as well as the politics of humanity becomes perverse, in a sense. Worldly ends govern things which ought, through beauty, to serve the good. From what glimpse of this that we can muster, then, this sea and land appears to be the realm of the imagination, such as poetry and music, and the realm of the visible human world of the city and politics.

Unless the devil is cast down twice with some angels, the Michael section (12:7-10) seems to be a retelling of 12:1-6, or more precisely of what occurs in heaven and on earth when Salvation becomes available. The war between Michael and the dragon occurs after the child is born and caught up, but before the dragon pursues the woman on earth. The portents are seen in heaven, but it is not clear when the action shifts to earth– as though heaven and earth were together during the incarnation.

There are three similar images in the scripture. First in Daniel, in the account of the little horn that appears to be Antiochus, and a type of the Beast, the growth of the horn is described in very strange terms, so that Scofield calls this "the most difficult line in all of prophecy" (1909, p. 912):

> It grew great, even to the host of heaven; and some of the host of the stars it cast down to the ground and trampled upon them. It magnified itself even to the host of heaven, and the continual burnt offering was taken away from him, and the place of his sanctuary was overthrown.

Here the stars cast down are like his prevailing over some of the saints. The example of fallen angels raises the possibility that the prevailing over the saints is not only over their bodies. The stars in the opening chapter are the angels of the seven churches.

But how is it that it is said "now woe to you, o earth and sea"? The metaphors are mixed. Those reading Chapter 12 as an end of the end times event may read that he is re-admitted, having once been cast out. Rather, we read that he is defeated in the crucifixion and resurrection, so that those who dwell in heaven are decisively freed of his reign, though those on earth, who dwell in the watery and the earthly, are even more endangered.

[12:13-14] Once he sees that he is on the earth, the dragon pursues the woman whose male child was caught up to God. "But the woman was given the two wings of the great eagle that she might fly from the serpent into the wilderness, to the place where she is to be nourished for a time, two times and a half a time." As Aune (II, p. 705) comments:

> The precedent for this is the well-known biblical association between the exodus from Egypt and the wings of an eagle, expressed in Exodus 19:4, "You have seen what I did to the

> Egyptians, and how I bore you on eagle's wings
> and brought you to myself"...

Unless, too, the woman went twice into the wilderness, 12:14 is a description in more detail, of the same flight into the wilderness of 12:6. When two images are given of the same intelligible, it is possible as by triangulation to separate image from object, and see through to the meaning of the images. The true church is nourished in the wilderness, like Israel under Moses, or John the Baptist, rather than in the city, and this reminds us of the constant retreat into the desert of monastic communities even before the time of Jesus, as the Essenes and John the Baptist, to escape the corruption of the human world including its effects on religion. The eagle is a symbol of Rome, ironically suited to the relation of Rome and monasticism after Constantine. This protection of religion might also make one think of how the United States, borrowing from Rome the senate, republicanism and the eagle, has protected religion from the European persecutions of the nations of the Roman Empire, and especially as a refuge from the movements of twentieth century tyranny.

[12:15-16]

> ...The serpent poured water like a river out of his mouth after the woman ... but the earth came to the help of the woman, and "opened its mouth and swallowed the river which the dragon had poured from his mouth.

This section presents something like the following possibility: The serpent attacks the church with a stream of speech, in a theoretical undermining something like the Enlightenment of the seventeenth and eighteenth century modern secular thought, for which the premises of History and natural history, Darwin, Freud or Skinner, Newton and Einstein, are *knowledge*, and the mysteries of faith appear to be at best fairy tales, and at worst, themselves the illusions of a "kingdom of darkness." The river is modernity, and the earth opens up to swallow the stream of speech. It may be that science and history themselves, the earthly things, come to neutralize the attack on the church undertaken by the dragon when he lost the spiritual warfare and was thrown to earth. Superstitious mankind discovers to our amazement, through archeology and Biblical archeology, that there really was a Troy, a Crete, an Achaia, a Jericho and Babylon, etc. It is surprising how often common persons now doubt that the people in the Bible, even Jesus, ever really lived, just because they have become convinced that science knows the incarnation and resurrection to be miracles, and miracles to be impossible. The more we consider, the things of history and science are not contradicted, and even confirm the things of faith. We see for example that the order of the creation in Genesis– land, vegetation, birds and fish, mammals and man– is roughly accurate. This is an astonishing achievement, regardless of who wrote it. The order of the cosmos presents itself accurately in a seven part unfolding. There are many things about the Bible that are like this. By contrast with every other ancient poetic text, it is astonishing how rarely the Bible even seems to contradict the more stable truths of science, such as the Copernican universe, Lyell's geology, and even Darwin.[92] Meanwhile, the teaching of power and the tyrannical ordering of the soul have flowed onto the earth, in politics and economics, and into the realms of the images and poetry, if these are something like the realms of earth and sea. This, a rise of evil, occurs when the myth and tradition that once upheld the ethical law and the restraint of the animal in man, is undermined by science. Science even appears to suggest these, for example through the assumption that if God is a myth, the true good is to ignore justice and pursue power, or the various teachings from Darwin's survival of the fittest that survival and reproduction, the animal ends, are therefore the true ends of man. These arguments assume what then seems to be demonstrated, as occurs also when neurology seems to teach that because neuron activity is discernable, we are therefore controlled by our brain cells. Socrates addresses these errors, as when joking that the reason he remained in prison rather than escape with Crito was because his arms and legs were bent in a certain way there on the bench (Plato, *Phaedo*, 98c). Indeed, it would be surprising if, when we are making choices, our brain cells were not doing *something*! But that *we*, as beings, *cause* anything is too difficult for this scientific philosophy, even as the principles that distinguish the many kinds of things become inaccessible, and all eventually appears to be reduced to a swirling and indiscriminate, and hence meaningless, soup of matter in motion. Galileo could not even explain why the ball he rolled, in his experiments on gravity, was one ball, a unity, or distinct being, let alone how plants might be living unities and animals move themselves. Does science know that *word* is not the cause of the intelligibility of things apparent to common sense? Rather, science ignores the intelligibility of things, even while assuming it, as Galileo could not have done his experiment unless the ball he rolled down the incline were one thing distinct from the other things around it. Thinking we knew what Genesis means, we think that Genesis, rather than our understanding of it, is undermined by science. What is gained, though, from the emergence of a science, is a purging of the air, as through the lightening of a thunderstorm. Mankind is freed from the superstitious understanding of the causes which allows, for example, the persecution of imagined witches. The air is not filled with spirits for us, as it was for Augustine and those of the Biblical age. But the spirits pertain to the soul, and evil enters the world or acts as a cause, through the error of the human souls. Though it is only a possibility, the event; the change in humanity in the West, and now most of the world, does correspond in symbol to the images shown here in lines 15 and 16 of Chapter 12.

> **[12:17]** Then the dragon was angry with the woman, and went off to make war on the rest of her offspring, on those who keep the commandments of God and bear testimony to Jesus. "And he" [or: "I"] "stood on the sand of the sea.

The woman is the mother of the offspring of God. The offspring of God are *begotten*, and this is in contrast to the created man, since begetting and making are different. We are born once by our mothers, and this is the Lord's creating. We are then begotten, as John writes, of the spirit (John 1:13; 3:16), in a mystery that is the original of the image of baptism. She is the Bride because she is the mother of the offspring of God. The woman is the mystical Church because she is, or may be something like the body of humanity redeemed. The Church is somehow the representative of this, the womb of the redemption of humanity that is somehow the bride of the Lord.[93] Those who keep the commandments of God and bear testimony to Jesus might be one group of Jewish Christians, or they might be two groups, the Christians and the Jews, or even all those who obey the commandments and love righteousness, including Islam. The Law might allow some to be aligned with the righteousness of the mystery while being not yet redeemed, to look for the Messiah, and to be known when he appears.

This is, or may be, the first of two suggestions that Jews and Christians are both together in the New Jerusalem in the reign of the Messiah, as though our second coming were the first advent of the Messiah for them, and all would then come to agree, as would occur were he seen coming on the clouds. The second place where the formula "those who follow the commandments of God and the faith of Jesus" occurs is at 14:12, in the call for the patience of the saints. The second place where the Jews and the Christians seem to be together is said to be in the twelve gates and twelve foundations (21:12), if not in the identities of the twenty-four elders before the throne, if there were 12 from each, such as Moses, Abraham, Enoch, Melchizedek, etc. A third reason for the suggestion of Jews and Christians together is that the prophecies of the Old Testament really do refer to Israel, to the gathering from worldwide dispersion to a restored Israel at the center of world conflict. A fourth is the account of the grafting of the olive tree (Rom 11:17-24).

The last line of Chapter 12 is "And he stood on the sand of the sea." There is a classic ambiguity in the text regarding whether *estathen* is to be translated "he stood" or I stood," since the Greek for either is identical. If it is "he stood," it is either the angel of Chapter 10 who straddles the sea or the dragon that stands on the sands of the sea, and then the Beast emerges. If it is "he," and he is the dragon, then it is as if he just emerged, and when the dragon comes on land he is the Beast. But the Beast emerges from the sea or the Abyss, while the dragon is an angel that fell down. If it is John who stood, then he is transported to the place where the Beast is seen to arise out of the sea. In either case, the line links Chapter 12 with Chapter 13, showing that the emergence of the Beast is fundamentally a continuation of the war of the dragon against the offspring of the woman in Chapter 12. Here Van Impe reminds that the chapter divisions were added in the sixteenth century (1982, p. 171). Yet it is a distinct vision that begins with Chapter 13.

ii: The Beast that Arises from the Sea
And the Beast that Rose Out of the Earth

The vision is introduced "And I saw...:

> ... a beast rising out of the sea, with ten horns and seven heads, with ten diadems upon its horns and a blasphemous name upon its heads.

[13:1-10] The twelfth chapter ends, and the thirteenth begins with the sea. This seems to be the same as the sea in Chapter 10, straddled by the angel. It also seems to be different from the many waters that are the peoples etc., though possibly the same as the sea in some other instances, as for example the sea containing the souls of the dead, with Death and Hades. It does not seem to be the same as the sea that is turned red like blood at the second trumpet and second bowl, which seems to be the literal sea. Henry Schaefer identifies it as the sea of humanity (class, 2010). The four beasts of the vision of Daniel "came up out of the sea," (7:3), the lion with eagle wings, the bear with three ribs in its teeth, and then the leopard with four heads, before the fourth, the terrible beast. The Beast of Revelation 13 may then come up out of the sea in the same way that these empires, of Babylon, Persia and Greece arose. In the interpretation to Daniel of one who stood there, this is synonymous with "four kings who shall arise out of the earth." This sea may be something more like the collective unconscious in the Jungian sense, the "realm" of the soul or spirits rather than the earth and the body, which we hold subordinate in a Christian metaphysical context.[94] Political powers might be said to arise from there, as all the human things belong to the middle realm, between the earth and sky. It is the soul of mankind, in one sense, but only as this soul of mankind is somehow the same as something more

The Beasts that arise from the Sea and the Earth

fundamental than man. There is a teaching in the eighth book of Plato's *Republic*, that the kinds of government arise from these characters in the human soul, as, for example, when the one part, the appetites or spiritedness, is dominant among the citizens collected together, this makes up the propensity of a regime (VIII, 544d-e). A people is in part responsible for the tyranny of its rulers, though the people are the victims of bad government.

Isaiah prophecies: "In that day the Lord with his hard and great and strong sword will punish Leviathan, the fleeing serpent, Leviathan the twisting serpent, and he will slay the dragon that is in the sea" (Isaiah 27:1). It is also the bottomless pit (17:8), the abyss, as was written at 11:7. When the witnesses "have finished their testimony, the beast that ascends from the Abyss will make war on them and conquer them and kill them." The events of Chapter 11 are then in part posterior to some of the events of Chapter 13, which would then appear to reach back into the sixth trumpet to describe the emergence of the Beast that kills the witnesses, before describing the Beast in greater detail.

The interpretation of the Beast is given later, in the seventeenth chapter of the Revelation, when the angel explains the mystery of Babylon. Of course, angels explain things cryptically, through yet other symbols:

> ...the seven heads are seven mountains on which the woman is seated; they are also seven kings, five of whom have fallen, one is, the other has not yet come, and when he comes he must remain only a little while. As for the beast that was and is not, it is an eighth, but it belongs to the seven, and it goes to perdition. And the ten horns that you saw are ten kings who have not yet received royal power, but they are to receive authority as kings for one hour, together with the beast. These are of one mind, and give over their power and authority to the beast. They will make war on the Lamb... (Revelation 17:9-14)"

The blasphemous name on its seven heads is like the claim of emperors from Egypt on to be the son of god or to represent God on earth. This beast is described as being like a leopard with bear's feet and a lion's mouth. It is somehow like Daniel's four beasts all together, or, as Aune notes, the first three, something like the culmination of human empire. It is fundamentally like a leopard, which is the beast that represents Greece in the vision of Daniel, and it is this beast in Daniel that has four heads, while the fourth beast in Daniel, the one with ten horns, has only one head. It is said that the combining of the beasts means that the Beast of Revelation will combine the powers of the first three beasts of Daniel (Oxford, p. 1504). One wonders too if, as the Alexandrian empire combined the territories and crowns of Egypt, Syria, Babylon or Persia, and Greece, this Beast will not combine these nations: the mouth of Babylon, the feet of Persia, into a Grecian sovereignty. There is presently a neo-Nazi party in Greece, which had been gaining from the bad economy, and this would be something like the leopard. Henry Schaeffer has suggested that the Antichrist will be Greek or Syrian (Class, 2010), and it is difficult to compare and distinguish the Antiochus prophecies in Daniel from those concerning the Antichrist, of which Antiochus is said to be a *type*. Aune (*Revelation*, p. 591) cites Lactantius, a writer of the late third century, writing that the "destroyer of the human race" will arise from Syria. An opinion with more scripture to support it is the teaching of Van Impe, citing Daniel 9:26: he will be of the people that destroyed the temple, Roman or Italian. Antiochus did not destroy the city and the sanctuary, but desecrated the temple, so that it was purified at Hanukkah. Hal Lindsey sees two Antichrists, one from the EU and one from the Jews (1973, p. 103). Britain, Norway, Germany, Spain, and even a corrupted United States are possibilities suggested, as well as the Islamic nations, and on occasion the communist nations, so that none but Australia and Switzerland are excluded from the suggested possibilities.

The seven heads and ten *horns* are somehow like the seven horns and seven eyes of the Lamb, which are the seven churches (5:6). So horns are something like organizations that manifest the

The Beasts that arise from the Sea and the Earth

powers in the world, whether of the Beast or Lamb. In Chapter 8 of Daniel, Alexander is the horn and the king of Greece is the goat, so that the horn is the ruler, while the animal to which it is attached is the nation. While in the previous chapter, the seven headed dragon with ten horns appeared as a red dragon, here the Beast seems to be distinguished from the dragon when it is written: "To it the dragon gave his power and his throne and great authority." The dragon is more something spiritual only, an angel and not a man, while the Beast is an incarnate something, an empire or a man. The dragon probably does not have the likeness of a leopard with bear feet and a lion's mouth, and so these two are distinct in their appearance. He is apparently able to influence the nations after the Beast and false prophet are defeated (20:8).

Aune writes: "There is wide agreement among scholars that the beast who is identified as the eighth king, who "is one of the seven," (17:11) is Nero *redivivus* (Lohse, 95), (or "alive again") but it is not immediately evident which (if any) of the seven (*Revelation*, lxii). Why scholars should agree to such a thing is not at all clear. The teaching that the Revelation is some pamphlet against the then current Roman Emperor is reassuring, teaching that the events are not *to come* at all, and has an air of having been deduced from an assumption, rather than arising out of the particulars. For most, this reading must coincide with a very early date for the writing of the Revelation, not under Domitian but under Nero, since it is said that "one is," or one *now* is. The reading otherwise must ignore the fundamental time outline of the text, according to which the sections following Chapter 4 address what is to come, and not what for John on Patmos occurred some thirty years prior. It is extremely awkward to stuff the Roman emperors, whether Domitian, Nero, Vespasian or some other, into a series according to which these appear seventh. In the year 69, there were three brief emperors, and no one knows whether to count them, nor whether to begin from Caesar or Augustus. Even Van Impe falls into an explanation in terms of the emperors, with the seventh as future and Domitian sixth (1982, p. 237-238). Further, it seems that the vision is part of the seventh trumpet, which is preceded by the six trumpets, and the destruction of one third of mankind and the world. One

Beast, seven heads, one *is*, i.e., the then current Roman Empire; five have fallen, and one is to come for a short while: It is to be an empire of the stature of the first six, ruling over kings and over Jerusalem or Israel, as did Rome, Alexandrian Greece, the Median-Persian empire of Darius, Nebuchadnezzar's Babylon, Assyria under Sargon, and ancient Egypt. It is as though the prophetic spirit were especially interested when empires rule over Israel, or especially sensitive to events concerning or surrounding Jerusalem and the temple. In history, Rome was followed by the Turks and then the British, though these do not seem to fit the interpretation. The focus, if correct, is on Rome, the revived Rome, and Israel. We will take up these questions again below, in the comment on Chapter 17.

Again, *horns* are something like organizations dedicated or in service to the heads from which they spring. The Lamb appears in the throne vision with seven horns and seven eyes, which are the seven spirits of God sent out into the earth, through the churches. The most revealing comment on the seven heads and ten horns of the Beast is the relation of the ten horns to the ten toes of the statue in the first vision of Daniel (2:33, 42; 7:7; Van Impe, 1982, p. 162). Both the seven heads and the ten horns are explicitly said to be kings, and this helps those who have sought seven emperors to match, thinking that both must be successive rulers. But if the five are not particular kings, the next leading possibility would be that they are successive dynasties of ruling nations, even the nations or kingdoms that, because of their empire, also ruled over Jerusalem. And it would still be so that, when John was addressed, "one now is." And it is obvious from twentieth century fascism what we might fear from the wrong kind of revived Rome. Jack Van Impe explains that there are seven world empires: Assyria, Egypt, and then the five from Daniel's image, Babylon (2:37-38), Media-Persia, Greece, Rome and a revived Roman Empire represented by the feet of iron and clay.[95] Hence, five have fallen, one, Rome, presently is, and another has not yet come. The woman who "is" seated on the seven mountains is Rome. The ten horns are identified with the ten toes, and the last world empire with the fourth beast that Daniel sees rise out of the sea. Further, the two legs of the statue in Daniel's vision may be the eastern and western Roman Empires. If the analogy can be extended, the ten horns or ten toes would be five kings from the Western and five from the Eastern Roman Empire, in something like a European Union, perhaps including Greece and Russia. In Daniel, the four beasts that came up out of the sea are each distinct, the first like a lion with eagle's wings; the second is like a bear; the third a leopard with four wings of a bird on its back, and four heads; and then the fourth. These are identified by Hippolytus as the Babylonian, Medo-Persian, Greek and Roman empires. The four heads of the third seem to depict the four divisions into kingdoms of the empire of Alexander after his death. The fourth beast is described not as like any of the great carnivores, but only as exceedingly terrible, "with great iron teeth." Iron is the fourth metal of the vision of the statue in the second chapter of Daniel. The angel explains to Daniel regarding the four beasts he saw rising out of the sea: "these four beasts are four great kings that shall arise out of the earth" (7:17). These are *successive* empires. The fourth kingdom shall be "different from all the kingdoms, and it shall devour the whole earth." The ten horns, and the story that occurs regarding them (7:8), are then explained: "Out of this kingdom ten kings shall arise, and another shall arise after them ...different from the former ones, and shall put down three kings" (Daniel 7: 23-24). It may be in this sense that it is an eighth that is one of the seven. It is this one that Daniel saw destroyed when he saw "the Ancient of Days, one like a son of man coming with the clouds of heaven (Daniel 7:13). It may be this one destroyed that devours "the whole earth," and will think to change the times and the law. In his destruction, the imperium of the worldly is destroyed, the same as began in the imperium of Egypt and continued through the seven heads. A story is then told about this Beast to which the dragon gave his throne. John **[13: 3-4]** writes:

> One of its heads seemed to have a mortal wound, but its mortal wound was healed, and the whole earth followed the beast with wonder. Men worshiped the dragon, for he had given his authority to the beast,

and they worshiped the beast, saying "who is like the beast and who can fight against it?

The relation of the dragon of Chapter 12 to the Beast of Chapter 13 is similar in pattern to the relation between the Father and the Son, where the Beast is like an incarnation of the dragon, given his throne and great authority.[96] For this reason he is called the Antichrist, though the text of the Revelation does not use this word. But his is like a satanic religion. Men worship both together, as is the case with the father and the risen son. But men do not worship the Beast because they think it is just or merciful, but because no one can fight against it– somewhat as people follow a fighting champion, only at war. He is in one way not opposable by men, and so it is said that those taken into captivity or slain will be thus. Yet, like a son of man, he is subject to mortal limitations, which is why his reign will only last a short while. Yet his being healed from a mortal wound is like a resurrection, and he continues to live:

> **[13:5-8]** And the beast was given a mouth uttering haughty and blasphemous words, and it was allowed to exert authority for forty-two months; It opened its mouth to utter blasphemies against God, blaspheming his name and his dwelling, that is, those who dwell in heaven. Also, it was allowed to make war on the saints and to conquer them. And authority was given to it over every tribe and people and tongue and nation, and all who dwell on earth will worship it, everyone whose name has not been written before the foundation of the world in the book of life of the Lamb that was slain...

The blasphemies are also mentioned in Daniel (7:25), and this again seems to mean that he will not pretend to be holy or righteous or pious, nor to be Jesus, but be openly satanic. There the horn has "a mouth speaking great things." and "In his own mind he shall magnify himself (8:25), and "he shall speak astonishing things against the God of gods" (11:36) and "magnify himself above all." (11:37). This, that he appears openly, seems to be so that the multitudes following this are in part guilty, rather than simply deceived.

Those who dwell in heaven will not worship the Beast, in contrast with those who dwell on earth. There is a revealing connection to "heaven" and "earth" in Chapter 12, and we see why those who dwell in heaven rejoice, though there is woe for those in sea and earth. Those with earthly concerns will submit to the necessity of the world rule, and not notice their submission to the dragon through the Beast. As Paul (2 Thess. 9-11) writes:

> The coming of the lawless one by the power of Satan will be with all power and with pretended signs and wonders, and with all wicked deception for those who are to perish because they refused to love the truth and be saved. Therefore God sends on them a strong delusion, to make them believe what is false, so that all may be condemned who did not believe the truth but had pleasure in unrighteousness.

The world rule, over every people, is established *before* the mark of the beast instituted by the false prophet. This world rule somehow coheres with the advance of the kings of the east and the gathering of the armies around Jerusalem, perhaps at some point in rebellion *against* the reign of the Beast, as though he had set himself in the temple, so that the world need come against him there. Another possibility is that the world rule and the mark of the Beast occur after the defeat of these armies of the north and east, as there would then be no competing powers.

If the heads are kings or empires, the mortal wound that is healed would be more like a revived Third Reich, or doubly revived Roman Empire. This would be the case if the Nazis were to take power in the new European Union. There is some question as to whether the trouble in the soul of Europe[97] that led to the ideological tyrannies of the twentieth century has been resolved by the victory of the free West in World War II. A sinister under-culture remains, similar to the Nazis in America, and this takes an explicitly satanic turn in Norway. This may be what it means that he arises out of the sea: it is not out of nowhere, but out of a cultural development among humanity that the Beast arises, just as Hitler arose amid a more general fascist movement, in a Europe primed for such a movement. The first thing we can do, then, is not to be a part of the people that calls for the Beast or is indifferent to the ascent of this. We will take the example of the World War II generation, with the added assurance of hindsight.

In a sentence that the Oxford edition notes some ancient authorities omit, it is added: "Also, it was allowed to make war on the saints and to conquer them" (13:7). Daniel relates: "And as I looked, this horn made war with the saints, and prevailed over them, until the Ancient of Days came, and judgment was given for the saints of the Most High, and the time came when the saints received the kingdom." (7:21-22). "He shall speak words against the Most High, and shall wear out the saints of the Most High…and they shall be given into his hand for a time, two times and a half a time" (Daniel 7:25). One wonders how this relates to the 1260 days in which the woman and her offspring are protected from the Beast. The best guess, since protection is the opposite of being given into his hand, is that it is the second half of the seven year period, so that the Christians or Jewish Christians are protected in the first half, but then the Christians are martyred and persecuted in the second half of the seven year reign of the Beast. The saints, and hence those endangered, are a group more broad than the 144,000 that are protected. Authority was given it over every tribe and people and tongue and nation, and all who dwell on earth will worship it, every one whose name has not been written before the foundation of the world in the book of life of the Lamb that was slain. There follows a call for endurance during captivity, and an apparent caution against armed opposition, which may for a time become futile. One begins to see what is involved in "to him who conquers." That he will make war on the saints and conquer them for a while may refer not only to their martyrdom, but to spiritual warfare, as though the saints, like some of the angels, could yet fall. The martyrs are said to conquer when they persevere, and so that he conquers some might mean that some give in. This is again stated "He will *wear out* the saints of the Most High" (Daniel 7:25).

The character is likely to appear different at the beginning than it appears from the time that the witnesses are killed and the world rule manifest. Since he will speak words against the Most High, the deception of the Beast will at least at some point not be to appear holy, but rather to present the more usual human deception, by which we are impressed with power, wealth, technical ability and success in worldly endeavors. It does not appear, then, that he will pretend to be the Christ returned. The character of the Beast is most clearly described in the brief glimpse provided in the concluding section of the eleventh chapter of Daniel. His end may be descried in the seventh chapter (7:11; 26) and in the fourteenth chapter of Isaiah. The section of the eleventh chapter of Daniel that is thought by Van Impe to refer to the character of the Beast reads as follows:

> And the King shall do according to his will; He shall exalt himself and magnify himself above every god, and shall speak astonishing things against the God of gods. He shall prosper till the indignation is accomplished; for what is determined shall be done. He shall give no heed to the gods of his fathers, or to the one beloved by women; he shall not give heed to any other god, for he shall magnify himself above all. He shall honor the god of fortresses instead of these; a god whom his fathers did not know he shall honor with gold and silver, with precious stones and costly gifts. He shall deal with the strongest fortresses by the help of a foreign god; those who acknowledge him he shall magnify with honor. He shall make them rulers over many and divide the land for a price.
>
> Daniel 11: 36-39

On the Revelation

Apparently, it will not be difficult to tell that the Beast is the Beast. Like Nietzsche, he is an atheist who proclaims himself God, and yet in place of gods honors the things concerning the holding of power. His end reminds of the end of Hitler, where his body was burned and then the council sat in judgment (Daniel 7:11; 26). Hitler too could be said to have put down at least three of ten kingdoms that arose out of the Roman Empire, such as France, Austria, Czechoslovakia, and Poland, Belgium and the Netherlands, Norway and Finland and Denmark. He also killed many more than 144,000 of the Jews and others. It may even be possible that among the nearly six million Jews, there would be some 2.4 percent that are Christian. Yet, though the rule of Hitler was openly tyrannical for about seven years, it never became literally global, and while the Nazis rolled over Italy, including Rome, there was not yet much action centered around Jerusalem, as seems to be the case in the apocalyptic prophesies. The fear is of course that the roughly seven year period during the worst part of the reign of the Third Reich was only a foreshadowing of what is to come. This one is like a Hitler that *succeeds*, and the head with the mortal wound that healed would fit a miraculous return of Nazism. Here, the head of the revived Roman Empire, in *Fascism (*named for the Roman *fasces*), received what is like a mortal blow, and yet the fascist teaching is strangely resilient. It may be like the villains of modern film who do not die in the end, but come back for a sequel. No one can well explain the reason for the rise of Nazism in America, though it now seems clear that communism never was our most significant internal danger. But this is the sort of thing we are dealing with regarding the Beast, and not some relatively pansy European liberal leading the E.U. by chance. In his rising, he may be undetectable. But in the example of the rise of the Third Reich, the world has seen what this looks like, and how it could ascend. Hitler, on an openly Nazi platform, took power by democratic means, winning a divided election with nearly forty percent of the vote, as the weak German Weimar Republic gave way to tyranny.

In the present context, world rule would of course be impossible in our age unless the sovereignty of the United States was overcome, and it is possible that a global weather catastrophe make universal rule from Europe somehow seem necessary. China, too, like the United States, would either prevent or must host any form of world rule, as would certain others, Russia, Britain and Israel. Van Impe reads Daniel 7:26 as implying that the Antichrist will come from the European Union, since this is a revival of what was called the Holy Roman Empire, the Austrian regime of the Middle Ages. This line, "...The people of the prince who is to come shall destroy the city and the sanctuary," seems to imply that he is not to be a ruler or resident of Israel. It may mean that he is to be an Italian, like Machiavelli or like some "Catholic" mobster. Machiavelli wrote in his *Prince* of the beast and man in the preceptor Chiron the Centaur (XVIII), in intentional contrast with the divine man Christ. More can be learned about these things too from the classical study of tyranny, as in the eighth and ninth books of Plato's *Republic,* and the work of Leo Strauss, *Thoughts on Machiavelli,* p. 78). The "people who destroyed the temple" may have a very broad possible meaning, covering most of the globe in some sense or another, since Russia too derived her tradition of czars from Caesars, and is a part of the Eastern Orthodox Church. The United States imitates Rome in some ways, such as having a Senate. This must either be overcome or be the origin of the Beast, if the Beast is to be a literal world ruler. There is the clear implication of a warning against taking global authority even if this were handed to *us* by necessity. As the Roman Empire quickly led to the reign of the mad, self-deifying emperors, so world rule would make political liberty impossible. Concentrated in one, it might quickly become a throne of madness. Perhaps such an event would be a national test of our commitment to republican government. In Rome, the principate was established when the republicans were killed off in the civil wars (Tacitus, *Annals*, I. i). But it would seem that as long as our constitution is in force, the world rule of any Beast will be restrained. The nations discussed prophetically do not include the United States in any clear way, in part because the nation was not founded yet, and the entire region of the world unknown. One catches occasional glimpses of some nation helping Israel, in the four corners of the earth, leaping across the sea[98] and on the "wings of eagles," as He brought them out of

Egypt (Ex. 19:5; Deut. 32:11). One would hope that it is somehow possible for us to avoid either complete isolation or the complete entanglement of our affairs in the fate of this other third of the globe. The Kingdom of the Beast (16:10) seems distinct from the nations at the four corners, though these are gathered for battle once or twice. Yet it is said that "authority was given it over every tribe and people and tongue and nation." Democratic or republican government, though, may simply go into hiding, so that as Lincoln said, it "shall not perish from the earth." Nations opposed to Israel do not fare well in prophecy, and there is a blessing on those that are helpful (Numbers 24:9). Islam accepts the books of Moses, and the whole of scripture, so that one wonders that these old brothers cannot manage to be neighbors or better friends.

[13:11-18] Then John saw another beast which arose out of the *earth*. The difference between earth and sea seems crucial here, though the beasts Daniel sees arise out of the sea are also seen arising out of the earth. The two realms are in contrast with the element of the *air* and the sky or heaven: Again, the sea is something like the source of myth and poetry in the soul of humanity, and of dreams, while the earth is more mundane and political, the world or the place of the actual regimes. What is said about the earth and sea would fit the matter if the first beast were something like Nietzsche, who did say that he was God, yet one who seeks political dominion, and holds a sort of spiritual dominion over modern thought. The second might be something like Hitler or Marx, although in identification with the false prophet it seems more like al Qaeda. And this may be the "foreign god" with whom he takes the strongest fortress: if Communism or some other in the future were to *use* the Islamic world against the West. That beheading is the favored Islamic method of execution is particularly ominous.

The earth beast "had two horns like a Lamb and it spoke like a dragon." It is sometimes speculated that this might be like the proverbial wolf in sheep's clothing, or that it ascends by pretending to be like a lamb or the Lamb. The Ram with two horns in Daniel is the Kingdom of the Medes and Persians, and so this would also be interesting if the false prophet were to arise out of Islam. Horns, we recall, are sometimes present kings, and the seven horns of the Lamb are in one vision the seven churches.

> "It exercises all the authority of the first beast in its presence, and makes the earth and its inhabitants worship the first beast, whose mortal wound was healed."

This too would be as if the followers of Hitler were to restore the Nazi regime, and honor the defeated fuehrer. Or it may be as the Nazi Reich presented itself, as a revived Roman Empire. Scofield (1909, p. 1342) writes:

> Fragments of the Roman Empire have never ceased to exist as separate kingdoms. It was the imperial form of government which ceased; the one head wounded to death. What we have prophetically in Revelation 13.3 is the restoration of the imperial form as such, though over a federated empire of ten kingdoms; the "head" is "healed," i.e. restored; there is an emperor again– the Beast.

Yet the restoration causes astonishment, which leads people to worship the Beast, as though it were a literal resurrection. The earth beast is somehow in the presence of the first beast. Is it a religious ruler that speaks the things of rage and war, like a dragon? In fooling mankind, it "works great signs, even making fire come down from heaven to earth in the sight of men." By these signs, the land beast deceives "those who dwell on earth," and in this deception, they make an image for the Beast which was wounded by the sword and yet lived.

Scofield (1909, p. 1342) writes:

> The many antichrists precede and prepare the way for the Antichrist, who is "the beast out of the earth" of Revelation 13.11-17, and the false prophet of Rev. 16.13; 19.20; 20.10. He is the last

ecclesiastical head, as the Beast of Rev. 13.1-8 is the last civil head. For purposes of persecution, he is permitted to exercise the autocratic power of the emperor Beast.

This is very interesting as a hypothesis, and may demonstrate the anomaly that we do not know just which beast the Antichrist is, since the word *Antichrist* does not occur in the Revelation. If the hypothesis is wrong, to state just why it is wrong might be revealing. The idea of a political and ecclesiastical beast is related to the idea of two Babylons, political and ecclesiastical, with which we will also disagree, and find revealing, below. The Antichrist is not likely to honor another above himself, unless it is the dragon, but not a man, since he will say that he is God. The land beast does, though, seem to lead the religious worship of the sea beast. The beasts do not die until they are slain by the word in Chapter 19, and so we know that the sea beast is still alive despite the mortal wound. And what if he directed his own worship in disguise?

The image is made to speak, when it, the earth beast, was "allowed to give breath to the image." This would describe television images of the fuehrer, though it may be some future hologram image. Would not a worship of Hitler through footage of his speeches be like this? All those who will not worship the image of the Beast are to be slain. This is like Roman emperor worship and like Nebuchadnezzar's attempt to force Daniel to worship their statues. This second beast, the land beast, is the one that causes all to be marked on the hand or forehead so that no one can buy or sell unless he has the mark, which is the name of the Beast or its number. It is here that the famous mark of the Beast is foretold:

> This calls for wisdom: let him who has understanding reckon the number of the beast, for it is a human number, its number is six hundred and sixty-six.

The mark is called a *chragma*, which can also be translated brand, as those associated with slavery or, cattle. The *chragma* is in contrast with the seal, a *sphragida*. This is the first of two things said to call for wisdom, before the angel's interpretation of the image of the Beast at 17:9. "Here is wisdom," may indicate that the answer to the riddle in Chapter 13 is given in Chapter 17, in an account dominated not by sixes, but by sevens. We are seeing just now the emergence of technology which makes such a thing possible, to mark each one and require such a thing for any transaction: it is the application of the same technology that will be required, or is the logical conclusion of, modern banking with anti-fraud measures. This is one aspect of the prophecy that is a clear possibility for us, but was not apparent to readers in earlier times, and so could not have been imagined, beyond what is said in the Revelation. We see in this not only the astonishing capacity given to evil by modern technology but the increased importance that these new powers be kept in the hands of liberty and out of the hands of tyranny.

While the mark of the Beast may be an actual number spun out of a name, the meaning becomes apparent in contrast with the seal by which the 144,000 have the name of the Lamb and his father written on their foreheads. The best clue so far as to the literal meaning of the marking and sealing is the passage of Ezekiel in which those are marked who "sigh and groan over all the abominations that are committed in" Jerusalem (Ezekiel 9:4). A mark on the forehead is what one sets his plans according to, and on the hand, that to which one sets his work. There seems to be no question of tricking the Beast, as one would otherwise advise for example women and children to do if one were caught under the reign of one like Hitler. Because of this famous passage, and its elaboration in the next vision (14:9, 11), Christians will know enough not to take such a mark, and prepare for the consequences. Similarly it is hoped that avoiding the deception of the Antichrist will be a matter of ethical common sense, rather than extraordinarily difficult. Yet those whose names are not written in the Book of the Lamb will be deceived.

One can see how the mark in the literal sense might be a self-fulfilling prophecy, as whole gangs in prisons now mark themselves this way on purpose. And what if one should name himself "Nero Caesar" because the name supposedly has such a number? One wonders if the strength of our prisons does not presuppose that such things as electricity will continue, or that there will always be fair weather.[99] And this, incidentally, is a practical reason for the death penalty: we cannot be assured of our ability to keep these extremely harmful sorts in prison, nor do we owe to them this risk. The reason against the death penalty is also practical: errors can be made, and the powers can be abused, which cannot be remedied after an execution.

The common attempt to spin the number out of gamatria formulas which exchange numbers for letters is probably mistaken because such a calculation does not call for wisdom and intellect, but rather calculation, which is accessible to all, and may be, as *logistikon*, a faculty different from *nous*. In addition to Nero, the number was said to apply to "Titan," Evanthas, Latinus, Reagan, Napoleon and others, and when the name does not fit the birth name, the birth name may be shuffled about until it does fit. *Visa* and *Computer* have also been suggested. These things seem at best fruitless and at worst harmful to persons like Reagan, to whom no apology is given when it becomes clear that there was never any reason to say such a thing. Reagan, together with the Pope John Paul II and Mikhail Gorbachev, dissolved the Berlin Wall and the most ominous aspect of the Cold War division. Aune (p. 769), citing Bauckham, notes that Greek word for beast transliterated into Hebrew has the value 666, making the gematria identity a statement of the obvious. More interesting is the meaning of three sixes in the text, the sixth seal, trumpet and bowl, which seem too to fit together, addressing the Euphrates and the martyrdom.

In scripture, the phrase "number of his name" comes from the book of numbers (1:3; 20), where the Lord told Moses:

> Take a census of all the congregation of the people of Israel, by families, by father's houses, according to the number of names, every male, head by head; from twenty years old and upward, all in Israel who are able to go forth to war, you

The Beasts that arise from the Sea and the Earth

and Aaron shall number them, company by company.

Each tribe is then listed "according to the number of names," and the total is over six hundred thousand. But in each of the twelve tribes, or eleven since Levi is not numbered, there would be an individual with the three sixes as his number. If the tribe of Dan were numbered but not sealed, this would fit.

But neither does this tell us what the number of the name means. More significant seems the fitting together of the lines "here is wisdom. Let him having intellect figure the number of the Beast for it is the number of a man" (*hode ha sophian estin, ho echon ton noun psaphisato*) and then: "Here is a mind with wisdom" or even "Here is the mind having wisdom" (*hode ho nous ho echon sophian*, 17:9). Is the answer to the number of the name somehow in the account explaining the *seven* heads, ten horns, and the woman that rides in on him, seated on seven mountains? Perhaps the sixth head, sixth horn and sixth mountain? But it is said that he is "an eighth," though "of the seven." We will have a chance to revisit these things below, when taking up the section of the text that contains the interpretation.

iii: Chapter Fourteen

[14:1-5] After the vision of the beasts from land and sea, John sees the Lamb with the 144,000 on Mount Zion, the holy hill of Jerusalem. Zion refers both to Jerusalem as a whole and to one of the four hills. Zion is the southeastern hill, distinct from Mount Mariah within the old city, now called the Temple Mount, and the Mount of Olives, the easternmost hill. It is thought, from Zechariah, that at his return his feet will touch the Mount of Olives, and separate sets of prophecies relate to Mount Mariah and Mount Zion. This is the prophesied appearance on Mt. Zion (Psalm 2:6), "I have set my king on Zion, my holy hill," and "the Lord of hosts will reign on Mount Zion and in Jerusalem, and before his elders he will manifest his glory" (Is. 24:23; 28:16).

The identity and character of the 144,000 is a difficult question. Five distinct groups are recognizable: 1) those martyrs shown in the fifth trumpet; 2) the 144,000 of Chapters 7 and 14; 3) the multitudes from every nation; 4) the two witnesses, called the two olive trees; and 5) those beheaded for refusing to take the mark of the Beast. The latter three may be identical. Other groups which may or may not be identical are a) those raptured; b) the millennial saints beheaded; c) the rest of the dead that rise after the millennium; and d) those that return with Christ for the battle of Armageddon.

This chapter is very complex, as Aune and others note. It is full of ambiguity, and questions that challenge and deepen our understanding of the whole. After he saw the beasts as described in Chapter 13, he sees again those sealed in the sixth seal, the 144,000, who appear on Mount Zion. These are heard singing a new song before the throne, the living creatures and the elders, as appeared in Chapter 4. The questions surround images that depend for their interpretation on our reading of the whole of the Revelation. That is, the teaching of the section assumes an account of the whole that is not clear. But for this same reason, Chapter 14 is valuable in that it *indicates* that whole account, the whole which would be required to make the section clear. The 144,000 who appear on Mount Zion also appeared in Chapter 7 just before those who had come out of the tribulation. It is not clear whether they appear here as martyrs or as survivors. They appear with the Lamb on Mount Zion, rather than, as in Chapter 15, beside a sea of glass, or in heaven. Are these, who have conquered the Beast and its image, the same as the 144,000 sealed? Or are these two different groups, the survivors protected from beheading for not taking the mark and those protected by the seal? All those whose names are not written in the book of life will follow the Beast (13:8), but the seal of Chapter 7 is different from the more general book of life. Do they appear in heaven with harps because they have just been martyred, or rather raptured? It is not clear whether the Lamb is shown as returned, nor whether the Lamb has returned to leave with them or has rather returned with them, on the clouds, as with all his saints (Zechariah 14:5), to conquer and reign with them. The chronological reading would seem to require the latter.

There follows a vision of six or seven messengers, six angels and one like a son of man, and then there is the *harvest* and the *winepress*. The connection of the six angels to the 144,000 is also not immediately clear. As Aune states the question, "Should the one like a son of man be identified with Christ or an angel, and does the harvest represent judgment or salvation?" The Lamb has just appeared on Mount Zion. Is he then shown coming on the clouds?

There may be a close relation between Chapter 14 and Chapter 13, continuing the same story. Hal Lindsey writes of the 144,000 that these have somehow managed to stay alive through the whole tribulation (1973, p. 197). Joel (3:5) writes: "For in Mount Zion and in Jerusalem, there shall be those who escape…," or, in the New American translation:

> Then shall everyone be rescued
> Who calls on the name of the Lord;
> For on Mount Zion there shall be a remnant, as
> The Lord has said,
> And in Jerusalem survivors

On the Revelation

Whom the Lord shall call.

The 144,000 of Chapter 14 sing a new song that only they can learn. The sound heard from heaven that preceded the sound of many harps was the sound of a voice from heaven like the sound of many waters and loud thunder. This recalls the statements of the seven thunders, which was also inaccessible, or not to be written down. It may involve a union of Israel and universal Christendom, as these 144,000 are said to be Israelis, and chaste. The Jews currently reject celibacy. But the 144,000 are of a different and very high order: we should not feel left out if we cannot adjust our reading to include ourselves. Nor does it seem helpful, as the Witnesses do, to identify them with the *aristoi* of a certain group or sect, nor again are all the saints or all the saved identified with them. They are distinguished from the multitudes, those that are seen coming out of the tribulation. The multitudes are presumably not celibate.

A new song is written in Chapter 7, as it is sung *by* the four creatures and the twenty four elders. This song (7:8-10) considers developments from the crucifixion through the apocalypse:

> Worthy art thou to take the scroll
> And to open its seals,
> For thou wast slain and by thy blood
> Didst ransom men for God
> From every tribe and tongue and people and nation,
> And hast made them a kingdom and priests to our God,
> And they shall reign on the earth.

There are, of course, priests of God who are not among the 144,000, and it is said that these will reign on the earth. If these are other than those beheaded, their reign on earth would be after the millennium. The song of the elders said that the Lamb was worthy to open the sealed scroll because of his conquest of death. The 144,000 sing their song *before* the elders, the living creatures and *the throne*. Those who appear beside the sea of glass in

Chapter 15 also appear with harps or guitars, and sing a song, here called the "song of Moses and the song of the Lamb." This is the song of the Old and New Testaments, or of the Jews and the Christians, different from the song in Chapter 14 that only the 144,000 can learn. This is another example of the union of things Jewish and things Christian that emerges as characteristic of the Revelation (12:17; 21:12-14). The word for song (*odon*) is similar to the word for "way," and the word for harps (*kitharodos*) is the same as the word for guitars. Because their song is open, these seem to be other than the 144,000. They may be the multitudes who were seen with the 144,000 as coming out of the tribulation. A second possibility is that the 144,000 are gathered on Mount Zion *for* their martyrdom, and so these then appear in the following chapter beside the sea of glass.

He hears a "voice from heaven like the sound of many waters," like a thunder and the sound of harps." The sound is a part of a new song that they sing before the throne and the living creatures and the elders, and only these could learn that song. There may be a contrast with the sound of the wings of the locusts in Chapter 9. These are virgins, a celibate priesthood that follows the Lamb wherever he goes, somewhat as the wheels follow the faces of the living creatures in the vision of Ezekiel. "These have been redeemed from mankind as first fruits for God and the Lamb, and in their mouth no lie was found, for they are spotless." This line, and the example of John, is among the main scriptures supporting the celibate priesthood. These are those made eunuchs for the kingdom (Matthew 19:12). The line is very similar to the answer recorded in the gospel of Luke (20:34), to the sophistic question of one's wife in the resurrection:

> The sons of this age marry and are given in marriage; but those who are accounted worthy to attain to that age and to the resurrection from the dead neither marry nor are given in marriage. For they cannot die any more, because they are equal to the angels and are sons of God, being sons of the resurrection.

On the Revelation

"Age" here is used in a sense outside of time. In this sense it may be right to say that John, who was literally celibate, is, and was, a son not of the present age, but of the resurrection, or of the Kingdom. Peter and Phillip, who were married, may also be so, though they were not so literally, in that age. The most holy sort *are* singular, as apparently were also James, Andrew and Thomas. The Greek Orthodox custom allowing two orders of Priests, and some to marry, may be more suitable, and reduce the attempt to hide the lack of a husband or wife by entering the orders. Nor is it made clear that those in the resurrection will be reunited with loved ones, though this is not impossible either. And we who seek to marry look to them for the example that frees us from the body, and even for the liberty of the love in our marriages.

The celibacy of John and the 144,000 is literal, and no reason appears to alter our reading to obscure this possibility. Similarly, while they follow the Lamb and have the names of the father and the son written on their foreheads, there is no reason to obscure the possibility that they are literally 12,000 from each of the 12 tribes, of Jewish Christians. It is, again, possible that these Jewish Christians were among the 6 Million Jews killed in the Nazi Holocaust. But even if Hitler is not the Beast, and only a precursor, still one sees something of what this event looks like. The thirteenth, fourteenth and fifteenth chapters fit together if, again, the tribulation caused the martyrdom while this precedes the seven bowls of Chapters 15-16, or at least the seventh bowl.

That the 144,000 are redeemed as "first fruits" would seem to mean that their resurrection was not preceded by a rapture of believers at 4:1. If these are the raptured, their rapture is also to be identified with their coming out of the tribulation. Jesus raised is called a first fruit. That the 144,000 are called "first fruits," though, is somehow consistent with the one raised by Elijah, Lazarus, and those who rose at the resurrection of Jesus.

[14:6-13] But what happens is that the 144,000 appear with the Lamb, then six angels appear, surrounding one that appears as a son of man, that is, as distinct from an angel. The six surrounding the central figure makes the section of the angels shaped like a menorah. The first three appear flying in mid heaven with statements or messages. With the first, an eternal gospel is proclaimed, and with the second, it is announced that Babylon is fallen. Then the third angel issues the warning not to take the mark of the Beast. This third establishes the connection of Chapter 14 with what has just been shown in Chapter 13. A blessing is announced on those who die in the Lord from this time forward, and this is difficult to understand. The one like a son of man is seen seated on a cloud, and an angel comes with a sickle, and another, coming "out of the temple" calls for the earth to be reaped. The human then appears with a sickle for the harvest, and an angel then calls for him to reap. Is this the same as the Lamb that was just seen on Mount Zion? Is the reaping of the harvest not a reaping of the Christians, in contrast with the winepress? Then another angel appears with a sickle and another calls this one to cut the grapes for the winepress, amounting to seven, and another series of sevens. These two, the fifth and sixth, come "out of the temple–"the latter explicitly out of the temple in heaven. The last angel comes out from the altar, and calls for the one with the sickle to gather the clusters of grapes, which are gathered and thrown into the winepress of the wrath of God. The winepress trodden outside the city is generally understood to be Armageddon, though Armageddon is not mentioned until the sixth bowl, and then as something that has not yet occurred, the same as the conquest of the army of the Beast and capture of the Beast and false prophet that occurs in Chapter 19. The text does not seem to intend to refer here to three Armageddon battles, but only one. Another possibility is that the winepress is the gathering of the harvest and the fall of Babylon both, the persecution of all Christians true and false, all at once.

Hal Lindsey recognizes what occurs in Chapter 14 to be two different harvests, a reaping, as of wheat, and another reaping that is a gathering of grapes for the winepress of the wrath of God. Chapter 14 is extremely difficult, with a depth and ambiguity of characters that is similar to the ambiguity of the rider on the first horse. It is possible that the harvest is that of the multitudes, while the winepress is the killing of those who follow the Beast, and that these occur simultaneously.

The winepress is also mentioned at 19:15, where it is said in the future tense, of the one who appears on the white horse, Jesus at his return, that he will "tread the winepress of the wrath of God the Almighty." Our reading of Chapter 14 must aim at consistency with these other instances. Similarly, the winepress is related to the wine of the impure passion of Babylon, and the wine that Babylon is given to drink because of the blood of martyrs spilled (17:6; 18:6). The treading of the winepress in Chapter 14 is the same instance as that in Chapter 19. That the last three angels come out of the temple in heaven reminds of the bowl angels, and the judgment of Babylon in the seventh bowl.

In more detail, the first angel is seen flying in mid heaven "…with an eternal gospel to proclaim to those who dwell on earth, to every nation and tribe and people and tongue." It is said that Joachim of Fiore thought this to be some new account based on the Holy Spirit that was to replace the New Testament, based on the Son (Jung, 1978, p. 85). But the message is to worship God the creator of the four realms that are about to be struck. As Henry Schaeffer suggests, and we have related above, the message is not, as the Christians have taught, that the hour is coming, but that it *has come*, or is now arrived, and the bringing of this message is the office not of human witnesses, but of the angel. It is not the Christians but an angel that is to announce this, when the time arrives. With a loud voice, this one says "fear God and give him glory, for the hour of his judgment has come; and worship him who made heaven and earth, the sea and the fountains of water." These are the four elements to be struck in the first four bowls of wrath below. This may be said as a reminder that the creation belongs to the Lord as a vessel to its potter, since the wrath of the Day of the Lord is to be so terrible for the whole world, and the world is so beautiful. The eternal gospel may be the same as the gospel till this time, which is not only for the people of Israel, but for all people.

A second angel follows, saying in the past tense as an event that has already occurred, what will again be shown in the 17th and 18th chapters: "Fallen, fallen is Babylon the great, she who made all nations drink the wine of her impure passion." The fall of Babylon may be distinct from her drinking the wine cup, or the punishment of Babylon. The third angel then delivers a warning against taking the mark of the Beast, and a call for the endurance of the saints, who are "those who keep the commandments of God and the faith of Jesus." The first three angels would then address three fundamental occurrences of the two millennia from the crucifixion until the present: the gospel, its corruption by Rome, and the cause for endurance, the imposition of the mark of the Beast. Is this not in some sense the last commandment of the Bible, not to take the mark? Eternal torment is the lot of "any one who worships the Beast and its image and receives a mark on his forehead or on his hand." This teaching is important, because under certain tyrannies, it is right to teach children and others to lie to avoid persecution. Here the rule of the Beast is contrasted with the Nazi tyranny, to which it would have been prudent to lie. In this circumstance, the mark carries with it more *earthly* torment than its refusal, and may be something, like allegiance, which cannot in any case be given by children.

The warning here implies something about the time sequence, as though the time were at the start of the last three and one-half years of the tribulation. There is a similarity of proportion between the sets of seven, where seals: trumpets :: angels : bowls. But the pattern of 4/3 that characterizes the seals, trumpets and bowls, appears reversed in the angels, which is more 3:4 or 3:1:3.

Here a voice is heard in heaven telling John to "write this:

> Blessed are the dead who die in the Lord henceforth. Blessed indeed, says the Spirit, "That they may rest from their labors, for their deeds follow them!"

Is there some new permanence to deeds that was not so for those who died in the Lord previously? That our deeds follow us, if the soul is immortal, is related to the book of life (20:12), to be considered in place below. Aune cites a teaching from the Mishnah: at the time of a man's death, neither silver nor gold nor precious stones nor pearls go with him, but only the law and his good works." 1998, p. 839). Does this occur in some new way from this time forward? Could the same be said of those who die in the Lord after the crucifixion? Eternal life may then have entered into the world, and colored deeds of life, as are written in the book of each. But the voice here may refer to those at the harvest, or to those who die in the Lord after the seventh trumpet, the latter day saints. Interestingly, this is the only appearance of the singular Spirit as a character in the vision of the Revelation, as distinct from in the greeting and signing off, and when John is in the Spirit. Elsewhere, the Spirit is present in the seven spirits before the throne, and in many vessels, such as are men and angels. The Spirit also speaks with the risen Christ to the churches.

This is the second of the seven blessings of the book of Revelation (see p. 29 above). The identity of the voice is a mystery, though it is followed by the voice of the Spirit and then a vision of "one like a son of man," thought to be the Messiah, coming on the clouds. This is the closest that the description in the Revelation comes to his arrival on a cloud, as is elsewhere prophesied (Acts 1:9-11; Daniel 7:13). It is possible then that this voice is a third example of the speaking of the Lord (with 1:8 and 21:6-8). The unidentified voice occurs also at 16:1 and 18:4-8. The other interjection is the one appearance of the rapture in the Revelation, when after the description of the three frogs in the sixth bowl, He, Jesus, says "behold, I come like a thief" (16:15).

[14:14-20] What is strange is that one like a son of man enthroned on a cloud, with a golden crown appears with a sharp sickle. Is this the same as the appearance on Mount Zion with the 144,000? The image is strange, because in contrast with our image of the grim reaper, the reaper is apparently the returning Messiah. It is possible that this one is in contrast with the Lamb on Mount Zion, as the Antichrist is also like a son of man and incarnates an angel. But that he is enthroned on the cloud, and has a golden crown seems to indicate that this one is rather the Messiah, coming with the clouds. He is told by an angel that "the time to reap has come, for the harvest of the earth is fully ripe." He swung his sickle, and the earth was reaped. This is a grain harvest, distinct from the grapevine harvest to follow. Another angel comes out of the temple in heaven, also with a sickle, and then the angel that has power over fire comes out from the altar and calls to the previous angel. The image is strange because the harvest of the wheat is an image of the gathering of the grain into the barn, an image of salvation. An example is "the harvest is plentiful but the laborers few" (Mt.9:37-38) and "look up, for the fields are already white for harvest" (John 4:35). The ripe grain would probably not occur as an image pertaining to those ripe for wrath, as are the grapes, although the grapevine is an image for both. Does the image here turn, and the harvest is of those who die at Armageddon, the unredeemed, to whom Jesus appears as a grim reaper? The winepress is that of the wrath of God, which those who take the mark will drink. So it seems that the harvest and winepress are separate because there are both martyrs and followers of the Beast that are killed. The blessing on those who die in the Lord henceforth might be because these are killed by friendly fire, as might occur if there were humans on the side of the Lamb at Armageddon, making sense of that very strange blessing.

Mixing the metaphors of harvesting grain and vineyards, the angel of fire tells the angel that came out of the temple to gather the clusters of the vine of the earth, for its grapes are ripe. The grapes are then gathered and thrown into the great winepress of the wrath of God. The winepress is then "trodden outside the city," reminding of the treading of the outside of the temple (11:1). Blood flowed from the winepress as high as a horses bridle for about 200 miles. This is thought to be a picture of the battle of Armageddon, and "outside the city" would seem to be outside Jerusalem. This impression is supported by the passage of Joel describing the winepress, in the context of the judgment of the nations around Jerusalem in the "valley of decision" (3:13-14). This valley is Jehosephat, just south east of Jerusalem, in the Kidron valley. Joel writes:

> Put in the sickle, for the harvest is ripe.
> Go in, tread, for the winepress is full,
> The vats overflow, for their wickedness is great.

Later, when the one on the white horse appears in Chapter 19, it is said that he will tread the winepress (19:15), so that here the one like a son a man does seem to be the Messiah.

The relation of the harvest and the winepress to the seven bowls of wrath is difficult. If the winepress afflicts the followers of the Beast, it would seem to occur *after* the first and fifth bowls, in which the followers of the Beast do not yet seem to have been crushed. If it afflicts Babylon instead, it would seem not to occur until the seventh bowl. It seems to occur either after the seven bowls or to be another symbolic description of the same thing, culminating in the slaughter at Armageddon described in Chapter 19.

The winepress is familiar from the prophets, from Isaiah, and Joel. In Isaiah (63:1-6), the Messiah appears after the winepress:

> Who is this that comes from Edom, in crimson garments from Bozrah,
> He that is glorious in his apparel, marching in the greatness of his strength?
> "It is I, announcing vindication, mighty to save."
> Why is thy apparel red, and thy garments like his that treads the winepress?
> "I have trodden the winepress alone, and from the peoples no one was with me;
> I trod them in my anger and trampled them in my wrath;
> Their lifeblood is sprinkled on my garments, and I have stained all my raiment
> For the day of vengeance was in my heart,
> And my year of redemption [or of my redeemed] has come.
> I looked, and there was no one to help;
> I was appalled, but there was no one to uphold;
> So my own arm brought me victory, and my wrath upheld me.
> I trod down the peoples in my anger, I made them drunk in my wrath,
> And I poured out their lifeblood on the earth."

Revelation Chapter Fourteen

This is quite terrifying, and it is perhaps done alone because vengeance does not belong to man, but to the Lord.

iv: The Seven Bowls of Wrath

The vision of the six angels and the son of man is followed by another, the sixth or seventh vision included in the seventh trumpet. The seven bowls of wrath complete the wrath of God. Chapter 15 introduces the seven bowls with a vision of those who conquered the Beast and its image and the number of its name, standing beside a sea of glass mixed with fire. They have harps or guitars of God, and are singing the song of Moses and the song of the Lamb. This song of praise to the Lord concludes: "All nations shall come and worship thee / For thy judgments have been revealed." The Song of Moses (Ex. 15:1-18) was sung by Moses and the Israelis after the Egyptians were drowned at the parting of the waters.

After this, he looks, and the temple of the tent of witness in heaven is opened, and seven angels with the seven plagues come out of it. Then one of the four living creatures gives the angels seven bowls of the wrath of God. The temple was filled with smoke, and no one could enter it until the seven plagues were ended.

In this fifteenth chapter, points about the time sequence become apparent. Those who had conquered the Beast and his image and number are seen standing beside the sea of glass, prior to the seven bowls. In 14:8, Babylon has fallen, past tense, *before* the warning not to take the mark of the Beast. The sea of blood in the second bowl is compared to wine, and men are given blood to drink, as is their due for shedding the blood of saints and prophets. In 17, when the fall of Babylon reported by the second angel is described, the dwellers on the earth have become drunk with the wine of her fornication. She holds a cup of her fornications, and a call is given out that she repay double for her deeds. From Chapter 11 through Chapter 18, the same event is described from different angles. There is a huge and severe, worldwide persecution of Christians by the Beast, something like the attempt of Hitler to wipe out the Jews, but directed at the

Christians as well. This may be something like divine retribution for the making of martyrs, as was done by the Church in the persecution of heretics and witches, which included the persecution of translators of the Bible and possibly of saints, even as Israel persecuted the prophets.

A word about divine retribution is in order, because people imagine God to be like a man with a will that is the cause of all things, and so would question why a just God would afflict the innocent for the crimes of the guilty. It is at least possible to suggest that it does not work this way, or that these things are impossible to understand from this assumption. That is part of why these things are hidden. It does not work in the way imagined, yet it does work, if in a more natural way, based on the human soul and the natures of human things. The sins of the Church in the making of martyrs set in motion the anti-Christian tendency of modernity and modern thought and philosophy. In America, this opened the way to liberty, but in Germany, the anti-Christian motion of modernity gave rise to communism and fascism, both the spawn of German "philosophy." These may be two of the three frogs that lead to the gathering of the nations at Armageddon. The law causes the reflection of its opposite, and when Christ was made into a law, with opinion to be legislated as belief, the opposite was caused to develop in humanity. This opposite is extraordinarily cruel, with an upside-down ordering of the soul, aiming at an inversion of the kingdom on earth, and their adherents exercise their cruelties in a religious vigor that cannot be explained from their self-interest as rational, or even as animal. These then afflict the world, as Nazism and Communism afflicted half the globe, and radical Islam now afflicts the nations under Sharia law. It–the ideologies to come out of the West– is the natural result of the anti-Christian, inspired by the making of martyrs. That seems to be how divine retribution works, and not by some god who is puppeteer of fortune and hence responsible for the cruelties of man afflicting the innocent. The Beast attacks the harlot. That is the key to Revelation. The Harlot is the worldly manifestation of religion, used as a cloak for human vice, though the affliction will likely be on anyone identifiable as Christian or biblical, even as the affliction of the Jews was against both the Jewish faithless and the Jewish faithful. Again, the rapture of the Christians prior to the bowls might appear from the worldly view to be persecution and martyrdom.

Chapter 15 is a throne scene, though the throne is not mentioned, and those who have conquered the Beast are the final completion of the throne with the number of the martyrs for which the martyrs of the fifth seal wait. Those before the sea of glass may have been completed in the harvest of Chapter 14, or in the survivors that appeared with the Lamb on Mount Zion, showing the inner connection of the events in these chapters.

Chapter 16

[16:1-11] A loud voice is heard from the temple telling the seven angels to pour out the seven bowls of wrath onto the world. This may be the voice of the Lord. When the first bowl is poured, "Foul and evil sores came upon the men who bore the mark of the beast and worshiped its image." The first bowl is like the first trumpet in that it affects the earth. As the fifth trumpet effects or torments all those that do not have the seal of God on their foreheads, with stings like that of a scorpion, the first bowl affects the followers of the Beast, leaving them with foul sores. And like the second trumpet, the second bowl is poured onto the sea, "and it became as the blood of a dead man, and every living thing died that was in the sea." The word mistranslated "thing" is psyche, soul. And like the third trumpet, the third bowl is poured out onto the fresh water. In the trumpet, this was turned to wormwood, while here, the rivers and fountains of water became blood. An angel is heard to say to God, addressed as O Holy One, that he is just in these judgments, "For men have shed the blood of saints and prophets, and thou hast given them blood to drink, it is their due." It is, to repeat, especially as a punishment for the making of martyrs, not only by the followers of the Beast but by all mankind, that the judgments of the Revelation come. It is all mankind in the sense that the waters on which she is seated are "the peoples and multitudes and nations and tongues" (17:15). One would think it obvious that we ought never to have anything to do with religious executions. The altar voices agreement with the judgment (16:7).

Again, none of the calamities seem to recognize any other of the calamities as having preceded them. The text does not say, for example, that the remaining two thirds of the sea were destroyed, after the thing like a great mountain was thrown into it and one third of the waters turned to wormwood. When men are given blood to drink, it is not understood to be in place of wormwood, but in place of fresh water. It is not the blazing but the normal sun that is darkened, and no reference is made even to one third of mankind having been killed prior to the seven bowls of Chapter 16, though it is said that even after one third is killed, they did not repent, so that the striking of one third in the great battle described through the six trumpets is not the end, but only the beginning of the end. Yet it is possible that we are to understand that one third of the world has been previously destroyed. The great tsunami was quickly forgotten in new concerns and new catastrophes, so that it is not impossible that the remaining two thirds of the world simply continue with what is next.

As in the fourth trumpet, the fourth bowl affects the sun. But while in the fourth trumpet, the sun, moon and stars were *darkened*, here the sun "was allowed to scorch men with fire; and men were scorched by the fierce heat, and they cursed the name of God who had power over these plagues, and they did not repent and give him glory." This of course reminds everyone of the effect of human chemistry on the ozone layer, as the sun does appear to have become noticeably hotter or more burning in the past two decades. The fragility of the whole earth was of course not appreciated, as technologies are applied when there is a short term benefit, regardless of our knowing that consequences or harmful side effects cannot always be foreseen. But to return, the fifth trumpet would alleviate the fourth bowl somewhat, if it were to occur after the sun became blazing, and if it occurred before, the sun would have to be very hot indeed to penetrate the smoke of a large volcano, unless the smoke were understood to have dissipated. As after the sixth trumpet, so here, and after the fifth bowl, men still do not repent.

Like the fifth trumpet and the first bowl, the fifth bowl affects the followers of the Beast. The bowl is poured out on the throne of the Beast, "and its kingdom was in darkness; men gnawed their tongues in anguish and cursed the God of heaven for their pain and sores, and did not repent of their deeds." The event of the sores is very similar to that described in the fifth trumpet and first bowl. Otherwise there is no explanation of the sores. Again, the bowls may cover the period of the three woes in greater detail.

[16:12-16] The sixth angel pours his bowl on the river Euphrates, "and its water was dried up, to prepare the way for the Kings of the East." This anti-exodus event seems to precede the scene described in the sixth trumpet, but could conceivably come after one third of mankind was killed in the sixth trumpet. The four angels bound at the Euphrates and then released may be the three frogs and the free nations of the West. Isaiah writes: They come from a distant land, from the end of the heavens, the Lord and the weapons of his indignation, to destroy the whole earth" (13:5). The Euphrates was the eastern limit of the Roman Empire, near where the angel seen by Daniel straddled the river. Even here, then, in Daniel, the question involves the division between East and West.

Here another vision, introduced with "And I saw," breaks into the scene of the sixth bowl:

> And I saw, issuing from the mouth of the dragon and from the mouth of the beast, and from the mouth of the false prophet, three foul spirits like frogs; for they are demonic spirits, performing signs, who go abroad to the kings of the whole world to assemble them for battle on the great day of God the Almighty.

This is not unlike the way that fascism, communism, and radical Islam are three *ideologies*, one possible effect of which is to gather the nations to come against Israel and perhaps all the people of the commandments of the Bible, including the entire

Christian West. The three frogs are each from one of the demonic characters, the dragon, the Beast and the false prophet, providing a clue to the identities of these. The description of the third frog or demonic spirit as the "false prophet," once conjectured to *be* Mohammed, makes more sense once Al Qaeda-like groups appear. Mohammed brought monotheism to the Arabs, and brought the Arabs and then the Persians to the God of Abraham and Moses. He is violent as a legislator, as is Moses, but he brought the law and justice to the Arab and Persian worlds, and so, as it appears, could not himself be the false prophet. Saint Paul was forbidden to go into Asia, and turned West (Acts 16:6), though Thomas preached in Parthia, or Iran. The missionaries do not penetrate the Arab world, so that these are polytheists when Mohammed arrives to convert them to the God of Abraham and Ishmael. There is some question about spreading Islam by the sword, and so forbidding free speech and religion, and some question of whether it sees itself as universal. Christian preaching is generally forbidden in the Muslim world, as it may be in Israel as well. Yet Islam itself follows the orders of chastity and peace, outdoing the West in purity of ethics in certain respects. Our old doctrinal differences, genuine as they are, look ridiculous and human in light of the genuine appearance of the diabolical in the political worlds. All that is needed for Islam to get along with other nations is the recognition that the God called Allah is the same as the God called Yahweh, or that the Jews and Christians worship no God other than God. Jews and Islamists have more in common with one another than they have with atheists and the polytheists of the East. That Jesus is the Messiah and God will be a bit more difficult, though Islam claims to accept the authority of the New Testament. Radical Islam is a kind of right wing fascism, different from the Nazi form in that it is apparently *theistic*, rather than atheistic, as are the other two frogs. There is some question as to whether the zeal of Muslims is not being used by something else, something other than Islam. Are the highest persons in radical Islam seeing themselves as obedient and dedicated to the Koran? Or do they use this as far as it will take them in a more secret and atheistic purpose of the destruction of the West, aiming at Islamic World rule? "He shall

On the Revelation

deal with the strongest fortresses with the help of a foreign god," though he himself will honor the "god of fortresses" (Daniel 11:38-39). This language is Machiavellian, although it is not clear that Machiavelli honored the god of fortresses. He seems to advise against relying on fortresses, which are for the weak who cannot meet the invader with an army in the field (*Prince* X). But then fortresses can be useful according to the times, as shown by the Germans and Machiavelli's advice for withstanding a siege. Then to have one's own arms is the strongest fortress or the true fortress (XX).[100] The Psalms sing that the Lord is a mighty fortress (18:1-2; 31:3; 71:3; 91:2). The Machiavellian language is a deliberate comment on the image in the Psalms, replacing reliance on God with reliance on one's own arms. But here the King James Version may have the better reading, substituting "forces" for fortresses, and we should await an appeal to the Hebrew original. Not having read Machiavelli, Scofield suggests that this means the forces of nature, and this too would be true in a sense. But it may be the god of "arms" or power in the politically relevant sense.

[16: 15] A voice breaks in to this vision: "Lo, I am coming like a thief! Blessed is he who is awake, keeping his garments that he may not be exposed!" One question would be why this voice says this here, at the sixth bowl, rather than somewhere else. This is the closest reference to the Pauline teaching of the rapture in the entire text. And why especially here is there the caution to keep from being exposed? It may be that if one can keep from being exposed, he might be raptured, but otherwise, martyred. When a thief comes in the night and one has no clothing, he would wish first to dress and then go to oppose the thief, so that he would not be exposed. One awake might already be there, unseen by the thief, awaiting his arrival. In one famous story, when a thief arrived to pick the lock of the gate of a master, he put his hand through the wood of the gate to grab the wrist of the thief. The nakedness of the body, clothed for our appearance in public among humans, is also clothed from above. It is also on the basis of our sins that the diabolical can prevent us from helpful actions, and so repentance frees us for the service of the Lord. It may be well then to hide our faith, and to teach others to hide. "And they assembled them at the place which is called Armageddon." The event described in the sixth trumpet, in which one third of mankind is killed, may be what follows here.

It is in the sixth trumpet and bowl that the Euphrates is mentioned, and, as we have suggested, what is like the rapture occurs at the end of the sixth, just before the seventh, in each case. The sixth seal, describing the sealing of the 144,000, and the seeing of those "who have come out of the Tribulation" may be simultaneous or continuous with the events of the tribulation described in the sixth trumpet and the sixth bowl. These are continuing accounts of the same thing surrounding the Euphrates. Opening the sixth seal, the four winds are held back, and these may be the same as the four angels bound at the Euphrates that are released (7:1; 9:13-20). The rapture seems to occur just before Armageddon, and just after the martyrdom at Jerusalem. Their gathering with him on Mount Zion, then the harvest and winepress, then their appearance with harps standing beside the sea of glass, opening Chapter 15, seems to indicate that they have already been raptured or martyred when the battle occurs. The martyrdom which completes the number of the servants of God, and has been the theme of the work, occurs in part preceding the rapture at the middle of the seven year reign, between the sixth and seventh of the trumpets and bowls, and then is completed in the seventh trumpet, under the order to take the mark of the Beast. The seventh of the trumpets and bowls do seem then to occur *after* these have come out of the tribulation. The teaching of the pre-tribulation rapture is then in part verified by the mid-tribulation rapture: it is the *seventh* that is avoided, by those martyred and those mercifully raptured prior to the seventh.

The bowl of the seventh angel is poured onto the air. The air was also struck in the fourth trumpet when one third of the sky was darkened, and the fifth, when the sun and air were darkened with smoke from the shaft (8:12; 9:2). "A voice came out of the temple from the throne, saying 'it is done.'" (16:17; 21:6). There follows lightening, voices, peals of thunder, and a great earthquake, "such as has never been since men were on the earth," apparently outdoing the worldwide earthquake of the sixth seal, the explosion of Toba in 70,000 B. C. The Toba volcano is thought to have reduced the human population to a few thousand, from a few hundred thousand, dwarfing Santorini. Isaiah writes: "I will make men more rare than fine gold" (Is. 13:12). The "great city," said to be Rome, "was split into three parts, and the cities of the nations fell, and God remembered great Babylon, to make her drink the cup of the fury of his wrath." Jerusalem is *now* divided into four sections and three religions, though this splitting in the earthquake may be literal in the geological as well as the human world. The islands then fly away, no mountains are to be found, and the plague of great hailstones occurs, for which men curse God. There is a great similarity between the seventh bowl and the seventh trumpet, in the hail and earthquake. What may be an outright textual difficulty may appear in the similarity with the sixth seal, because there "every mountain and island was removed from its place" (6:14), while here, also with earthquake and hail, "every island fled away and no mountains were to be found" (16:20). The most likely reading seems to be that there are two earthquakes, at the start of the sixth and the end of the seventh, the second one later, and even worse, than the first. The mountains may be leveled in the first, when the crust of the earth moves about, causing friction at the plates, where all the mountain ranges are. Another scenario would be a ripple in the crust of the earth, which floats on molten lava. The islands will disappear if the sea level rises, and enormous hail may result from great earthquakes. Great hail may also result in the burning of the atmosphere from the reentry of particles, as would occur from a meteor or super-volcano.

Rather than a series of twenty one successive judgments, the series of three Revelations show seven parts of a single event, which does have a chronological succession, though this is either hidden or is not the topic of what is shown. When each part of the world, earth, sea, freshwater and sun are struck, the picture seems to describe a single catastrophe in four different aspects. Then the fifth of each, the trumpets and bowls, describes something that happens to the throne of the Beast, while the sixth of each describes the Euphrates, the gathering toward Armageddon, and the martyrdom-rapture, before the seventh describes the completion of the judgment. This seems to be why the voice

The Seven Bowls of Wrath

breaks in at the sixth bowl saying he comes like a thief in the night: The rapture occurs between the sixth and the seventh, when the eastern nations move against Israel and the Antichrist martyrs the two witnesses. Babylon is then punished, as the land beast orders the mark and attacks every remnant of the people of the Biblical God.

The pattern of the text is not of disconnected parts, but an unfolding of parts within parts, the seven trumpets within the seventh seal, the seven images within the seventh trumpet, and six or seven messengers in the third and fourth images, then seven angels with seven bowls of wrath. Adding up the seals, trumpets and bowls, Van Impe writes of 21 Judgments, which are 19 if the sevens are included in the seventh. At the same time, there is a curious repetition of the first half in the second half, as if going over the same events detailing a different aspect, or perhaps the same aspects, as sea and land and freshwater, in a different event, or an unfolding of the event. There is a curious repetition of the pattern of the seals in the trumpets, in the sets of four and then three. Then there is the repetition of the aspects affected in the trumpets and the bowls. This is especially evident in the fifth, sixth and seventh trumpets and bowls. The Euphrates is the topic of the sixth seal and the sixth bowl. Earthquakes conclude each of the sevenths, the trumpets and bowls. It is not simply clear that for example the sixth trumpet occurs historically prior to the sixth bowl, and so on. That is, it is not clear that the events prophesied are always written chronologically in the book of Revelation. Nor is it clear that we are always shown images that refer to the same time scale, and there is no reason to assume so. The sixth trumpet may come after the sixth bowl, though it is not impossible that one third of mankind has already been killed when the Euphrates is dried up for the kings. In the trumpet, the four angels bound at the Euphrates are released, with 200 million troops, and they kill one third of mankind. In the bowl, the Euphrates is dried to prepare the way for the troops of the kings of the east. Is this after one third of mankind have been killed, and still prior to Armageddon? The sea turns to blood in both the second trumpet and the second bowl. Another pattern, evident from the similarity of the trumpets and bowls, is suggested: We can look for things in the comparison of the seals and the seven angels, and compare the two sets of fourteen things that are in the first and then the second half of the text. Does the first half follow events to their conclusion, with the end summarized when the ark is seen in the temple (11:19)? How then do the series of images that follow the ingestion of the small scroll relate to the two sets of fourteen of the first and second halves? Are they a part of the sixth and seventh trumpets, both containing them and being contained by them? And where does the seventh trumpet end? Chapters 17 and 18 are an elaboration of the fall of Babylon described in the second bowl. Does the judgment of Babylon occur *after* the seven bowls? Or is it not included in the seven, as the seventh? Does the arrival of the one on the White Horse and the defeat of the Beast and the kings of the earth occur after the seventh bowl? Or is it not an elaboration of the fifth through seventh bowls?

One large question is whether we are shown the destruction of one third of the world in the trumpets and then the *whole* world in the bowls, or whether the unspecified extent of the destruction in the bowls refers to the *same* series of destruction over one third of the earth. There is, again, no acknowledgment in the bowls that a previous destruction has occurred, such as a saying that the remaining two thirds of the waters were turned to blood, etc. There is a recognition in the fifth bowl of the sores on the followers of the beast from the first bowl, but no recognition of sores given them previously, in the fifth trumpet. The only point preventing the reading that these destructions are the same is that the sun is *dimmed* in the trumpets but *scorching* in the bowls, though the kingdom of the beast is left in darkness. This would occur if the earth stopped spinning, or even wobbled, so that the sun went down at noon, etc. Otherwise, the reading of the two as describing the *same* event would be simply consistent, and even so, that they are nearly consistent seems to indicate something. The first beast kills the two witnesses in the sixth trumpet, so that the fake resurrection may occur in the middle, as the abomination, and the earth beast and the mark of the Beast occur in the seventh trumpet.

The Seven Bowls of Wrath

To summarize, then: the chronological reading, though, assuming 21 consecutive judgments, is not consistent. The fact that an element is described in the text later than another element does not imply that it literally comes afterward in time. For example, at one point, those who refuse the mark of the Beast are slain (13:15), at another there is the warning not to take the mark (14:9); At one place it is reported that Babylon has fallen, (14:8), while at another, the description of the fall of Babylon (17-18) is related. In Chapter 11, the two witnesses are slain by the Beast but the Beast, in Chapter 13 is shown first rising from the sea (13:2). In the bowls, the way is prepared for the kings of the East, while in the trumpet they *have slain* one third of mankind, etc. Similarly, while it is true that what is shown is what is yet to be, there is no principle preventing some of the images addressing large periods of time, the whole of what is to be from the time of John forward, providing the context of what is to occur at the very end. This appears to be what happens in Chapter 12, describing the birth of the Messiah, and in the first five horns of the Beast, if this describes five previous empires over Jerusalem. What is chronological is that the events described after the letters to the churches are future to them, but even this does not exclude the possibility that it is the birth of the Messiah that is shown in Chapter 12, prior to and into the time of these churches. The four seals seem successive, but the four trumpets might be simultaneous, contained within the seventh seal.

A final parallel to look for is this: What if the seven years of years (2520 years), the seven years of the tribulation, and then a period of seven days, were telescoped like the seven seals, trumpets and bowls, where the latter sets of seven are contained in the seventh of the previous set? Seven ages, ending in seven years, ending in seven days, (or seven sevenths of a 365 year period and then seven years) would then be the time of the prophecy of the seals, trumpets and bowls.

Finally, we should look, as Victorinus says, to *what is occurring* in each of the sets of sevens. The seals show the Four Horsemen, then the martyrs, a completion of their numbers, and then, in the seventh, the introduction of the seven trumpets. The seven trumpets show four tiers of destruction, then the locusts sting those without the seal of God in their forehead, in the fifth, answering the martyrs as in the fifth seal. Then in the sixth, an army is unleashed at the Euphrates to kill one third of mankind and the two witnesses, apparently still within the sixth trumpet, are killed by the Beast, before the seventh angel blows his trumpet. Then the temple in heaven is open, and visions are shown before the seven bowls are poured. The vision is of the mass martyrdom of those who would not worship the Beast, who institutes the mark, apparently within the seventh trumpet. This is the completion of the number of the martyrs, the cause of the seven bowls, and the judgment of Babylon. The Lamb appears on Mount Zion, and prepares the final victory. The angels set the time as during the order of the mark of the Beast, after the gospel has been proclaimed and before Babylon has fallen. The harvest and winepress occur, after the command not to take the mark of the Beast, and then the seven bowls are delivered from the temple, completing the judgment. In the bowls, the first four again describe tiers of the creation that are struck, the earth, sea, freshwater and sun, before the throne of the Beast is struck and his kingdom left in darkness, in the fifth. Then in the sixth, the nations are gathered to Armageddon. In the seventh the greatest earthquake of all time occurs and judgment is inflicted on Babylon, though not until the seventh. Chapters 17-20 then present the detail of these things barely outlined in the seven bowls.

v: The Judgment of the Great Harlot

[17:1-2] The Whore of Babylon is in contrast with the Bride and with the woman of Chapter 12, whose offspring are those who obey the commandments and follow Jesus (12:17). After the seven bowls, or included in the seventh, one of the angels that had the bowls comes and says to John: "Come, I will show you the judgment of the great Harlot, who is seated upon many waters, with whom the kings of the earth have committed fornication, and with the wine of whose fornication the dwellers on earth have become drunk." It is also a bowl angel that, in a parallel construction (Aune, p. 1020), says, "Come, I will show you the Bride, the wife of the Lamb (21:9), for which he is transported not to a desert but to "a great, high mountain." Here the parallel construction clearly indicates the contrast intended. Here, to see the harlot, John in the Spirit is carried away into a wilderness, and this reminds us of the wilderness in the sign or portent seen in heaven in which the woman with the crown of twelve stars was nourished "in the wilderness" or "in the desert," away from the face of the beast (12:5, 14). One wonders if the wilderness is not the same as that where the woman was to be nourished, or, whether this vision is seen in the same wilderness.

These are the two contrasting women of the Revelation, and the identification of the one as Israel-Mary-true Church leads to the obvious suggestion that the Harlot, the whore of Babylon, is an opposite woman, the secular city opposite the Church / bride / woman, and possibly the false church. While some suggest she is the Roman church, and Van Impe suggests she is a future, now emerging, ecumenical church (1982, p. 235),[101] yet she seems more universal, so that these might participate in her, along with the Protestants who made martyrs and those for example prosecuting the witches in Salem. The woman must be broad enough to include "all those slain on the earth," (18:24) as those slain by Jerusalem and even Athens: something like "the city," as the authority by which these are slain. Incidentally, this too is why the whore of Babylon is not, or is not only, something that emerges in the seven year tribulation period. The fornication of the kings of the earth is past tense. It has been going on for quite some time. Herod, for example, is a king in fornication with Rome.

Leo Strauss has done much to recover the original meaning of the conflict between philosophy and the city. There is a conflict between the orthodoxy required to have a political unit and the liberty required for the pursuit of truth. Socrates, *the* philosopher, was put to death in *democratic* Athens for supposed impiety and the corruption of the youth (Plato, *Apology*, 24 b-c). The conflict between philosophy and the city is not unlike the conflict between Jerusalem and the prophets, between the Temple and the Christians, and between Rome and the Christians. Yet, just as the image in the statue is the same through the five parts, so this empire thing is the same through each of the particular empires. The city of man, contrasted with the city of God, as by Saint Augustine[102] is close to this in meaning, though the city is also, for the Greeks and the pre-Christian world generally, of higher dignity than it is for Augustine or the Christians generally. Virtue, education, and indeed love, flourish especially through, and just outside, the city. These empires are cities that have grown into universal empires, something quite different from the particular cities that make up the pre-imperial world. The ancient cites were kingships, but these expanded cities have become the kings of kings. Human worldliness enters a different manifestation in the empire, becoming Babylon, as she is seated on the waters that are the peoples (17:15). The Augustinian view of the city of man is conditioned by the example of a universal city, that is, Rome. Is Babylon then some *particular* universal embodiment of *"the city?"*

Other particular possibilities include the 1) literal Babylon, where Daniel was taken, or Iraq, should it even now become a base; 2) Italy as a nation with Rome as its capital, in something like what occurred under Mussolini, or even; 3) when Rome fell in the fifth century; 4) Rome as a religious organization, where the blood of martyrs is indeed also found, and finally; 5) The United States as a nation, or something like secular liberal democracy. Equal to all these combined in weight is 6) some future city that persecutes the saints and embodies universal empire as Rome does. Something like this might occur if, as seems impossible, the Inquisition were to be somehow revived, so that the final generation manifests the errors of the past, and so is punished then for these. As we read through the text, we will indicate what readings might be supported by what appears.

[17:3-6] In the wilderness, John saw…

> …a woman sitting on a scarlet beast which was full of blasphemous names, and it had seven heads and ten horns. The woman was arrayed in purple and scarlet, and bedecked with gold and jewels and pearls, holding in her hand a golden cup full of abominations and the impurity of her fornication; and on her forehead was written a name of mystery; "Babylon the great, mother of harlots and of earth's abominations." And I saw the woman drunk with the blood of the saints and the blood of the martyrs of Jesus.

Another translation is "…a name: Mystery of the great Babylon, mother of whores and of the abominations of the earth." The image as a whole is the mystery of Babylon. The mystery of Babylon is that the one seated on many waters (17:15) is also seated on the Beast. There is a relation of the Beast too to the waters, as these things could not come to be were it not from something in the people that admires and desires tyranny. The mystery is that the woman that is attacked by the Beast entered riding on the Beast, or conversely, that the woman that entered riding on the Beast is to be attacked by the Beast and the ten horns. The woman that is the Roman Church entered riding on the Roman Empire, even as the last living part of the Roman Empire. A fine example of what is intended by the text occurs regarding Nazi Germany: As a revived Roman Empire and a third German Reich, the Nazis attacked the Jews, and were beginning to expand their target to the Christians. The Communist regimes of Russia have especially attacked all theism, especially that of the Christians and the Jews. The Jews of the temple, who persecuted Christians, beheading James and throwing James from the pinnacle of the temple, could be called not truly Jews but a "synagogue of Satan," so the Roman Inquisition could be said to enter riding on the beast of universal Roman Empire. Yet when the Beast, perhaps a revived Rome in some sense, persecutes religion, he will attack the Roman Church, and perhaps every other religion that is drunk with the blood of saints and martyrs. The Inquisition inspired the anti-Christian motion of modernity, which led in Germany to the atheistic totalitarian visions, which in turn attack all religion, but especially Rome. That is why the key to the mystery of the Harlot is that she enters riding on the Beast, but the Beast will attack her, and that is her judgment. The Messiah returned does not inflict the judgment and punishment of Babylon, but destroys the Beast after the Beast has attacked Babylon.

For this reason, we hold it to be of primary importance that the Church *repent* the Inquisition, and think these matters of the authority of opinion through more thoroughly. There is of course no Christian establishment of doctrine by law in Christian nations, in the sphere of political rule, and there is no reason the citizens should be forbidden the philosophic ascent, even through many errors, toward the truth. It is not at all clear that a thoughtful heretic or atheist is inferior to a thoughtless believer, in the sense of piety toward ancestral custom, which Christendom has in common with the idolatrous nations. The banishment of two things that are divine– philosophy and love– are the reason for the error of the Babylonian authority. These banishments occur because man-made custom or convention cannot contain the truth of the Spirit, but can at best reflect it and be open to it. It is especially in America, following Roger Williams and the founding of Rhode Island, right through to the Declaration and the Bill of Rights, that the Christian religious problem is addressed with some success. But this would be a digression, and another history.

From beginning to end, the Revelation is about the martyrs, the making of martyrs and the reaction or result of the making of martyrs. The result is in a way natural, and it is stated in terms of divine judgment and the answering of the call of the martyrs for vengeance, in the fifth seal. Another way of stating the matter might be to say that the religious killings were an abomination deeper than could then be imagined by the persecutors, who in some cases may even have thought of themselves as fulfilling a religious obligation. Many mere humans were killed, along with a few who gave their lives for the faith at the hands of the faith. Men cannot do such things without the severest of consequences, which for the most part cannot be foreseen, nor can they be avoided in the natural order of things.

To men who do not see the diabolical, merely human things, and even unintelligent accidents, that oppose them, often appear to be diabolical. But when the diabolical appears, these things of mythic demonology appear as fairy tales. The projection of evil[103] in the normal human factions is dissolved, and the commonality of the human things, if not the Christian things, appears more prominent. So suddenly, after the Second World War, all the races are friends, the veil is lifted and anti-Semitism dissolved, relativism flourishes because it allows us to accept other cultures, ecumenism arises in religion, and all the sects are better friends, etc. Like the imminence of death, the appearance of the diabolical has a way of putting things into the proper perspective. The Christian world has always tossed around the attribution of the diabolical. The suggestion is that, this having been false in almost every way and case, we ought learn something from this, and be more humble about such things.

[17:6-8] John relates that when he saw her, he marveled greatly, but that the angel asked him "Why do you marvel?" He offers to tell John the mystery of the woman and the Beast that carries her. And it is here that the angel explains the Beast, as was described in place with Chapter 13 above, beginning: "The beast you saw was and is not, and is to ascend from the bottomless pit and go to perdition." The reason that the Beast *is not* is not explained until the explanation of the punishment of Babylon. The reason may be that in attacking the Harlot, his character is revealed. Those who dwell on earth, and the names of whom have not been written in the book of life from the foundation of the world, will marvel to behold the Beast *because* it was and is not and "yet is," or is to come. This formulation, contrasting with He who is, was, and is to come (1:8), is said to mean that he "has returned from the dead" (Aune, 1998, p. 940). This seems to describe the marveling or wonder (13:3) caused when the mortal wound appears to have been healed (13:12; 14), or when something like an aping of the resurrection is displayed, leaving the impression that the Beast is unconquerable. This would also fit a revived Nazi Reich, the Beast having received its mortal wound in the Second World War. We are already amazed at the resilience of this defeated teaching. Fascism even arose on its own in one branch of modern music. But the scene may occur just as it is depicted, with an individual faking or performing something like a resurrection.

[17:9-10] Again, here for the second time, the angel says that something calls for intelligence and wisdom (Here, or this is for the intelligence and those having wisdom (*ode o nous o echon sophian*"). It is just a bit different from the similar statement introducing the number, "Here wisdom is, and for the one having intelligence (13:18)." The seven heads are seven mountains on which the woman is seated (17:9). These are also seven kings, five of whom have fallen, one that presently is, and one that is not yet come, and will remain only a little while, or, "when he comes he must remain a while." The woman is seated on the heads of universal empire. She is somehow both Rome, that Rome that *is* when John is talking to the angel, and the five "universal" empires that have fallen. In reading Daniel, Van Impe counts these as Egypt, Assyria, Babylon, Medo-Persia, Greece and Rome: Empires that have ruled not literally over the whole world, but were universal in a sense, and ruled over Israel. The one that is to come will be a seventh and an eighth, as might fit either a revived Nazi Germany or Fascist Italy, different from ancient Rome.

[17:11-14] Cryptically, it is then said: "And the beast which was and is not, he is also eighth, and is of the seven, and goes into perdition." This would fit, for example, if the German Reich, claiming to be a revived Rome, were itself revived, though other things would fit as well. The ten kings go along with the one head that is yet to come, for these have not yet been given a kingdom, but are to "receive authority" to reign with him for "one hour" (17:12). This would be something like a world empire divided into ten regions ruled as subject kingdoms, made out of tenths or regions instead of keeping the previous national divisions. The nations of Europe, though parts of the Roman Empire, had not yet been given kingdoms when the angel spoke to John. The Arab nations had not yet been carved out by the British, nor were the nations of the old Soviet empire quite so distinct. The eighth that is of the seven would also fit if the horn that is the Beast put down three kings of the ten, leaving seven, of which he would be an eighth (Daniel 9:24). The head of the seventh empire is one of the ten kings of that same empire, and overcomes three kings, leaving seven, with himself as an eighth. He is then one of those he overcomes, or another holds office in the one of the ten, and he remains as emperor after the murders. If a "day" were also a year of 360 days, one twenty-fourth of a day, or an hour would indicate a period of fifteen days. If these are the same as the ten kings in the book of Daniel, the beast puts down three kings, and would then be an eighth of the ten that is of the seven successive empires (7:8; cp. 8:9-11). A revived Nazi Germany would also be an eighth as a revived Rome, if old Rome were sixth and Hitler's Germany seventh. British fascism, as that addressed in Roger Water's *The Wall*, is yet another possibility, as is American fascism. The liberty of thought and religion that is the American answer to the problem of church and politics allows an opening to fascist teaching that can only be overcome because the people choose against it. Similarly, there is nothing in our constitution to prevent the entire nation from becoming communist or Islamic, should we so choose, and are not otherwise persuaded. The experiment in self-government means that we are responsible in private for the care of virtue.

One feature that the angel does not explain directly is that the dragon in Chapter 12 has diadems on his seven *heads*, while the beast in Chapter 13 has ten diadems on the ten *horns*, and a blasphemous name written on his seven heads (13:1). Our suspicion is that this is related to the different time scales of the visions of Chapter 12, with empires and many centuries, and Chapter 13, which we hope is no more than the literal seven years. Diadems are different from crowns (*Stephanos*). Crowns are mentioned in the letters to the churches (3:11), and belong to the twenty-four elders, as those crowns they cast before the throne (4:5, 11). A crown of the twelve stars is seen on the woman, (12:2). The reaper wears a golden crown (14:14) But the diadems are the same as the diadems when the rider on the white horse is seen in the nineteenth chapter. That the horns are ten kings who have not *yet* received royal power may be what this means, and it implies that the seven heads with diadems *did* receive royal power, although the seventh is yet to come, and *is not*, while the ten horns have yet to receive power. Yet if so, if diadems indicate royal power once given, why then would the seventh head in Chapter 12 also be shown with a diadem? In Chapter 17, we are told, one "was, is not and is to ascend..." These ten are said to be "of one mind," and to give their authority over to the Beast, who is one of the seven heads of the dragon. True royal power is sovereign, and this may be why they wear diadems instead of crowns: diadems may be subjected kingships. The diadems on both the antichrist and the rider on the white horse may indicate that specific nations are under them, even in the battle of Armageddon. This would fittingly describe some tyrannical empire of ten kingdoms, such as the Soviet Union once was, or as the Third Reich almost was, when it had conquered Poland, Austria, France, Italy, etc. But the ten seem not to yet exist, in contrast with the way for example that Greece and other nations that were once great still exist, though these have their power diminished (Daniel 7:12). But the ten are to arise "out of" the fourth beast of Daniel, which is the Roman Empire (Daniel 7:24).

To conclude, these, the Beast and the ten kings, will make war on the Lamb, and the Lamb will conquer them (13:13-18; 17:14). This kingdom of the Beast will attempt to wipe out all Christians in a purge that will be like the attempt of Hitler to wipe out the Jews. In this, he may persecute all associated with the Biblical God, not only the true Christians but also all those who use the Christian things for worldly benefit. But the victory of the Lamb, shown as the rider on the white horse in Chapter 19, is what occurs.

Digression: On the Meanings of *Babylon*

Babylon is first the city where the language of man was confounded, after the first attempt to build a skyscraper (Genesis 11:1; 7). Its name means confusion, according to the Bible, though in the Sumerian language, it is said to mean "gate of God." It was, even before Egypt and Assyria, the first empire, now called the Sumerian. Nimrod was the great grandson of Noah, through Ham and Cush. Egypt was an uncle of Nimrod, a brother of Cush (Genesis 10:6), though the Egyptian *Empire* may have come later. Of Nimrod, it is written, "The beginning of his kingdom was Babel, Erech, and Accad, all of them in the land of Shinar" (Genesis 10:10). The eleventh chapter relates that as men migrated east, they "found a plain in the land of Shinar and settled there." Enoch, the son of Cain, had settled the aria when Cain built the first city and named it Enoch for his son, prior to the flood (Genesis 4:17). The wheel originates in Sumer, apparently after the flood, over five thousand years ago, before 3000 B.C. And "Abraham came forth from Ur of the Chaldeans" (Genesis 11:31). So it is fitting for all seven of the empires in the statue or five parts of the statue in the vision of Nebuchadnezzar to be named after Babylon.

Second, Babylon is the city that conquered and destroyed the two remaining tribes and Jerusalem, after the Assyrians had scattered the northern tribes. The fundamental prophecy of the fall of Babylon is of course that given by Isaiah (21; Jeremiah 50) and Daniel, foretelling the fall of Babylon to the Medes and Persians that resulted in the return of the Jews to Jerusalem by Cyrus in 539 B.C. Isaiah, about the time of the fall of the Northern Kingdom and the ten tribes to Assyria, foresees: "Fallen, Fallen is Babylon and all the images of her gods he has scattered to the ground." In Isaiah, a watchman is to be set, and when he sees two riders approaching,[104] he may know that Babylon has fallen (21:6-9). The Jews are then able, under Cyrus, to return to Israel and Jerusalem. So Babylon is at first the barbarian empire that prevents the return to the Promised Land,

and then under Cyrus, the empire is the beneficent King of Kings who enables their return. Isaiah (47:7-9) prophesies regarding Babylon:

> ...You said 'I shall be mistress forever...
> I am, there is no one besides me;
> I shall not sit as a widow
> or know the loss of children'
> These two things shall come on you in a moment,
> in one day...

The prophecy of Isaiah is of the literal destruction of Babylon, and this occurred. She is even to remain uninhabited, as also occurred (Jeremiah 50:3).

Third, Babylon is the mysterious Babylon of the Revelation. That Babylon is fallen is said in Chapter 14 (14:8), with the angel that is second of the seven. The Judgment is indicated in the seventh bowl, and so Chapters 17 and 18 are an elaboration of what was described in the seven bowls or seventh bowl. Prior to the second angel of Chapter 14, there was apparently no mention of the mysterious Babylon in either the account of the seals or the trumpets. One thing this means is that the rule of the Antichrist can be described without Babylon, which in turn supports the contention that the Antichrist does not rule Babylon. His kingdom is struck in the first and fifth bowls, while Babylon is addressed in the seventh bowl. But his character is revealed when he attacks Babylon (17:16). The dragon with seven heads and ten horns and seven diadems on its heads is likewise described in relation to the woman of Chapter 12, and the nature of the Beast of Chapter 13 is explained in the description of the fall of Babylon. The Beast and Babylon are two distinct organizations or powers, whose symbols are opposite as male and female, and this distinction is evident when the Beast and the ten horns attack Babylon. What this Babylon *is* is the question of the next section.

The Judgment of the Great Harlot

Digression: The Book of Daniel on the Beast

The fundamental point in the reading of Daniel and the Revelation together is that the ten horns of Revelation 12-13 and Daniel 7 are the same as the ten toes of the statue seen in the dream of Nebuchadnezzar. A second key, following Dr. Gaebeline, is that the five parts of the statue are the latter five of seven successive empires that make up the head of the Beast, with the addition of Egypt and Assyria, the five are Babylon, Media-Persia, Greece, Rome, and a revived Rome. A third key may be to look for the two legs of the statue in two parts of the Roman Empire. It is the Jewish and Christian readings together, of Daniel and the Revelation, that is the key to Bible prophecy. One sometimes wonders if Daniel were not written concerning the Jews and the Revelation concerning the Christians pertaining to the end times.

Did the scepter not depart from Judah until Jesus came (Genesis 49:10)? There was no monarchy then, but Judah was the leading tribe. Still, what must the Israelites have thought of this prophecy when Zedekiah was blinded and Jerusalem fell to Babylon? Herod was near to the last king, although sovereignty had departed and been regained. The obedience of the peoples is given to Jesus when He brings the God of the Jews to the nations. The five empires are five that will rule over Jerusalem until the city is returned to Jewish sovereignty, as occurred in 1967. Van Impe calculates 2,553 years,[105] and one should compare the Jewish calendar of 360 day years. The number is again very close to the 2,520 that is twice 1,260, converted into solar years.

The book of Daniel alternates between the story of Daniel in Babylon and the apocalyptic prophecy, presented as it arises in the context of the exile. The chapters of the book of Daniel that are not apocalyptic, Chapters 1, 3, 4, 5, 6, are also connected with the apocalyptic Chapters 2, 7, 8, 9, 10, 11, 12 by providing points necessary to understand certain things in the apocalyptic prophecy. One meaning of "times" is given in Chapter 4, when Nebuchadnezzar is given the mind of an animal until "seven times" come over him, and this seems to be seven years. From this a "time" two "times" and a half a "time" seems to be three and one-half years. But the connection between the story and the prophecy appears especially in the comparison of the refusal of Daniel to eat the food and worship the gods of the Babylonians with the refusal of the latter day saints to take the mark of the Beast. We note that it is Daniel, the one who was especially pressed to worship the Babylonian god, and who refused, or would not bow at peril of his life, that is the one who sees the Old Testament equivalent of the Revelation. It is also Daniel who, under the last Babylonian king, openly prayed when this was forbidden. In these two, Daniel shows examples of the first two clauses of the first Amendment to the U. S. Constitution, forbidding the government establishment of religion and allowing free expression. That Daniel is the one who sees the apocalypse as John did is something like the anomaly that it is the persistently questioning Job who enters the divine presence (Job 42:5-6) and intercedes for his friends. Daniel is a precursor of Western Liberty, a surprising example of the spirit of liberty outside of ancient Greece. His example is the example for the martyrdom of the Christians, and of those to be killed for not taking the mark of the Beast. There is also a similarity of the coming through the fire of the furnace by the three and the coming through the fire of the conflagration. There is a connection with this insistence on political liberty and the circumstance of the end times. Josephus reports on a fourth sect among the Jews, following one Judas the Galilean:

> These men agree in all other things with the Pharisaic notions; but they have an inviolable attachment to liberty; and they say that God is to be their only Ruler and Lord. They also do not value dying any kinds of death, nor indeed do they heed the deaths of their relations and friends, nor can any such fear make them call any man Lord.
>
> Antiquities, XVIII, ii. 6

As Elaine Pagels makes clear, there is an unbroken tradition of religious liberty from Daniel in Babylon through the Jews under the Seleucids and the Maccabean revolt of 164 B.C., through the Jews under Rome, after 63 B.C., to the Jews and Christians under Rome after the crucifixion. She cites Tertullian, "It is a fundamental right, a power bestowed by nature, that each person should worship according to his own convictions, free of compulsion."[106] This is an amazing statement for the second century, though evident enough to the common sense of the Christians prior to Constantine.

Also incidentally, the contrast between the two women is the reason that it is not right to require obedience simply, or why, for example, the Church should not require oaths of obedience of teachers in philosophy and the other human disciplines. In this light, we question the apparent teaching of Paul in Romans (13:1-5) that one must simply obey the governing authorities, and the apparent teaching of the Revelation, that one must never lie (21:8; 14:5). One must explain how we are to avoid acquiescence in the fornication of the kings of the earth with Babylon. What does Paul think of the refusal of Daniel to worship the God of Nebuchadnezzar and his son? Paul was killed by Nero along with Peter, and may soon have had to face the question of whether one should betray others upon command in a persecution. And when the Nazis asked "do you have any Jews hidden here," how many risked their lives and lied to prevent horrible injustice? One is obligated in these cases to disobey, especially if one can get away with it, and maybe even if one cannot. The decision in the Nuremberg trials and again in the case of Mi Lai, in the Vietnam War, set a very fundamental precedent: Soldiers are sometimes obligated to disobey rather than commit the outrages of war upon command. Patriotism sometimes involves concern for the *justice* of one's nation, for its own true good, rather than its apparent advantage. Commanders who enact justice in war appear to lose short term advantages, but gain in spirit and allegiance, becoming indomitable, other things being equal. Throughout history these are very rare, commanders who for example would not allow their soldiers to rape and pillage, and would protect the conquered people. Aristocracy and knights who are noble are rare. But obedience is not tenable as an absolute principle because of the cave, which even the light that enters into the world has not been able to dispel. It is for this reason, as we have argued elsewhere, that Jefferson and limited government is superior to Constantine, and the ignorance of Socratic philosophy superior to the belief that passes in the world for faith. In the teachings of natural liberty and knowledge of ignorance, Jefferson and Socrates both are consistent with the truth of the human condition, that human authority is fundamentally ignorant regarding the first things or the highest, or the most important things. We know, too, what John means by liars, and that this is different from always telling the truth to everyone. Those who betrayed others for gain would be the liars, even while telling the truth. Pastors and priests may be asked for lists of their parishioners, but then modern marketing has made this superfluous. As is made clear by the discussion that opens Plato's *Republic*, we do not owe the truth about everything to any and all people.

[Daniel 1] Daniel is like Joseph, rising in the court of the foreign empire as Joseph and Moses rose to prominence among the Egyptians. Babylon has captured the Jews and the vessels from the temple. The effect of this will prove to be the destruction of the world rule of Babylon. As was prophesied by Jeremiah, Babylon had conquered Jerusalem, destroyed the temple, and taken most of the Israelis captive. Nebuchadnezzar commanded that certain of the outstanding Hebrew youth be educated in the Chaldean language (Daniel 1:4).

Though it is not clear that the liberal arts flourished in Babylon, Daniel might have had the opportunity to study and compare the epic of Gilgamesh with the story of Noah in the Torah. The youth are chosen as children "in whom was no blemish, but well favored, and skillful in all wisdom, and cunning in knowledge, and understanding science, and such as had ability to stand in the king's palace" (1:4). He might have then been able to see what Abraham and Moses had done with the story since Abraham left Ur, since the flood story does not come from Egypt. Through this education, the four youths were given "learning and skill in all letters and wisdom," by God. Daniel in addition "had understanding in all visions and dreams."

Proscribed a rich diet, Daniel asks the chief eunuch, with whom he has become friends, if he might be allowed to not defile himself with the food of the King. The Eunuch states his fear that he will lose his head when Daniel appears thinner than the others. Daniel asks to be allowed to try eating only "pulse" for ten days. After the ten days, Daniel and his companions appear to be fatter than the others, and so Daniel is allowed to eat. It is not clear that the food of the king was dedicated to idols, but it is likely that the request of Daniel was in order to observe Jewish dietary laws. This is then the same as the conflict with Hebrew law that will emerge in a larger way when there is an attempt to force the companions of Daniel to worship the statue in Chapter 3, or to make Daniel worship none other than Darius for thirty days, as in Chapter 6.

[Daniel Chapter 2] The whole apocalyptic prophecy is encapsulated in the first image in the Book of Daniel, when Daniel interprets the dream of the King. The dream is of a statue that is a head of gold, arms of silver, midsection of bronze, and legs of iron and feet of iron and clay. In the first apocalyptic image of the book of Daniel, a stone cut out by no human hands smote the image on its feet of iron and clay. But the stone that struck the image became a great mountain, and filled the whole earth. Daniel tells the King both the dream and its interpretation. Daniel tells his dream:

> As you looked, a stone was cut by no human hand, and it smote the image on its feet of iron and clay, and broke them in pieces…But the stone that struck the image became a great mountain and filled the whole earth…

After describing this last kingdom, he interprets:

> And in the days of *those kings* the God of heaven will set up a kingdom which shall never be destroyed, nor shall its sovereignty be left to

another people. It shall break in pieces all these kingdoms, and it shall stand forever.

(Daniel 2:34, 35, 44).

The stone reminds of the tablets first inscribed by the finger of God, the tables that were broken (Ex. 31:18). This is the beginning of apocalyptic prophecy, and a concise snapshot or capsule of the whole. Most simply stated, this is what occurs. The first sentence of the dream interpretation of Daniel reminds us of the last sentence, in some editions of the Lord's Prayer: "You, O king, the king of kings, to whom the God of heaven has given the kingdom, the power, and the might, and the glory…" That is, we say "For thine is the Kingdom and the power and the Glory," The phrase "king of kings" is the nearest ancient equivalent of "empire," and we conclude the Lord's Prayer by giving this authority over to God.

The rest of the prophecy in Daniel and the Revelation is an unfolding of this simple message. Babylon is both the head and the whole image, and this is a key to reading the Babylon of the Revelation. Rome *is* Babylon in the sense that each of the parts belongs to the man in the statue. It is also, like the Alexandrian empire, a universal empire that rules over Israel. The feet of iron and clay are the manifestation of Babylon when it is struck. The feet and toes are of iron mixed with clay. This is interpreted as meaning that "it shall be a divided kingdom," "with some of the firmness of iron in it," though mixed with "miry clay." The toes are partly strong and partly brittle, or, in the King James Version, broken. The Revised Standard Version then, for 2:43, reads: "As you saw the iron mixed with miry clay, so they will mix with one another in marriage, but they will not hold together, just as iron does not mix with clay." Here, the King James translates "…they shall mingle themselves with the seed of men." The Catholic New American translation has: "The iron mixed with clay tile means that they shall seal their alliances with intermarriage, but they shall not stay united, any more than iron mixes with clay." There is a similarity to mixed marriage, and the failure to dissolve racial divisions as the background to the end times. "One another" may also refer to the toes, and an attempt to unite the ten into one empire through mixed marriage, as in a European Union, which fails. Marriage customs, and with these marriages, have been especially destroyed in the modern West, due to the destruction of tradition caused in part by modern science. But "in the days of those kings" indicates that the ten toes are ten kings.

[Daniel 7] Some years later, after Nebuchadnezzar and Darius have passed, in the first year of Belteshezzar, Daniel sees four beasts arise "out of the sea." These correspond to the latter four parts of the statue seen in the dream. The fourth, exceedingly terrible, has ten horns. The ten horns of the fourth beast (Daniel 7: 24), or ten kings that arise out of the Roman Empire, the ten kings of the diabolic empire in the Revelation, are the ten toes of the statue seen by Nebuchadnezzar. Again, the identification of the ten horns and the ten toes is one of the keys to the reading of the ten horns, and hence the seven heads, of the Beast in the Revelation.

Hippolytus, writing at the beginning of the *third* century, says:

> As these things, then, are in the future, and as the ten toes of the image are equivalent to so many democracies, and the ten horns of the fourth beast are distributed over ten kingdoms, let us look at the subject a little more closely, and consider these matters as in the clear light of a personal survey.

The fourth century statement of Hippolytus appears shockingly prophetic, since there is nothing in the text to suggest that the people are sovereign in the ten, and every indication that they are monarchies. Then the nations which emerged from the Roman Empire became democracies, even all at once, following the American experiment. These are easy to number if one includes the new world democracies of Australia, the U. S. and Canada, though ten European democracies can be counted if these are Britain, France, Germany, Italy and Greece, Switzerland, Belgium, Sweden, Denmark and Austria. Notice that as Hippolytus reads, kingdoms or "kings" are not monarchies but sovereignties, since these might be nations with a democratic regime. There was a time when democracy was known to be the worst and most unstable of the three forms. Yet, since the good forms of the other two, aristocracy and kingship, are so rare, what usually occurs is some form of oligarchy or tyranny. These can often be moderated by the introduction of a popular element and a constitutional way of hashing out the interests of the parts, securing these interests as an approximation of the common good. Hence, as Churchill said, democracy is indeed the worst of all forms of government, "except for those others that have been tried from time to time." Among the actual forms, some near to the best for nations are constitutional democracies.

Hippolytus is shocking for a second reason: the ancient Greeks present a descending order of regimes: kingship-aristocracy, timocracy (based on honor), oligarchy, democracy, anarchy, tyranny, from Book VIII of Plato's *Republic*. These kinds of regime are described in a different schema by Aristotle, adding clarity: rule by one, few, or many is divided according to whether the regime aims at the common good (*Politics*, III.5-7). Six forms result, though the descending order is implicit. This is the archetype of the kinds of constitution, and it is based on the kinds of souls found among mankind. At least since the myth of metals in *The Republic*, metals, gold, silver, bronze and iron, are associated with the various regimes and with the parts of the soul: the gold with reason or intellect that is her crown, the silver with the courageous spirit, and the baser metals with the third part of the soul. The noble lie told to the guardians by the rulers in the beautiful city is that these metals were literally mixed into the souls of the citizens of each class in the regime (*Republic*, 414c ff). Now, one strange thing about Nebuchadnezzar's dream and the interpretation given to Daniel is that, if anyone from the Greek or Western tradition were to take up the dream alone, they would begin with the comparison of the metals to the corresponding souls. The souls in which the gold is dominant are those in whom the pursuit of wisdom rules, the silver their spirited powers, and the bronze and iron, two different sorts of the baser metals, such as the aim at wealth or at the objects of the appetites, women and other things thought to be pleasures of the appetites we share with the other animals. Copper corresponds to the first age of metals in archeology, though gold was first discovered and worked, and probably silver second. Then the alloys, bronze or tin, and iron, with the Iron Age beginning about the first millennium B.C. Lead too is an image of the baser metal of the soul. There at first appears to be no connection between the image seen by Daniel and the ancient Greek regimes. At the time of Daniel, the Jews had as yet little or no contact with the Greeks, and Plato had not yet written. The metals in Hesiod's *Works and Days* do follow this order, the golden age coming first and then descending in some order through silver, bronze, Age of Heroes, then iron, and then a foretold sixth age that is very bad (*Works and Days*, 103-201). Jeremiah does write of the baser metals in analogy with the baser souls (6:28-30), while gold and silver are the metals refined through the fire (Zechariah 13:9; Proverbs 25:11-12). But suddenly in the interpretation of Hippolytus, the fifth regime reveals some connection with the kinds of government. The connection is made regarding the iron and clay, as the fifth and baser metal. But is there any reason to think Babylon related to gold, Persia to silver, Greece to bronze, Rome to iron, and these to the kinds of regime? The great democracies that come from the Roman Empire are clear to us to some extent, and some now compose the European Union. These would be something like the U.S., Britain, Canada, Australia, Germany, France, Italy, Denmark, Switzerland, Austria, Belgium, Luxembourg, Greece, Spain. All these can be said to come from the Western Roman Empire, and five of these may be in the ten horns. Five too may come from the East, as Russia, Greece, Romania, Hungary, Ukraine, Poland, Estonia, Latvia, Czechoslovakia, or now, Serbia, Macedonia and Croatia.

It is also a classical teaching to notice that one way in which tyranny arises is that it comes out of the degeneration of democracy. This was the case with the Weimar republic in Germany, though the tyranny in Russia came quickly from a monarchy. Something similar happened in Rome, after the introduction of the popular element near the end of the Republic. As in the famous account of Polybius, Rome descends from monarchy through aristocracy toward democracy, in a descending cycle of regimes, before arriving at tyranny, though in the reigns of the more descent emperors, the empire or city of Rome might to some extent recover. The character of monarchy, and whether it is a tyranny, depends upon the character of the king or emperor. Tyranny and kingship are first orderings of the soul, and orderings of regimes only secondarily.

Some detail is given here about these horns (7:8):

> I considered the horns, and behold, there came up among them another little horn, before which three of the first horns were plucked up by the roots. And behold, in this horn were eyes like the eyes of a man, and a mouth speaking great things.

The eyes in the horn, and the mouth, remind a bit of the KKK hood, and the "speaking great things" is of course like Hitler or perhaps Nietzsche, or both. Nietzsche is the one to say that he *was* God. The four Zoa had eyes all over, as did the Lamb, indicating what for us would be a perception beyond our nature. The eyes in the horn surely is like our modern spy-tech system in the service of a tyrannical power, introduced for marketing purposes and quickly used by governments good and evil to spy on every single person through our televisions, telephones, computers, and now every thing connected to the internet.[107] There next occurs a vision of the throne, as begins the Revelation of things to come, and Daniel sees the judgment, and books opened (7:10). The one seen looks again like Hitler because of the sound of the great words that the horn was speaking...

> And as I looked, the beast was slain, and its body destroyed and given over to be burned with fire. As for the rest of the beasts, their dominion was taken away, but their lives were prolonged for a season and a time.
>
> Daniel 7:11-12

That their dominions were taken away but their lives prolonged means that while the Babylonian, Greek, Persian, Italian, nations had their empires destroyed, they continued as recognizable nations for over two millennia. All these have now re-attained sovereignty in the last two centuries. But the last beast is distinct from these in that its body is burned, and, unlike Germany after the Nazis, it apparently does not continue. The mouth speaking great things and the body being burned remind of Hitler, as does Isaiah 14, and we must consider whether Daniel is not the prophecy to the Jews regarding Hitler. While Hitler is probably really dead, Nazism is not, and next time may begin with the Christians. Though he was in power nearly ten years, his fury, and World War II, lasted about seven, from 1938 to 1945, and the exterminations about three and one-half years, beginning in 1941. He too shall "go forth with great fury to exterminate and utterly destroy many" (Daniel 11:44), and would "think to change the times and the law" (7:25). This may be the nearest to a prophecy of the holocaust in the books of Israel. Otherwise, *the* people of prophecy were strangely blindsided by the Holocaust: no one saw it coming until it was too late, in part because it is so unbelievable. It was once beyond the limit of the human imagination, except for that referenced symbolically in the books of the apocalypse.

Yet Germany too continues. While he caused the Jews to be marked, this was yet *unlike* the mark of the Beast, which will bring damnation and allow one to buy and sell. Hitler too was stopped short of devouring the whole world, stopped by the allied nations, and not directly by the word of God. Yet an alternate reading is that the Roman kingdom did devour the "whole earth," even more than Alexander, though neither conquered China, and Rome never reached India, not to mention America.[108] Britain extended the Western empire over China and India, in the opium trade and tea wars. These two nations now contain three-eighths of all the people in the world. Yet Britain still did not quite literally achieve world empire, being limited by many other European empires. Britain ruled over the Palestinian authority and Jerusalem, from 1914 through World War II. The Balfour Declaration of 1917 stated the purpose of a Jewish homeland in Israel, and in 1948, both Jews and Palestinians were given land and a state, with Jerusalem to be an international capital. The

On the Revelation

Arab world attacked and lost, leaving hundreds of thousands of Palestinian refugees. Another war in 1967 led to the capture of Jerusalem by Israel. But here we move ahead of our logos.

The visions of Daniel 7 are unlike a prophecy of Hitler in that these are both final, with the arrival of the "Ancient of Days," and the receipt of the Kingdom by the saints of the Most High. And so it is like the vision of John on Potmos, a vision of the same "last things," last for us, though the world and humanity continue in a new age.

In a separate vision introduced "Then I saw," Daniel sees "one like a son of man" come on the clouds to be presented before "The Ancient of Days," and he is given everlasting dominion and kingdom so that "all peoples, nations and languages should serve him." (7:13-14). Daniel then approached one who stood there in the vision and asked the meaning of these things. In explanation, he is told that the four beasts are four kings that will arise "out of the earth" but that "the saints of the most high" will receive and possess the kingdom forever (7:15-18). The rest of the beasts are the first three, the Babylonian, Mede-Persian, Greek and Roman empires. The Oxford Bible note has the Mede and Persian separate and successive, and the fourth the Alexandrian. Yet one can discern the four wings and four heads, as the empire was split up after his death. Then one like a son of man is presented before the Ancient of Days. And to him was given dominion so that all nations, people and languages should serve him, an everlasting dominion and a kingdom that will not be destroyed. A son of man is a human being, as was Jesus, who is called *the* son of man, that is, among divinities, in contrast with an angel.

Here we have a summary again of the same apocalyptic snapshot as in the dream of Nebuchadnezzar, and the stone hewn by no human hand that fills the earth and becomes an everlasting kingdom is the same as the reign of the Messiah, and is also like the spreading of the word throughout the world. The dream of Daniel is an amplification expanding the vision of the King into greater detail about the same topic.

When the angel explains the vision, he says that the four beasts are four kings that will arise "out of the earth." One of course thinks of the two beasts of Chapter 13 of the Revelation, how the first arises out of the sea and the second out of the earth. In Daniel, sea and earth seem to be equivalent, or, there is no clear difference between the two, for in the image, the beasts arise out of the sea, and then in the explanation, these arise out of the earth. When Daniel desired to know the truth about the fourth beast, as he looks...

> ...this horn made war with the saints, and prevailed over them, until the ancient of days came, and judgment was given for the saints of the Most High, and the time came when the saints received the kingdom.

In explanation, the one standing there then says "As for the fourth beast, there shall be a fourth kingdom on the earth..." The possibility arises that "out of the earth" means on the earth, so that the dominion of the sea beast in Revelation may not be "on the earth," but rather a spiritual dominion, perhaps in the realm of thought, like that of Machiavelli or Nietzsche. The fourth kingdom, on the earth, will be different from all the others, and will "devour the whole earth, and trample it down, and break it to pieces." When Daniel restates the vision in posing the question to one who stood there, he adds that the fourth beast had "claws of bronze," which from the image of Chapter 2 would indicate that the parts harmful are Roman and Greek. He then (7:23-25) explains the horns:

> As for the ten horns, out of this kingdom ten kings shall arise, and another shall arise after them; he shall be different from the former ones, and shall put down three kings. He shall speak words against the Most High, and shall wear out the saints of the Most High, and shall think to change the times and the law; and they shall be given into his hand for a time, two times, and a half a time...

That he will think to change the times and the law is an important clue to the character of the Beast as an ideological anti-

On the Revelation

Christianity, rather than the more usual thoughtless strongmen we get for tyrants. Hitler too intended, of course, to change the calendar. That he was seen to make war with the saints and prevail over them, and "shall wear out the saints of the Most High" is the first hint, and these lines are the first time this conflict, significant in the Revelation (13:7), is mentioned. He will "mislead if possible even some of the elect" (Matthew 24:24; Mark 13:22). That they shall be given into his hand for a time, two times and a half a time" also enters scripture for the first time in this Chapter 7 of Daniel. It is thought to be, and hoped to be only three and one-half years, half of seven years, but may also be half of 2,520 years, 1260, (or even 1,260,000, if each of 1260 days were a thousand years). In the following chapter, a period of 2,300 evenings and mornings is said to be the time until the sanctuary is restored. The restoration might be the beginning of the end times, but it is not a restoration following the abomination of the Antichrist, since there is no temple at all in the New Jerusalem.

There is no necessity that the empire that devours the whole earth be *dissolved* into ten, but rather it is *divided* into ten. It seems here *not* to be the eleventh horn that itself devoured the whole earth, but that he is the offshoot of the ten nations that arise from this empire. We count the nations that came out of the Roman Empire, and few are kingships. These are nations such as Italy, Greece, France, Germany, Libya, Algeria, Tunisia, Britain, the U. S., Australia, Israel, Syria, Lebanon, and Jordan. Spain remains a monarchy. If there were, though, suddenly a world government established and divided into ten new regions, no one would think any longer of the European Union.

The Soviet Union was an empire that arose out of the Eastern Roman Empire in one sense, and has now broken into many nations, Russia, Estonia, Latvia, Ukraine, Georgia, Azerbaijan, Moldavia, Kazakhstan, and the satellites, Poland, Romania, Albania, etc.

That the little horn arises after the ten nations is similar to Israel arising as a nation later than the others from the dominions of the old Roman Empire, and fits with the theory of Hippolytus, that the Antichrist is from Israel. The United States, too, is similar in that it is a new nation.

There is a cumulative effect of the successive empires, as each conquers the previous, and is included in the next. The exception is the Persian part of the empire of Alexander, not included in the Roman Empire. Will, then, the Egyptian, Assyrian, Babylonian, Persian and Roman be included in the seventh head of the Beast that is this empire?

But he will put down three kings, perhaps as Hitler took over Austria, Czechoslovakia and Poland before coming against France, Russia and Great Britain. "But the court shall sit in Judgment" reminds one of Nuremberg, though this is not where the dominion of Hitler was taken away. The court also sat in judgment in the vision of the coming of the Ancient of Days and what is like the last judgment (7:26; Rev. 20:4), and so this seems more likely to be like the last judgment. The kingdom and dominion, apparently over the greatness of the kingdoms, will then be given to the "people of the saints of the Most High." There is a default kingdom over kingdoms, which would appear to be Israel, except that "people of the saints of the Most High" might include "all peoples, nations and languages." The Kingdom will be ruled through the saints of the Most High, or by Him through his presence in them. That this is described as a rod of iron (Revelation 2:27; 12:5; 19:15; Micah 4:13) might be explained as the rule of force over tyranny, preventing diabolic atrocities. Such rule is only sanctioned after this cruelty has emerged and been revealed and defeated.

In summary, a dual reading of Chapter 7 appears, according to 1) whether the little horn describes Antiochus and the coming of the son of man like the incarnation, or; 2) whether the little horn arising from among the ten describes the Antichrist of the end times, the slaying of the Beast synonymous with Revelation 19, and the throne and the receipt of dominion in the image like the last judgment, when books are opened, and the second coming, when the kingdom is to be received. In the explanation, it is clear that the fourth kingdom, with teeth of iron and claws of bronze, will devour the whole earth before ten kings arise from it. Then there is another, who will put down three kings. That the saints will be given into his hand, for a time, two times and a half a time indicates that this is the Beast of Revelation 13:5. This is in a different, unique sense, although the same might be said in some sense of numerous persecutions, of Antiochus, Herod, Nero, Diocletian, the medieval Inquisition or Ferdinand of Spain, Hitler, Stalin, and others.

[Daniel 8] Two years later, Daniel sees in a vision, recorded in Chapter 8, the Greek and the Median-Persian empire of Darius as a two horned ram and he goat, who is broken when he is strong, and replaced by four "conspicuous" horns, the four divisions after Alexander, the Ptolemaic, Seleucid, and those of Lysimachus and Cassander. Out of one of these comes a "little horn," like the little horn that arose after the ten horns in Chapter 7. *This* little horn of Chapter 8 is reportedly Antiochus Epiphanes who came from the Seleucid dynasty and defiled the sanctuary in 167 B.C. The continual burnt offering is taken away, and it is said to be for two thousand three hundred evenings and mornings, or one thousand one hundred fifty days, almost three and one-half years. Josephus (*Antiquities of the Jews*, X. xi) writes that Daniel prophesied that from one of the parts of Alexander's empire, a king would arise that would overpower the Jews and...

> ...spoil the temple, and forbid the sacrifices to be offered for three years time." And indeed, it so came to pass, that our nation suffered these things under Antiochus Epiphanes, according to Daniel's vision, and what he wrote many years before. In the very same manner, Daniel also wrote concerning the Roman government, that our country should be made desolate by them.

Josephus also writes 1296 days, just over the 1260 days. But was the offering not restored when the temple was purified and rededicated, as is celebrated in Hanukkah? The Oxford edition notes that the temple was purified on December 14, 164, having been desolated in 167, which may be 1,150 days or nearly the three or three and one-half years. The reason for the difference between 2,300 and 2520, or seven years of days, may be that

The Judgment of the Great Harlot

Chapter 8 refers directly to Antiochus, and through his example to the beast of the end times. By what they have in common, in different sizes, these examples, such as Antiochus, Nero and Hitler, show things about the Beast.

One wonders why it would be stated this way, as evenings and mornings instead of days. In the explanatory section, the vision is said to pertain to "many days hence," the "latter end of the indignation." While possibly distinct from the end times, it "*pertains* to the time of the end" (8:17). The vision is not concluded with the statement that it is about the end times, but rather "pertains to many days hence." Elements of apocalyptic prophecy then enter the description, for at the latter end of the rule of these four, which were replaced by the Roman Empire, a king "of bold countenance" is to arise, one who "understands riddles." He will destroy many men, including the "people of the saints," or Israel. This one will magnify himself, and even "rise up against the Prince of Princes," but "by no human hand he shall be broken." (8:25). This could not refer to the incarnate Jesus if the one who rises up is Antiochus, before the incarnation. Scofield writes that verses 24 and 25 are about the little horn in Chapter 7, though the phrase may refer to both.

[Daniel 9] The fourth apocalyptic image of Daniel is a visitation, rather than a dream or vision. The visit came in the first year of the reign of Darius, or just after the Babylonian has given way to the Mede and Persian Empire. Daniel has just now perceived in the Prophecy of Jeremiah (Daniel 9:2; Jeremiah 25:11-12; 29:10) that the time of the desolation of Jerusalem is to be seventy years. Desolate just means deserted, as Israel was before the modern emigration began.[109] In the Babylonian conquest this desolation was not caused by an abomination, but was due to foreign conquest of the temple. Seventy years later, Cyrus allowed the Jews to return to Jerusalem, as foretold by Jeremiah. The Edict of Return was issued in 538, while the prophecy of Jeremiah is dated 607 B.C., before the 586 fall of Jerusalem, about seventy years before the decree to rebuild under Cyrus. After a prayer of penance, Daniel is visited by Gabriel and told of the seventy weeks of years, apparently 490 years. A prince is apparently said to come in "seven weeks," in the

Revised Version, though the King James reads "seven weeks, and threescore and two weeks." Nothing special appears 49 years later, in about 394 B.C., near the date of the execution of Socrates. Plato was then alive, though Aristotle was not yet teaching Alexander, who lived from 356-323. The second temple was completed in 515 or 16, and the walls in 443, some 110 years before the beginning of the Alexandrian conquest. Antiochus comes in 167 B.C., and the Messiah comes about 511 solar years later, which is near the 490, though not exact in either lunar or solar years.

There follows the section of Chapter 9 (9:24-27) describing the seventy weeks in a division of 7 / 62 / 1 weeks. An "anointed one, a prince" or in the King James, "the Messiah, the prince" was to come in 49 years, or seven weeks of years, and this does not yet make sense. Regarding the 69 weeks, Hal Lindsey includes the calculation of Sir Robert Anderson, converting 483 (69 x 7) lunar years and solar years into their common denominator of 173,880 days from the going forth of the word to Nehemiah to rebuild the temple (Nehemiah 2:8), in 444 or 445 B.C. to the day Jesus rode into Jerusalem on the donkey, the first palm day (Lindsey, 1973, p. 100; Van Impe, 1998, p, 167), in about 32 A.D. The second anointed one is understood to be Jesus while the first anointed one that came after seven weeks or 49 years cannot then be Jesus. Both are translated Messiah in the King James Version. Scofield notes that three decrees to rebuild were issued, and the prophecy "undoubtedly refers to the last one," though he was not then sure whether it was 454 or 444 that was the twentieth year of Artaxerxes (1909, p. 915.)

Then, after 62 weeks,

> ...an anointed one shall be cut off, and shall have nothing; and the people of the prince who is to come shall destroy the city and the sanctuary. Its (or his) end shall come with a flood, and to the end there shall be war; desolations are decreed. And he shall make a strong covenant with many for one week; and for half of the week he shall cause sacrifice and offering to cease; and upon the wing

of abominations shall come one who makes desolate, until the decreed end is poured out on the desolator.

Scofield reads:

> The seventy weeks are divided into seven = 49 years; sixty two = 434 years; one = 7 years. In seven weeks, Jerusalem was to be rebuilt in "troublous times." This was fulfilled, as Ezra and Nehemiah record. Sixty two weeks = 434 years, thereafter Messiah was to come. This was fulfilled in the birth and manifestation of Christ. Verse 26 is an obviously indeterminate period. The date of the crucifixion is not fixed. It is only said to be after the threescore and two weeks. It is the first event in verse 26. The second event is the destruction of the city, fulfilled in 70 A.D. "Then unto the end," a period not fixed, but which has already lasted 2000 years.

After 62 weeks, or x 7= 434 years, the people of the Prince who is to come shall destroy the city and the sanctuary. This is held to have happened in 70 A.D. when, under the emperor Vespasian, the general and future emperor Titus destroyed Jerusalem. The destruction, though, was not with a flood.

Does the difference between the figures 2520 or 2555 and 2300 relate to the difference between 167 and 586? Approaching the year from which Van Impe reasons to the entrance into Jerusalem, 167 + 220= 387, and 167 + 255= 422, Hence 2555 is almost 2300 from Antiochus. Is this a clue to relating the seventy weeks of years from the Persian restoration of Jerusalem to the coming of an anointed one, on one hand, to the 2520?

The final week is identified with the seven year reign of the Antichrist. "He shall make a strong covenant with many for one week," the very 70th week we had expected from the 69. Van Impe expects this week to begin with a peace agreement for Israel to last seven years, which will be broken after three and one-half years. The seven years are to coincide with the week, divided in half, that the witnesses preach in Jerusalem. It is thought that they, knowing the scriptures, preach against the Antichrist as he rises. He causes sacrifice to cease for the first half of the week. This is strange because sacrifice has not yet been restored. In order for sacrifice to be restored, it is said that the temple must be rebuilt. Then, upon the wing of abominations shall come one who makes desolate, until the decreed end is poured out on the desolator." "Poured out" reminds us of the seven bowls in the Revelation. It is not said that this one is the same as the "Prince that is to come," and the anomaly in the text, introducing the one who makes desolate as though he were another, is consistent with the two beasts of the thirteenth chapter of the Revelation. The ninth chapter of Daniel does not describe the Second Advent, as did the seventh chapter, but only ends "…until the decreed end is poured out on the desolator." This line coincides with the eleventh line of Chapter 7 of Daniel, where the Beast was seen slain.

None of the dates match up, if the anointed one cut off is the Messiah and the desolator the Antichrist. The Oxford notes say that the reference is to the desolation of Antiochus, though this does not fit an easy calculation of dates either. Other desolations occurred, when Pompey conquered Jerusalem for Rome in 63 B.C., and when the temple was destroyed in 70 A.D., though none of these are thought to be *the* desolation. As Scofield indicates, Jesus speaks of "the desolating sacrilege spoken of by the prophet Daniel" as future, demonstrating that the events of the seventh week had not then yet come to pass (p. 1081). Van Impe reads the one cut off to be the Messiah, and calculates the days up to the entry of Jesus into Jerusalem. The final seven year period is thought to refer to the seven years that the Antichrist will hold power, and no account is given of the apparent suspension of the clock of the weeks of years for two millennia. This suspension is like the delay, until the number of martyrs is filled. The strong covenant made with many is thought to be a Middle East seven year peace agreement, and the prophecy is thought to allow for a two millennium leap to the last week. The reasons to think so are especially in Chapter 12 of Daniel. One half of the week is "a time, two times and a half a time," and the time between the cessation of sacrifice and offering to the desolation, thirty days into the second half (Daniel 12:11). Also, the events are said to refer to the time of the end and are to be accomplished "When the shattering of the power of the holy people comes to an end" (12:7).

Van Impe reads the "people of the prince that is to come" as implying with certainty that the Antichrist will come from the Italian people, and with equal assurance that he will head the European Union. This is possible, and may even be the best reading. Another possibility is that he come from the Jews, as in the reading of Hippolytus and others. Hal Lindsey writes of two antichrists, the Beast and false prophet, from the E. U. and the Jews respectively (p. 103; Revelation, Chapter 13).

There is an interesting question which arises between the Christians and the Jews, which occurs from considering Maimonides *The Days of the Messiah*. It is a peculiarly Christian teaching that the Second Advent is a coming with the clouds, and hence the Messiah will not be born and grow up again in this age. This means that the Jews gathering in Israel are especially susceptible to a false Messiah, and the one born in this age who claims to be the Messiah would seem to be a false Messiah. As in the case of Rome, it does little good to warn them, because they will not admit such a reading. *We* are concerned about the rebuilding of the temple, because the Mosaic laws regarding animal sacrifice and the stoning of adulteresses and other violators of the especially severe Mosaic Law, would seem then to be required. Isaiah 66:3 seems to us to suggest that animal sacrifice be set aside, as does Hosea (2:18; note 117 below). It is presently forbidden for Christians to proselytize in Israel. One wonders if the killing of Christians will not again seem to some to be required by Mosaic Law, so that the temple might pick up where it left off, as when James, the most legalistic of the Christians, was thrown from the pinnacle of the temple. One sees the scenario of the end times developing where both the Jews and Rome are given a circumstance wherein they are called to renounce a fundamental error, regarding the Messiah and the Inquisition, and there will not be the ability to do this, simply because those able to do this have left the Jews or Catholics respectively. It may be a theme of the end times that the fundamental questions again are presented, and the characteristic errors of the ages brought to bear in a present circumstance.

Jack Van Impe is convinced on the strength of a single passage that the Antichrist must come out of the European Union, since he is to be of the people that destroyed the temple, and these are the Romans (Daniel 9: 26. "...and the people of the prince who is to come shall destroy the city and the sanctuary"). In the passage, the prince previously mentioned is the anointed one who was to come seven weeks after the call to rebuild Jerusalem. Hippolytus, a third century Bishop and anti-pope, writes that he will be from the tribe of Dan, and that he will deceive the Jews into receiving him as the Messiah (Treatise, 209).

> For he will call together all his people to himself, out of every country of the dispersion, making them his own, as though they were his own children, and promising to restore their country, and establish again their kingdom and nation, in order that he may be worshiped by them as God...

One notes how close this reading is to what actually occurred, if Hitler was inadvertently the cause of the gathering of the Jews and the restoration of Israel, though he did not call, but chased them to return to Israel. Yet some future and more complete gathering might occur, with a false Messiah calling all Jews to return, into a trap. But the restoration of Israel seems to have occurred without the things foreseen by Hippolytus. Hippolytus next cites an apparently apocryphal prophet in support of his gathering theory: "He will collect his whole kingdom, from the rising of the sun to its setting." The reasons given by Hippolytus for identifying Dan as the tribe of the Antichrist are generally not demonstrative, but rather, things such as that he will lead an army of noisy horses, etc. That is, they are not good clear reasons drawn from the prophecies regarding the tribe of Dan, and worse things might be said of Benjamin from the histories. The best of these is citing Genesis 49:17, where Jacob delivers oracles for each of the twelve tribes from his deathbed. After the famous Judah oracle, foretelling the birth of the Messiah from the line of Judah, it is written "...Dan shall be a serpent in the way, a viper by the path, that bites the horse's heels, so that the rider falls backwards..." This of course reminds of the curse on the serpent in Genesis, (3:15) "I will put enmity between you and the woman, between your seed and her seed; he shall bruise your head and you shall bruise his heel." Hippolytus presents little else beyond the tradition that this is the reason that the tribe of Dan is excluded from the 144,000 sealed in the seventh chapter of the Revelation. That the eleventh horn arising out of the Old Roman Empire could refer to Israel, as one of the newest of these nations, is a further interesting possibility. A part of the tribe of Dan was lost among the Ethiopian Israelites, and is now being returned. There are, though, other suggestions, and no necessity either to these.

It is comforting that the nation of Israel has already been reestablished and the generation that did so passed, but it is important, we think, to teach Israel that he is coming with the clouds, because he is the one that was born two millennia ago. In speaking of the horns being like a Lamb, Hippolytus writes: "By the beast coming out of the earth, he means the kingdom of Antichrist; and by the two horns he means that he will make himself like the son of God, and set himself forward as king." We consider what would occur should the temple be restored, animal sacrifice resumed, adulteresses stoned, the preaching of Jesus banned, as at the fall of the temple, the Jews picking up where they left off when the temple was last destroyed. That is how such a thing might begin if Hippolytus were correct, the Antichrist from the tribe of Dan, and his rule an Israeli rule. The teaching of Jesus set aside the severity of the Law of Moses, and if he is considered false this teaching too will be rejected. This would make a mockery of the new tolerance for the Jews that has developed since World War II, and make the world regret that Israel had been supported, only to itself impose a racist or fascist universal dominion. Susceptibility to fascism, and immunity from fascism, need not follow race. This, though, might have something to do with education done rightly or wrong. It would then come from the quarter least expected, since the Jews before all are thought to understand the result of racial ideologies, and from a people who, with the Greeks, would have one of the better arguments for the superiority of a people. But, while there is some communism in the Kibbutz movement, there does not seem to be an Israeli fascism, some thought of atheism combined with racial superiority. To be the chosen people means something different.[110] And the prophecy *is* one of some sort of guidance to the nations from Jerusalem during the millennium. But the pattern would then make sense, as it is in the overcoming of tyranny that royal rule can then be established on the basis of its defeat, and the universal dominion of the Antichrist will prepare, if in a macabre way, for the universal dominion of the true Messiah from Jerusalem. The rod of iron makes more sense as the compulsion that prevents diabolical crimes and tyranny. It is like the call of warriors to end the Holocaust by defeating its perpetrators- for at some point these questions are decided in the battle field. The thought of a wrathful God, in the Revelation, long misapplied to mere human deficiency, makes more sense with regard to twentieth century tyranny.

There is very little detail about Rome, the fourth beast of Chapter 7, except that the people of the Prince that is to come will destroy the sanctuary. It is not likened to a known animal, but is terrible and strong, with iron teeth, and has ten horns. The ten horns, ten kings that will arise out of this kingdom, do not characterize Rome at all in ancient history, but only make sense when the nations are left after the dissolution of the empire.

[Daniel 10-12] The last three chapters of Daniel record a single vision that is very strange because in parts it is a prophecy that is so detailed that it looks like post-diction, rather than prediction. Porphyry and others noticed this long ago (Scofield, p.1077). Something may have been inserted, perhaps discernable by following out the interrupted account of the angel Michael, as at 11:2 and 12:1. It is commonly said that the book of Daniel was written about 167 B.C., though it seems entirely possible that it was seen as written in the very years that are written in it, and passed on either orally or in unpublished manuscripts.

The Judgment of the Great Harlot

Josephus includes a story about Alexander which supports the contention that Daniel was written when it says it was written. When Alexander was approaching Jerusalem on his way to conquer Darius and the Persians, Juddua the high priest refused to swear an oath to serve Alexander, having previously sworn an oath to Darius. The high priest was in great fear. But then he had a dream, which told him to receive Alexander, and in the clothing usual for his office, rather than white robes of submission. He was dressed in purple and scarlet, with a golden plate engraved with the name of God. Alexander adored that name. Asked why, when all people adored him, he adored the high priest of the Jews, Alexander answered:

> I did not adore him, but that God who hath honored him with his priesthood; for I saw this very person in a dream, in this very habit, when I was at Dios in Macedonia, who, when I was considering with myself how I might obtain the dominion of Asia, exhorted me to make no delay, but boldly to pass over the sea thither, for that he would conduct my army, and would give me the dominion over the Persians.

(Josephus, *Antiquities of the Jews*, XI, viii. 3-5)

Alexander then offered sacrifice in the temple of the Jews. "And when the book of Daniel was shown him, wherein Daniel declared that one of the Greeks should destroy the empire of the Persians, he supposed that himself was the person intended." As a favor, Alexander was asked to allow the Jews to follow their own laws, and he granted this, though he soon died and Jerusalem fell under Ptolemy of Egypt, and later (198 B.C.) the Seleucids took over the area. The early opposition of the Jews to Hellenizing or Greek influence is conditioned not by access to the writings of Plato and Aristotle, but by Antiochus. The text that Alexander was shown may be that in Chapter Eight of Daniel, lines 1-7. One wonders, then, whether the Jews did not show him lines 8 and following, or warn him against magnifying himself exceedingly.

On the Revelation

The apparent post diction characterizes Chapter 11, but not Chapter 8, and the brief section may have been added by the Jews for publication. But Chapter 11 has another characteristic that is related: The post-dicted prophecy of Antiochus is in turn a prophecy of the Antichrist. One flows insensibly into the other, beginning from the description of the desolation, when the continual burnt offering is taken away and the abomination set up (11:31). Van Impe writes that the little horn of Daniel 7 is the Antichrist, coming out of the fourth beast from amid the ten horns, while the little horn of Daniel 8 is Antiochus, out of the four horns of the third beast that is Alexandrian Greece. Antiochus is said to be not the Beast himself, but an "archetype" of the Beast (1998, p. 143). After the desolation of the temple, the descriptions of Antiochus and of the Beast merge. There is a description of his character and thought (11:36-39), and then the section following "At the time of the end... The Oxford note interprets the events foretold here, but says that none of this occurred. These things, though, will be considered in connection with Chapter 19 below.

Revelation 17:15-18

We return to an attempt to understand the harlot and her judgment. The woman seated on the Beast is also seated upon many waters (17:1; 15). The angel says that the waters on which she is seated are "peoples and multitudes and nations and tongues" (17:15). Are these then the same as those who worship the Beast (13:7-8)? She is seated on the popular opinion that also upholds universal empire, as when "every tribe and people and tongue and nation" excepting those named in the book of life, worship the Beast (13:7-8).

[17:16] The ten horns and the Beast will hate the harlot. This seems to be the key to the identity of the mysterious Babylon, and the reason that the nature of the Beast is discussed here, rather than in the thirteenth chapter. Like the United States and like the Roman Church, the mysterious Babylon is hated by both forms of twentieth century totalitarianism. And like both, she is

The Judgment of the Great Harlot

seated on a sort of universal popular opinion: secular democracy and popular piety. The ten horns and the Beast will attack her, as Israel was attacked by the Nazis:

> They will make her desolate and naked, and devour her flesh and burn her up with fire, for God has put it into their hearts to carry out his purpose by being of one mind and giving over their royal power to the beast, until the words of God shall be fulfilled. And the woman you saw is the great city which has dominion over the kings of the earth.
>
> (17:16-18)

The woman is seated on the Beast, on the waters that are the peoples, and on the seven hills or mountains. She is a city, one that has dominion over kings and one responsible for the blood of all those slain on the earth. This is thought especially to indicate Rome, but again, could also mean the seven empires, Rome being the one that *is*, while Hitler or the Antichrist are yet to come, and to remain only a while. The eighth, then, might be the Beast or the dragon conquered after the millennium.

[17:17] That God is using the Beast and the ten horns is beyond difficult. For when Babylon is burned, if this is the meaning, just as it was for the Jews under Hitler, many are killed who had nothing to do with the inquisition, little girls dressed for Easter, perhaps, any who have not been sealed. We admit that this raises the question of faith, as to how there could be a God and yet these things occur. This has led many Jews to science and philosophy, and yet away from faith, in the middle third of the last century. And this may be part of why these things are foretold: we know God knows they are occurring. They have something to do with what is required in order that man be free to choose Him and his righteousness, yet man does it, and there is a sense in which it truly need not have been done: man freely does this, and we must be penitent for our species. Yet it reveals that He, the Lord, is Lord, and his people truly his people, because they are persecuted, and even by the Beast. There is the teaching that we, the Christians, are the bait in the trap, leading him to come forth to be defeated, so that a new time can come to be, in which the fall has been overcome.

The United States does not have dominion over the kings of the earth, nor does Rome any longer, though when John was writing, this, the one that now *is* would have meant Rome if it meant any particular great city that had dominion over kings. Jerusalem could not then have been referenced as one that "now is," if we understand the sentence correctly, nor did that great city ever have dominion over kings or other cities as did the empires of Cyrus, Alexander and Caesar, or even as the empires of England, France, Spain, Holland and Portugal.

The Great City could also be the earthly kingdom, the city of man, although this does not have such dominion simply. The heart of the king may be as a spring of water in the hand of the Lord (Proverbs 21:1) and kings might pray as Solomon did, for wisdom to govern the people of the Lord (1 Kings 3:9; Proverbs 14:24). In support of this, the Augustinian and more universal reading, it is written that in her was found the blood of prophets and saints, and of "*all* who have been slain on the earth."(18:24). It is the earthly city of man, in which the earthly cities of Rome, Athens and Jerusalem participate, that is the mysterious whore of Babylon. It is connected with the Beast through the topic of universal empire. Five have fallen, one is, and one is yet to come. So this conclusion does not exclude the possibility that a universal religious institution occur in the future, so that the whore is not identical with any institution yet founded, but that this future Babylon is somehow more than those past, an incarnation of the earthly city of man. The beast that is empire may be defeated in the defeat of a particular empire. One would not like to see some new world government setting up some universal church centered literally in Babylon, fitting the name, nor in Rome, fitting the seven hills. There is talk of some new ecumenical world religion, and it is not impossible that this is yet to come, and is the essential manifestation of Babylon. But the Bride is not something made by man.

For John, the worldly reign of the Roman Church was also yet to come. Did John ever suspect that it was even possible that

The Judgment of the Great Harlot

Rome become the Catholic Church, or that the Church, attempting to hold political imperium, would make martyrs as the Roman Empire once did of Christians? The translators of the Bible, the Jews of the Spanish Inquisition, and many of the leading or most thoughtful Christians, as well as scientists, were *burned alive* by *Christian* Rome, even as, or worse than, the Christians were persecuted, by the Jews and then by Rome. Christians also persecuted the Jews, in the Spanish Inquisition and in Pogroms. It is fair to say that these actions were seated on general popular support, that is, it is the people, if misled, who give seat to this drinking of the blood of the saints and martyrs. Hence, the religious killings do not end with the arrival of Protestantism, but people continued to do these things until the enlightenment dispelled both faith and superstition. The numbers tortured and killed as heretics and witches by the *Protestants as well*, may be a part of the Rome wherein the blood of martyrs is found. The kings of the earth are said to have committed fornication with her, and the blood of saints and martyrs is found in her (16:6; 18:24). This particular is unlike the United States, though like many other possibilities. The U. S., ruled democratically, is, as Tocqueville notices, characterized by a *soft* despotism and a slow, drawn out martyrdom. Herod in his relation as king of the Jews toward Rome comes to mind as an example of a king in fornication with the Whore of Babylon, and the participation of kings in the Inquisition, from Ferdinand of Spain to Henry of England, might be another example. For about three hundred years, or more, as it seems, the way to wealth and power was through the offices of the Church, and the royalty of Europe shared a tenuous co-Sovereignty with the universal Church of Rome. And this has been the cause of the Reformation, Counter-Reformation, and continuing monastic reform. The fornication of kings with the harlot describes a form of idolatry, as when Hosea is wed to a harlot to show Israel what she is like in going after other gods (Hosea 3:1-5). "For I desire steadfast love and not sacrifice, the knowledge of God rather than burnt offerings" (Ibid, 6:6). The woman described as a Harlot may be related to the use of religion for profit, as the harlot uses the things that ought to be things of love and beauty– when the bride and groom enter into the chamber and the harmony of Eden together– for the subject purpose of money and power. And even without prostitution, the emphasis on the animal parts of love in modern America has made the sound of bride and bridegroom rarer, as we too mix but do not hold together. But this is said of the iron and clay, the strong and the miry.

Babylon then seems properly to be a symbol because it points to something that is, yet is unknown. Rather than be identifiable as a particular empire or the Roman Church, it is somehow what is present in all seven, or the last five universal empires that are the whole statue seen in the dream of Nebuchadnezzar. It is nearer to the earthly city addressed by Augustine, though just a bit more particular: these five empires are something, some one thing, and something with which the kings of the earth commit fornication in killing the martyrs. It is not synonymous with either the kings of the earth or the peoples or the merchants, but is seated on the peoples, nations and tongues, and is responsible for the deaths of all who are slain on the earth. It is almost like the cave in Plato's allegory. It is the permanent dusky darkness of the human condition, related to the idea of original sin. One sees that Rome, as an extension of the Roman Empire, participates in this but is not synonymous with it. This thing– which includes the assumption that the empire can govern a man principally, and so, as we say, govern belief– is contrary to the first amendment of the U. S. Constitution. This is when "the city" as those following Leo Strauss discuss this, claims she is no widow, as though she were the Kingdom, ruled presently by the logos or the Christ. The truth is that this thing, the kind of universal empire that entered with Babylon and continued through the Persians, Greeks, and Romans, rode in on the Beast, who in the end attacks her. It still seems that she is also conventional religion, in so far as this participates in the assumption that human government can take authority over belief. If each is an image of God, these things are, as Madison presents, owed not to any government, but rather to the Lord. Human government, under the principle of Babylon, assumes the authority of God, as though it were God or the rule of the saints in the kingdom. This is why the apocalyptic sections of Daniel are recessed with stories of how Daniel refused to

The Judgment of the Great Harlot

worship the Babylonian God under either the Babylonians or the Persian Darius. The U.S. Declaration and Bill of Rights allow the people to "come out of her," and so the U. S. founding may be at least potentially, outside the borders of Babylon.

Beginning at 17:8, the angel, then, tells the mystery of the woman and the Beast with seven heads and ten horns that carries her. The key to the reading of the relation of these, and their identification, seems to be especially that the Beast will hate and destroy the Harlot (17:16). Hence, contrary to Luther, there is no suggestion that the Antichrist or the Beast *rules* the mysterious whore of Babylon, though she enters riding on it, much as the universal church entered world domination riding on the Roman Empire, or these riding upon the principle of empire in all five or seven empires. This is evident in Chapter 16, where the kingdom of the Beast is afflicted in the first and fifth bowl, while the fall of Babylon and her punishment are announced in the seventh bowl. Rather, the suggestion is that he *persecutes* her, much as Hitler persecuted the Jews and the Roman emperors persecuted the Church. Three or four possibilities have been suggested for the identification of the mysterious Babylon. These are 1) literally Babylon, the modern Iraq; 2) The United States, or Western liberal democracy; 3) Rome; and 4) the earthly city of man in general. And it could of course refer 5) to some dominion over the kings of the earth that has not yet arisen, or something beyond our imagination, as the medieval church would have been for John beyond imagination. Scofield notes that the possibility of a literal Babylon is contradicted by Isaiah 13:19-22, which says that Babylon will never again be inhabited (1909, p.1347). Victorinus writes, regarding the seven thunders, that among the things they might contain is "the overthrow of Babylon, that is, the Roman state." It is Rome that most made martyrs. When the Roman Empire joined with the church, the political empire fell, and then the spiritual empire continued. The apocalypse is *about* world empire and especially about the making of the martyrs, and the cause of the wrath of God is especially the making of the martyrs. One suggestion is that Babylon is guilty of the blood of the martyrs that appeared under the throne at the fifth seal, while the Beast is responsible for the martyrs of the tribulation.

On the Revelation

The Roman Empire continues through the Eastern and Western Churches, so that the martyrdom of the two witnesses is also related. The Beast attacks *both* women, *both* the true and the false Church, going after every people related to the word of the Biblical God, apparently as a way of striking at God. Yet if he honors the god of fortresses rather than the god of his ancestors, he may in some sense not even know that God *is*.

One might begin with this by considering the significance of nothing or "the nothing" in nineteenth century German thinking, which says something like this: at the bottom of everything is nothing, and what *is* is due to a creative act of a will, a so-called "will to power." Here, the sense in which both the Lord and the Beast are to come is the topic of the work. The Lord *was,* present ruling at the creation, and will be in the end, because He *is*. The Beast *was* in some similar or strange sense as well– not in the sense of a previous incarnation, but some sort of having been. In what way can it have been and be to come when it *is not*? It is said that those who dwell on the earth, whose names have not been written in the book of life from the foundation of the world, will marvel to behold the Beast *because* it was and is not and is to come. What will this look like? Why is the cause of wonder evident to earth dwellers particularly that it was and is not and is to come? This strange appellation of the Beast is set in contrast to the name of God unique to the Revelation. Here, the Greek is more directly translated "that it was something (*en ti*), is not, yet now is." Is it that Rome was, is not and yet returns that causes people to be so amazed that they follow? Or is it rather the false resurrection of a particular person? As discussed below, this may also refer to the Beast with the mortal wound that was healed, as though he *were not* because he died, and yet somehow returns. Could he deceive even some of the saints by his apparent resurrection, even though he is followed as unbeatable in *war*?

Chapter 18

Scofield, Van Impe, Lindsey and Macarthur present a teaching of two distinct Babylons; one religious, in Chapter 17, and one

The Judgment of the Great Harlot

commercial, in Chapter 18. While this calls attention to the difference in the image between the two chapters, the distinction or the reading that there are two Babylons does not seem to be called for by the text. The text, rather, appears to challenge us to see the same thing through two different images. Scofield writes: "Two Babylons are to be distinguished in the Revelation, ecclesiastical Babylon, which is apostate Christendom, headed up under the Papacy, and political Babylon. Ecclesiastical Babylon is "the great whore" (Rev. 17.1) and is destroyed by political Babylon (Rev 17.15-18), that the Beast alone may be the object of worship (2 Thess. 2.3, 4; Rev. 13.5). The power of political Babylon is destroyed by the return of the Lord in Glory.

But Scofield has misread the attack of the Beast and the ten kings. These are not a part of Babylon, but rather attack her. There is no suggestion that the political Babylon of Chapter 18 has attacked the ecclesiastical Babylon of Chapter 17, but rather, these are called by one name, and the commerce of the Tyre-like city in the literal reading of Chapter 18 is *symbolic* of the "ecclesiastical" Babylon. It is, again, rather the Beast and his armies that are struck in separate instances in the first and fifth Bowls of Chapter 16, separate from that addressing the fall of Babylon, after the third bowl warning not to take the mark. There is no suggestion in Chapter 16 that the kingdom of the Beast *is* Babylon. The persecution of those refusing to take the mark of the Beast is different than the complicity of Babylon in the blood of the saints through her fornication with kings. It is possible that Babylon is the persecutor of the saints throughout history, though this was also shown as pursuit of the woman by the dragon, while the Beast is the persecutor of the tribulation. It, the Beast with ten horns, attacks Babylon, and this, we argue, is key to understanding what is occurring. It is the basis for distinguishing the two, which otherwise merge, as in the Babylon statue of Daniel and the empires as heads of the dragon.

[18:1-3] "After this," after the Mystery of Babylon seen in the image and explained in Chapter 17, another angel is seen coming down from heaven, not said to be one of the seven, but "having great authority." We might look for Gabriel and Michael and archangels throughout the Revelation. The earth was made bright with his splendor, and he calls out in a loud voice, describing this Babylon and why it is fallen. She *had become* a dwelling place for demons and foul spirits and birds, and so it appears that she *once was not* such a dwelling place. The nations, kings and merchants have, respectively, drunk the wine of her impure passion, committed fornication with her, and grown rich "with the wealth of her wantonness." She is then something different from the nations, kings and merchants, and something in whose idolatry or fornication the kings and nations can participate, as in allowing the making of martyrs while using the church and human religion for worldly wealth and power. It is interesting to follow the kings: while ten are ruled by the Beast; many fornicated with the harlot. After digesting the scroll, John was to prophecy about peoples, nations, tongues, and *kings* (10:11). So the second half of the Revelation is especially political, concerned with nations, or as we say, foreign policy.

This universal corrupting influence upon nations, kings, and merchants from a number of countries might be said to describe either a nation like the United States or Rome, on their worst side. In the prophecy of Isaiah against Tyre, the commercial republic is said to have fornicated with kings (Is.23:17). Jerusalem too is said to have "played the harlot" with the Egyptians, Assyrians, and Chaldea (Ezekiel 15:26, 28; 23:3-5). The image occurs in Jeremiah (51:7-8), regarding the fall of Babylon to the Medes:

> Babylon was a golden cup in the Lord's hand,
> Making all the earth drunken;
> The nations drank of her wine,
> Therefore the nations went mad.
> Suddenly Babylon has fallen and been broken...

What does it mean for the kings of the earth to commit fornication with Babylon? The tree here is known by its fruit, as the effect is similar to idolatry, and the result is the making of martyrs. How is it then that Rome made martyrs? Is it the same as the way Israel made martyrs of the Christians, and the Christians of others? It is somehow the assumption of knowledge or supremacy that allows the city to persecute the saints and prophets of God? It assumes for itself possession of the first principle and what follows, or assumes that having in the scripture revealed principles, it also has what follows. One sees the wisdom of the Socratic revelation that divine wisdom is not the possession of man, but of "the God" (Plato, *Apology*, 23 a-b). What follows from *this,* Socratic ignorance, are the principles of Jefferson, though their conclusions were arrived at independently. Jefferson writes: "I doubt whether the people of this country would suffer an execution for heresy, or a three years imprisonment for not comprehending the mysteries of the trinity" (*Notes on Virginia*, XVII). Human government simply is not good at setting doctrine, governing men in their natural essence, or governing reason. The attempt to govern doctrine leads unavoidably to the exclusion of some instances of the Holy Spirit, the subjection of the image of God in man, on which it is said "you are gods..." These *especially* will not submit, and in the worst cases, the persecution of the saints of God occurs.

The presence of the divine in man requires that political rights are more fundamental than political duties, as distinct from spiritual duties. This seems to be more so regarding nations and states, though the theoretical question could only be resolved in the ancient city, if not the best regime, where interest and service coincide. That rights are prior to duties was for modern political theory based on self-preservation, but the idea persists because the true natural principle in man is above man made governments and institutions of every kind. The very requirement of obedience or submission to the will of God requires absolute liberty regarding the rule of men. Daniel cannot obey Nebuchadnezzar and worship the Babylonian god, or stop praying for thirty days, because of a prior obedience. Madison writes that religious liberty is required due to our prior obligation: "What is here a right towards men, is a duty towards the creator, preceding civil society (*Memorial and Remonstrance Against Religious Assessments*)." Socrates tells the Athenians that if he were told to cease philosophizing, he would have to obey the God rather than them (*Apology*, 29 d).

On the Revelation

The modern solution is supposed to have been unimaginable to the ancient Greeks. Even Plato's second best regime persecutes unorthodox doctrine. The thought that there not be religious orthodoxy upheld by the threat of death is apparently entirely modern, made necessary by Christianity. The separation of Church and State has been required as a practical solution to the peculiar difficulties of Christian Europe. But the Greeks considered the sovereign city, and the Greek *polis*, rather than the non-Greek nation or empire. *Empire* such as Babylon was considered inherently barbarous, as were the non- Greek cities. The *polis* is more natural, and nearer to the family, where duties may in theory precede rights. It is not impossible that the Greeks, had they considered the modern nation or nation-state, would have quickly thought of something like contract theory (*Republic*, II, 358e) and the purpose of government to secure rights. Christianity heightens the tension, though it is the same perennial tension: The rule of men in spiritual matters is, for almost all practical purposes, the rule of ignorance, while the cultivation of nature in these matters requires something like the recognition of the individual sovereignty of the divine image present somehow in each. Otherwise, men must attempt by custom to rule over the Holy Spirit, and this is not advisable. The precedence of rights over duties is in truth based not on the self-preservation of the body, but the life of the soul and mind. Montesquieu explains that political liberty consists in not being prevented from doing what is right, nor compelled to do wrong (*The Spirit of the Laws*, XI.3). The offended spirit of liberty is always this, that we are prevented from doing what we ought, and forced to do what we ought not. Liberty, then, is a right of doing what *constitutional* laws permit, since laws forbidding what are natural rights may be enacted, though these are not going to be constitutional.

The connection between the prophets oracles of literal Babylon and the Mystery Babylon of the Revelation is that Rome is the final empire on the statue seen by Nebuchadnezzar, the head of which was Babylon, so that the image as a whole, including the legs, feet and toes of iron and clay, in some sense, the most important sense, *is* Babylon.

[18:4-8] John hears another voice, from heaven, saying "Come out of her, my people, …" so that they not partake in her sins and share in her judgment (18:4). This may be the voice of God, since it says "my people," although line 5 says "for God has remembered..." This would leave Jesus and the Archangel Michael, if "my people" were Israel. But what is most likely is that it is the Christ, which means that "Come out of her my people" refers to the Christians. As 18:2 requires that Babylon was once not a dwelling place of demons and foul birds, so 18:4 requires that His people were once in her, and the suggestion is strengthened that in our age this was the medieval church. The call sounds like the exodus from the Church at the Reformation, and should the Inquisition again arise, it might be the best one could do to come out of the orthodox churches in order to avoid participating in such a thing. The matter may not be simply in the past. It may be that the sins of the past are again repeated in the end times, in a modern persecution, as impossible as this sounds. The Roman Church, through the Counter-Reformation, has also been greatly reformed, so that these persecutions no longer occur. The Inquisition as an institution still exists. Yet this, a new Inquisition, does not seem especially to be what is foretold, but rather, a persecution of the church that matches or doubles the medieval persecution inflicted by the Church:

> As she glorified herself and played the wanton, so give her a like measure of torment and mourning / Since in her heart she says, A queen I sit, I am no widow, mourning I shall never see, so shall her plagues come in a single day, pestilence, and mourning and famine, and she shall be burned with fire; for mighty is the Lord who judges her.

(18:7-8)

The prophet Zephaniah (2:15) wrote:

> This is the exultant city that dwelt secure
> That said to herself: 'I am, there is none else'

On the Revelation

> What a desolation she has become
> A lair for wild beasts
> Everyone who passes by her hisses and shakes his fist.

The church, of course, cannot be warned about such an event, because she cannot see herself in the account of the Whore of Babylon, little more than John himself could believe that such a thing as the medieval persecutions could occur. What we are saying too sounds incredible: That a persecution of Christians comparable to that of the Jews may occur, and this may be the result, causally, of the medieval errors. We do not think that a just God would do such a thing, but it may not make sense to think of the will of God that way. We are permitted to do political things, like entertain slavery, which bring about grave consequences generations later. In the nature of human things, there is a causal repercussion of what we do to every one of our fellow humans, aside from any direct or deliberate vengeful intention. For one who would strike at the Biblical God, the institutions of Christianity are especially exposed, because these *appear*.

[18:7] The assertion that she is a Queen and no widow reminds us of the assertion of Thomas Aquinas that theology is the "Queen of the sciences," at the opening of the *Summa Theologea* (Question 1). Aquinas brought Greek philosophy into the Latin Medieval church, but, as for Clement of Alexandria, philosophy is approached as a "handmaid to theology," rather than as a way of life. Revealed doctrine becomes the first principle of a syllogism that ends up sanctioning every authority. Wonderful it is to have Revelation, yet the difficulty is that we cannot read it or apprehend it, and so we both have and do not have it. The four corners imply that the earth is flat and not round. How do we know that God does not literally have a right hand, when this is stated in revealed scripture more clearly than any injunction to read with understanding? So then all who do not believe that God is corporeal are contrary to scripture, and heretics. The assumption of *certainty*, on the basis of revealed principles supported or buttressed the Inquisition and the killings of heretics. How do we know that an illiterate old woman who loves righteousness needs also to hold correct doctrine regarding consubstantiation in order to be loved by the Lord, and saved? Or the Muslim who for righteousness protects his Christian neighbors? Amid human ignorance, the church has a responsibility to free the people from doctrinal issues that cannot concern them, or to present a simple and believable faith. Following the recovery of Aristotle in the West, suddenly everyone must be a theologian in order to find heaven, be saved, or avoid damnation. The fact may be that humans do not know the truth about the divine, cannot read what is revealed, and do not have divine wisdom, which is not the possession of men but of the God. If so, then our mortal opinion ought to go along with our humility, and our assumption of its supremacy be sacrificed continually. This is however impossible for the city, for men in the cave, or for tradition, which is required for man to live, and is the place into which created men are born. The city apparently must base itself on the assumption of knowledge which Socrates begins by destroying. The Socratic destruction is in order to prepare us not for the *justifiable* assumption of the possession of wisdom, but for the quest, or for fundamental inquiry regarding the first principle that may result in an ascent of knowledge. But the union of Christianity and Rome caused the union of the guiding church opinion with the power of opinion in the cave and city. While heresy is a concern of John, he did not foresee the conjunction of Christianity and the city. This conjunction, though, seems as necessary, in hindsight, as it was unforeseen by the early church. Introduce the terms of the true Messiah into the human condition as described in Plato's allegory of the cave, and would one not expect soon to see men chained to viewing shadows of its image held up by other men before the fire in the cave? And if they would try to kill the man who leads up above (*Republic* 517 a), would they not also try to kill the prophets and the Messiah?

The vengeance of God on Babylon may include the punishment of Rome, if she has said "a Queen I sit," and participated in the larger Roman making of martyrs. The Revelation is from start to finish about the martyrs. Modernity and twentieth century totalitarianism may have resulted from the inversion of the images, due to the hatred of the light, fueled by the anti-Christian ire of modernity, by hating its reflection in the Church and in law, because the Church caused people to be burned alive while claiming that it was the vessel of the Holy Spirit. This seems to have confused the world. Paul says that the law causes it's opposite (Romans 7:7-12). We conclude something like this: that we ought not have made a religion of law out of the light. But this is almost unavoidable, given human nature and the true Messiah. The persecution will be of the true woman and her offspring *and* the false woman that is or participates in Babylon.

As Aune reads Chapter 18, three speeches, by another angel, another voice, and a mighty angel, speak regarding three groups: all nations, the kings of the earth and the merchants of the earth. The voice says, "Come out of her, my people, lest you take part in her sins…". "Come out of her, my people" also reminds of the ascent from the cave in Plato's *Republic*, if the city is the cave. In Biblical terms, the allegory of the cave is stated by Isaiah (42:6-7):

> I am the Lord, I have called you in righteousness,
> I have taken you by the hand and kept you;
> I have given you as a covenant to the people,
> A light to the nations, to open the eyes that are blind,
> To bring out the prisoners from the dungeon,
> From the prison those who sit in darkness…

As Alan Bloom writes regarding speech generally,[111] the word of the Lord in scripture is especially a light in the cave of human ignorance. This cave, though, involves our highest faculties and the opinion of the first principle, and is intended to describe the original condition of all of us–as could be expected of something like a fallen nature.

The assumption of political and divine authority by the Catholic Church ignores not only the Eastern Church and others, but the problem of the cave: that it is the permanent human condition, and cannot be transformed, at least by us. The church was told to spread the gospel to the ends of the earth until he comes (Matthew 24:14; Acts 1:8), or to preach repentance and forgiveness of sins (Luke 24:47), but was not especially told to rule the world as though he were here, or she were not widowed in the crucifixion, until his return. Nor was the church told to set up doctrines to be believed by law and root out heresy with the secular sword. The punishment of heretics was officially left to the kings of the nations, as in the circumvention of the prohibition against the church drawing blood. This involvement of the church with the kings may even *be* the fornication of the kings with the Whore of Babylon.

It is not that the Church, or the churches, are an entire failure. The conjunction ought to have been a great blessing, and in some ways, it has been. Violence and barbarism in war have in some ways decreased.[112] Philanthropy and hospitals have spread across Europe and throughout the world. There is at least some escape from the dreary sorrow of the private despotisms that commonly characterize the family. The church is the only one to respond to the circumstance of the cave in any way that can directly affect the people generally, as at the crown of every household. This is so if the relation of image to object provides a ladder of ascent, awakening the soul to the mysteries. An analogy is in the following case: the church or the teaching of the Christians was, in the latter half of the nineteenth century, frequently criticized for being "world-rejecting," and was thought to ignore the "real existence" of the human body. Upon reflection, though, it is the church that introduced the whole idea of the hospital, which with modern medicine gives us the modern medical system. In history, the greatest teacher of charity regarding food and clothing for the poor, caring for the true needs of the body, have been the churches and the institutions of religion. The importance of the body is the ground of charity. The wealthy of the United States, and the Protestant missions, might easily be the second greatest teacher of charity. The two, the woman and Babylon, are both present in the human institutions, the worse the more it is denied, or the more the peoples and nations acquiesce in Babylon. The great modern rejection of Christianity under the banner of the needs of the body leads in theory to the *life* of the body, from self

-preservation and pleasure to power, or, to tyranny, which ends up destroying the body.

Yet, as the Salem witch trials indicate, the change to Protestantism does not solve the problem of the spirit of persecution and Christian orders.[113] Augustine writes that both the regenerate and unregenerate are together in the church. In its sincerity, the church preserves the closest remnant of the teaching of the Apostles, against many errors. Its symbols and ceremonies, the food of the imagination, aligned toward the word of God, and the celebration of mysteries, awakening these things in the nature of the soul. Her achievement is a cultivation of humanity or an education of humanity unrivaled in extent by any organization in human history, except the education of the Jews and perhaps the Greeks. These educations make love and friendship more possible, as we seem to have noticed among these communities. The loss of these things in the Protestant world has left an impoverishment of the imagination and intellect, a void that may be filled by worse ways of spending time. Similarly, the secular world does not realize that something we *can* do to minimize drug addiction is to cultivate the genuine liberal arts. The Catholic Church participates in both the Harlot and the Bride, the Harlot the more it is unrecognized, and the Bride more in recent centuries, having greatly reformed in some ways. Not the change to Protestantism, but the teaching of religious liberty that is behind the First Amendment, is what seems to have ended religious persecution, and in only a small though expanding section of the Western world. The persecutions, it is important to remember, were very popular. She is seated on peoples, multitudes, nations, tongues. Outside the West, the nations do not believe in "tolerance," but are "ethnocentric," just as animals do not believe in animal rights.[114] It is, as in the case of the crucifixion, we as mankind that are guilty of these things, and, as in the Stations of the Cross and passion play, we participate in the sin of mankind. The Protestant churches too participate in both the Bride and Babylon. Even those attempting to be most scriptural add much without realizing this, and one sees how difficult it is to transmit the true teaching from Jesus and the Apostles. Prohibitions of beer and cigarettes, dancing like David, and of many things, without support or scriptural backing, are thought to be implied by misreading.[115] Indeed, it may be because of these things that the witnesses have been held to be a torment to the world. These prohibitions may indeed be best, and it may be fine to have different characters and traditions develop, but let us be clear about the source of their authority, from *outside* the scripture, and among the things that Jesus did not think important enough to mention in recorded teachings. The only sins he rails against are those of the Pharisees.

That the Bible is the word of the Lord is not stated directly in scripture, and surely not as clearly as this is stated in the work of Mohammed, a medieval teaching nearer in time to the authorization of scripture than to Jesus. Jesus is more ancient than medieval. The teaching which gives absolute authority to scripture is a Protestant replacement for the authority of the Holy Spirit recognized by the Catholic Church. The Bible is often vastly superior to the authority of humans claiming the Holy Spirit to authorize despotic rule. It was a standard for the Reformation, once the word was printed and translated, or became accessible. Something occurred with the printing press that is like what occurred when Josiah found the book of the law buried in the floor of the temple (2 Kings 22). But the Bible says that the word of God *was* in the beginning (John 1:1). It is by speaking that the Lord creates, on each of six days, and three times on the sixth day. As Leo Strauss comments on the opening of Genesis: "We have no right to assume that God said it, for the Bible introduces God's sayings by expressions like 'God said.'[116] So there are many senses of "word of God." The Bible was written only two and three thousand years ago, and the canon was of course not agreed upon until the fourth century. It is an articulation of the word that is always, but the articulation has of course come into being at a certain time. To give even the Bible divine authority may be an idolatry, to take a thing that has *come to be* to be worthy of the honor of the Most High. There are scriptures cited for the authority of scripture (2 Timothy 3:16). Upon reflection, only the Old Testament was canon or "scripture" when these were written, so that although a teaching about the Christ is referenced, the New Testament as we have it cannot be

On the Revelation

what is referenced. The New Testament *contains* the word of God, but need not be without editorial errors or mistranslations in order to be or to contain the word of God. We must read and understand it in order to gain what access we have to this word, and be assisted. Nor should the Bible be used as a biology textbook. The concern with editorial errors, and even with historical accuracy, indicates a misunderstanding of what it means to say that every inspired word of scripture is the word of God, based on an unexamined assumption about what must be so if it is inspired. There is a difference between the narrated text and the text where God speaks, as in the two instances in the Revelation, or in the prophets. One reason for the teaching against idolatry is that we already have an image of the Most High that is not man-made. To try to know ourselves is to seek this image.

While it is true that the Bible is the word of God, we do not know what this means. Do we make an idol out of something that has come to be? A similar confusion can arise in Israel, with reflection upon the eternal Torah. One must accept Jesus as his "personal" Lord and savior? This too is true, and yet it is not *in* the scripture in just this way, but a teaching that arises in contrast to the impression of an "impersonal" savior. Yet how quickly could such a profession become a prerequisite for inclusion, or to avoid excommunication? The freest American sects– even those that are the source of the abolitionists and the rights of women– practice a vigorous ecclesiastical and political exclusion on a religious basis that is simply not there. If the authority claimed for itself and the obedience required by each of the Protestant sects were heeded, they must all renounce their disobedience and return to the authority of Rome. Similarly, if we deny that humans ought to found Christian churches, we must be Catholic or Greek Orthodox by default. And would this not be better than by heredity? Soon popular opinion and the cultivation of reputation in light of this have become confused with the ministry of the word and the teaching of Jesus. He taught that adultery was sin, but also showed that we are *all* guilty. He shows the highest purity, and the deepest forgiveness. If one were to judge Christianity by what is seen on the television, it is a constant

The Judgment of the Great Harlot

appeal for money with occasional teachings of various degrees of weakness. The imagination of divine control of fortune is harnessed to make money for the preacher. One wonders that the Christians do not do something about *this*, with our moralizing and inquisitions. But it is characteristic of the claim to authoritative opinion that it misses the mark anyway, and cannot suppress vice and viciousness as this would be done by a true prince. They slaughter scientists and Albigenses, while the most severe diabolism emerges unseen. Babylon is the necessary consequence of the fallen condition, in combination with the age of man. Yet the Bride is not without presence in the world. "The spirit blows where *it* will," and not where human convention says it can or must. In practice, about 400 years must pass before the church explicitly corrects any error, as in the case of Galileo. In the meantime, to believe that the errors are errors is considered as though it were contrary to law, and those swearing oaths to follow the hierarchy in belief are obligated to believe what is not true. The Church must be able to repent, but is it theoretically or doctrinally able to repent? Pope John Paul II repented any omission of the Church regarding the holocaust, in 2003, and this may be the first time in history that the Church has been able to do this. The current Pope Francis has renounced the tolerance and influence of the Mafia, and considered the molestations to be a diabolic influence. In humility, must the church not leave off compelling oaths to obey in the face of such things? In scripture a lamp stand is not so sovereign, and can be removed, and an olive branch cut off.

[18:9-20] The kings of the earth and the merchants stand far off in fear of her torment (18:10, 15). The merchants are identified by the mighty angel with the great men of the earth. (18:22). Seeing her judgment come "in one hour," the kings lament, as then do the merchants and the sea traders (11-20).

One reason for the drawing out of such detail as to the cargo of the merchants and the things not ever to be found in her anymore would be to suggest the meaning of the mystery. Aune notes the similarity of phrase between 18:16 and 17:4, "dressed in purple and scarlet and adorned with gold and precious stones and pearls." The two Babylons of Chapters 17 and 18 are the same.

In these lamentations are particulars that might lead the reader to think of either the United States or Rome. If the U. S. were destroyed, as by the super volcano under Yellowstone, the merchants would similarly stand off and lament, as would the merchants of these particular wares, many of which are used in the divine service. The merchants would then be like the moneychangers of the temple or the salesmen of statues of Diana at Artemis. Among their cargo is said to have been "slaves, that is human bodies," as in the early history of the United States, and especially in ancient Rome. This line is more literally translated "and of bodies and souls of man." In Greek, the word for bodies (*soma*) was also used for slaves. The Roman Church has never traded in slaves. It is a city and not a nation, in the age not of cities but of nations. And the United States has renounced slavery and made very few martyrs.

[18:21] A great millstone is taken up by an angel, who says, "so shall Babylon the great city be thrown down with violence." In the prophecy of Isaiah of the fall of Babylon, the millstone and grinding refer to the work of slaves, into which Babylon is cast from her present luxury (Is. 47:2). It is also related to threshing out the grain (Is. 27:12). The millstone occurs elsewhere in the New Testament when Jesus addresses the punishment fitting anyone who would "cause one of these little ones who belong to me to sin" (Matthew 18:5; 18:1-14; Mark 9:42; Luke 17:2). The meaning of the gospel passage seems generally to refer to all leading astray the children that belong especially to Jesus. Yet one is reminded of the molestation especially of male children by members of the priests, and the possible destruction of the church by lawsuits and the loss of authority that results from this. This circumstance was encountered by Rousseau, as related in his *Confessions*. It may have influenced his separation from that education, and so affected the history of the West at a crucial branching of modern thought. While these things are a risk in all the helping professions, the priesthood seems to have attracted pedophiles and homosexuals because it offered the cover of celibacy to these deviant home lives, or granted a public persona and a great deal of trust and camaraderie to those who were not interested in raising a family. The use of the cloak to cover shames will occur so long as man is fallen, though it will be worse or better according to what we do. A revolution in honesty about these things, in our age, has allowed us to address a problem that is also much worse in our age. Something entered hiding beneath the "sexual revolution."

One further note on this issue: It is an anomaly of Nazi and Klan "ethics" to hold an especial hatred for child molesters, attacking them in prison, though the same indignation is not exercised by them for even the *murderers* of children of some race or another. The white Anglo Protestant tendency of twentieth century American racism had always included Catholics among the persecuted groups, so that the elemental tendencies already appear. What is odd about this extreme vengeance is that on other issues, ethical purity has been replaced by racial purity. That is, Nazis do not especially care about ethical purity.

The things that will be in her no more, such as musicians and craftsmen, millstone and lamps, fit the Church, although the milling activity in a more literal sense reminds more of a commercial nation, as the U. S. The voice of bride and bridegroom reminds more of the church. The removal of their lamp is what is threatened for the church of Ephesus, if they do not recover the love they had at first (2:5). This possibility is incomprehensible from the self-understanding of the Roman church: that a church might have its lamp removed, and that the church ought to repent. Similarly, the final statement fits each in part, though neither completely:

> For thy merchants were the great men of the earth,
> and all nations were deceived by thy sorcery. And
> in her was found the blood of prophets and saints,
> and of all who had been slain on earth."

(18:23-24)

On the Revelation

This last line reminds again of the earthly city in general, Rome or worldly political theory that guides the great men of the earth. Even here, one wonders if this city is universal enough to include literally everyone ever killed on earth. The first murder came before the first city. Is it the darkness of mankind? It is the merchants, though, of Rome or the ideals of the Roman Empire, who were the great men of the earth. Scofield notes the connection to Matthew 23:35, "That upon you may come all the righteous blood shed upon the earth," from Abel to Zechariah. A logical difficulty in scripture occurs unless the Babylon of the Revelation, in its connection with Rome, is broad enough also to include the guilt of Jerusalem for slaying the prophets prior to Jesus, and indeed the guilt of mankind in the crucifixion. Both Jerusalem and Rome participate in Babylon. The connection between post Christian Rome and pre-Christian Jerusalem is the orthodoxy of the church and temple, claimed as the reason for killing the saints and prophets. It is stunning to think that John, having seen the persecution inflicted by the Roman Empire, could not imagine that Rome would become the church, and the church continue the tradition of the making of martyrs. The third level of development, when fascism revives the Roman image, could further not have been foreseen or imagined. And yet, when one attacks the other, the image is shown fulfilled.

This line may be another great clue wherein the text is self-interpreting. Can the merchants in the whole chapter, then, be read as the great men of the world, the Caesars and Napoleons whose ambition leads them to seek power and conquest? The corruption of the Church, in the age of the making of the martyrs by the Church, is attributed to the priesthood having become the principle way for men of ambition to rise in power and fortunes in the world. Babylon would then be, as Augustine suggests, the earthly city of man in contrast with the kingdom of God. As such, we might see how it could be guilty of all those slain on the earth. Cain, the first murderer, is also the first to found cities (Genesis 4:17). It is not the Church of Rome that is Babylon, but the earthly city, that *same* thing in all of the seven empires, in which the Church of Rome, and all the churches participate following, even in the assumption of divine knowledge. The earthly woman that is contrasted with the heavenly woman, who is guilty of the blood of the martyrs and is to be attacked by the Beast, is not a kingdom of the Antichrist, but is the worldly city in general, in which worldly religion participates. When the Beast attacks the people of the Biblical God, he attacks both the false and true, as much as these appear. This may even be the harvest and the winepress.

vi: Chapter 19

The vision of Chapter 19 seems also to be an elaboration of the winepress of the Lord, announced by the last three angels of Chapter 14. Its three parts are 1) the Hallelujah chorus; 2) the Revelation of the rider on the white horse; and 3) the disposal of the Beast and False Prophet. The action follows immediately upon the destruction of Babylon in Chapters 17 and 18. The defeat and destruction of the Beast and false prophet is obviously distinguished from the fall and destruction of Babylon

The Hallelujah Chorus

[19:1-10] Next John hears what seemed to be the single loud voice of a great multitude, who praise God and the justice of the judgment of the Harlot. These announce, for the first time in the text, the marriage of the Bride and the Lamb. This is another indication that these two women are to be understood in contrast to one another. The Bride is first mentioned just after the account of the judgment of the Harlot.

The loud voice says "Hallelujah! Salvation and glory and power belong to our God." The servants of God appear praising the Lord and agreeing that his judgments are just: "He has judged the great Harlot, who corrupted the world with her fornication, and he has avenged on her the blood of his servants." The statement is past tense, clearly distinguished from the defeat of the Beast about to be shown. "Hallelujah," they say again, "The smoke from her goes up for ever and ever." Alleluia, from Hebrew, is said to mean "Praise ye Ja," Or, "Let us praise God." The twenty-four elders and the four living creatures worshiped God, who is seated on the throne, saying "Amen, Hallelujah." "Amen," spoken to voice agreement in both Greek and Hebrew, simply means "Truly." Then a voice comes from the throne, saying: "Praise our God, all you his servants, you who fear him great and small." This raises the question of where the 144,000 are in the scene. Then John again hears what is like the voice of a great multitude and the sound of many waters, with the addition that it is also like many thunders (perhaps as many as seven). This voice says:

> Hallelujah! For the Lord our God the almighty reigns
> Let us rejoice and exult and give him the glory,
> For the marriage of the Lamb has come,
> And his bride has made herself ready;
> It was granted her to be clothed with fine linen, bright and pure. For the fine linen is the righteous deeds of the saints.

An earlier voice, or voices, said that God had begun to reign (11:17). The restoration of providence may be synonymous with the marriage of the Bride and Lamb. The Bride seems to be something like the true church or redeemed mankind, clothed with the righteous deeds of the saints, though it is important too that this is not written. Here an angel tells John "write this: Blessed are those who are invited to the marriage supper of the Lamb." Those invited to the marriage supper may be different from the bride herself, but that these are blessed might suggest that these are the bride herself. If they are different from the Bride, a further extension of blessedness, including not only the Church but also her guests, may be indicated. John and the angel are called fellow servants. Angels may be included in the Bride. Then the angel said to John "These are the words of God." And it is here that John fell down at the feet of the angel to worship him. The angel tells him:

> You must not do that! I am a fellow servant with you and your brethren who hold the testimony of Jesus. Worship God. For the testimony of Jesus is the spirit of prophecy.

This scene is interesting in a number of ways. The angels are fellow servants with the men who serve god, indicating that the angels are not above us, and suggesting that the men *are* angels, or, as in the image, in heaven men become angels or like angels (21:17). We are revealed to be like angels in becoming what we are. Of the children, it is said that "in heaven their angels always behold the face of my father" (Matt. 18:10). One wonders if one's own immortal soul were not his guardian angel. So the multitudes of angels into the sixth seal around the throne may somehow be related to the multitudes seen with palm branches (5:11; 7:9), though there are myriads of each. A second interesting point is that we are not to bow down before our fellow servant. A third is that the holy John himself has erred on this point, and been corrected, by an angel.

[19: 11-16] So, Babylon has fallen and is punished before Armageddon, and the scene that follows upon the invitation to the wedding is the feast of the birds and wild animals on the flesh of the armies of the Beast.

Now for the third time, John sees the heaven opened. He has seen a door (4:1) and the vision of the throne and of the temple open in heaven (11:19). Here when he sees the heavens opened, he sees the son of man, Jesus the Messiah, and his army of saints prepared to come for the battle with the sea and land beasts, the Beast and the false prophet. Something like this was foreseen amid the six angels of Chapter 14 (14:14-16), when one like a son of man came on the clouds. John sees, and says behold, a white horse! Without naming him, he describes him:

> He who sat upon it is called Faithful and True, and in righteousness he judges and makes war. His eyes are like the flame of fire, and on his head are many diadems; and he has a name inscribed which no one knows but himself. He is clad in a robe dipped in blood, and the name by which he is called is the Word of God. And the armies of heaven, arrayed in fine linen, white and pure, followed him on white horses. From his mouth issues a sharp sword, with which to smite the

nations, and he will rule them with a rod of iron; he will tread the winepress of the fury of the wrath of God the almighty. On his throne and on his thigh he has a name inscribed: King of Kings and Lord of Lords.

Jude writes that Enoch prophesied: "Behold, the Lord came with his holy myriads, to execute judgment on all, and to convict all the ungodly..." Enoch wrote in the seventh generation from Adam.[117] Zechariah too writes: "Then the Lord your God will come, and all the holy ones with him." The many diadems on his head remind one of the ten diadems on the ten horns of the Beast. This is a rare suggestion that there are certain nations with him for the battle. But, as the Beast has ten horns with diadems, and these are sovereignties, so the word of God has sovereignties. He has a hidden name that only he knows, although his open name, in addition to faithful and true, is "The Word of God." The name written on the white stone, received by him who conquers, is like this name in that it is known only to he who has it. As he appeared from the start, "his eyes were like a flame of fire" (1:14). The open name "Word of God" is also in the opening of John's gospel, though it would be more correct to say that John uses the "characteristic phrasing and diction" from the vision, rather than the reverse. The armies of heaven are those who washed their robes in the blood of the Lamb, or who have been given white robes, and it seems significant that linen was just mentioned in relation to deeds or righteous actions. The white horses may symbolize the purity of the body and spiritedness of these, and they appear like the knights of the temple, as though the medieval knights dressed intentionally for the part. It is not said that those who come with him fight, but he conquers by the word. The sword that issues from his mouth was said to be two edged (1:16), and is elsewhere said to be the word (Ephesians 6:17), as the word both kills and brings to life. Yet it would be surprising if the literal meaning of the winepress were bloodless. That he will touch the Mount of Olives and tread the winepress is the only indication that his feet touch the earth. The rod or crook of iron presents a similar question, since, if it means what it says,

On the Revelation

it seems to suggest despotic and very forceful rule. The rod of iron may be the major obstacle to the attempt to argue that the messianic kingdom is not a world empire. The final name of the description, inscribed on his robe and on his thigh, indicates that he is the king of earthly kings and the Lord of other Lords. The rod of iron may be used in the destruction of diabolical evil, as the Nazis were once already defeated and pursued afterward, as the court sat in judgment. The saints are said to participate too in this rule with the iron rod.

Is this the appearance prophesied by Zechariah, when his feet split the Mount of Olives and the nations recognize him and mourn? The prospect of imminent defeat in the refutation of the Beast might lead his armies to fall apart on their own, accomplishing the victory by his Revelation. This would be especially so if the Beast taught, and even half believed, that He did not exist. The appearance of the one on the white horse contradicts that the Beast is God, and this may cause his collapse, as though his power depended on this illusion. This is the smashing of the statue on its feet of clay by the stone cut by no human hand, which is the Word of God (Daniel 2:34-35; Scofield, p. 1348).

> At the latter end of their rule, when the transgressors have reached their full measure, a king of bold countenance, one who understands riddles, shall arise. His power shall be great, and he shall cause fearful destruction, and shall succeed in what he does, and destroy mighty men and the people of the saints. By his cunning, he shall make deceit prosper under his hand, and in his own mind he shall magnify himself. Without warning he shall destroy many; and he shall even rise up against the prince of princes; but, by no human hand, he shall be broken (8:23-25).

[19:17-21] After the Revelation of the one on the white horse, an angel is seen standing in the sun. He calls all the birds that fly in mid-heaven to come to eat the flesh of all men, described as seven kinds: kings, captains, mighty men, horses, their riders, slaves and freemen. The list is very similar to that at the sixth trumpet catastrophe, where it is kings, generals, rich and strong, slave and free (6:15). Horses are added, and there are other slight changes from the people that hid after the earthquake. Has there been a devolution following the earthquake, so that the battle is literally fought with horses? The last word in the prophecy of Isaiah (66:24) is this feast:

> And they shall go forth and look on the dead bodies of the men that have rebelled against me; for their worm shall not die, their fire shall not be quenched, and they shall be an abhorrence to all flesh.

John saw the beasts and the kings of the earth gathered with their armies to make war on the "Him who sits upon the white horse," and against his army. The battle is uneventful, or not described in detail. The beast and the false prophet are not killed but captured, and thrown alive into the Lake of Fire. The rest, the nations and armies that accompanied the Beast and the false prophet, are slain with the sword that issues from his mouth, and "all the birds were gorged with their flesh." This seems to be the same as the event of the winepress described in Chapter 14, where blood covers the ground to the height of the bridle of a horse (14:20).

Isaiah writes: and he shall smite the earth with the rod of his mouth, and with the breath of his lips he shall slay the wicked" (11:4). An example of slaying with the word is in Hosea 6:5-6:

> Therefore I have hewn them by the prophets
> I have slain them with the word of my mouth
> And my judgment goes forth as the light.
> For I desire mercy, not sacrifice;
> The knowledge of God rather than burnt offerings.

Elsewhere, at 2 Thessalonians 2:8:

And the Lord Jesus will slay him with the breath of his mouth
And destroy him with the brightness of his coming (*parousias*).

When Jesus returns at the battle of Armageddon he slays with the word, rather than with weapons. It is possible that the nations gathered against Jerusalem and the Antichrist become confused and destroy one another. While the word is not a literal but a symbolic weapon, the armies of the beast are literally slain. This may be related to how the Voice of God can be visible, or by His Word He creates. The divine does not need weapons.

The history leading up to the Revelation is described by the prophets in some detail. In an oracle against Babylon, Isaiah wrote:

> …hark, and uproar of kingdoms
> Of nations gathering together!
> The Lord of hosts is mustering a host for battle
> They come from a distant land,
> From the end of the heavens,
> The Lord and the weapons of his indignation,
> To destroy the whole earth.

Then the stars, sun and moon are darkened, the earth shaken from its place, and men made more rare than fine gold (Isaiah 13: 10-13). Zechariah (14:2-5) writes:

> For I will gather all the nations against Jerusalem to battle, and the city shall be taken…half of the city shall go into exile, but the rest of the people shall not be cut off from the city. Then the Lord will go forth and fight against those nations, as when he fights on a day of battle. On that day, his feet shall stand on the Mount of Olives which lies before Jerusalem on the east; and the Mount of Olives shall be split in two from east to west by a very wide valley, so that one half of the Mount

> shall withdraw northward, and the other half southward. And the valley of my mountains shall be stopped up, for the valley of the mountains shall touch the side of it. And you shall flee as you fled from the earthquake in the days of Uzziah king of Judah. Then the Lord your God will come, and all the holy ones with him.

It is "the Lord" whose feet will stand on the Mount of Olives, and here all Israel will see that the Messiah is the Lord. Zechariah (14:12-14) describes the plague that strikes the armies that come against Jerusalem:

> Their flesh shall rot off while they are still on their feet, their eyes shall rot in their sockets, and their tongues shall rot in their mouths And on that day a great panic from the Lord shall fall on them, so that each will lay hold on the hand of his fellow, and the hand of one will be raised against the hand of the other; even Judah will fight against Jerusalem...

And Joel (3:2) writes:

> ...I will gather all the nations and bring them down to the valley of Jehoshaphat, and I will enter into Judgment with them there, on account of my people and my heritage Israel, because they have scattered them among the nations, and have divided up my land, and have cast lots for my people, and have given a boy for a harlot, and have sold a girl for wine, and have drunk it.

Jehoshaphat is traditionally identified with the Kidron valley, just east of Jerusalem. Armageddon is toward the coast, northwest of Jerusalem, about fifty miles. The sun and moon are darkened around this time, and there may here be the earthquake and plague that occurs with the seventh bowl. Already the followers

On the Revelation

of the Beast have been smitten with sores in the first bowl, and scorched by the sun in the fifth bowl.

The mention of the Beast when it is thrown alive into the lake of fire (19:20) is the first definite statement implying that the Beast is alive following the mortal wound that appeared to be healed, or following Chapter 13. Prior to this mention, it was possible that the false prophet was exercising the rule of the Beast that appeared slain.

What has apparently occurred since the time that he appeared is that he has taken over ten nations, and rules a revived Roman Empire. When he becomes tyrant over the empire, he may be both the seventh head and an eighth horn. At the middle of the seven year period, there is a great persecution of Christians, and all the nations gather at Jerusalem for battle. Van Impe and others assert with assurance that he will enter with a seven year peace plan for the Middle East, and this peace will be broken in the middle.

> And he shall make a strong covenant with many for one week; and for half of the week, he shall cause sacrifice and offering to cease; and upon the wing of abominations shall come one who makes desolate, until the decreed end is poured out upon the desolator.
>
> Daniel 9:27

It is especially the conclusion of Daniel that is thought to describe things regarding the reign of the Beast. From the profanation of the temple and the abomination that makes desolate, it is said that he will magnify himself above every God. It is also said that he will honor not the god of his fathers but the god of fortresses, or "forces," and will "deal with the strongest fortresses by the help of a foreign god" (11:39). This last part would fit if he were to use Islam against Christendom.[118] He will give rule to those who honor him, and "shall divide the land for a price" (11:39). Van Impe reads the division of the land here in relation to the contemporary question of the division of Israel to include a place for the Palestinians who are able to live with Israel.[119] Van Impe considers the last five lines of Daniel 11 (40-45) to describe the end of the Beast:

> "At the time of the end the king of the south shall attack him, but the king of the north shall rush upon him like a whirlwind...He shall come into the glorious land. And tens of thousands shall fall, but these shall be delivered out of his hand: Edom and Moab and the main part of the Ammonites. He shall stretch out his hand against the countries, and the land of Egypt shall not escape. He shall become ruler of the treasures of gold and of silver, and all the precious things of Egypt; and the Libyans and the Ethiopians shall follow in his train. But tidings from the east and the north shall alarm him, and he shall go forth with great fury to exterminate and utterly destroy many. And he shall pitch his palatial tents between the sea and the glorious holy mountain; yet he shall come to his end, with none to help him.

The statements regarding Antiochus in Chapter 11 of Daniel increasingly become statements about the Beast, just as occurred in Chapter 7. It is interesting to read this backwards, looking for the point at which this convergence might begin. The abomination of desolation is one such point, where the account of Antiochus merges into the prophecy of the Beast (11:31). He rules Egypt by conquest, and has as allies Ethiopia and Libya. Cush and Put may well indicate much of Africa. He does not attack, and so may be allied with, Edom and Moab, and one wonders if these are related to the Palestinians.

It may be safe to say that if the Ethiopians are with Gog coming against Israel, they revolt from Gog here, unless of course the Beast *is* Gog of Magog. This is because the Ethiopians are with him when the king of the North rushes against him. Many will fall in what is a sudden or surprise persecution: "Without warning he shall destroy many"... (8:25) and the horn "made war with the saints, and prevailed over them." (7:21). Again, what is foretold appears to be a mass martyrdom of the people of the biblical God, at the hands of the Beast, when the kings of the East move their armies toward the Euphrates, and the king of the North also comes at him like a whirlwind. There will, though, be survivors, and some will escape.

He apparently has a sort of world government, but in the three frogs (16:13-14) we see from comparison to our world that there may be three ideologies that lead the armies to gather at Armageddon. It seems that what is written in Daniel (7:23), that the fourth kingdom would "devour the whole earth" might be *ancient* Rome, since out of this kingdom ten kings arise, before three are put down by the little horn. It is contradicted when all the nations come against him, though it may be that these revolt after the mark of the Beast is instituted. Universal rule is suggested only by the statement in the thirteenth chapter of the Revelation, that authority was given it over every tribe and people and tongue and nation, and that *all* tribes, peoples, tongues and *nations*, would worship him, everyone who dwells on the earth, except those whose names were written in the book of life of the Lamb (13:7-8). This may be similar to saying that those with life in them will see through the things that captivate and deceive the lot of humanity concerned with money, power and worldly advancement. Its authority might be trans-political, something like the way modern science holds authority over nearly every people amid the political authorities, which are something different.

The gathering of all the nations (Zech 14:2) surrounds the question of Jerusalem:

> Lo, I am about to make Jerusalem a cup of reeling to all the peoples round about; it will be against Judah also in the siege against Jerusalem. On that day I will make Jerusalem a heavy stone for all the peoples; all who lift it shall grievously hurt themselves. And all the nations of the earth will come together against it.

Revelation Chapter Nineteen

Here we see again the Jews or tribe of Judah is against Jerusalem, and the possibility is increased that the Beast controls Jerusalem. The eye of prophecy is especially sensitive to Jerusalem and to the martyrs, as though the window to the seeing of these things were through what occurs to Jerusalem and to the martyrs. The wonder is not that more is not seen, but rather that anything can be seen at all of these things.

There is surprisingly little detail presented in the Revelation regarding the battle in which the Beast and False Prophet are defeated. The prophecy of Ezekiel regarding Gog and Magog is read as referring to a pre-millennial battle, and as we will see, this looks very much like the battle concluded by the second coming in Chapter 19 of the Revelation. But Gog and Magog are mentioned in the Revelation only regarding the *post*-millennial battle, and this is described very briefly (20:7-10): Satan loosed deceives Gog and Magog, the nations that are at the four corners of the earth, and they *again* surround Jerusalem. Here, Jerusalem is, at the close of the millennium, "the camp of the saints and the beloved city." By contrast, in the pre-millennial battle, there may have been the abomination in the temple. In the circumstances of Armageddon, it is a question central to our reading of the scene, whether, when the whole world comes against Jerusalem, the Beast is ruling there, rather than the saints. In the post-millennium battle, they are consumed by fire from heaven, and the Devil is thrown into the lake of fire where the Beast and false prophet *were,* where they apparently had been since the start of the millennium. So, while the Beast and false prophet are defeated here in Chapter 19, the Dragon is apparently not yet finally defeated. It is very to difficult to see what this might mean.

The battle of Gog and Magog after the millennium is distinct from the first battle, as it seems, and if we think the millennium will occur, we can consider how we are to distinguish the pre-millennial and post-millennial battles in the prophecy of Gog and Magog in Ezekiel (38-39). Fire from heaven is common to both, as Ezekiel writes "I will send fire on Gog and Magog, and on those who dwell securely in the coastlands, and they shall know that I am the Lord" (Ezekiel 39:6). What is common to Chapter

19 and the prophecy in Ezekiel is the feast of birds and wild animals that is described as a sacrificial feast (Ezekiel 39:17; Revelation 19:17). It is difficult in prophecy to distinguish the things that pertain 1) to the incarnation, resurrection and fall of Jerusalem, 2) the pre-millennial wars surrounding the battle of Armageddon, and 3) the post-millennial truly final battle. The question draws us into a three dimensional picture of these great changes, and humbles us, we who study these things. As Jewish scholars have had difficulty separating the prophecies regarding the incarnation and the second coming of the Messiah, so Christian scholars will have difficulty separating out the pre-millennium and post millennium occurrences. The church, or, the people of Yahweh, will be different in the millennium, with the olive branch of the Jews and the respect of Jewish thought restored, and Gentiles included, from every sort of people.

After describing the restoration of Israel, Ezekiel is told to set his face toward Gog, of the land of Magog, the chief prince of Meshech and Tubal, and prophesy against him." The identification of Magog with Russia is not obvious, and needs to be demonstrated, because it is not the nation most obvious to the prophets themselves, to whom the utter parts of the north might mean the Assyrian, and the kings of the East, the Persian or even Babylonian. The Oxford note to Ezekiel 38 and 39 states: Since the foe from the north in Jeremiah (25.9) and Ezekiel (26.7) was Babylon, it is probable that the foe here described is a grandiose surrogate for Babylon..." The identification suggested is (p. 1049):

> ...Gog, king of Magog, both unidentified, though the general location is to the north. Meshech, Assyrian "Mushku," south of Gomer...Tubal, Assyrian "Tabal," south of Beth-togarmah...Cush, Ethiopia, Put [with Cush, Ethiopia], Gomer, Assyrian, "Gimirrai," Cimmerians in central Asia Minor (Gen. 10.2-3). Beth-togarmah, Assyrian "Tilgarimmu, east of the southernmost Halys River...

Tubal and Meshek are trading partners with Tyre (Ezekiel 27:13). They are elsewhere mentioned in the table of nations of Genesis 10. Magog, Tubal and Mechek are three of seven sons of Japheth, the son of Noah. The others are Gomer, Madai, Javan and Tiras, north of Israel and Mesopotamia. On the map printed in some Bibles, Javan is Greece; Gomer the area of the Ukraine, Tubal is placed south of the black sea, in Turkey, and, Tiras is the area of Yugoslavia, Hungary and Romania. They may easily have spread north from Ararat and around from there, to become the nations at the four corners of the world. The "Caucasian" Europeans are likely to be descendants of Japheth, rather than Shemites or Hammites, who would be the Semitic and African peoples respectively. Asian, Pacific island and American peoples are either unknown to Genesis, or derived from these. Scofield, (1909, p. 833) notes:

> ... That the "primary reference" in Ezekiel 38:2-3 "is...to the northern (European) powers, headed up by Russia, all agree. The whole passage should be read in connection with Zech. 12.1-4; 14.1-9; Mt. 24.14-30; Rev. 14.14-20; 19. 17-21. "Gog" is the prince of Magog, his land. The reference to Meshech and Tubal (Moscow and Tobolsk) is a clear mark of identification. Russia and the northern powers have been the latest persecutors of dispersed Israel...

Van Impe often states that a longitude line drawn north from Israel goes through the center of Moscow. He, Gog, is told that the Lord will "put hooks into your jaws," as though he were the sea beast, and "I will bring you forth...Persia, Cush and Put are with them...Gomer (Cimmeria) and all his hordes; Bethtogarmah (Turkey?) from the uttermost parts of the north with all his hordes, many peoples are with you" (38:4-6). "In the latter years, you will go against the land that is restored from war, the land where people were gathered from many nations and now dwell securely" (38:8). Then, as Isaiah wrote: "In that day, the Lord with his hard and great and strong sword will punish Leviathan the fleeing serpent, Leviathan the twisting serpent, and he will slay the dragon that is in the sea."

The destruction of Gog of Magog looks much like a description of the battle that is Armageddon in the nineteenth chapter of the Revelation. This has been done so that He might vindicate his holiness before their eyes, and has been long prophesied (38:16-17). There will indeed be a great earthquake in Israel, and worldwide, and "all the men that are upon the face of the earth shall quake at my presence, and the mountains shall be thrown down...every man's sword shall be against his brother...torrential rains and hailstones, fire and brimstone...I will give you to the birds of prey of every sort and to the wild beasts to be devoured" (38:20-39:8). For seven years, the people of Israel make fires of the weapons, which we do not believe are literally shields and bucklers and such. For seven years they will be burying the corpses in a cemetery of Gog. Ezekiel is told to summon the birds for a sacrificial feast (39:17), the same as that in Revelation 19. "You shall eat the flesh of the mighty and drink the blood of the princes of the earth." There follows in Ezekiel the measuring of the temple.

It is obvious that the world is not destroyed here, in one sense, since there is clean up work occurring for seven years. This seven years may extend into the start of the millennium.

Citing the Midrash Tehillim, Jack Van Impe and Hal Lindsey distinguish three phases of the battle. "There will be three different attacks against Jerusalem at the time of the end." (Van Impe, 1998, p. 206). Van Impe considers the attack of Gog to be the first of these three waves. The first begins when Russia attacks Israel, and is "bombed back to Siberia." Here Van Impe cites Joel (2:20, Ibid, p. 207). The second is indicated by Daniel (11:44), when the Beast must turn back from a campaign in Egypt because of news that the armies of the east and what is left of Russia, the 200 million man army, is approaching. Van Impe then has him killed by Russia, and resurrected to rule for 3 and one-half years in Jerusalem (Ibid, p. 207-208). A third phase is identified as the battle of Christ and the Antichrist that ends in Armageddon (Ibid, p. 209).

Van Impe's reading is interesting for its detail, as well as for the explanation of how Daniel and the Revelation fit together. If the death of the Beast at Daniel 11:45 is the death from which the mortal wound on one of the heads of the Beast seems healed, and the second half of the Tribulation period were then to begin, with the abomination, things would fall into place. It would make sense how the rule of the Beast becomes worldwide and yet Russia and the Kings of the East come against Jerusalem, and why it is said after the end of Chapter 11 *"At that time*, there will be a time of trouble, such as there has never been since there was a nation (12:1). One would think that the time of the greatest trouble would have passed. But from the time the continual burnt offering is taken away to the abomination would be 1290, that is, thirty days into the second half of the tribulation, and those who wait and come to 1,335 days, 75 days into the second half, are called blessed. This, though, may conflict with the reading that none of the blessed will see the second half of the tribulation.

That "all the world" should come against Israel would make more sense if the Antichrist were to rule from Jerusalem, though we now see one third or half the world as though it were being gathered, as by the three frogs of 16:13, to do just this: to attack Israel. It has become imaginable that Europe would again come against Israel, if there were an attempt to impose a settlement of the wars with the Arab world, or, especially, if the Nazis were to reemerge. The resilience of the Nazis, or of fascism, as in the presence of various groups in the U.S from prison gangs to the Klan and Order and Aryan Nations, make this appear to be a possibility. We, too, hold that Europe has not overcome the spiritual tensions that led to the emergence of the Nazis in Germany. Europe is now shockingly atheistic, as the result of entertaining modernity, the torch of the Reformation, and philosophy. Greece has a fascist group called "Golden Dawn." There is a dark undercurrent, evident in the persistence of archaic anti-Semitism as well as in the worst strains of modern art and music to emerge from there. Germany and England host a neo-Nazi punk movement, while Norway hosts a strain of satanic heavy metal to make the American seem marginal and tame. Carl Jung teaches that the artists show what is emerging in the

On the Revelation

collective mind of a people, and Plato, that changes in music foreshadow changes in the regime (*Republic*, IV, 424c). Yet there is plenty of fine music too, both human and divine.

The nations are gathered from the four corners of the world, which would seem to include the United States, assuming that we are not in the third of the world that may have been destroyed. Scofield states: "Prophecy does not concern itself with history as such, but only with history as it affects Israel and the Holy Land" (1909, p. 918). For this reason, it is not clear what the United States might be doing in such a battle. Attempts to describe the role of America in prophecy seem to me a hoax. The United States, and indeed the allied nations, would defend Israel against such an attack, and so we might be included in the nations that are at the four corners of the world, gathering for such a battle. We might also join the other nations to come against the Antichrist. One can see all the nations very rationally moving toward the great gathering, and we could find ourselves there as soldiers, even as the just entered into the Second World War. And here we should recall the statement that if anyone slay or takes captive, he will be slain or taken captive (Revelation 13:10, citing Jeremiah 15:2). Is this a teaching of end times pacifism? That the United States come *against* Israel is not yet imaginable, and the hope is that we will continue to share the blessing of the nations that help, and avoid the curse of those who come against Israel (Numbers 24:9; Genesis 12:3; Deuteronomy 32:8-10). In this way, the beginning of these wars could only occur if the United States were no longer a power, as though some catastrophe, an earthquake, power outage or surprise attack had made us ineffective. And if this were to occur, one could see the elements remaining in the worldwide balance of power all working toward this event and this conclusion. Europe tends by itself toward fascism. The North East and East are Communist, and the Islamic world, oblivious to their inner conflict with atheistic communism, already intends the destruction of Israel. If we are still here, we as a nation would be much as we were in World War II, and this may be the third war of this series. Russia will not see this prophecy, and walk into its result, nor will the Arab world see the prophecy against he who harms Ariel, the "apple" of his "eye" (Zechariah 2:8; Deuteronomy 32:10). It would be wonderful if the Islamic world would see this and simply become a good neighbor. But Islam does not have access to the prophecies, or these are ignored. The Russians similarly do not seem to be able to see these prophecies, or, one would think, they might just not attack Israel, and avoid their own destruction. But this would be as likely an occurrence as Hitler seeing his own prophesied destruction and avoiding it: the ability to see these things is opposite the nations and characters that fall into them and bring them about.

It is possible that the end of the Beast is described in the fourteenth chapter of Isaiah. In the context of a taunting of Babylon, it is written (14:12-19):

> How you are fallen from heaven, O Day star, son of Dawn!
> How you are cut to the ground, you who laid the nations low!
> You said in your heart, "I will ascend to heaven; above the stars of God
> I will set my throne on high;
> I will sit on the mount of assembly in the far north;
> I will ascend above the heights of the clouds,
> I will make myself like the Most High."
> But you are brought down to Sheol, to the depths of the pit.
> Those who see you will stare at you,
> And ponder over you;
> "Is this the man that made the earth tremble? Who shook kingdoms,
> Who made the world like a desert
> And overthrew its cities, who did not let his prisoners go home?"
> All the kings of the nations lie in glory, each in his own tomb;
> But you are cast away from your sepulcher,
> Like a loathed and untimely birth

On the Revelation

> Clothed with the slain, those pierced by the sword
> Who go down to the stones of the pit, like a dead
> body trodden under foot
> You will not be joined with them in burial,
> Because you have destroyed your land,
> You have slain your people.

The conclusion of the prophecy against Tyre in Ezekiel also reminds of the death of one who said "I am God" (Ez. 28: 9-10):

> Will you still say, 'I am a god,' in the presence of those who slay you,
> Though you are but a man and no god,
> In the hands of those who wound you?
> You shall die the death of the uncircumcised
> By the hand of foreigners;
> For I have spoken, says the Lord God.

This prophecy is against Babylon and Assyria, but these prophecies open out into the foreseeing of the day of the Lord and the coming of the Kingdom. As Ezekiel writes (14:26):

> This is the purpose that is purposed
> Concerning the whole earth;
> And this is the hand that is stretched out
> Over all the nations:

One of the clearer summaries of what is here occurring is found in the *Didache*. The increase in iniquity will lead men to hate, persecute and betray one another, demonstrating the connection between lust and cruelty. "And then the world deceiver will appear in the guise of God's son. He will work "signs and wonders" and the earth will fall into his hands and he will commit outrages such as have never occurred before. Then mankind will come to the fiery trial, "and many will fall away" and perish, "but those who persevere" in their faith "will be saved" by "the curse himself," which may mean the one hung on the cross. Then there will appear the "signs" of the truth; first the sign of hands stretched out in heaven, then the sign of "a trumpets blast," and thirdly the resurrection of the dead, though not of all the dead, but as it has been said: "The Lord will come, and all his saints with him." Then the world will see the Lord coming on the clouds of the sky."

In the twelfth chapter of Daniel, the prophet is told that at that time, Michael, "the great prince who has charge of your people" will arise. It is the time of the worst trouble since there was a nation, but that his people will be delivered, "Every one whose name shall be found written in the book" (12:1). Apparently ignoring the millennium, he says that many in the earth will then rise, "some to everlasting life and some to shame and everlasting contempt" (12:2). This may be the best scriptural support for reading the millennium as instantaneous. In a very hopeful note, Daniel is then told (12:3):

> And those that are wise shall shine like the brightness of the firmament, and those who turn many to righteousness, like the stars for ever and ever...

And when he asks "How long?" and "What will be the issue of these things," he is told (12:9-10):

> Go thy way, Daniel, for the words are shut up and sealed until the time of the end. Many shall purify themselves, and make themselves white, and be refined; but the wicked shall do wickedly; and none of the wicked shall understand; but those who are wise shall understand...

One practical suggestion is to consider how we would respond to an attack on Rome, and the emergence of genocidal enemies of Israel and the free nations, which tend to be Christian. It is good policy, when two possibilities appear, to prepare for both.

Another point of policy is to consider how we will uphold the human character should civilization break down, and protect ourselves and others from the animal that will arise in man. In political theory, we consider the self-interest that, as Hobbes and Locke imply, lies beneath all civilization. What will most men do, especially in our age, if the power goes out and there is no food? The earthbound vision of Hobbes is impressed by how thin the civilized character is revealed to be when most are put to the test, as by siege or civil war. Yet it is possible to remind us of the "better angels of our nature." And here one can see the benefit of the liberal arts and the cultivation of the human character. After World War II, Jung wrote regarding the effect of the mob on individual restraint. We, however, can resolve to remain human, band together with others who make a similar decision, and guide our bands to uphold humanity when disasters occur. We can foresee these challenges, and, like the Pilgrims with the benefit of hindsight, take steps to prevent the worst of these things.

Another such question is regarding the mark of the Beast, and how although it may seem sufficient to lie in giving allegiance, one suspects it may be worse for those who do take the mark, even in the world. They might escape torture to be altered and enlisted in the service of torture, only to suffer the sores and other things as bad as torture. We conclude that even children ought to be taught not to take the mark.

It is often said that prophecy is useless, since we cannot know what is to occur, but only see in hindsight that an occurrence was prophesied. One part of the answer to this is that when a prophesied thing occurs, we gain comfort, understanding and stability by knowing that it was foreseen, and is part of a larger picture, a bit more of the meaning of which might then appear. Imagine attempting to understand the horrors of the modern tyrannies with neither political theory nor the apocalyptic prophecies. Even if there were no connection between these two, holocaust and apocalypse, to know that such things can occur, that it is known that these things can occur, and are even prophesied to occur, is a great benefit. As is written in Daniel, "he will go forth to persecute many" and "wear out the saints of the Most High" (7:25). Many Jews lost faith on the question of how the Almighty God could allow such a thing. Must he allow that the birth of his Messiah result in the slaughter of the innocents, as recorded in Matthew, was done by Herod (Mt. 2:16-

18)? All that can be said is that in asking the question, we assume something about the divine that is not so, namely the he is such that it makes sense to ask why he allows them. What appears is that human suffering is more significant to *us* than to eternity, and the world yields a harvest from amid the thorns of accident and malice. It is apparently the work of man, through government, to protect the rights of the people from the self interest and malice of the people. This seems even to be the great work of civilization, common to every political order: crime fighting and the prevention of tyranny, as when the strong oppress the weaker. It is difficult to do this if the government is also engaged in things that are not its business, ruling the people as though it were God, or worse, using its authority and office to fleece the people or practice malice, harming the rights that government is intended to defend. And it is difficult to see these things even with the comfort of prophecy. There is a sense in which the Lord had not yet begun to reign, if it also must be said that it is because we rejected Him, or do not invite Him to reign. Let us return the earth to the Lord!

Another part of the answer to the value of prophecy is the comprehensive picture of foreign policy accessible through the texts. It is at first useful to read so that one is not blown about by the winds of things said to relate to these matters. Yet the Bible does provide a background for understanding, for example why so much of world politics swirls around Jerusalem. The four thousand year history of these nations and their interrelations is accessible through the history and prophecy of the Bible. It is also significant that the statue is destroyed by no human hand, and earthly armies are not called to battle the Beast, but rather, to refuse the mark and face martyrdom. The ridiculousness of those who arm themselves as though to fight for Jesus out of the Biblical prophesies is apparent. Much of this will happen as by necessity. Russia is not going to see the prophecy and simply avoid attacking Israel, nor the people through education just not fall for tyranny and the Beast. Nations will act as nations do, but it is a marvel that their development was foreseen. The sense in which we cannot influence these affairs indicates what limited things might be done by human action and foresight. Nations can also do what it is right for nations to do.

vii: Chapter 20: The Millennium

It is the twentieth chapter that presents difficulty of the millennium. Again, this is the only place in scripture where a thousand year reign of the saints with Christ is foretold. The difficulty would not appear if the thousand years were simultaneous with the events of the judgment of Babylon and the defeat of the earth and sea beast described in Chapter 19. But the impression is that the events are successive, and that when the Devil is finally bound and thrown into the pit, the two beasts are already in the lake of fire, having been defeated in the winepress of Armageddon. And it is clear in what follows that the saints have already been beheaded. While James was beheaded by Herod Agrippa, these saints are those beheaded during the reign of the beasts, for refusing to take the mark. Here we are told for the first time that those killed in Chapter 13 were beheaded. We are eerily reminded of the method of execution favored by Islamic warriors against the United States and the West, and should they gain the power to do these things, they may have the intention to do them.

[20:1-3] John sees an angel descend holding a key to the bottomless pit and a great chain. This scene is similar to the fifth trumpet, when a star fell from heaven and was given the key to the shaft of the bottomless pit (9:1-2). The Beast that arises from the sea is also said to arise from the abyss. Here, the angel seizes the dragon, "who is the Devil and Satan," and "bound him for a thousand years, and threw him into the pit, and shut it and sealed it over him, that he should deceive the nations no more, till the thousand years were ended. After that, he must be loosed a while." The loosing means he *is* able to deceive the nations.

[20:4-6] There follows a separate vision of those to whom judgment was committed, something like the 24 elders with 24 thrones (4:4). Jesus said to the Apostles that they would sit on twelve thrones, judging the twelve tribes of Israel (Matthew

19:28; Luke 22:30). With these, John sees the souls of those beheaded for their testimony to Jesus and the word of God, who had not worshiped the Beast nor received the mark on their foreheads or their hands. There follows the description of the millennial reign:

> "They came to life, and reigned with Christ a thousand years. The rest of the dead did not come to life until the thousand years were ended. This is the first resurrection. Blessed and holy is he who shares in the first resurrection! Over such, the second death has no power, but they shall be priests of God and of Christ, and they shall reign with him a thousand years."

The reading of these two resurrections is crucial, and very difficult. The Baptist teaching assumes that all the saved are raised here to rule during the millennium, while the "rest of the dead" judged in the Great White Throne Judgment (Lindsey, 1998, p. 279) are those who are to suffer damnation. The "rest of the dead" would seem not to include the Twelve Apostles, if these are among the twenty-four elders, so that at least these are also alive with the beheaded during the millennium. It seems that those raptured, as we read, at the seventh trumpet, are not among the dead at all. Paul writes: then the dead in Christ shall rise, then we who are alive..." The place of those raptured in the Revelation of John may even be when He comes, at 19:19, "his army," on the clouds with his saints (Zechariah 14:5). Do these too "share in the first resurrection," if they are raptured and not martyred? The text does not address the raptured, but if the resurrection and rapture have occurred when those beheaded are raised, it would seem that they and the dead in Christ, raised just before them, are, according to the Baptist reading, not judged in the Last Judgment.

That some are saved during the millennium and judged at the last judgment would mean that the latter cannot be identified with the resurrection of judgment in contrast with the judgment of life. Those saved might somehow not die, but otherwise, these would be among "the rest of the dead," though they would not yet have lived and died when those beheaded are raised. These may have been somehow in the earth and sky that fled away before the sea and Death and Hades gave up the dead in them (20:13).

The reading of this chapter has given rise to three distinct opinions in the division of modern theology called eschatology. In a fine summary by John E. Walvoord, "Some take it we are in the millennium now (a-millennialism); others expect it to come to pass in the future before Christ comes (post-millennialism); still others expect that Christ must return first before this kingdom can come (pre-millennialism). Aune associates these readings with different sects: Following Augustine, Catholic, Reformed and Presbyterian Churches hold a-millennialism, Lutherans hold a postmillennialism, while the pre-millennialists are the Dispensationalists (p. 1089) and the early Chiliasts. And so, if these things were obvious or easy to settle on from the text, these three different readings would not exist. The first two hold that the thousand years is symbolic, and not literally a thousand year period of time, while the Dispensationalists and the early chiliasts look for a literal millennium.

St. Augustine finds the key to this passage in the understanding that the first resurrection is spiritual, and not bodily, while the second is bodily, and not the resurrection of the spirit (*City of God*, XX. 6-9). Victorinus also writes: There are two resurrections. But the first resurrection is now of the souls that are by the faith, which does not permit men to pass over to the second death." If this, the rebirth in life that baptism is, or is an image of, is this "first resurrection," then it could be understood that all Christians participate in the millennial kingdom. But this would mean that all these are those beheaded, in some symbolic sense. Augustine writes that the binding of the Devil occurred with the spread of the church, following the crucifixion and resurrection. The binding of Satan occurred when the church began to spread (p. 43 above), and the first resurrection is the birth of souls out of the world. In the sixth section of his twentieth chapter, Augustine explains a line from the Gospel of John, "The hour is coming and now is, when the dead shall hear the voice of the Son of God; and they that hear shall live…(John 5: 22-24). Augustine comments:

> As yet He does not speak of the second resurrection, that is the resurrection of the body, which shall be in the end, but of the first, which now is. It is for the sake of making this distinction that He says, "The hour is coming, and now is." Now this resurrection regards not the body, but the soul…For in this first resurrection none have a part save those who shall be eternally blessed; but in the second, of which he goes on to speak, all.

In John, Jesus goes on: "Do not marvel at this: for the hour is coming in which all that are in their graves shall hear His voice and come forth, those who have done good to the resurrection of life, and those who have done evil to the resurrection of judgment" (5:28-29). This famous argument, perhaps the most influential in the history of commentary on the Revelation, is worth citing at even more length than what follows:

> …So there are two resurrections, the one the first and spiritual resurrection, which has place in this life, and preserves us from coming into the second death; the other the second, which does not occur now, but in the end of the world, and which is of the body, not of the soul, and which by the last judgment will dismiss some into the second death, others into that life which has no death.
> …The evangelist John has spoken of these two resurrections in the book which is called the Apocalypse, but in such a way that some Christians do not understand the first of the two, and so construe the passage into ridiculous fancies.
>
> *City of God*, XX.6-7

It seems that the ridiculous fancy to which he refers includes the belief in something like a bodily resurrection during a literal millennium, and literally not taking the mark of the Beast.

But the first resurrection in Chapter 20 of the Revelation is not baptism. Rather, it is something different: the raising of the martyrs who refused the mark of the Beast.

One difficulty is that as angels can fall, it is apparently possible for some of the saints to be conquered or to fall. Baptism, then, or being saved would not prevent the second death with certainty, while the second death has no power over the martyrs beheaded and literally raised. This may be because of their literal victory in facing literal death, so that unlike the baptized as a whole, these can no longer become like fallen angels. This martyrdom would then be like a sacrament. Each of the sacraments are based on mysteries of the soul.

Augustine then cites the entire text of Revelation 20:1-6, and comments:

> Those who, on the strength of this first passage, have suspected that the first resurrection is future and bodily, have been moved, among other things, specially by the number of a thousand years, as if it were a fit thing that the saints should thus enjoy a kind of Sabbath rest during that period, a holy leisure after the labors of the six thousand years since man was created, and was on account of his great sin dismissed from the blessings of paradise into the woes of this mortal life, so that thus it is written, "One day is with the Lord as a thousand years, and a thousand years as one day."

Those who believe those asserting this are called Chiliasts or Millenarians, and Augustine adds "for I myself once held this opinion." Irenaeus, for example, wrote:

> For in as many days as this world was made, in so many thousand years shall it be concluded...For the day of the Lord is as a thousand years (2 Peter

3:8); and in six days created things were completed: it is evident, therefore, that they will come to an end in the sixth thousandth year.[120]

(*Against Heresies*, III, xxviii.3).

There is also the two days and the third day addressed by Hosea (6:2), cited previously as one of the rare scripture references to the millennium outside the Revelation. The thousand years is, according to Augustine, not a literal length of time at all, but indicates the completion of some development of the Church. This may be so, and still not solve the millennial difficulty. The millennial difficulty is that the saints are beheaded, come alive when Satan is bound for 1000 years, and then Satan is loosed again and comes out to deceive the nations at the four corners of the earth and gather them for battle, in what appears to be a separate gathering and a separate battle from the one in which the beasts from the sea and land are defeated. In this second battle, depicted as if coming after the seventh day or seventh millennium, Gog and Magog are gathered in great numbers after marching over the "broad earth" to surround the beloved city *yet again*. The battle is described in less than half a verse: "but fire came down from heaven and consumed them." The Devil is then thrown into the lake of fire "where the beast and false prophet were," to be tormented forever. The last Judgment is separated from the Revelation of Chapter 19 by a thousand years of human history yet to come.

Consistent with the key points of St. Augustine, the other possibility regarding the millennial reign of the saints is that it literally is one thousand years and has occurred already, in the reign of martyrs such as John's brother James and all the saints who did reign in the Middle Ages, and for some of us still do in some sense reign, as teachers and examples. Something like this is said in the Fatima vision, where the blood of the saints is sprinkled on the pilgrims making their way up the hill. The example of the martyrs may be what rules during the millennium. And with the sword of his mouth he might be said to have overcome those who would reject him, and even to have established worldwide recognition of himself as the leading figure in all of human history, with no other figure even coming close to the one or two billion followers of the Lamb. But then, as it appears, the Beast and false prophet would have come already, and the battle in which they were defeated and thrown into the lake of fire would have already occurred. The mark of the Beast would somehow refer to emperor worship, required in the Roman persecutions, and the name too fitted to Nero Caesar. And one would wish that the whole story of the apocalypse were only a bad dream, and that it is symbolically about purely spiritual warfare, or like the fate of Nineveh could be averted by our penance. Though it will call forth virtues unique to the end times, and allow a vast perspective, it is not a time we hope to be alive during (Amos 5:18). The twentieth century has shown that spiritual things have "literal" or political consequences never before imagined.

What Augustine seems to consider to be the millennium– the reign of the Church based on the rule of the martyrs of the first three centuries– is accounted for in the Revelation by the martyrs seen under the throne in the fifth seal. It may have been an impious error for the church to act as though she were not a widow, and to participate in the persecution that characterizes Babylon. Jesus told the Apostles, not to set up a spiritual authority over all the kings and nations, but to spread the gospel throughout the whole world, and then the end would come. It is a long way from "on this rock I will found my church" to the authority to beat ones fellow servants because the master is delayed, or to judge heresy and exercise the sentence of death. While he may have alleviated the spiritual difficulties that attend chiliasm, what did not appear to Augustine any more than to John is the possibility of the corruption of the church through the conjunction of church and empire.

The essay of Victorinus is concluded by a statement associating the millenarians with heresy: Therefore they are not to be heard who assure themselves that there is to be an earthly reign of a thousand years; who think, that is to say, with the heretic Cerinthus. For the Kingdom of Christ is now eternal in the saints, although the glory of the saints shall be manifested after the resurrection" (p. 360). The statement, though, may be a post Augustinian addition to the essay of Victorinus.

Nor does it seem that Satan is bound in Chapter 11, nor in Chapter 12, when the woman gives birth to the male child that is caught up to God, nor in Chapter 13 or anywhere until his beasts are defeated in Chapter 19. In our reading, this appeared to show in symbol the incarnation, resurrection, and the pursuit of the church while she is nourished in the wilderness. This might be consistent, though, if the binding were synonymous with the Devil being cast out of heaven, so that while he is bound in heaven, he can be loose on earth, persecuting the church and deceiving the nations. It is possible that Chapter 12 and Chapter 20, the only two chapters that depict the dragon, go together as representing the *same* sort of time scope, different from all other chapters, more fundamental or more comprehensive, involving centuries rather than the lives of particular kings. But it is possible that both descriptions of Armageddon, the battle with the Beast and the battle with Satan loosed, are simultaneous or semi-simultaneous, describing two *levels* of the same battle, even at a slightly staggered chronology and with an altered time scope, as has seemed characteristic of the text throughout. This altered time scope seemed to occur when the scene of the witnesses, their execution, resurrection and rapture, was immediately followed in Chapter 12 by what appears to be a symbolic representation of the incarnation, or the events of the first century. Though the Beast is defeated, it is not explicitly said that the Messiah returns to reign on earth in Chapter 19. Nor is it clear that his feet have touched the Mount of Olives (Zach. 14:4) in the image of the winepress

The impression that the events are successive may create the millennial difficulty. One possibility that preserves a smooth and coherent reading is to consider the reign of the saints as occurring not over one thousand years, but more instantaneously, between the beheading of the martyrs and the conquest of the Beast, when the Messiah returns. The sea and land beasts may be the manifestation of the dragon, and so the dragon defeated in their defeat. This may be no more than to say we could have a more coherent reading if we got rid of the millennial reign of the saints, and better satisfy our expectation, if mankind did not have to wait yet another one thousand years after the defeat of the Beast for the New Jerusalem to arrive.

And yet it would solve the difficulty that otherwise the Judgment Day appears to occur one thousand years after the "end times" or "end of days." There seem to be two battles of Armageddon, and the figure of the Beast, the one who brings the dragon into the world, or is the incarnation opposite the Christ, is not involved in the post-millennial, truly final battle. The New Jerusalem too would otherwise come one thousand years after the defeat of the beasts and the establishment of the millennial reign. The return of Jesus might even be another thousand years delayed, until the New Jerusalem after the millennium, and the millennial rule exercised through the saints of the first resurrection, those beheaded for refusing to take the mark of the Beast.

The coming of the beasts might, then, occur at the same time as the final loosing of the Devil, and be encapsulated in it. Aune includes a piece from the work called *Pistis Sohia*, which purports to be a statement of Jesus:

> Nevertheless, at the dissolution of the all, namely when the number of perfect souls is completed, and the mystery, for the sake of which the all came into existence, is quite completed, I will spend 1000 years, according to years of light, as king over all the emanations of light, and over the whole number of perfect souls that have received the mysteries.

One can see how this thousand years might be in heaven, and so be separate from the earth and earth time, so that relative to the earthly, the millennium is instantaneous. But that is the lesser of the two possibilities. The contradiction of the sequence of events seems still to prevent this reading. The resurrection of those killed by the Beast for not taking the mark of the Beast requires the binding of Satan. Satan is bound 1000 years, while those beheaded for not taking the mark, not of some emperor, but of the

Beast, reign 1000 years, then after the thousand years Satan is loosed and gathers the nations for battle from the four corners of the earth, and is consumed by fire from heaven, before the resurrection and the Last Judgment. The battle of Gog and Magog, when Satan is *again* loose, could then not be the same as the battle in which the armies of the Beast are slain by the word, though both might be described as fire coming down from heaven. In one, all the nations seem to come against the Beast in Jerusalem. In the second, Gog and Magog come against *the saints* in Jerusalem, just as though the saints had been there for one thousand years (20:9). Lindsey writes that the later are the ancestors of the former, which is possible and makes some sense. He also places the passage of Peter, saying that the elements are dissolved with fire, at the end of the millennium (1973, p.18). The final loosing of Satan is separated by one thousand years from the martyrdom of those who refused the mark. To read the millennium as simultaneous with the conquest of the sea and land beasts requires the ending for its beginning. The only consistent reading would seem to be the chiliast or literal.

That there is a spiritual resurrection is entirely consistent with the literal beheading of the saints, who may have already found this first resurrection in their lives, leading them to become saints prior to being martyred or beheaded in a separate incident. Are we to understand all those who die to sin to be killed for refusing to take the mark of the Beast, as those beheaded for their testimony? For in a sense this could be said, and yet it is entirely possible, viewing modern politics and technology, that there will be such a mark and such a persecution, a literal order and beheading.

The beheading of the martyrs is different from the martyrdom described in Chapter 11, when the two witnesses are killed, also for their testimony. Both are killed by the Beast, though it is not said that the witnesses of Chapter 11 were killed for not taking the mark of the Beast, nor that they were beheaded, as in Chapter 13. It seems the leading possibility is that these two were the Eastern and Western legs of the Roman Empire, martyred in the sixth trumpet, separate from those beheaded for not taking the mark in the seventh trumpet. There was the additional possibility that the 1,260 days refer also to 1,260 years, or that the period of the Antichrist presents a seven year capsule of the broader history, and the recognition of Victorinus that *two* three and one-half year periods are referenced, amounting to a total of seven years. The beheading of the millennial saints may occur not in the first but the second half of the seven year period.

Millennialism implies an astonishing circumstance: a thousand year period of human history is foretold in its outlines, yet is barely described in scripture. The earth is not wholly destroyed in the first battle of Armageddon, but is to be ruled from Jerusalem until the general resurrection. There are still independent nations, and the New Jerusalem has not yet come. Gog and Magog still exist at the four corners of the world, and after one thousand years, attempt to take Jerusalem again. This book, the Revelation, might be read during the millennium, as both prophecy and history, and the final battle prophesied then. The Lord, though, has begun to reign, and it is not clear in what way the rider on the White horse, having returned, will remain or abide in Jerusalem with all the resurrected saints. Because Satan has been bound, there may be no war, because the nations will no longer be deceived by him. Is it here then that the swords are beaten into plows, for nearly one thousand years, though not finally? Considered literally, a one thousand year period of restoration and development, after the example of the catastrophe of human civilization,[121] might naturally prepare men to inhabit a city that literally comes down from heaven. Prudence would seem now to suggest a sustainable satellite made to endure a period when the earth is uninhabitable.

[20:11-15] The vision of the Judgment opens with a vision of the throne, as in Chapter 4. It is here a great white throne, and John sees Him who sat upon it. The earth and sky fled from His presence. Strangely, it is added "and no place was found for them." This is similar to what was said when the dragon and angels were defeated and cast out of heaven, where "their place was no more in heaven." John sees...:

> ...the dead, great and small, standing before the throne, and books were opened.

On the Revelation

> And also another book was opened, which is the book of life. And the dead were judged by what was written in the book of life, by what they had done.

The books that are open are the books of the deeds of men (Daniel 7:10). The book of life (Daniel 12:1; Exodus 32:32; Malachi 3:16; Psalm 61:28; Isaiah 4:3) may record each of the souls that have through penance died and been born anew into Life. The book of life is a symbol for what we have written with the lives of our immortal souls. Enoch reads the "heavenly tablets," which includes the "book of all the deeds of mankind, and of all the children of flesh that shall be upon the earth to the remotest generations" (Enoch, 81; 103; 47). After reading this, he blessed the Lord, creator of the works of the world, and said:

> Blessed is the man who dies in righteousness and goodness
> Concerning whom there is no book of unrighteousness written
> And against whom no Day of Judgment shall be found.

The seven holy ones then tell him to declare to Methuselah and all his children that "no flesh is righteous before the Lord." In the Revelation, those whose names were not written in the book of life were thrown into the lake of fire, which is called "the second death." But prior to this casting into the lake of fire, the sea, Death, and Hades also give up the dead in them, and all were judged *by what they had done*. Earth and Sky had already fled away from the presence, and it does seem to be suggested that there may be souls "in" these as well. It is not otherwise said that the living are here taken up, after the millennium. It is not impossible that some of the souls be saved out of purgatory, or the sea, Death and Hades, though this is doubted in a number of places.[122] One wonders for example if here, in something like a purgatory, a pious Jew who saw the Christians kill his friends and family, and having heard we ought not to worship any created being, and thought the story about Jesus being the Messiah could not possibly be true, might be allowed to receive the Savior. If for this reason in life he were never born out of the world, still Purgatory might allow things to be seen in their proper light, if one were to look. We who praise our own attachment to tradition should understand the reluctance of other traditions to be abandoned for a savior and a sect, even without clear demonstration from the prophets. For who knows the secret science that the Lord imparted to the two on the road, and then to others (Luke 24:27, 32), when he opened the scriptures to them, and showed how they referred to him? Because he tied his foal to a tree, or because they parted his garments, we are to set aside the teaching that the reign of the Messiah is forever when he comes, or the teaching not to worship any created being? If the calculation of Van Impe were correct, concluding that Jesus rode his donkey into Jerusalem on the exact day foretold in Daniel, then this might have been guessable, if one first gets past the order to rebuild Jerusalem being identified with the order of Cyrus.[123] From prophecy, the Essenes were expecting something more like the images of the *second* coming, a genuine war between the sons of light and sons of darkness. The logic of coincidences is not deductive, but rather like induction, it suggests a possibility. Humans almost always misunderstand the meaning of prophecy when applied to the particular event, the part that is "literal" and the part "symbolic," or in what way each is so. Prophecy is particularly misunderstood, and fulfilled ironically upon, those attempting to use it for self-interested purposes. One is reminded of the saying of Lao Tzu (#15), on gazing into the pool of the ancient wise: "Who can wait calmly till the mud settles." When prophecy is fulfilled, as when miracles occur, a symbol occurs in action. The blind are healed. It is symbolic in our lives, but for the man healed by Jesus, an image occurs in action, and he is also enlightened regarding salvation and the Messiah. That particular events surrounding a very significant event can be foreseen is different from knowing what this means, or how we should act in the face of it. How difficult would it be to separate the prophecies regarding the first and second coming, so that the fact that Jesus was killed would not seem to refute his claim to be the Messiah who reigns forever? For particular coincidences, we should now believe the Lord is incarnated, killed and raised? He did not establish the heavenly Kingdom, as it is said the Messiah will do. They do not see that he is not finished yet. Set aside the covenant through Moses, when setting aside the Torah and the Law has been the cause of so many evils that have come upon our nation? But to see that Jesus ought to be worshiped as the son of God? To see that worshipping Jesus is not idolatry, worshiping other gods, but rather is in the whole purpose of the creation? One wonders too about the philosophers of justice who similarly know that the eternal cannot become incarnate (*Republic,* Book III), and find in reason itself the logos and the light. Do these yet have a chance to see themselves and what they have become in the light of the truth, and choose the Messiah if that is the choice of their souls, given a clear view of the matter in its proper light? The statement that salvation is *only* through Jesus simply turns around, if it might also mean that any who *do* find the eternal way and logos *have* found him. It is difficult to see such figures as Socrates or Lao Tzu being in any way deficient as humans, let alone below every believing Christian. He has others that are "not of this fold" (John 10:16). Do we know that this does not mean that these others are not recognizably Christian by name in the world? If salvation means to be born out of the world, then these are saved. Some, those most identifying the way with their own way, will see this sort of universalism as a corruption, but the question is whether or not it is true.

Following the reading of C. I. Scofield, Jack Macarthur presents a reading according to which "The dead in these verses can refer only to those left behind at the first resurrection and who constitute those raised unto damnation" (*Revelation*, p. 431). The reading is based on John 5:29, where the "resurrection of "life" is distinguished from the "resurrection unto damnation." But there is no basis in John or anywhere else for identifying these with the first resurrection and the post-millennial resurrection respectively. As the fourth of a seven part summary on the resurrection, Scofield (1909, p. 1228) writes:

> "Two resurrections are yet future, which are inclusive of "all who are in graves" (John 5:28). These are distinguished as "of life" (I Cor. 15:22-23; I Thess. 4:17; Revelation 20:4), and "of judgment" (John 5:28-29; Rev 20:11-13). They are separated by one thousand years (Rev. 20:5). The first resurrection, that "unto life," will occur at the second coming of Christ (I Cor. 15:23), the saints of the O. T. and church ages meeting Him in the air (I Thess. 4: 16-17); while the martyrs of the tribulation, who also have a part in the first resurrection (Rev. 20:4), are raised at the end of the great tribulation.

Van Impe too writes that the last Judgment "is only for those whose names are not found inscribed in the book (see verse 15)" This is very strange, since it would again imply that from the literal text of the Revelation, without inserting a rapture of those other than the martyrs, that *only* martyrs are saved (20:5). There are two ways of escape from this conclusion. One might reverse the categories and say that all the saved *are* symbolically martyrs, having sacrificed the attachment to the earth, seeking not to save their own lives and entered with Christ into the grave. Another is to say that those who died in Christ and those alive at the rapture are not among the dead but are in these terms *alive*. "The *rest of* the dead did not come to life until the thousand years were ended" (20:5). So it is *explicitly* stated that those other than the martyrs among the dead are raised *at the end* of the millennium. One wonders how this coheres with the teaching that the dead in Christ rise first, "then we who are alive..." (1 Thess. 4:16-17). That anyone whose name was not found written in the book of life were thrown into the pit would seem to imply that some names *were* here found written, and so these were *not* thrown into the lake of fire. The Scofield reading requires too that none born during the millennium be among those whose names are found in the book of life, which does not seem to be true. No one asserts this, but if some are saved, then the resurrection to judgment after the millennium is not only of the damned, and the separation by the one thousand years of the two judgments written of by John in his gospel is an error. Of everyone who sees the son and believes in him, Jesus says: "I will raise him up *at the last day*" (John 6:40).

Yet there is ancient support for the thought that others among the dead and those then presently alive will be included when he gathers his elect from the four corners of the earth. The last two sentences of the *Didache* (16.6-7)[124] reads:

> ...then the sign of "a trumpet's blast," and thirdly the resurrection of the dead, though not of all the dead, but as it has been said: "The Lord will come and all his saints with him." Then the world will see the Lord coming on the clouds of the sky.

While it does not explicitly say that the living are here judged, those on earth and in the sky would seem to be those not dead yet, on earth, and those dead but whose souls are not in Hades, earth or sea, but in the sky, or, in heaven. They come before judgment at this time, when the "places" they are in fly away. There is otherwise no rapture here, and one is reminded again that the closest thing to a description of the rapture in the Revelation is the ascent of those killed for their testimony, described in Chapter 11. The rapture is replaced by martyrdom, and the rest of the dead are not raised till after the millennium.

Here is an argument: A) The dead are raised before the rapture; B) the dead are raised after the millennium, therefore c) the rapture comes after the millennium. But Paul says that the rapture occurs at the "seventh trumpet," which is when the Beast and false prophet are about to be defeated, *prior* to the millennium. The resurrection and thousand year reign of those beheaded for not taking the name and number is not the rapture, because the rapture occurs *after* the dead are raised (I Thess. 4:16-17), which does not occur until after the millennium. The only resolution that appears is that the martyrs *are* the dead said to rise before the rapture, while the general resurrection does not occur for a millennium after. This millennial paradox would also be resolved if, in literal terms, the millennium were instantaneous, rather than a thousand years from the earthly view. Could it be that the seventh trumpet lasts one thousand years? Or that the "dead in Christ" refers to the martyrs only? Or that there are multiple resurrections, as appears from the dead that were said to have risen at the crucifixion (Matthew 27:52; Henry Schaeffer)?

But what is written by St. Augustine on the basis of this passage seems unsurpassed. Regarding the plural *books* that John saw opened, Augustine writes:

> We must understand it of a certain divine power, by which it shall be brought about that everyone shall recall to memory all his own works, whether good or evil, and shall mentally survey them with marvelous rapidity, so as this knowledge will either accuse or excuse conscience, and thus all and each shall be simultaneously judged. And this divine power is called a book, because in it we shall as it were read all that it causes us to remember.
>
> *City of God*, XX.14

It is commonly said that before our death our whole life flashes before our eyes. The wonder of the books and the book of life leads one to consider the significance of each thing regarding the soul, each action and each good thing we might have become, as though what we had been in our lives determined what our eternal soul would be, in its character and conformity with what is and what is true. And Jesus would teach them, that whatever we do to one another, we do to him (25:31-46), as though our own immortal good were secured when we love one another, but when we harm one another, in the light of truth we harm ourselves, or our true selves. Because the soul or the man is an image of God, our nature is this way, and we gain or lose the opportunity to participate in the eternal light, by our regard for others, and how this leaves a harmony or discord in the soul. And here he described how when the son of man comes in all his glory, he will separate the sheep and goats according to this principle. When we forgive others, we may be forgiven, but if we do not forgive others, we will not be forgiven (Matthew 7:14-15). But robbers in truth lie in wait for their own blood, the light of the wicked is withheld, and their uplifted arm is broken (Proverbs 1:18; Job 38:15). The saints intercede and petition the Lord with prayers for unrepentant sinners, and for the wicked, that they might cease to be, but what we have done is done, and this is what we have become, through the actions and the life in which our immortal souls have been engaged. If the soul or man is immortal, the wonder is not that actions, in their imprint, are retained, but that sins can be forgiven.

A clue to the millennial difficulty might be found in the promises to the churches. This occurs to me because Hal Lindsey has erroneously stated that Thyatira is promised that a remnant of these "will be co-ruler with Christ over the Kingdom that will be established for one thousand years on earth" (1973, p. 58). If this were true, it would demonstrate that some other than the martyrs beheaded by the Beast are to rule with Christ during the millennium, but this is not demonstrated. Sardis is told that those who conquer will not be hurt by the second death, but there is no reason to assume that this exemption is true exclusively of the millennial saints, as all those raised later whose names *are* found in the book of life might also not be hurt by the second death.

Lindsey also writes: If a person does not receive Jesus Christ as savior by the time he dies, his name is blotted out of the book of life" (Ibid., p. 62). The text does not quite say this, because it is not quite true. If Abraham and Moses knew the Messiah by this name, it would be a miracle, though it is not impossible. To have one's name written in the book of life is the birth of the soul out of the world, and a natural mystery that can occur without words. We hold that some even before Christ was born, are saved, as Abraham and Moses. "Before Abraham was, I am" (John 8:58). Any others might find the logos without naming it this, though it may be rare and more difficult. The point is worth laboring, because it demonstrates the importance of genuine philosophy, or the openness of faith to genuine philosophy. We seek to have faith not in the walls of a man made prison, even with the names and colors of the Christ. In the second book of Plato's *Republic (357b)*, there is a famous distinction between things we seek because they are good for their own sake; things good for what comes out of them, and things good for both. There is some question about the effectiveness of faith chosen to avoid punishment, rather than for its *own sake*, or for both. Those, for example, who gave him clothing and food when they saw him naked and hungry, though they do not know to take his name, may not have their names blotted, while those who do take his name, waving it like a banner, but do not feed and clothe him when they see him, may. The reverse logic, though, is true: Those who do truly receive him, we think, will not have their names blotted out. A further question is whether some of the saints or the elect, those conquered by the Beast, will have their names blotted out though they *did* receive Jesus while they were alive, and whether there is a purgatory, in which the souls, given the characters built up in their earthly lives, will be allowed to see the choice in its proper light. The Witnesses make this second chance a character of the millennium, and in the old Catholic imagery, this was thought of as purgatory. And if the soul is immortal, it would be a difficult thing to tell that it were impossible that it be born out of the world somehow after death. But these images refer to natural realities. We receive him and the spirit of truth enters our souls.

Another reason for looking in this direction is the strangeness of time in the other depiction of the dragon. The dragon appears in the twelfth chapter, the first chapter of the second half of the book, and this chapter seems to fill in the background for the events of the sixth and second trumpets by describing the incarnation, crucifixion and persecution of the early church. It concludes at the sands of the sea, and then the woe to these appears as a beast emerges from each, from sea and then earth. It is possible that Chapter 12 and Chapter 20 go together, both in that they depict an action done to and by the dragon and in being of a different time scale, outside and around the events on earth described in the rest of the end time story, providing something more like a thousand year context of the same events of the final century of the age. The concluding tenth of each would then be

On the Revelation

nearer to simultaneous the nearer the description came to the end. The saints beheaded, especially Peter and Paul, did in one sense come to life and reign, even about one thousand years, if one considers the extent of the medieval Church from Constantine into the Middle Ages until the start of the Inquisition, from 313 through till about 1215, and even to the present, in a sense. This is not beyond the possibility of symbolism, to present one who is dead but reigns through writing as having died and come to life, and this is one of the possible readings of the dry bones prophecy of Ezekiel, as depicting the new flowering of Israel as the resurrection of the Israelis.

We should not let pass the opportunity to address the strangeness of the image of our immortality. The dead are seen standing before the throne, books are opened, and the book of life. The dead are judged by what was written in the books, by what they had done. Any one whose name was not found in the book of life is thrown into the lake of fire. Then there is a new heaven and a new earth, and the Lord is present in the New Jerusalem, which is a light to the nations (21:24). The water of life is there, and the tree of life is given for the healing of the nations. These nations are outside the city, and yet are neither thrown into the lake of fire nor do they dwell there, only they are no longer deceived by the Devil. Does this not mean that the human world of births and deaths, of people neither saints nor demons, writing their deeds into the book of life, continue on when the new heaven and the new earth come to be? And is this not simultaneous with the life of the immortal spiritual bodies or the beings who lived, died, and were resurrected? There are no resurrected bodies in the picture of the New Jerusalem. Its walls are men, but there are not houses described. Since the walls are men, the measuring allegorical, and the lamp replaced by the Lamb, it is possible that the city is allegorical of the presence of God and the Lamb in the souls of men. It is right to say that this is more beautiful than the more literal depiction. There is a street, and a river, orchards, and gates that are never shut but that the clean may enter. "And his servants shall worship him; they shall see his face, and his name shall be written on their foreheads." And will there be sun and moon outside the city? This is very strange, because in the description, heaven and earth come together, and Jerusalem appears as both an immortal paradise and an earthly nation that leads the world out of the time of evils that we know and into a timeless age governed more directly by the divine.

The immortality of the soul seems not to be a thing that can be known for certain, but a teaching given to us in images, in which we have hope and faith, but not certain knowledge. Near death experiences provide common evidence enough, and if these occurred to some in ancient times, it would not be surprising if these should be enough to give rise to the hope and the belief in immortality, as among the ancient Egyptians. It will always be suspected that the teaching is a dream we tell ourselves because we are afraid to die, and there is a great courage in facing the possibility that immortality may be no more than dreams[125] or images caused for the human imagination by the more mundane truth of the higher intellect. One way of presenting the question of the immortality of the soul is that in some sense, though we *were not*, we now *are*, and hope to *be* in the kingdom. It is difficult to see even how such a thing could be possible. We would be a strange cross section of the immortal, like the angels, and our coming to be would be a coming to be immortal. Immortality may not be the same as eternity, in the way that 2+2=4 is always the same, was and will be, or in the sense that the Lord is always the same. The past is unchangeable, but is no more, except as it lives on through the present. In one image, the soul dies and goes to heaven, as Jesus said to the thief crucified next to him: "This day, you will be with me in paradise" (Luke 23:43). Jesus himself ascends some*where*, as does Enoch, so that his body has literally escaped. Must there not be some *where* like place to receive the body? It is also said that "flesh and blood cannot inherit the kingdom" (I Cor. 15:50) but we will all be changed, so that it is a resurrected body. "Flesh" here has an analogical meaning that is synonymous with soul, as in "the two become one flesh" (Genesis 2:24; Matt. 19:5), where we do not mean literally one body, but through the body, one soul, which is in part true literally. In another image, the body lies in the earth until the resurrection, and the kingdom is future: it was and is not

On the Revelation

now, but is yet to be. What is the relation of the *yet to be* to the eternal? If our deeds are written in the book of life, our eternal soul is shaped or affected by what we do here, at least for some, if not for all. If the souls are *always*, and immortal backward in time, one would think we would remember this, though we may have forgotten, as though having crossed some river of forgetfulness. In the images of reincarnation and of recollection, the soul is immortal backwards, or always, which would seem to include the past. If the soul is immortal, and this is always, it would seem to be so *now*, as well as in the past and future. Some think the soul immortal "only while it is alive," and thus from the perspective of time, to *be*, yet only for a while. Hence the Joke implied by the saying that Plotinus became one with the first principle– four times! These are the difficulties thought encounters when we attempt to consider what we mean by saying that the soul is immortal. And what do we mean by *soul*? Modern thinkers often deny the existence or causal significance of the soul, so that we must say "it is that with which you are considering this!" or that with which you are denying. It is that which is considered in three parts, reason, the heart, and the appetites. Is this not part mortal, our changing thoughts and emotions, and something different from the immortal life or light in us? And which are *we*? One of its many meanings is your true self as distinct from that in us that is more ephemeral. So difficult is this to say that many give up, resting in the assurance that the immortality of the soul is an expedient fairytale. But Christian philosophy, if this is possible, genuinely takes up from start to finish the question of whether the soul is "to be or not to be," setting aside the couch of the assurance either that we know immortality to be true in just such a way, as it is imagined, or that it is obviously a fairytale because of the ways in which the teaching might be useful or salutary. For it may in the end be even more difficult to show how such a thing could *not* be so, and we, with no part in us that is akin (Plato, *Republic,* 490b2-3; 532 c4-5), have access to things that are always.[126] Human speech is said to be evidence of the immortality of the soul. Immortal life is likely to be an astonishing thing we do not expect and cannot imagine. But if we can know it, it may be indirectly, as in the metaphysics implied in the saying that the soul is an image of God. The possibility is that in the soul something rises as in the cosmos, and what rises is redeemed mankind. The body is redeemed, as mankind is redeemed. Particulars can be eternal, contrary to the expectation of philosophy.

And it is a good question, whether we will then be at liberty to pursue all sorts of studies, as Socrates imagined, speaking with the great minds of the ages (*Apology* 41 a-b), who would then have enough time for us, or perhaps to read the history of the earth, man and all things that have been, like an open book, in the sense that what has been *is*, and in certain unalterable way. Maybe it is as an instantaneous sharing in the knowledge of the Lord, including all that has been, the knowledge of all the beings that ever lived and what occurred to them. If the Lord is like that, it seems to us unimaginable to perceive and know that many particulars, as though what is must have trouble apprehending and being concerned with, for example, so many ants, etc.

There are two images of immortality that do not fit together. One is that immortality is attained, and another that it characterizes the souls from the beginning. Again, in one, the meaning of immortal life is the good and just, the bread that sustains the life in us is the word. In another, the souls of the evil are unfortunately also immortal.

The mystery of damnation is very difficult. The Apostles are sometimes inclined to intercede for the damned, in a high and rare sort of compassion which is sorrowful for the fate of the souls even of the wicked. Damnation can be understood from the equation of the elements 1) that the soul or spirit, or spiritual body, is immortal and 2) what we do to one another is done in truth to ourselves. The cruel then seal their own torment, and it is to their misfortune that the soul is immortal. In their compassion, the saints wish they might simply cease to be. As Mary says in the vision of Fatima: "This is hell, where the souls of poor sinners go." This compassion, and the absence of vengeance, is, by the way, an indication that the vision of Fatima is genuine. As at the conclusion of the *Epistula Apostolorum*, it is questionable whether this intercession has any effect at all. There Jesus answers that the Father has so determined these things, and that he himself agrees.

vii: The New Heaven and the New Earth

Chapter 21

[21:1-4] John next sees the new heaven and new earth, "for the first heaven and the first earth had passed away, and the sea was no more." Earth and sky had fled from the presence as described at 20:11. There is no other description of the passing of the former heaven and earth, and it is not clear whether it is a complete or partial destruction.[127] Augustine writes: "For this world shall pass away by transmutation, not by destruction." (*City of God*, XX.14). This, though, would seem to be when the elements are dissolved with fire, as written by Peter. He sees the New Jerusalem, "coming down out of heaven from God, prepared as a bride adorned for her husband." A voice from the throne is heard to say, "Behold, the dwelling of God is with men. He will dwell with them, and they shall be his peoples, and God himself will be with them." As was promised, he will wipe away every tear (7:17; Is. 25:8). That He will dwell with man (Is.7:14) might be fulfilled if the Messiah were to return and reign.

[21:5-8] He who sat upon the throne then speaks, saying: Behold, I will make all things new." He also told John to write this, for his words are trustworthy and true:

> It is done! I am the Alpha and the Omega, the beginning and the end. To the thirsty, I will give from the fountain of the water of life without payment. He who conquers shall have his heritage, and I will be his God and he shall be my son. But as for the cowardly, the faithless, the polluted, as for murderers, fornicators, sorcerers, idolaters, and all liars, their lot shall be in the lake that burns with fire and sulfur, which is the second death.

The New Heaven and the New Earth

This is the second of the two places, together with 1:8, where the Lord explicitly speaks directly. The river of the water of life (Isaiah 55.1) is shown flowing from the throne of God, and the Bride and Lamb too invite all to drink the water of life without pay, as the last word of the revelation (22:17).

That the first heaven and the first earth had passed away raises the question of the sense in which these pass away and the sense in which the earth "abides forever." The new heaven and earth, after the passing of the old, comes not at the millennial reign, but after the thousand years, and it is this condition foretold in Isaiah (65:17-25), where the lion and ox will live together peacefully:

> For behold, I create new heavens and a new earth;
> And the former things shall not be remembered or
> come into mind.

Here the new creation is not unfamiliar, but is like a restored or uprighted version of the old. People who build houses and plant vineyards will inhabit and harvest them, rather than have another inhabit and harvest them. There will be death, but in ripe old age, and even sin (Is. 65: 20-22).

[21:9-27] Next one of the angels that had the seven bowls of wrath comes and says to John "Come, I will show you the Bride, the wife of the Lamb." The phrase parallels the phrase "Come, I will show you the judgment of the great whore" (17:2; Aune, 1998, p. 1202). John is carried away in the spirit by the angel, to a great high mountain. Its radiance is like Jasper clear as crystal, a rare jewel. In the vision, "It had a great high wall with twelve gates." Angels are at each of the gates, and the names of the twelve tribes of Israel were inscribed on the gates, three on each of the four sides of the wall. The wall also has twelve foundations, probably also three on each side, on which are written the names of the Twelve Apostles of the Lamb. One wonders why it is the tribes and not the patriarchs, and why these are not reversed, the foundations being the tribes and the gates the Twelve Apostles, where the Gentiles enter. The foundation of the Christian teaching is the twelve tribes, while the apostles are gateways of salvation. The tribes reminds of the 144,000 sealed, and the place of the nation of Israel in the City of God. This question points toward the meaning of gates and foundations. The foundations are of twelve different jewels, the gates each of a single pearl, and the street of transparent or glass-like gold. The wall, as well as the first foundation, is jasper, as was the radiance of the city (21:11, 18). The twelve gates and the twelve tribes may culminate the theme of Jewish and Christian together that is involved in the 144,000 from the twelve tribes, and in the grafting of the olive branches apprehended prophetically by Paul. The theme, as we have argued, is suggested by the formulation "those obeying the commandments and following Jesus" (12:17), and "Song of Moses and of the Lamb" (15:3). The suggestion is that the future belongs to messianic Judaism, or a Christian Israel moderated by penance for the execution of the Messiah and the example of the things that led to war prior to the millennium.

[21:17-21] One of the seven angels then gives John a measuring rod of gold, and tells him to measure "the city and its gates and walls." The city is a cube, its length, breadth and height all equal, "12,000 stadia," the number being the same as that of those from each of the twelve tribes that were sealed, multiplied by the cube of ten, one thousand. We recall from Chapter 11 that John was told to measure, but did not then actually measure. The measuring here is of the city rather than the temple. The city, the New Jerusalem has no temple or lamp stand, and the lamp is the Lamb (21:24). The law has cultivated man, who through the ordeal has become holy, where he once was merely obedient. His civilization has become natural, and his civilized character divine. He also measured the wall of the city, 144 cubits, "by a man's measure, that is, an angel's." This, again, is a suggestion that the men have become angels, or even that the angels *are* men, or the same as men except for not having had their immortal souls disturbed and cultivated by their incarnation. It even appears that the men, having become angels, *are* the walls of the city. 144 multiplied by the cube of ten would remind of the 144,000. There are no immortal souls described in the city, and it is not clear what the saints who came with him on the cloud and ruled during the millennium are *doing* in the city. Do they live there in immortal bodies, or live elsewhere? If the city of God is so much like the current earth renewed, are there simultaneously souls in heaven, in a condition that is not described? Or is the city a description of the heavenly condition? It is a city and not a garden, a post-civilized condition.

The stones adorning the foundations of the wall are also addressed by Isaiah (54:11-14):

> Behold, I will set your stones in antimony,
> And lay your foundations with sapphires
> I will make your pinnacles of agate,
> Your gates of carbuncles, and your wall of precious stones.
> All your sons shall be taught by the Lord
> And great shall be the prosperity of your sons
> In righteousness you shall be established...

The foundations have something to do with the presence of the Lord and with teaching.

Zechariah (2:1) saw a man with a measuring line, who, when asked, tells him that he is going to measure Jerusalem, to see what is its breadth and what is its length." Another angel comes to meet an angel that spoke to him previously, and tells him to run and say to that young man that because of the multitude of men and cattle in her, "Jerusalem shall be inhabited as a village without walls, "For I will be to her a wall of fire round about, says the Lord, and I will be the glory within her." Zechariah (2:10-11) continues:

> Sing, and rejoice, O daughter of Zion, for lo, I come and I will dwell in the midst of you, says the Lord. And many nations shall join themselves to the Lord in that day, and shall be my people; and I will dwell in the midst of you, and you shall know that the Lord of Hosts has sent me to you."

Ezekiel (37:27-28) prophesies:

> My dwelling place shall be with them; and I will be their God, and they shall be my people. Then the nations will know that I, the Lord sanctify Israel, when my sanctuary is in the midst of them for evermore....

[21:22] The name Emmanu'el means "God with us" (Is. 7:14; Ez. 48: 35). There is no temple in the city, for its temple is the Lord God the almighty and the Lamb. There is said to be no sun and moon. Its lamp is the lamb: there are no churches or other lamps needed. One wonders how, cosmically, to imagine there being no sun and moon, but only the light of the presence.

[21:24] The next section of the description of the heavenly city concerns the nations, and seems to provide a window or clue to what is occurring:

> By its light shall the nations walk; and the kings of the earth shall bring their glory into it, and its gates shall never be shut by day–and there shall be no night there; They shall bring into it the glory and the honor of the nations.

As Aune, citing Strothmann, notes, this line presupposes the continuing existence of the nations and the presence of the New Jerusalem on earth (p. 1171). Interestingly, the time is an age of nations rather than cities, as before the Roman Empire, in the age of the ancient polis, before Christ. The key passages of the prophets describing the New Jerusalem and the nations are Isaiah 60 and Zechariah 14. Selections of Isaiah 60 are:

> ...darkness shall cover the earth, and thick darkness the peoples;
> But the Lord will arise upon you, and his glory will be seen upon you.
> And nations shall come to your light,
> And kings to the brightness of your rising...
>
> ...who are these, that fly like a cloud,

The New Heaven and the New Earth

And like doves to their windows?
For the coastlands shall wait for me,
The ships of Tarshish first,
To bring your sons from far,
Their silver and gold with them,
For the name of the Lord your God,
And for the Holy one of Israel,
Because he has glorified you
Foreigners shall build up your walls,
And their kings shall minister to you;
For in my wrath I smote you,
But in my favor I have had mercy on you.
Your gates shall be open continually;
Day and night they shall not be shut;
That men may bring to you the wealth of the nations,
With their kings led in procession.
For the nation and kingdom that will not serve you shall perish;
Those nations shall be utterly laid waste.
The glory of Lebanon shall come to you,
The cypress, the plain and the pine,
To beautify the place of my sanctuary;
And I will make the place of my feet glorious.
The sons of those who oppressed you shall come bending low to you;
And all that despised you shall come bow down at your feet;
They shall call you the city of the Lord,
The Zion, the Holy One of Israel

(Isaiah 60: 2-3; 8-14)

Zechariah too, writes:

> And it shall come to pass, that every one that is left of all the nations which came against Jerusalem shall even go up from year to year to worship the king, the Lord of hosts, and to keep the feast of tabernacles. And it shall be, that

On the Revelation

whoso will not come up of all the families of the
earth unto Jerusalem to worship the king, the Lord
of hosts, even upon them shall be no rain.

This circumstance in which there are nations appears from Revelation 21:24 to continue beyond the millennium and into the time of the everlasting Kingdom and the New Jerusalem. One is reminded of the description of Maimonides of the days of the Messiah. Maimonides writes:

> Nothing in existence will change from the way it is now, except that Israel will have a kingdom. The text of the sages is as follows: There is no difference between this world and the days of the Messiah, excepting subjection to the kingdoms...which hinders us from acquiring the virtues.
>
> (Pereq Heleq, *Days of the Messiah*, p. 166)

The law will be written on the hearts of men, and livelihood will come much easier, but there is no fundamental change in the nature of things, nor do the immortal souls appear dwelling on earth. It is as though what has changed is man, so that man comes into the presence of the Lord. "On that day, the Lord shall be one, and his name one" (Zechariah 14:9). Indeed, there is no God but God.

As in Isaiah 60:11, it is striking that there are still nations, and they have their own sovereignties. It is said that the nations that do not bring their offering to Jerusalem will be deprived of rain. If what is shown is the post millennium city in a new heaven and new earth, *there are still nations*, and perhaps some of the same nations that were. Perhaps even the words of Lincoln concluding the Gettysburg Address, will continue true, that government of the people shall not perish from the earth. To be playful: as an American patriot, one imagines a scene in which the supreme court, after a severe drought, decides 5-4 that it *is* constitutional for the United States to send their offering, since it is not so much

The New Heaven and the New Earth

establishment of religion as our free religious expression as a nation. Such an event is possible, unless the United States is the throne of the Antichrist, and destroyed. It is possible that we suffer a disaster and become politically irrelevant, or that we help Israel in the war, if neither are the throne of the Antichrist. The nations come to Armageddon from the four corners of the world, and though the "whole world" is said to come against Israel, it is not necessary that all come to Armageddon as enemies, rather than as diadems of the word. But there is otherwise no suggestion that Christians participate as armies in apocalyptic warfare, though we can participate in spreading the word.

At the conclusion of Isaiah, there is the suggestion that the offering of the nations is the return of the Jews to Israel. In a summary of prophecy, Isaiah (66:18-21) writes the saying of the Lord:

> ...I am coming to gather all nations and tongues; and they shall come and see my glory, and I will set a sign among them. And from them I will send survivors to the nations, to Tarshish, Put and Lud, who draw the bow, to Tubal and Javan, to the coastlands afar off, that have not heard my fame or seen my glory, and they shall declare my glory among the nations. And they shall bring all your brethren from all the nations as an offering to the Lord...to my holy mountain Jerusalem...just as the Israelites bring their cereal offering in a clean vessel to the house of the Lord. And some of them also I will take for priests.

There is an argument that the Kingdom of God is not a world empire, or that the rule of the nations from Jerusalem is more voluntary. Though there is the throne, the city is nowhere called a kingdom. The city is similar to the philosophic kingship in Plato's *Republic*: it is the kingship of the Good, so that the regime is a kingship, although visible persons rule not in a kingship, but in an aristocratic republic. Yet it was said that he would rule the nations with a "rod of iron," and this seems to mean forceful rule in the just suppression of what is really evil. The saints too participate in the rod of iron: "He who conquers and who keeps my works until the end, I will give him power over the nations, and he shall rule them with a rod of iron" (2:27). This is left out of the description of the city at the end of the Revelation. World empire is what was destroyed, as in the first apocalyptic teaching, in Daniel's interpretation of the dream of Nebuchadnezzar, in which a stone cut by no human hand smashes the image on its feet of iron and clay. It is the same iron, and it is only after the destruction of the world by the principle that led to world empire that the City of God, guiding the nations, becomes possible. Isaiah (2:1-4; 11:6-9) writes:

> It shall come to pass in the latter days
> That the mountain of the house of the Lord shall
> be established as the highest of mountains,
> And shall be raised above the hills, and all the
> nations shall flow to it,
> And many peoples shall come, and say,
> "Come, let us go up to the mountain of the Lord,
> To the house of the God of Jacob;
> That he may teach us his ways and that we may
> walk in his paths."
> For out of Zion shall go forth the law;
> And the word of the Lord from Jerusalem.
> He shall judge between the nations,
> And shall decide for many peoples;
> And they shall beat their swords into plowshares,
> their spears into pruning hooks; nations shall not
> lift up sword against nation,
> Neither shall they learn war any more.

Isaiah also writes (42:1-4):

> Behold my servant, whom I uphold,
> My chosen, in whom my soul delights;
> I have put my Spirit upon him,
> He will bring forth justice to the nations.

The New Heaven and the New Earth

> ...He will not fail or be discouraged
> Till he has established justice in the earth;
> And the coastlands wait for his law.

Micah (4:2-3) seconds the statement of Isaiah, and adds that the Messiah will mediate disputes between the nations, somewhat as the U. N. is supposed to do today:

> For out of Zion shall go forth the law,
> And the word of the Lord from Jerusalem
> He shall judge between many peoples,
> And shall decide for strong nations afar off;
> And they shall beat their swords into plowshares,
> And their spears into pruning hooks;
> Nation shall not lift up sword against nation,
> Neither shall they learn war any more...

Here the Messiah is shown giving law and just rule to the nations, and this must be either in the millennium or in the New Jerusalem. If it is in the city, the meaning of new heaven and new earth is consistent with "the earth endures forever," and what is destroyed is the surface, which may be total enough for man. The earth might still grow men, though they have become rare. But the old division in man after the fall may be gone, and the place of man different, with something healed. That is how fundamental a change is indicated.

That nothing unclean will enter the temple, but that there are still the nations means too that there is still the human world. The tree of life, in the next chapter, is given for the healing of "the nations." The tree is like one grafted with twelve different fruiting branches, like those seen in ornamental gardens. Its twelve fruits are twelve like the Apostles, and the saying "leaves of the tree" makes one think of the leaves of a book or even the leaves of the great books, including the Bible. There are the writings of the Apostles currently known, John and Matthew, and works that may be by Thomas and some letters of Peter, and his teaching is preserved in the gospel of Mark, though we do not have twelve teachings of twelve apostles. These leaves are going to be different from the fruit of the tree of life, which, had they taken of it in the garden, would have made them not die, or live forever. It is in the promise to Ephesus that it is explicitly said that it will be granted to he who conquers to eat of the tree of life, and this would seem to be of the fruit. The leaves are the parts of this plant, and they are medicinal for the nations, which reminds *us* of the leaves of the book and of the great books of the pursuit of wisdom, or political philosophy. It is akin to prophecy in that it is critical of the highest worldly authority, the city and the human temples, by an appeal to the truth and what is right by nature. Because it flies between the actual human political things and the truth about what is best even for them, it is capable of being medicinal for the nations, devastated by what has occurred on the face of the earth.

At the opening of Chapter 11, in which the martyrdom of the two witnesses is described, John was also given a rod and told to measure "the temple of God, and the altar, and those who worship there." There he was told to leave out the outer court, since this was to be trampled by the nations, but now in Chapter 21, this large measure, said to be about 15,000 miles, would seem to include the outer court. The city is a cube, equal in its length, height and breadth (21:16). Its length and breadth and height are 12,000 stadia. While in Chapter 11, John is told to measure, in Chapter 21, the angel measures, also the walls of the city, which is said to be 144 cubits "by the measure of a man, that is, that of an angel." As has been noted, this suggests that the angels are the same as men, or also sons of God (21:7). The number is again the same as the number of those sealed, if a cubit were the same as a thousand. The Bride and the elect are identified only by this, while the multitudes are the servants of the Bride.

The wall was built of jasper, and the city was "pure gold, clear as glass" The foundations, on which the names of the Twelve Apostles are inscribed, are adorned with twelve different jewels, and each is listed. The twelve gates, on which a name of one of the twelve tribes is inscribed, are each made of a single pearl. There are two separate Jewish traditions regarding the gates hewn out of huge pearls.[128] The street, like the city, is pure transparent gold.

The New Heaven and the New Earth

While in Chapter 11, John was told to measure the altar and temple, in Chapter 21 there is no temple seen in the city, "For its temple is the Lord God the almighty and the Lamb." This of course does not mean that we are to take this mention of the temple as a clue to the date of the composition of the text. It underlines the reading that the olive trees are the Christian churches, the Christian attempt to imitate the Jewish temple. The Jews expect the restoration of the temple in the New Jerusalem, and according to John misunderstood Jesus when he said "destroy this temple and I will rebuild it in three days." He spoke of the temple of his body, as here the temple *is* the Lord and the Lamb. Nor is there any need of sun or moon to shine on it, for the glory of the Lord is its light, and its lamp is the Lamb. The churches in the opening section are the lamp stands. The heavenly Jerusalem is where the intelligible light is received, and a literal one: that visible light or even the sun and moon will be replaced by invisible light, or the presence may result in literally visible light. Isaiah (60:19) writes:

> "The sun shall be no more your light by day, nor for brightness shall the moon give light to you by night, but the Lord will be your everlasting light, and your God will be your glory. Your sun shall no more go down, nor your moon withdraw itself; for the lord will be your everlasting light, and your days of mourning shall be ended. Your people shall all be righteous; they shall possess the land forever.

Chapter 22: The River and Tree

The river of the water of life flows from the throne of God and of the Lamb, through the middle of the street or plane of the city. It is that from which we are offered to drink for free (22:17). Of the 144,000, it was said: "...and he will guide them to springs of living water." The tree of life is "in the midst of its plane, here and there," as though many trees are intended. The water and the tree are distinct as spirit and word are distinct. The water of life is told of in the story of the woman at the well (John 4:7-39):

> If you knew the gift of God, and who it is that is saying to you, 'Give me a drink,' you would have asked him, and he would have given you living water... Everyone who drinks of this water will thirst again, but whoever drinks of the water that I shall give him will never thirst. The water I shall give him will become in him a spring of water welling up to eternal life.

Enoch (48) writes:

> And in that place I saw the fountain of righteousness,
> Which was inexhaustible,
> And around it were many fountains of wisdom
> And all the thirsty drank of them,
> And were filled with wisdom
> And their dwellings were with the righteous and holy and elect.

    The tree of life is that of which ones share will be taken away if he adds or detracts or from the words of this prophecy (21:19). To eat of the tree of life is one of the seven promises to him who conquers, in the first promise, to Ephesus. All seven characterize the New Jerusalem. The other promises were 2) to not be harmed by the second death; 3) that they be given some of the hidden manna and a white stone with a new name; and 4) power over the nations and the morning star; 5) to be clothed in white garments and not have his name blotted out of the book of life; 6) to become a pillar of the temple, and have the name written of God and of the city and his own new name, the savior; and 7) to sit with his Father on the Throne.

    Tree of life and river of the water of life are added to the description of what was seen by Ezekiel (47:12),

The New Heaven and the New Earth

> And on the banks, on both sides of the river, there will grow all kinds of trees for food. Their leaves will not wither nor their fruit fail, but they will bear fresh fruit every month, because the water for them flows from the sanctuary. Their fruit will be for food, and their leaves for healing.

In Ezekiel, the tree of life is not yet explicitly shown as present in the city. The tree confers immortal life, as in Genesis, it is said, "Lest he put forth his hand and eat of the tree of life and live forever" (Genesis 3:22). The tree of life was not at first forbidden (Genesis 2:16). It has fruit that sustains us, beyond milk and grain. It is the same as the tree that was present in the garden, and not forbidden, though Eve reports to the serpent that the tree "in the midst" is forbidden (Genesis 3:3). She takes from the tree of the knowledge of good and evil, and man is banished from the garden. Were it not so, all things may have never left the unity, which is restored at the wedding of Bride and Lamb. There is no separate tree of the knowledge of good and evil in the New Jerusalem.

One of the finest passages I have seen attempting to interpret the trees in the garden is that found in the Letter to Diogenes, describing to the emperor Hadrian (117-138 A. D.) "…what God has prepared for those who love him as they ought:"

> (these) have become a paradise of delight, cultivating in themselves a flourishing tree, rich with all kinds of fruit, while they themselves are decked out (adorned) with a variety of fruits; for in this Garden a tree of knowledge and a tree of life have been planted. But it is not the tree of knowledge that destroys; it is disobedience that brings destruction. Indeed, there is a deep meaning in the passage of scripture which tells how God in the beginning planted a tree of knowledge and a tree of life in the midst of paradise, to show that life is attained through knowledge. It was because the first men did not use this knowledge with

clean hearts that they were stripped of it by the deceit of the serpent. For there cannot be life without knowledge any more than there can be knowledge without genuine life, and so the two trees were planted close together.

The thought that it is not knowledge itself that is harmful, but disobedience.... That life is attained through knowledge, or as the proverb states, "by knowledge are the righteous delivered" from the folly of injustice toward a neighbor (Prov.11:9). The letter elaborates that knowledge without *life* is what is harmful, knowledge understood as ethically neutral science, and life as the aim at the good. Knowledge is spoke of in the prophecies in a different way:

> For I desire steadfast love and not sacrifice,
> The knowledge of God rather than burnt offerings. (Hosea 6:6)

> There is no faithfulness or kindness,
> And no knowledge of God in the land. (Hosea 4:2)

> My people are destroyed for lack of knowledge
> Because you have rejected knowledge
> I reject you from being a priest to me,
> And since you have forgotten the law of your God,
> I will also forget your children. (Hosea 4:6)

> For the earth will be filled with the knowledge of the glory of the Lord
> As the waters cover the sea (Habakkuk 2:14).

Here knowledge is obviously different from that conferred by the eating of the tree of knowledge of good and evil. The tree does not seem even to refer to ethical knowledge or political science. Solomon, in a dream, was told by God "Ask what I shall give you," and Solomon asked for "an understanding mind to govern thy people, that I may discern between good and evil." So he was given a wise and discerning mind (1 Kings 3:9-12). Socrates, famously, teaches that when we are immoderate, what we have is not knowledge but opinion, since it would be strange if knowledge were "dragged about like a slave" (*Protagoras* 352b). If we truly knew what was good, we would choose it. So this is a different sense from that in which eating of the tree confers knowledge of good and evil. The effect is not that they suddenly study justice or the parts of the soul and the regimes, become wise or philosophers, know what to do or have political science. This need be said because the pursuit of knowledge involves the questioning of the authority of law, and a certain disobedience, to human if not also to divine authority, and the replacement of a trust and security with questioning and restlessness. But the effect of the tree of knowledge is the emergence of shame, our recognition that we are naked. Outside the marriage chamber, shame is felt before members of either gender, but is related to our sexual nature, its stimulus by sight or vision, and another sense of the word "know." Hence, we wear clothing. This is a mystery that is with us daily, though no one understands it fully. Unless one's nature has been preserved, the sight of the beautiful stimulates a usurpation that destroys the ordering of the thoughtless and uncultivated soul. The story of Gyges, in the *Inquiries* of Herodotus (I. 8-12) demonstrates this, when the sight of the Queen causes the compulsion of Gyges to murder the king and seize the throne. The ordering is restored through scientific knowledge, as when, in a later story, the physician of Darius is able to cure the Queen Atossa, able to treat a lump on her breast in the transcendence of our sexual nature and shame that occurs in science and medicine (Ibid, III.133). Still, it is as though the only immediate effect of the turning on of perception for these creatures is conscience, and the only activity of conscience shame, as though this were the only place in human life where intelligence is active or *alive*. In this way, the story is similar to the sense in which love sometimes seems to be the only way that most humans awaken at all, and most are incapable of romantic love. Beauty, says Socrates, is the only one of the intelligibles to be visible with any luster, due to the mysteries in which all souls were initiated prior to our incarnation (*Phaedrus*,

250b-c). It causes death, though, because now, in order to restore the harmony, the humans must ascend through death, or the sacrifice of penance, overcoming what is called original sin. It is as though the new intelligence were surprised to find it has a body, and a soul of animal appetites. The best thing written on the tree of knowledge and the tree of life may be that found in the work called the *Gospel of Phillip*, found in the collection at Nag Hammadi. In a very strange passage, the author makes clear that the death caused by the tree of knowledge of good and evil is the death of penance that leads to rebirth, caused by the law, so that the law, the Torah, is the tree of knowledge. The passage reads:

> ...This garden is the place where I will eat all things, since the tree of knowledge is there. This one killed Adam, but here the tree of knowledge made men alive. The law was the tree. It has power to give knowledge of good and evil. It neither removed him from evil, nor did it set him in the good, but it created death for those who ate of it. For when he said, "Eat this, do not eat that," it became the beginning of death.

The death of the tree of knowledge is related to the way in which the law causes death, the death that leads to birth (*Nag Hammadi Manuscripts*, p. 144, Romans 7:7-25). Adam was told they would die in the day that they ate of it (Genesis 2:17), but as the serpent said to Eve, they did not literally die, but lost innocence. In this sense, the serpent tells the truth while God lies. But they do not really become like God, knowing good and evil, either, as Solomon was for a while after his prayer. Rather, they are to be acquainted with this divine perception of a dimension of reality they were not before acquainted with, seeing like angels while having a human body. The knowledge of the tree would then be the beginning of self-knowledge. For man it causes death in a symbolic, not a literal sense. The serpent works with the literal sense, not in which God spoke it, but the sense in which Adam and Eve understood it, since these are not wise but innocent. The

Serpent uncovers the earthly truth hidden in the beliefs of the obedient. This belief, though, would have been sufficient for happiness, and is true in any case on the highest level. The disobedience of Adam made man aware of the body, and he hides himself from God, showing what must now be overcome for man to know himself, and again stand naked in the garden.

This, then, is the reason that the tree of knowledge does not appear in the New Jerusalem. Maimonides writes: "As for the tree of knowledge, The Holy One, blessed be He, has never revealed that tree to man, and will never reveal it. This is correct in as much as the nature of existence requires it" (*Guide*, II.30). This Tree is not some mysterious knowledge pursued, but rather, that presupposed by the human condition.

Still, the two trees are related in the Genesis story, in the midst of the Garden, and the tree of life is not forbidden. Only the tree of life appears here in the New Jerusalem. It is as though the tree of knowledge were no longer needed, and its effects are presupposed, though now, the victory of the Lamb and the martyrs is required in order to have access to the tree of life. Life means that the eating of the fruit of this tree, the very tree whose leaves are given for the healing of the nations, confers immortality, or is the same as immortal life. It also means the higher nourishment of the immortal soul, not what confers immortality but vivifies the life in us. "In Him was life, and the life was the light of men" (John 1:4).

The fruit is mentioned in the description of the city as of twelve kinds, and is implied, in the Ephesian promise to him who conquers (2:7). Enoch writes: "Its fruit shall be for food to the elect" (Enoch 25). There is a connection to the eating of the Eucharist and drinking of the wine, and one thinks of the tree that is the cross. The tree of knowledge of good and evil is the beginning of self knowledge, in self perception that is the natural motion of the perception we call conscience, inseparable from our social or political nature. That the leaves of the tree of life are to be given for the healing of the nations appears in its most visible form, as a foretelling of the possibilities for medicine and genetics properly used, or as a prophecy of bodily healing, possibly from the poisons of a nuclear war. Genetic medicine might literally be a giving of the biological tree of life for the healing of the nations, even from nuclear poisons. It may also or especially be a prophecy of the place of political philosophy. The *basis* of the knowledge of good and evil, or the *cause* of the law, is the image of God that is man (Genesis 9:6). It is this image that lies asleep in the soul, but is what each most is, awakened through baptism, and fed by milk and grain, before fruit. The leaves of the tree of life are the pages of the Bible, and maybe also any other of the great books that reflect the eternal Torah. Enoch saw another mystery, that "books shall be given to the righteous and the wise, to become a cause of joy and uprightness and much wisdom" (Enoch 104). The liberty of the nations to bring tribute or not may indicate that, despite the rod of iron, philosophy will not be proscribed during the millennium, as it has been in the "age of grace."

The tree of life appears elsewhere in scripture, as in the Psalm, but the most important instance is in the Proverb, which explains of Wisdom:

> Her ways are ways of pleasantness, and all her paths are peace.
> She is a tree of life to those who lay hold of her;
> Those who hold her fast are called happy... (3:17-18)
> Prize her highly and she will exalt you;
> She will honor you if you embrace her,
> She will place on your head a fair garland;
> She will bestow on you a beautiful crown. (4:8-9)

The statement in the Proverbs identifies the tree of life with wisdom. This is the source of the invisible crown. Another teaching is that the tree is the Torah, in the sense in which the Torah is identified with the eternal word. The pursuit of wisdom is the same as the quest for the apples of immortality. The fruit is the knowledge or the acts of oneness with God. Jesus said, "My food is to do the will of him who sent me" (John 4:34). When we are able to serve Him, doing our work well, the division is overcome. The unity of all things appears, not as though the things had lost their distinction, like a glass of water poured into the sea, but as beings with a place in the whole, moving as parts of one (being) that is the creation in union with the Creator. The good is seen when we participate in it, or, it may be visible, to the extent that it is visible, only from within it, when we are serving it, and then, like the plan of a master, not entirely. Socrates, too, is like a spirit working between God and man. We sense the Presence above us, and there is a prayer that He remain hidden while we serve, so that we are not harmed by the Presence. It is more accurate to say we are *known by* Him, than that we know Him or It, as the lesser thing, from within It, which of course cannot be called It, and barely can be called Him. Plato's Socrates famously called the Good "beyond being," (*Republic*, VI, 509b) whereas an "it" or even a "He" is *a* being. A contemporary formulation is "Beyond the difference between the personal and impersonal," or a person and more, the original or cause of what it means to be, to be alive or to be a person. The vision of the good that completes philosophy comes in philosophic kingship, which is a participation in rule, if only of the highest sort (*Republic* 540a-b). Socrates was midwife, and we may work in this, even to assist the offspring of the Lord. This mystery, the tending of the garden of the Lord, is the goal of education, and the highest prudence, while the second highest sort is rule over the family, city, and nation involved in statesmanship and royal rule.

Finally, there is a teaching from a work attributed to Joseph of Arimathea,[129] who begged and buried the body of Jesus in his own tomb. This Joseph reports things said by Jesus to the robber Demas, crucified next to Christ, to whom he said "This day you will be with me in paradise" (Luke 23:43). Jesus said to him:

> And thou alone shalt dwell in Paradise until my second appearing, when I am to Judge those who do not confess my name...And He said to the robber, Go away, and tell the Cherubim and the powers that turn the flaming sword, that guard paradise from the time that Adam, the first created, was in paradise and sinned, and kept not my commandments, and I cast him out thence.

And none of the first shall see paradise until I am come a second time to judge the living and the dead.

The robber puts on an incorruptible body in order to "go into paradise, where no one has ever been able to dwell." Here, it is only in the resurrected body that we are able to eat of tree of Life, otherwise guarded by the Cherubim. Joseph may have heard this story, like his account of the betrayal of Judas, from "one of his disciples called John," the fullest witness.

The Bride

There is a history of consent in the marriages of Abraham and Isaac, to Sarah and Rebecca. Although both are chosen by the divine, their wedding waits upon the consent of the woman (Genesis 24:58). The same is evident in the Magnificat (Luke 1:38). This consent is a characteristic of royal, as opposed to despotic, rule, and is related to what is called "free will," as well as to its image in political liberty.

She is the bride, the wife of the Lamb. The wedding of the Bride and Lamb is the most complete image of God in all of scripture. The deeds of the saints are the bright, pure fine linen of the garment of her wedding dress, which it was granted she be clothed (19:8). Paul wrote to the Ephesians (2:19-22; 3:18):

> ...So then you are no longer sojourners, but are fellow citizens with the saints and members of the household of God, built upon the foundation of the Apostles and the prophets, Christ Jesus being the cornerstone, in whom the whole structure is joined together and grows into a holy temple in the Lord; in whom you also are built into it for a dwelling place of God in the Spirit.

Israel is the bride of the Lord (Is. 62:2-5; 61:10; 49:18; 54:5, Jer. 2:2; 31:32; Ez. 16; Hos. 2:6) and through the Messiah, people of every nation are added, as was prophesied by Isaiah (66:18; 55:5;

49:6). The New Jerusalem *is* the bride (21:2), made up of redeemed mankind. Paul writes: "But the Jerusalem above is free, and she is our mother" (Galatians 4:26; Is. 54:1). The temple has become mankind in that when the Spirit dwells in us, we *are* in a sense members of His body and the Bride, not as individuals but as collective mankind. She is the Church that is the womb of rebirth, and also wisdom, in whom we might participate, but who belongs to the Lord. Paul writes: "I betrothed you to Christ to present you as a pure bride to her one husband..." (2 Cor. 11). The mystery is that man is somehow one with the creation, and in the wedding, redeemed man *is* of the body of the Lord, uniting all things in the restored harmony of the whole. Human marriage is an image of this most complete image of the divine, and its truth is related to the metaphysical truth by natural analogy. Human marriage is also like the invisible image, the knowing soul. Hence, there is the Song of Solomon. And it is strange that Christendom has not cultivated the love or *eros* that leads to marriage, but has generally suppressed all *eros*. Paul (Ephesians 5:25) writes:

> "Husbands, love your wives, as Christ loved the church and gave himself up for her, that he might sanctify her, having cleansed her by washing with the water of the word, that he might present the church to himself in splendor, without spot or wrinkle or any such thing, that she might be holy and without blemish. Even so, husbands should love their wives as their own bodies. He who loves his wife loves himself. For no man ever hates his own flesh, but nourishes and cherishes it, as Christ does the church, because we are members of his own body. For this reason a man shall leave his father and mother and be joined to his wife, and the two shall become one flesh. This mystery is a profound one, and I am saying that it refers to Christ and the church..."

On the Revelation

This had been the theme of his letter to the Ephesians, to which John would have had access, assuming that it was kept in the church there:

> For he has made known to us in all wisdom and insight the mystery of his will, according to his purpose which he set forth in Christ as a plan for the fullness of time, to unite all things in him, things in heaven and things on earth (1:10).

Heaven and earth are joined when the Lamb and Bride are wed. It is not said that the creation is wed to the Lord through this, as though the creation sprung from within him like Eve from the rib of Adam. The creation is one with the mystical bride that somehow is the body and the mother of redeemed mankind. The bride is the womb of the sons of God, the baptismal font. In a sense the creation is also the womb of the sons of God, but in this roundabout way, not as though the creation were the mother of created man, but of begotten man. Created man is begotten by parents but made by the Lord. The children of God, though, are made by their forbearers, shaped by tradition and law, but begotten by the Lord (John 1:13). Yet it is so in the same way that the trinity is so. In the Bride and Lamb, all things are united in Him. The most complete image of God in scripture is a trinity joined, or a quaternity.

The new name is related to the marriage: Isaiah 62:2-4:

> The nations shall see your vindication,
> And all the kings your glory;
> And you shall be called by a new name
> Which the mouth of the Lord will give.
> You shall be a crown of beauty in the hand of the Lord,
> And a royal diadem in the hand of your God.
> You shall no more be termed forsaken
> And your land shall no more be termed desolate
> But you shall be called 'My delight is in her'
> And 'your land married.'

The New Heaven and the New Earth

[22:3-4] The throne of God and of the Lamb will be in the city, and his servants will worship him. They shall see his face, and his name shall be on their foreheads. His face is singular, in a Johannine allusion to the identity of the persons of the trinity. And the throne is singular. There is a long history regarding the question of whether a man can see the face of God and live. To Moses, God says "you cannot see my face; for man shall not see me and live" (Ex. 33:20). God hides Moses in a cleft of the rock when he passes by, so that Moses is not harmed, and Moses wore a veil because of the brightness of his face after speaking with the Lord on Mt. Sinai. Yet Hagar, seeing an angel, says "Have I really seen God and remained alive after seeing him (Genesis 16:14)? When Jacob wrestles with the angel, he calls the place the face of God, saying "For I have seen the face of God and lived" (Genesis 32:30; 33:10). On two other occasions, the angel of the Lord is seen, and those who see fear that they will die (Judges 6:22-23; 13:22).

That the saints will eat from the tree of life and see the face of God are things inconsistent with the mortal body, and contradicts the impression, made by the continuing of the nations, that the city is not in heaven but on the new earth. The mortal and immortal, heaven and earth, are joined in a way that was impossible after the fall, though it may have been possible in the garden. The garden is not quite on earth, as is evident from the contradiction between Genesis 2:4 and 1:26 as to which day man was made.

The city of God is shown from the earthly perspective, and this is similar to the second sentence of Genesis, where the heaven is set aside to discuss the "earth," meaning here the visible realm, since what it refers to is prior to the dry land called "earth," and it is clear that there is something above the firmament called Heaven, above that in which the stars are set, namely the waters above. This is shown by Maimonides (Guide II.30). However, when he writes of "out of nothing," we wonder how he will answer when we ask him on which day was the water created? And is there not a heaven prior to the first day, just as there is an earth without form and void and a deep over which the spirit moves? Is this not addressed by John in the first three sentences of his gospel? And was part of the movement of the spirit of God on the face of the deep prior to another part of the movement, so that movement implies that time is present before the first day?

[22:5] That they have "no need of Lamp or sun, because the Lord illumines them" is a repetition of 21:22, and a place where one gets a glimpse of the intelligibility in the images. The lamp stand, the churches, were an intermediate institution, no longer needed when the Lord is with us, but are here now because the Presence is hidden, or hides from us, beneficently. "And they shall reign for ever and ever." This is the only mention, in the description of the city in the last two chapters, of the saints sharing in the throne.

[22:6] The text of the revelation in one sense ends at 22:5, and the angel begins the signing off or farewell section. First the angel testifies that the words of the prophecy are true, and that he has been sent by "the Lord, the God of the spirits of the holy prophets," "to show his servants what must soon occur." The ending parallels the opening, except that the opening followed the order of the delivery of the message, from Jesus and God through the angel to John, while the conclusion is less hierarchical. Some characters have been added to the farewell section: the (singular) Spirit and the Bride.

[22:7] At 22:7, the speaker is Jesus, saying, "Behold, I am coming soon. Blessed is he who keeps the words of the prophecy of this book." More literally, it says "the one keeping," or, as was said, "those watching (1:3)" To keep the prophecy might also mean to pay heed to it. It may also refer to care for the text and the message of the Revelation. Or it may be that "those watching" is the better translation. This is the sixth of the seven blessings of the Revelation. What this means, though, is a question, once one thinks about it. The book commands us only to not take the mark of the Beast, though to keep the book would also mean to obey the purity implied not only by the exclusions from the Kingdom here in Chapter 22, and also in the letters to the churches. "Come out of her" is another thing we are told to do (18:4).

The New Heaven and the New Earth

[22:8-9] John is again the speaker from 22:8, before Jesus speaks again at 22:12. John testifies that it is he who saw and heard these things. He repeats that when he did so, he fell down to worship the angel, but was told that the angel is a fellow servant, and he should worship God. One significant addition from the very similar lines at 19:10 is "your brethren the prophets." At 19:10, the angel said "for the testimony of Jesus is the spirit of prophecy." John especially is himself among the prophets, so that again we say that John the apostle may have been the only one then alive who was able to receive the vision.

[22:10] When Daniel asked "What is the issue of all these things" he was told that the words are "shut up and sealed until the time of the end" (Daniel 12:9). John is told *not* to seal up the words of this prophecy, because the time is near. The Apocalypse of John may be the answer to the question of Daniel. Some of what occurs in the revelation may not yet have been set when Daniel saw, before the crucifixion. But this is the scroll.

[22:12-16] Astonishingly, Jesus delivers a brief summary and farewell address, until he appears:

> Behold, I am coming soon, bringing my recompense, to repay every one for what he has done. I am the Alpha and the Omega, the first and the last, the beginning and the end.
> Blessed are those who wash their robes, that they may have a right to the tree of life and that they may enter the city by the gates. Outside are the dogs and sorcerers and fornicators and murderers and idolaters, and everyone who loves and practices falsehood.
> I Jesus have sent my angel to you with this testimony for the churches. I am the root and the offspring of David, the bright and morning star.

The seventh blessing is a summary of the Christian knowledge of the human soul: Happy are those who through repentance join to the Christ through death to find the proper food for the immortal part of them that is our true being, and enter into the life of the city, the presence of the light, and the worship and service of the Lord.

The root and offspring of David is both the progenitor and the descendant. The Messiah is understood to have been before the Creation.

[22:17] Astonishing, too, is the farewell: "The Spirit and the Bride say 'Come.'" And let him who hears say "Come." And let him who is thirsty come and let him who desires take the water of life without price." The Spirit and the Bride are, again, as if persons of a quaternity, and him who hears also participates in the divine invitation to the water of life.

[22:18] Considering the warning not to change any words of the text, it is astonishing too that the modern readers are so ready to assume the work of many hands. It is "the tree of life and the holy city," as at 22:14, from which one would lose his share if he took away anything, while to one who adds will be added the plagues.

[22:20] That he is coming "soon" is the last word from the divine in the Revelation, as it was almost the first word. For as we say in the Creed, "He will come again in glory to judge the living and the dead, and of his kingdom there will be no end."

ix: Summary and Conclusion

The Messiah and the coming of the Beast are like two essential points in the time of earth and man, points that are so because of the way things *are*, and reveal the way things are. Then something else can come to be. It is for this reason that the reading of the Revelation is for all ages, not only for the Church of the end times as a warning. The prophesied event is the essential event, and reveals the permanent nature of things. It is because God is true and man in sin rejects God and justice that these things occur. The world we know will be gone, and so we know in every age that in this sense our works do not last, give or take a few thousand years.

To summarize, the teaching of this commentary has been: that John is the writer of the Revelation; that it is worth reading for its own sake, as well as for our worries about the future; and that the reading confers a blessing. It is addressed not to everyone, but to those already turned by the gospels, the servants. It is about the martyrs and the avenging of their martyrdom in the end times. The rapture, like the desolating sacrilege, is not directly addressed. The fourth chapter is a vision of the throne that continues throughout, so that the completion of the number of the saints or martyrs is a completion of the throne. The seals are of a different time scale than the trumpets, addressing centuries following the incarnation, up through the making of the martyrs seen in the fifth seal.

There is some conjunction of Jewish and Christian things foreseen, a re-grafting in of Israel. The Messiah will not be *born* in the end times, but is coming on the clouds, having already been born, died and resurrected. Israel may be set up to receive the false messiah, having missed the first incarnation, but will surely see the Messiah at the second coming, and then the two will agree. The two witnesses may refer not to individual prophets but, as the olive trees, to two bodies of the faithful, whether the Eastern and Western Churches or the Jewish and

On the Revelation

Christian. The two legs of the statue in the vision of Daniel correspond to the areas of the Eastern and Western Churches.

The twelfth chapter describes the incarnation and the consequent pursuit of the woman and her offspring, who are the Christians. This pursuit has led to the martyrs seen under the throne with the opening of the fifth seal. The worldwide earthquake destroys the present political orders, while the advances of civilization are retained, allowing after a profound silence for the emergence of the apocalyptic things concerning the Beast. The pursuit of the woman and her offspring is continued by the sea and land beasts of the thirteenth chapter, and provides the context. Meanwhile, there are survivors, and these gather on Mount Zion. The harvest and the winepress may be two different occurrences. The return is addressed in Chapters 14, 15 and 19, focusing on different aspects. The Beast is distinct from Babylon, and his kingdom is distinct. He attacks Babylon, and at the same time makes martyrs of the true offspring. The identity of Babylon is a mystery, but it is something like world empire, or the assumption made by the seven world empires, concluding with Rome and then the worldwide worship of the Beast. The two books of Daniel and the Revelation together provide the Biblical apocalyptic teaching. Babylon is the whole of the statue seen by Daniel, named after its head. In the worst period of all human history, the Beast will attack Babylon and make martyrs of the witnesses before the mark of the Beast is required. This will continue in the martyrdom of what become the millennial saints: those who refuse the mark and are not conquered by the Beast. The extent of the world rule is not clear, since his control does not prevent the nations of the four corners of the world from gathering at Armageddon. Nor is it clear that the millennial reign of the saints is literal from the earthly point of view, though this does seem to be the most consistent reading. Babylon is contrasted with the woman that is the true Bride. The New Jerusalem is mystically identified with the body of the faithful, who have no church as we do now. No lamps are needed because the Lord is present. The marriage of the Bride and the Lamb is the most complete image of God in the scriptures, mystically including mankind in the throne. The harmony of the whole, lost

Summary and Conculsion

from Eden, is restored in the union of God and His creation, through those not only created, but begotten, by Him and by the Bride. The saints even of this age are from this union, and are a foreshadowing or foretaste of the heavenly city. The new earth is like the former one in that there are nations. The story of their paying tribute indicates the difference, if the rod of iron indicates the similarity of the New Jerusalem to a world empire. The need for the rod of iron indicates the difference between the new condition and the simple imagination of perfection or of heaven, which remains the mystery that heaven has always been.

On the Revelation

Appendix A: The Three Secrets of Fatima[130]

1. After she showed the children a terrifying vision of hell, she said to them: "You have seen hell, where the poor sinners go. To save them, God wishes to establish in the world devotion to my Immaculate Heart. If what I say to you is done, many souls will be saved, and there will be peace."

2. "The war [World War I] is going to end; but if people do not cease offending God, a worse one will break out during the pontificate of Pius XI. When you see a night illumined by an unknown light, know that this is the great sign given you by God that He is about to punish the world for its crimes, by means of war, famine and persecutions of the church and of the Holy father."
"To prevent this, I shall come to ask for the consecration of Russia to my Immaculate Heart, and the communion of reparation on the first Saturdays. If my requests are heeded, Russia will be converted and there will be peace, if not, she will spread her errors throughout the world, causing wars and persecutions of the church. The good will be martyred, the Holy Father will have much to suffer. Various nations will be annihilated. In the end, my Immaculate Heart will triumph. The Holy Father will consecrate Russia to me, and a period of peace will be granted to the world. In Portugal, the dogma of the faith will always be preserved," etc.

3. After the two parts which I have already explained, at the left of our Lady and a little above, we saw an angel with a flaming sword in his left hand; flashing it gave out flames that looked as though they would set the world on fire; but they died out in contact with the splendor that our lady radiated towards him from her right hand; pointing to the earth with his right hand, the Angel cried out in a loud voice: Penance, Penance, Penance! And

we saw in an immense light that is God, 'something similar to how people appear in a mirror when they pass in front of it' a bishop dressed in white. 'We had the impression that it was the Holy Father.' Other Bishops, Priests, men and women religious going up a steep mountain at the top of which there was a big cross of rough-hewn trunks as of a cork tree with the bark; before reaching there the holy father passed through a big city half in ruins, and half trembling and with halting step, afflicted with pain and sorrow, he prayed for the souls of the corpses he met on his way; having reached the top of the mountain, on his knees at the foot of the big cross he was killed by a group of soldiers who fired bullets and arrows at him, and in the same way there died one after another the other Bishops, Priests, men and women Religious, and various lay people of different ranks and positions. Beneath the two arms of the cross there were two Angels each with a crystal aspersorium in his hand, in which they gathered up the blood of the martyrs and with it sprinkled the souls that were making their way to God."

Appendix B: The Apocalyptic Texts

The Revelation
Daniel

Matthew 24; 13:39-43; 25, 26:29, 64
Mark 13; 9:1; 12:25; 14:25, 62
Luke 21; 17:20-37; 18:6-8; 22:18, 30; Acts 1:11
2 Thessalonians 2
1 Thessalonians 4:13-5:11
John 5:22-28
2 Peter 3:8-13

Genesis 49: 1-2
Exodus 32:32;
Numbers 24:14
Deuteronomy 4:30

Deuteronomy 31:29
Ecclesiastes 4:15-16
Psalms 102: 25-26; 93:1-2
Isaiah 2; 9:7; 10:17-27; 11-14; 17; 24-27; 42:4; 49:6, 51:6-60-62
Ezekiel 36-40, 47
Jeremiah 25
Jonah
Hosea 6:2
Joel 2-3
Amos 5:18-20; 8:8-10; 9:11-15.
Micah 4
Zephaniah
Zechariah

Apocryphal:
Enoch,
Thomas # 51, 59, 113
2 Esdras
Epistula Apostolorum 34-38
Didache

Index

Abraham, 9, 14-16, 38-39, 101, 195, 232, 248, 253, 339, 365, notes 85, 88, 89, 92, 118
Acts, the Book of, 3-8, 18-20, 31-32, 47, 56-57, 73, 80, 91-2, 129, 138, 179, 223, 232, 290, 376, note 35
Acts of John, 4, 7-8, 25, 27 notes 5, 11, 23
Adam viii, 42, 58, 66, 302, 3612-2, 364, 367
age, viii, 1, 14, 33, 37, 47, 51, 57-60, 69-70, 77, 105, 130, 143, 154, 158, 178, 190, 194, 207, 218, 258, 261, 270, 286, 294-5, 297, 319, 340, 342, 349, 363, 372, 374 notes 38, 67
ages, 31, 47, 49, 53, 58, 64-66, 68, 72, 80, 83, 96, 102, 114, 129, 208, 238, 271, 327, 336, 341, 344, 379
Akiva, Rabbi, note 120
Alvarez, Leo Paul s. de, notes: 16, 49, 100
Amos, 38, 138-9, 328, 377
Anselm, Saint, 78
Andrew, the Apostle, 3-43, 7, 22, 219, note 4
Anna, grandmother of Jesus, 117
Antichrist, 9-10, 53-4, 56, 64, 68-71, 78, 112, 123-125, 135, 140, 153-4, 163, 166-7, 171-186, 188, 199, 203, 208, 210-212, 223, 236, 247, 249, 263-4, 268-272, 275-76, 280, 305, 313-315, 332, 352 notes: 61, 67, 91
Aquinas, Saint Thomas, 287, note 1
Aristotle, vi, 12, 257, 267, 274, 288
Assenmacher, Keith vi
Augustine, Saint, ix, 10, 41-42, 63, 67, 72, 165, 194, 241, 279, 291, 297, 324-28, 338, 345, notes 67, 102, 120, 126
Augustus, 16-17, 20, 180, 200, notes 9, 75
Aune, David, ix, 2, 23, 75, 77-79, 82-83, 100,-101, 140, 142, 144, 161-2, 177, 191, 199-200, 213, 215-16, 222, 240, 245, 289, 294, 344, 330, 346, 349 notes 1, 56, 127
Assyria, Assyrian, 108, 201, 245, 248, 250, 264, 311, 317, note 67
Athens, 14-5, 240-1, 277, note 116
Azerbaijan, 263

Babylon, 25, 64, 83-84, 95, 129, 144, 163, 165, 176-7, 179, 186, 193, 197-8, 201, 220-22, 225, 227, 235-250, 252-3, 255, 258, 275-6, 282-291, 294-5, 297, 299, 301, 305, 311, 316-7, 322, 328, notes 67, 89, 95, 102, 104
Bacon, Sir Francis 47 note 45
Balaam, 88, 91, note 72
Balak, 91, note 72
Baptist, v, vii, 103, 178, 187, notes 15, 105
Bartholomew, the Apostle, 5
Bauckham, Richard, ix, 68, 77-8, 80, 83, 94, 128, 146, 154, 156-7, 163, 213 notes 60, 73, 87
bear 130, 139, 197, 199,-200, 202
Beast, 19, 44, 56, 58, 60-64, 67, 76, 83-84, 91, 101-02, 107, 110, 112-113. 115, 118, 127-128, 132, 140-41, 144, 149-151, 153, 155, 159, 162-3, 165, 167, 170-71, 173, 176, 179, 181-183, 185, 191, 195-212, 214-216, 219-220, 222, 224-225, 227-29, 231-32, 245, 251, 256, 259-60, 262, 264-266, 269-270, 272-73, 275-7, 279-283, 298-9, 301-310, 312-313, 316, 319-20, 322, 326-31, 337, 339, 369, 372, notes 61, 85, 109, 114
Belgium, 207, 256, 258
Benjamin, 25, 271
book of life, 93, 96, 134, 203, 205, 216, 222, 244, 275, 281, 309, 333, 336, 338-9, 341, 343, 357
Bride, 5, 72, 96, 107, 176, 179-80, 183, 195, 240, 277-79, 291, 294, 296, 299-300, 345-46, 355, 358, 365, 367, 369, 371, 373-74 note 94
Bronze, 49, 83, 87, 92, 100, 254, 257-8, 262, 264
Burnet, John, 23
Bustamante, Frank, vii

Calendar, vii, 40-42, 44-45, 52, 54, 187, 250, 263 note 48
Caligula, 7, 10, 16-18, 180-181 notes 9, 61
Calvin, John, 65
Casey, Edgar, 52
Cerinthus, 22, 91, 328, note 28
Chiliast, 42, 62, 324, 326, 331
China, 208, 260

Clay, 153, 201, 254-255, 258, 279, 285, 303, 353
Collins, Adela Yabro, 177, notes 66, 71
cork tree, 242
Dan, 140, 214, 271-72 note 79
Daniel, vii, 32, 34, 36-38,43-49, 53, 59, 80, 82, 84, 92, 100, 102, 111-113, 115-16, 121, 124, 127, 129, 135, 141, 153, 155, 158, 162-3, 166-7, 184-6, 191, 197, 199, 201-3, 205-9, 211, 223, 231, 233, 241, 245-48, 250-275* 279, 282, 284, 303, 307-9, 313-14, 318, 333, 353, 370, 373, 376 notes 40, 67, 81, 95, 98, 100, 108, 109
Darwin, Charles, 192-3, note 92
David, 10, 21, 41, 87, 93, 116-17, 291, 370-71, note 72
Death, 53-54, 77, 82, 128, 210, 216
Devil, 60-1, 132, 188-9, 310, 322, 324, 327, 329-30, 341, notes 102, 113
Didache, 22, 317, 337, 377 note 124
Dionysius, tyrant of Syracuse note 51
Dionysius Exiguus, 41
Dionysius, Bishop of Alexandria, note 1
Domitian, 17, 19, 20-22, 57, 76, 180, 200 notes 9, 11, 95
Dragon, 61, 63, 78, 156, 176, 178-184, 187-8, 190-98, 200, 202-4, 209-11, 231-2, 246-7, 249, 276, 282, 313, 322-3, 329-30, 332, 340
Drewes, Christopher, 12, note 22
Drosnin, Michael, note 72
Drusus, 17

Eagle, 101-2, 127, 191-2, 197, 202
Earthquake, 67, 115, 135, 137, 139-40, 147, 149-51, 153, 155, 158, 161, 172, 187, 234-5. 239, 304. 306, 313, 315, 373, notes 86, 99
Easter, 41, 276
Easter Island, note 121
Eden, 90, 279, 374, note 65
Edom, 225, 308, note 72
Eleazar, Rabbi, note 120
Elijah, 16, 27, 111, 162, 164, 219 note 87
Elizabeth, kinswoman of Mary, 3, 25, note 4

Enoch, 16, 25, 27, 41, 44, 49, 100, 111, 115, 131, 162, 187, 195, 248, 302, 333, 342, 357, 362-3, notes 44, 79, 117
Ephesus, 7-8, 20, 22, 24-25, 76, 83, 87, 138, 296, 355, 357
Epistula Apostolorum, 22, 134, 168, 344, 377, note 122
Essenes, 4, 62, 192, 334, notes 75, 117
Exodus, the, 51, 92, 191
Exodus, the book of, 51, 77-78, 82, 92, 142, 149, 164, 191, 333, 376
Ear, 88, 94, 96
Egypt, Egyptian, 51, 108, 138, 142, 165, 178, 183, 191, 199, 201-2, 209, 245, 248, 250, 253, 274, 309, 313, notes 4, 41, 67
eye, 4, 10, 12, 26, 62, 66, 76, 80, 95, 110, 114, 310, 316, note 103
Ezekiel, 36, 38-9, 82, 99-102, 141-2, 147, 155, 157, 212, 218, 283, 310,-313, 317, 341, 348, 357-58, note 67

Fatima, 52, 122, 126, 129, 135, 146, 327, 344, 375, notes 43, 67, 130
fig tree, 33, 39
fire, 18, 46-7, 51-2, 58-61, 70, 75, 83, 87, 95, 100, 110, 127, 139, 142, 147, 154-55, 164 210, 223-4, 227, 230, 251, 258-9, 276, 286, 288, 301-2, 304, 307, 310, 313, 322, 327-28, 331, 336, 341, 345, 348, 375-6
France, 64, 207, 247, 256, 258, 263-64, 277

Galileo, 194, 294
gematria vii, 213

Genesis 23, 59, 61, 89, 116, 119, 131, 162, 193-4, 248, 250, 272, 292, 297, 312, 315, 342, 358, 361-3, 365, 368, notes 72, 88
Germany, German, 33, 48, 70, 127-8, 131, 134, 199, 207, 228, 233, 242-3, 245-6, 256, 258, 260, 263, 281, 314, notes 38, 113
Germanicus, 17
gold, 85, 87, 95, 101, 138, 206, 222-3, 235, 242, 247, 254, 257-8, 294, 305, 308, 347, 355
golden 83, 146, 151, 223-4, 242, 258, 274, 283
Gnostic 10, 66, 89, note 34
Greece, 197, 199-201, 245, 247, 250-51, 2567, 258, 263, 275, 312, 314

Greek, language and culture, x, 9, 14, 23, 48, 62, 66, 75, 77, 101-2, 105, 141, 151, 174, 195, 199, 202, 213, 219, 257-8, 261-2, 265, 274, 281, 285, 287, 293, 295, 299, notes 1, 3, 11, 67
Greeks, v, 7, 9, 14-5, 90, 241, 257-8, 273-4, 279, 285, 291, notes 75, 112

Habakkuk, 40, 359
Hades, 82-83, 119, 127, 197, 324, 333, 337
hear, hearing, 18, 22, 24, 26-7, 29, 34, 36, 70-71, 75, 79, 82, 88, 95-6, 99-100, 105, 111, 118-120, 125, 140, 151, 155-7, 165, 170, 215, 217-8, 222, 225, 229, 276, 299-300, 325, 328, 333, 345, 351-2, 359, 365, 370-71, notes 61, 70, 53, 57-58, 60, 62, 65, 69, 72, 81, 107, 210
heart 38, 63, 93, 104, 131, 163, 189, 225, 276-7, 286-7, 316, 343
Hebrews, the book, 2, 10, 58, 83, note 68
Hebrews, the people, 41
Heidegger, Martin, 70
Herod Antipas, 6
Herod Agrippa, 9, 322
Herod, King 10, 16, 21, 41, 178, 180-1, 183, 241, 250, 265, 278, 319, 322, 360, notes 43, 79
Hesiod 77, 258
hindsight vii, ix, 28, 32, 47, 64, 126, 205, 288, 319,
Hitler, Adolf, 23, 29, 34, 40, 43, 72, 104, 120, 132-3, 136-38, 143, 148, 160, 168-72, 177, 179, 181, 204, note 38
Hobbes Thomas, 173, 319
horn, 191, 200, 203, 205, 214, 246, 259, 262-4, 266, 272, 275, 307-8
horns, 13, 79, 84, 86, 118, 151, 179-81, 197-9, 201-2, 209-10, 214, 238, 242, 238, 242, 246-7, 249, 50, 256, 258-9, 262, 265, 272-3, 275-6, 280, 282, 302
Hopi, 52, note 48
Hosea, 43, 270, 278, 304, 327, 359, 377, note 114

Inquisition, 33, 242-3, 265, 270, 278, 286-7, 341
Insight, 66, 367
Irenaeus, Saint, 24, 42, 62, 66, 91, 326, note 1
Iron Age, 258

iron, 49, 131, 153, 176, 182, 192, 201-2, 254-5, 257,-8, 264, 273, 279, 285, 302-3, 334, 352-3, 363, 374
Isaiah, 3, 34, 36-7, 39, 53, 77-8, 81-82, 93, 100, 102, 107, 117, 120, 137-8, 141, 176-77, 181, 198, 206, 225, 231, 235,248-9, 260, 270, 280, 283, note 67

Jacob, 81, 178, 272, 353, 368, notes 72
Jacob, Rabbi, note 120
Jacobovich, 51
James the Just, 3, 5-7, 9, 19, 76, 243, 270, note 75
James Zebedee, 3-4, 6-8. 24, 26, 219, 243, 322, 327
James, the book of 2
Jehovah's Witnesses, 9, 45, 65, 167, 217, 340, note 15, 83, 104
Jefferson, Thomas, v, 12, 253, 284, note 112
Jerome, St., 22, 24, 105, notes 66, 71
Jerusalem, 5-9, 15, 18, 23-4, 31, 33-6, 41, 43-6, 51, 53, 56-7, 60-2, 67, 76, 80, 90, 94, 96, 107-9, 112, 114, 119-121, 136, 138, 141-4, 149, 153, 160-3, 167, 177, 179, 184-5, 195, 201, 204, 207, 212, 215-6, 224, 234, 238, 240, 248, 250, 258, 260-269, 271, 273-4, 277, 283, 297, 305-314, 330-4, 341-2, 345-358, 362, 366, 373-4, notes 61, 88, 120
Jew, Jews, Jewish, v, 4, 6-10, 16, 18-20, 35-9, 41-45,52-54, 62, 68, 77, 90, 93-4, 101, 105, 109, 111, 113, 117, 121, 141-3, 161, 163-4, 167-8, 178-9, 182-3, 185-6, 195, 199, 205, 207, 217-9, 227-9, 232, 242, 247-8, 250-254, 258, 260, 265-6, 270-278, 280-, 287, 291, 310-11, 319, 333, 346-7, 352, 355, 372, notes 16, 40, 41, 42, 67, 75, 85, 96, 113, 114, 118, 120
Jezebel, 92
Joachim, Grandfather of Jesus, 117
Joachim of Fiore, 64, 66, 68, 70, 221
Joel, 31, 135, 139, 216, 224-5, 306, 313, 377
John the Apostle, See especially Chapter One. Also, 31, 35-6, 38, 52, 57, 60, 62, 66-7, 75-77, 79-83, 91, 93, 99-103, 105-108, 110, 116, 118, 123, 126, 130, 132, 140, 143, 146, 149, 151-2, 154, 156-61, 169, 195, 200-202, 209, 215, 218-9, 222-3, 238, 240, 242, 214-6, 251, 253, 261, 277, 280, 283, 286-7-8, 297, 299, 301, 304, 322-3, 325, 327-8, 332, 335, 337-8, 345, 347,

355-65, 365, 367, 369-70, 372, notes 1, 4, 11, 28, 29, 78, 85, 117, 124
John, The Gospel, 2-5, 10-11, 15, 19, 22-3, 25-8, 35, 65, 68, 73, 79, 92, 99, 111, 118, 141, 155, 158, 180, 188, 195, 292, 302, 324-7, 339, 354, 362-3, 369 notes 1, 28, 29, 70, 75
1 John, 28, notes 1, 61
2 John, 8,-9, 71, notes 1, 61
3 John, 2, note 1
John the Baptist, 3-4, 9, 25, 118, 162, 192, notes 1, 4, 75
John Paul II, Pope 54, 213, 294
Joseph, the patriarch, 178, 253
Joseph, the tribe, 140
Joseph, the father of Jesus, 3, 6-7, 117, note 4
Joseph of Arimathea, 364-5, note 129
Josephus, 16, 18, 34-35, 181, 251, 265, 274
Judah, 25, 116-7, 125, 186, 250, 272, 306, 309-10 notes 4, 79
Jung, Carl G., 8, 68-71, 120, 132, 188, 190, 197, 221, 314, 319, notes 1, 12, 50, 52, 93, 94, 97, 103
Justin Martyr, 14, 62, 94, note 1

key, 68, 83, 87, 93, 115, 149, 164, 187, 228, 322, 324, 327, 349, note 43
keys, 82-3, 127, 256
King James Version, x, 101, 175, 223, 255, 267

Lamb, 4, 29, 58, 79, 83, 86, 89, 98, 107, 113, 118-120, 123, 126-9, 137, 143-44, 154, 156, 166, 187-8, 198-201, 203, 205, 209,-10, 212, 215, 223-4, 227, 229, 239, 2450, 247, 259, 272, 299-300, 302, 309, 328, 341, 346-7, 349, 356, 358, 362, 365, 367-8, 373, note 1
lamb 32, 209, 349
lamp, 77-8, 82, 85, 107, 147, 296, 341, 345, 349
lamp stand, 78-9, 82, 84-88, 163, 168, 185, 294, 347, 356, 369
Lao Tzu 334-5
Laodicea 8, 83, 87, 94-5, 99
leopard, 197, 199-200, 202
Levi, 25, 117, 214, notes 4, 79
Lincoln, Abraham, 209, 351

lion 101-2, 125, 116, 123, 139, 150, 155, 197, 199-200, 202, 346, note 85
logos, 11-2, 14-5, 23, 140, 261, 279, 335, 339
Luke, the gospel notes 14, 29, 35, 64
Luther, Martin 64-5, 68, 280
Lutherans, 324
Luxembourg, 258

Macarthur, Jack, 20, 76, 103, 281, note 59
Machiavelli, Niccolo 171, 173, 189, 208, 233, 262, note 100
Maimonides, 25, 37-8, 40, 82, 100, 270, 351, 362, 368, notes 37, 40
Madison, James, v, 133, 165, 279, 284
Malachi 162-3, 333
Melchizedek, 162, 165, note 88
Manasseh, 140
manna, 92, 96, 357
Mather, Cotton, note 18
Mather, Increase, notes 18, 113
Matthew, the Apostle, 3, 24, 354, note 3
Matthew, the gospel 3-5, 10-11, 23, 26-7, 31-35, 40-41, 54-55, 57-59, 73-74, 79-80, 95, 101, 109 111-12, 114, 116, 123, 135-6, 162, 176, 218, 263, 290 295, 297, 319, 322, 338-9, 342, 354, 376, notes 3, 14, 29, 61, 64, 103
Maya, 52, note 48
Mede, Joseph, note 79
Medes 124, 126, 209, 248, 261, 266, 283
Merlin, 62
Messiah, 5, 10, 32, 36, 38, 40, 42-3, 57-8, 60-62, 69, 80, 92, 112, 115, 117, 119, 121, 128-30, 162, 173, 176, 178-9 182-4, 195, 223, 226, 232-238, 243, 261, 267-273, 288-9, 301, 306, 311, 319, 329, 334, 339, 345, 347, 351, 354, 365, 371-2, notes 37, 39, 40, 41, 75, 85, 117
Micah, 100, 177, 264, 354, 377, note 41
millstone, 295-96
moon, 33-5, 41, 43, 52, 54, 67, 98, 112, 135, 137, 139, 147-8 158, 175-8, 230, 305-6, 341, 349, 356
Mother Shipton, 52

Mount Mariah, 160, 215
Mount of Olives, 60, 180, 215, 302-3, 305-6, 329
Mount Sinai, 78, 368
Mount Zion, 39, 60, 108, 115, 143, 160, 166, 168, 215-16, 218, 220, 223, 229, 234, 373 note 85
Moses, 9, 16, 38, 78, 82, 85, 101, 1623, 164-6, 192, 195, 209, 213, 218, 227, 232, 253, 272, 335, 339, 347, 368 notes 75, 87, 89

Nag Hammadi Manuscripts, 85, 361, notes 14, 64, 70, 77
nakedness, 95, 233
Newton, Isaac, vii, 44, 186, 192, note 90
Nero Caesar viii, 7-10, 17-21, 61, 67, 180, 190, 200, 213, 252, 265-6, 328, note 9, 61, 95
Nerva, 21-2, notes 9, 95
Nietzsche, Friedrich 189, 207, 209, 259, 262
Nicolaitans, 88, 91

olive tree, 84-86, 141, 163, 195, 215, 356, 372

Pagels, Elaine, 2, 16, 252, notes 20, 106
Patmos, 8, 20-22, 24-26, 28, 68, 76, 81-2, 105, 200
Paul, vii, 3, 5-8, 14, 18, 23-25, 31, 55-56, 67, 76, 83, 99-100, 106-7, 110-11, 141, 154, 157, 163, 204, 232-3, 252, 289, 323, 337, 341, 347, 365, note 14
Pergamum, 88, 91, 94
Peter, 2-10, 12, 18-9, 24-5, 27-8, 31-2, 421, 52, 58-9, 67, 76, 110, 115, 219, 252, 331, 341, 345, 354, note 14
1 Peter, 31
2 Peter, 2, 10, 32, 42, 58-9, 115, 326
Philadelphia, 88, 90, 93-4, 105, 109, 143
Phillip, 3, 7, 85, 219, 361
Philosophy, vii, 11-15, 48, 77, 90, 121, 128, 165, 189, 194, 228, 241, 243, 252-3, 276, 287, 314, 339, 343-4, 355, 363-4, notes 38, 67,
Plato, v, 7, 9-10, 15, 32, 46, 50, 58, 60, 110, 126, 128, 135, 156, 164, 167, 173, 178, 181, 184, 187, 204, 220, 222, 228, 236, note 66, 54. 62, 111, 116

Plutarch, 50, 81
Poland, 141, 207, 247, 258, 263-4
Polycarp, 22, 24, 90, note 1
Portugal, 277, 375
Proverbs, vii, 90, 176, 258, 277, 339, 363
Psalms 42, 92, 156, 215, 233, 333, 363, 377

Quaker 131

rainbow, 59, 100, 154-55
rapture, 24, 39, 54-7, 103-116, 124, 137, 144, 151, 157, 166, 168, 178, 183, 187, 215-6, 219, 223, 229, 233-6, 323, 329, 336-7, 372, notes 67, 78
Rome, 7, 10, 16-19, 22, 24, 52, 54, 62, 64, 66-7, 72, 76, 90, 107-8, 124, 127, 129-130, 163, 165, 183, 192, 201, 207-8, 241, 243, 245-6, 250, 252, 255, 258-60, 269-70, 273, 276-81, 283, 285, 288, 293, 295, 297, 309, 313, 373
Rome, Republic of, 65, 124
Roman Empire, 13, 16-7, 20, 62, 67, 124, 129, 181, 186, 192, 201-2, 204, 207-8, 210, 231, 242-3, 246-7, 250, 256, 258, 261, 263-4, 266-272, 278-81, 297, 307, 331, 349, notes 67, 95
Roman, 9-13, 21, 37, 40, 42-43, 49, 50, 58-59, 80, 83-84, 93, 106-7, 117-8, 121, 125, 129- 137, 150, 156-160, 162-63, 166-67, 169, 172, 175, 178, 180, 182, 185, 187, 191-2, 213, 215, notes 9, 15, 67, 93, 95, 112
Romans, v, vii, 18, 20, 57, 90, 180-1, 271, 279, notes 21, 75, 112
Romans, the Letter of Paul, vii, 90, 141, 163, 165, 252, 289, 361, note 115
Romania 258, 263, 312
Rousseau, Jean-Jacques 49, 295
Russia 25, 132, 152, 202, 208, 242, 258, 263-4, 311-316, 320, 375, note 113
Russell, Charles Taze, 45, note 83
2 Samuel, note 72
Sardis, 88, 93, 104, 107, 339
Satan, 22, 60-61, 67, 980-91, 93, 101, 132, 178, 184, 188, 190, 203-205, 243, 310 322, 324, 327, 329-332
satanic, Satanists, 13, 189, 203, 205, 314

387

Schaeffer, Henry, vii, ix, 33, 106, 179, 199, 221, 338
Scofield, C.I., ix, 96, 103, 114, 121, 166, 177-8, 191, 210, 233, 266-9, 273, 280-82, 297, 303, 312, 315, 335-6 notes 95, 108, 109
sea, 3, 51-2, 58, 83, 101, 108, 119-20, 136, 140, 147, 150, 152, 155-7, 159, 164, 166, 173, 179-80,184, 188-95, 197, 201,204, 208-9, 211, 215-7, 221, 227, 229, 234-6, 338-9, 256, 262, 274, 294, 301, 308, 312, 322, 324, 327, 329, 331, 333, 337, 340, 345, 359, 364, 373, notes 35, 85, 92, 117, 121
sight, the faculty (see also hindsight, foresight, insight 88, 95, 98, 120, 166, 210, 360
sight (a spectacle) 98
silver, 138, 206, 222, 254, 257-8, 308, 350
Smyrna, 7-8, 24, 88, 90, 93-4
Snobelen, Stephen, note 90
Socrates, vi, 9, 11, 14-15, 72, 92, 121, 170, 189-190, 193, 241, 253, 267, 284, 288, 335, 344, 360, 364
soul, souls, 12-3, 17, 50, 68, 70, 72, 84, 87, 89, 95, 99, 102, 112, 121, 127-8, 133-4, 146, 149, 162, 173, 189, 193-4, 197-8, 204, 209, 222, 228-9, 257-8, 285, 90-1, 295, 301, 323-5, 330, 333, 335, 337-44, 347-8, 351, 353, 360-2, 366, 370, 375-6, notes 68, 126
Spain, 7, 199, 258, 263, 265, 277
star, 41, 96, 147, 149-50, 187, 316, 322, 357, 370, notes 41, 72
stars, 43, 77-8, 84, 87, 93, 135-6, 139, 147, 175, 178, 181, 188, 190-1, 230, 240, 247, 305, 316, 318, 368
stone, 10, 92, 94, 96, 153, 254-5, 261, 302-3, 309, 353, 357, note 75
stoning, 6, 10, 270, note 75
sun, 33-35, 40-41, 43, 52, 54, 61, 67, 98, 100, 112, 135,40, 147-9, 154-7, 158, 175-8, 187, 230, 2345-5, 237, 239, 303, 305-7, 341, 349, 356, 369, note 48
Switzerland, 199, 256, 258
sword, 23, 47, 63, 71, 83, 87-89, 91, 126-7, 129, 198, 210, 232, 290, 301-2, 312-3, 317, 327, 353-4, 364, 374, notes 40, 51, 68, 114
Syria, Syrian, 2, 76, 100, 199, 263, note 124

Temple 4-7, 18-9, 23, 31, 33-36, 39, 43, 45, 55, 57, 67, 76, 85, 90-1, 94, 96, 98, 100, 112, 136, 159-63, 166-7, 172, 185-6, 199, 201, 204, 208, 215, 220-24, 227, 229, 234, 2327, 239, 241, 243, 253, 263, 265-70, 272, 274-5, 292, 295, 297, 301-2, 307, 310, 313, 347, 349, 354-7, 365-6, note 75
Thomas, the Apostle, 3, 5, 7, 9, 24, 68, 219, 232, 354, note 30
Thomas, the book, 3, 74, 88, 354, 377, notes 34, 35, 64, 70
Thyatira, 92, 339
Tocqueville, Alexis de 48, 278
Trajan, 24, notes 9, 95
Titus, 20, 35, 268, note 9
Tree of life, 29, 58, 89-90, 96, 132, 341, 354-8, 361-3, 365, 368, 370-1, note 92
Tree of knowledge, 358-362,
tree in general 283, 334
Trees, 140, 149-50
tree, the cross, 362, 376
(See also olive tree, fig tree)
Tribulation, 31, 34-6, 40, 54, 56-8, 84, 90, 93-4, 98, 103-114, 119, 123, 126, 128, 135-6, 142-4, 151, 158, 166-172, 185, 216-9, 222, 234, 238, 241, 280, 282, 314, 336, notes 67, 78, 85

United Nations, 167, note 119
United States 46, 111, 192, 199, 207-8, 241, 264, 275, 277-8, 280, 283, 290, 295, 315, 322, 351-2, 367
Usher, Bishop, 42

Van Impe, vii, ix, 33, 39, 42,-44, 58-9, 63, 103, 105, 108, 113-15, 121, 123-4, 163-4, 167-8, 172, 178-9, 196, 199-201, 206, 208, 236, 240, 245, 250, 268-71, 275, 281, 307-8, 312-4, 334, 336, notes 43, 67, 78, 95, 120
Victorinus, ix, 21-2, 76-7, 91, 99, 101, 103, 117, 123, 137, 148, 152, 154, 157, 160, 166, 188, 186, 238, 280, 324, 328-9, 332, note 95
Voegelin, Eric, 66

White stone 92, 94, 96, 302, 357

Williams, Roger, v, 243
Wine, 65, 126-9, 153, 221, 227, 240, 283, 306, 362, notes 15, 16, 88
winepress, 60, 216, 220-1, 224-5, 234, 239, 289, 302, 304, 322, 329, 373
Wycliffe, John, 64, 68

Yellowstone, 53, 295

Zechariah, 39, 60, 79-80, 84-5, 140-1, 163, 215-6, 258, 297, 302-3, 305-6, 316, 323, 348, 377
Zephaniah, 286, 377
Zion, (See Mount Zion) 40, 177, 215, 348, 353-4

Bibliography

A. Bible Texts

1. Bible. *The Pocket Interlinear New Testament.* Edited by J. P. Green, Grand Rapids, MI: Baker Book House, 1979.

2. Bible. *The New Oxford Annotated Bible with the Apocrypha.* Edited by Herbert G. May and Bruce M. Metzger. New York: Oxford University Press, 1977.

3. *The Catholic Study Bible.* (The New American Bible). General Editor Donald Senior New York: Oxford University Press, 1990.

4. *Holy Bible.* Rockford, Ill.: 1881.

5. *The Holy Bible.* Scofield, C. I. New York: Oxford University Press, 1909.

B. Classic Works

1. Anonymous 1. *The Acts of John.* In *The Ante-Nicene Fathers* edited by Roberts, A., and Donaldson, J. Grand Rapids: Eerdmans, 1985-1987. (Vol. VII, p. 563).

2. Anonymous 2. *The Acts of John* in *The Other Gospels.* Edited by Ron Cameron, Philadelphia: The Westminster Press, 1982.

Bibliography

3. *Anonymous 3. Authoritative Teaching.* Translated by George W. MacRae, in *The Nag Hammadi Library in English*, pp. 278-283.

4. Aquinas, St. Thomas. *Summa Contra Gentiles.*

5. Augustine. *City of God.* Translated by Marcus Dodds, D. D. New York: Modern Library, undated.

6. Bettenson, Henry. *Documents of the Christian Church.* New York: Oxford University Press, 1963.

7. Burnet, John. Plato: Euthyphro, Apology, Crito. London: Oxford, 1979.

8. Charles, R. H. *The Book of Enoch.* London: The Chaucer Press, 1966.

9. Didache. In Early Christian Fathers, edited by Cyril B. Richardson. New York: Macmillan, 1970.

10. Eusebius, *History of the Church.* In *The Nicene and Ante-Nicene Fathers.* Edited by Alexander Roberts and James Donaldson. W. B. Eerdmans Publishing Co: (no date).

11. Gibbon, Edward. *The Decline and Fall of the Roman Empire.* Chicago: Encyclopedia Britannica, Inc. 1952.

12. Hesiod. *Works and Days.* Translated by R. M. Frazier. Norman: University of Oklahoma Press, 1983.

13. Hippolytus. In *The Ante-Nicene Fathers.* Edited by Roberts, A., and Donaldson, J. *The Ante-Nicene Fathers* Grand Rapids; W. B. Eerdmans Publishing Co, Vol. VII, 1985-1987.

14. Irenaeus, *On Heresies*, III. In *The Ante-Nicene Fathers.* Edited by Roberts, A., and Donaldson, J. *The Ante-*

Nicene Fathers Grand Rapids: W. B. Eerdmans Publishing Co, Vol. I, 1985-1987

15. James M. R., ed. *The Apocryphal New Testament.* Oxford, Clarendon Press, 1924.

16. Josephus, Flavius Joseph. *The Complete Works of Josephus.* Translated by William Whiston. Grand Rapids: Kregel Publications, 1981.

17. Justin Martyr *Dialogue with Trypho.* in *The Ante-Nicene Fathers.* Edited by Roberts, A., and Donaldson, J. Grand Rapids: W. B. Eerdmans Publishing Co, Vol. I, 1985-1987.

18. Lao Tzu Tao Te Ching. Translated by Gui Fu-Feng and Jane EnglishNew York: Vantage Books, 1972.

19. Malachy, Saint. *The Prophecies of St. Malachy.* Rockford, Ill: Tan Books, 1973.

20. *The Nag Hammadi Library in English.* Translated by Members of the Coptic Gnostic project of the Institute for antiquity and Christianity, James M. Robinson dir. New York: Harper and Rowe, 1977.

21. Plato. *Apology.* In Three Texts on Socrates, ed. by Thomas G. West. Ithica, NY: Cornell University Press,1984.

22. _____. *Republic.* Translated by Alan Bloom. New York: Basic Books, Inc. 1968.

23. _____. *Phaedo.*

24. _____. *Meno.*

25. Suetonius. *The Twelve Caesars.* Translated by Robert Graves. New York: Penguin Books, 1989.

Bibliography

26. Tacitus. *The Annals of Imperial Rome*. Translated by Michael Grant. New York: Penguin Books, 1985.

27. Tocqueville, Alexis de. *The Old Regime and the French Revolution.* Translated by Stuart Gilbert. Garden City: Doubleday Inc., 1955.

28. Victorinus. *Commentary on the Apocalypse of the Blessed John.* In Roberts, A., and Donaldson, J. *The Ante-Nicene Fathers* Grand Rapids; Eerdmans, Vol. VII, 1985-1987.

C. Recent Commentaries

1. David Aune. *Revelation*. Word Biblical Commentary. Dallas, TX: World Books, 1997.

2. Bauckham, Richard. "Revelation," in *The Oxford Bible Commentary*, pp. 1287-1306.

3. Brother Michael of the Holy Trinity. *The Third Secret of Fatima.* translated by Gardiner, Anne Barbeau, Rockford, Ill; Tan, 1991.

4. Cradock, Fred B, and Tucker, Gene M. "Bible," in Microsoft, Encarta encyclopedia, 2004.

5. De Conick April D. "What's Up with the Gospel of Thomas?" In *Biblical Archeology Review*, Vol. 36 no. 1, 2010, pp. 28, 85-86.

6. dc Talk and the Voice of the Martyrs. *Jesus Freaks. Stories of those who stood for Jesus: The Ultimate Jesus Freaks.* Tulsa, Oklahoma: Albury Publishing, 1999.

7. Drewes, Christopher. *Introduction to the Books of the Bible*. St. Louis, Missouri: Concordia Publishing House, 1970.

8. Johnson, Paul. *A History of the American People*. New York: Harper-Collins, 1997.

9. Jung, Carl G. *The Portable Jung*. Edited by Joseph Campbell. New York: The Viking Press.

10. _____. *Symbols of Transformation*. Translated by R. F. C. Hull. New York: The Bollingen Foundation, 1956.

11. Lindsey, Hal. *Planet Earth*: The Final Chapter. Beverly Hills, CA: Western Front Ltd., 1998.

12. _____. *There's A New World Coming*. Santa Ana: Vision House Publishers, 1973.

13. Macarthur, Jack. *Revelation*. Eugene, Oregon: Vernon L. Iverson Co., 1973.

14. Mails, Thomas E. *The Hopi Survival Kit*. Arcana: Welcome Rain, 1997.

15. McBirnie, William Stuart. *The Search for the Twelve Apostles*. Carol Stream, Ill.: Tyndale House Publishers, Inc., 1973.

16. Mede, Joseph. A Key to the Apocalypse (Clavis Apocalyptis). Christian Classics Etherial Library. (Undated).

17. Newton, Isaac. Observations Concerning the Prophesies of Daniel and St. John. London: J Darby and T. Browne 1783.

18. _____. 1704 letter, Snobelen edition

19. Reagan, David R. "What Year is it?" Lion and Lamb Ministries. http: // www.lamblion.com.

20. Scofield, C. I. Notes, in The Holy Bible. New York: Oxford University Press, 1909.

Bibliography

21. Smith, William. In *The Holy Bible*, Rockford, Ill., 1881.

22. Snobeln, Stephen D. Cosmos and Apocalypse. In The New Atlantis,

23. _____. Statement on the Date 2060. July, 2003.

24. Strauss, Leo. *Thoughts on Machiavelli*. Chicago: The University of Chicago Press, 1958.

25. Van Impe, Jack. *Revelation Revealed Verse by Verse*. Troy, Michigan: Jack Van Impe Ministeries, 1982.

26. _____. *Final Mysteries Unsealed*, Nashville: World Publishing, 1998.

27. _____. *11:59 and Counting*. Jack Van Impe Ministries, 1983.

28. Voegelin, Eric. *The New Science of Politics*. Chicago: The University of Chicago Press. 1987.

29. Walvoord, John E Walvoord. *The Millennial Kingdom*. Grand Rapids, Mi.: Academic Books, 1959.

28. Watch Tower Bible and Tract Society of Pennsylvania. *Revelation: Its Grand Climax at hand.* Brooklyn, NY: U.S.A., 1988.

On the Revelation

Notes

[1] References to ancient authors are to text and section number, and occasionally to the modern texts where these can be found, while modern authors are indicated by referring to the author and the year of publication, the full title being available in the bibliography at the conclusion below.

Contemporary readers think it to be conclusive that the Revelation could not have been written by John the apostle (David Aune, *1997*, pp. xlviii-lx). And so this question has seemed to us a good place to begin. The tradition seems otherwise to always have assumed that John the apostle is the author, beginning in preserved writings about 155-160 A.D., with Justin (*Dialogue with Trypho*, 81; p. 40 below). It is not clear whether Justin cites the book or an oral report of the teaching of John, or how widely circulated the book was. It may have been a secret work in the first half of the second century, or the preserve of the churches in Asia. Dionysius the Great, Bishop of Alexandria, writing in the fourth century, seems to be the first of preserved writers to doubt that the apostle John wrote the Revelation. Dionysius suggests that the Apocalypse was seen by a different John (Roberts, A., and Donaldson, J. *The Ante-Nicene Fathers* (Vol. VII, pp. 82-84). One reason for his doubt is that in the gospel and first letter, John the apostle does not refer to himself by name. And so it is thought, since the John of the Revelation does call himself John, that this is likely to be another John. Yet surely John might identify himself in one writing and not do so in another, and this is less an argument than a hunch. Dionysius also comments that in the Revelation, none of John's characteristic "phrasing or diction" appears to be present. The writings "share hardly a syllable in common," and unlike the gospel and letters, the Revelation employs "barbarous idioms" and a dialect and language that are "not of the exact Greek type." We will consider in place below certain symbols, such as the door, the way of speaking about *being*, and about the divinity of Jesus, that seem nearer to John than anyone else known in history. A characteristic phrase is "to prepare a place," in the Gospel of John 14:2-3 and Revelation 12:6; Aune, 1997, p. 691). Modern linguistics notes that the rate of the use of words unique to the text is similar to the Gospel of John, and the use of the preposition *ek* is similarly higher in the Gospel of John and the Revelation than in any other Greek Biblical text (Aune, ccvii; cixxix). The identification of Jesus with the Word, though, is the most obvious similarity (Revelation 19:13; John 1:1), and it may even be safe to say that no one else in the history of humanity is able to speak and write in this way. The "Lamb of God" is another characteristic name from John the Baptist, as reported in the Gospel of John (1:29). Aquinas notices the light in the gospel (John 1:9), letter (1John 1:5) and Revelation (22:5, *Summa Contra Gentiles*, III. 53). There *is*, though, quite a difference between the Gospel of John and the prophetic vision of the Revelation. One wonders how much of the difference might be due to the dictated and descriptive character of the Revelation, or to John having been told what to write. He is simply shown what he saw, and told to write this. We need not presuppose that it is impossible for these things to have occurred just as they are written. So in the dictated letters to the churches, there are different concerns, for example regarding heresy and idolatry, than in the three letters of John. If one compares, for example, the writing preserved of Polycarp and Papias, or even Justin or Irenaeus, it is difficult to believe that anyone capable of the height of thought in receiving the Revelation was alive in the first or Second Century other than the author of the Gospel of John. Jung believes John to be the author of the gospel, the Revelation and the letters as well, writing that "psychological findings speak in favor of such an assumption" ("Answer to Job," in *The Portable Jung*, p. 625, 636 note 177).

[2] Cradock, Fred B., and Tucker, Gene M. "Bible," in Microsoft, Encarta Encyclopedia, 2004.

[3] According to the list of Hippolytus, Jude, Simon the Zealot and Matthias are other apostles to fall asleep rather than be killed (Roberts and Donaldson, p. 255). There is a Greek legend that Matthew died a natural death, in contrast with the Western tradition that he too was martyred. *The Search for the Twelve Apostles*. McBirnie, William Stuart, p. 180.

[4] *Ibid*, p. 108. Upon return from Egypt, Joseph goes to Galilee instead of Judea, to the area of the relatives of Mary (Mt. 2:22-23), who include her aunt or Great Aunt Elizabeth (Lk.1:39, 65) and sister Salome. Elizabeth seems to have lived across the great plain in the North of Judea, so that John and Andrew would be disciples of John the Baptist. She may have been the sister of Ann the mother of Mary, except that John the Baptist and his parents are Levites, while Jesus is of the tribe of Judah. How Elizabeth is the kinswoman of Mary is then a question.

[5] The *Acts of John*, in *The Ante-Nicene Fathers* edited by Roberts, A., and Donaldson, J. Grand Rapids; Eerdmans, 1985-1987. (Vol. VII, p. 563).

[6] Ibid, p. 108.

[7] William Stuart McBirnie, *The Search for the Twelve Apostles*, p. 108.

[8] *The Gospel of the Nativity of Mary*, in Roberts and Donaldson, *The Ante-Nicene fathers*, vol. pp. 384-387.

[9] The Roman Emperors, following the death of Caesar in 44 B. C., are: Augustus until 14 A. D.; Tiberius from 14-37, Caligula (37-41), Claudius (41-54); Nero (54-68), Four in 68-69 (Galba, Otho, Vitellus and Vespasian (69-79), Titus (79-81), Domitian (81-96); Nerva (96-98), Trajan (98-117)...

[10] *The Acts of the Holy Apostle Thaddeus*, Christian Classics Ethereal Library.

[11] *The Acts of John*, in *The Ante-Nicene Fathers* (Vol. VII, pp. 560- 564). This seems to be the first seventeen sections of another book called the *Acts of John,* which also contains numbered sections. The book is said to be written by Leucius, a companion of John. Sections 85-105 were uncovered in 1896 in a Greek manuscript copied in 1324. It is said to be Docetic, and was condemned as heretical in 787 (Ron Cameron, editor, *The Other Gospels,* pp. 87-98). This condemnation, possibly of the thought or emphasis of a companion of John, may have led to the rejection of the stories of the

On the Revelation

generation that knew John and the lack of historical material about the life of John, for there is very little otherwise. The clearest statement of what has occurred regarding the *Acts of John* is the suggestion that the apocryphal acts of the second century in general were later condemned and purged of some of their content, retaining the accounts of the deaths and portions of the original acts of the apostles (Oxford Bible Commentary, p. 1322). The purged content was later restored, leading to the possibility that the sections of the three *Acts of John* may somehow fit together. M. R. James, ed. *The Apocryphal New Testament* (Oxford, Clarendon Press, 1924) prints what are called sections 18-115; Cameron prints sections numbered 87-105, while Roberts and Donaldson print the story of John's appearance before Domitian and his speech at his death. The first section here may be sections 1-17 of the original *Acts of John* by Leucius.

[12] Jung, C. G. *The Portable Jung*, edited by Joseph Campbell, pp. 624- 625.

[13] McBirnie, 1973, p. 91-93.

[14] In the gospel of Luke (9:46-50), when the question arose which one of them was the greatest, Jesus places the child before them, and says "Whoever receives this child in my name receives me...he who is least among you all is the one who is great." John answers "Master, we saw a man casting out demons in your name, and we forbade him because he does not follow with us." Jesus answers him, "Do not forbid him; for he that is not against you is for you." Similarly, since this is to be philosophic reading, we can wonder whether the teaching of Paul that members of the church should avoid association with sinners is the same as the teaching of Jesus, that he came not to save the righteous but the sinners (Matthew 9:11-13; 11:19; Mark 2:13-17; Luke 5:27). Jesus some times speaks against those who "drink with the drunkards." This may be a difference of emphasis, suited to the different persons and their different circumstances. But it is a difference. He himself is like one who scorns the contempt of public opinion, while Paul uses this opinion to preserve purity among the flock. Here again, it is important too that the church be kept pure, and not be "yoked unequally with sinners" (II Cor. 6:14-16). But it is a different teaching, pointing toward a different concern. We wonder whether we ought not go among mankind, if we can avoid corruption, embrace humanity, bring light, lead out, even without regard for reputation, as Jesus was with Mary Magdalene, despite her seven demons (Mark 16:9). He did not say "Let us not be yoked with prostitutes." The tradition that she was a prostitute has become unfashionable, thought to be a chauvinistic invention. The Apostles do not otherwise record it, because she was their friend. But the whole point of this tradition is that he receives penance, forgives sins, and received this saint into holiness. That he even taught women was a novelty, questioned by Peter in the Nag Hammadi *Gospel of Mary Magdalene*. But after Mary and Mary Magdalene, women become saints.

[15] The Witnesses were the leading sect to face Nazi persecution directly, and they have also been at the forefront of legal cases to assure the observance of

the First Amendment to the U. S. Constitution. Because religion is based on custom or convention, religion is not always the first to oppose the tyrannical imposition of authority if this holds certain conservative principles and opposes enemies they have in common. The Witnesses are also leaders in a certain part of carrying out the things we *were* told to do, namely, spread the gospel. But if we would settle for doctrinaire assumptions of authoritative opinion, or first principles that equate one's own, man-made group with the elect, we should have remained simple Catholics. The same would seem to hold for the Baptist argument that the whole congregation should sing the same song, or say the same things, for example regarding alcohol prohibition. But Jesus is not a legislator, and the Jews know no such law. The wine of the wedding at Cana, and the new wine, are turned back into grape juice, miraculously making the miraculous mundane. Their own separation from the Roman Church is undermined, and it becomes clear that each sect is impelled to repeat the Roman error.

[16] Alvarez, Leo Paul S. de. of the University of Dallas is the source of this particular metaphysical formulation.

[17] Leo Strauss, *The History of Political Philosophy*, edited by Leo Strauss and Joseph Cropsey, p. 5.

[18] Increase Mather, the father of Cotton Mather, arrived at the same thought (Paul Johnson, *A History of the American People*, p. 82-83, note 116 below).

[19] Consider the bulk of the Christian things appearing on television, and the percentage of time spent asking for money. Why do the genuine programs or the teachings not succeed in this media?

[20] Elaine Pagels, *Revelations*, p. 109.

[21] Eusebius, *History*, II, 2, citing Tertullian, *Apology for the Christians*, writes:

> And when the wonderful resurrection and ascension of our Savior were already noised abroad, in accordance with an ancient custom which prevailed among the rulers of the provinces, of reporting to the emperor the novel occurrences which took place in them, in order that nothing might escape him, Pontius Pilate informed Tiberius of the reports which were noised abroad through all Palestine concerning the resurrection of our Savior Jesus from the dead. He gave an account also of other wonders which he had learned of him, and how, after his death, having risen from the dead, he was now believed by many to be a god. They say that Tiberius referred the matter to the Senate, but that they rejected it, ostensibly because they had not first examined into the matter (for an ancient law prevailed that no one should be made a god by the Romans except by a

vote and decree of the Senate), but in reality because the saving teaching of the divine Gospel did not need the confirmation and recommendation of men. But although the Senate of the Romans rejected the proposition made in regard to our Savior, Tiberius still retained the opinion which he had held at first, and contrived no hostile measures against Christ.

[22] Christopher Drewes, *Introduction to the Books of the Bible*, p. 154.
[23] The *Acts of John*, in *The Ante-Nicene Fathers*, Roberts and Donaldson. p. 561.
[24] This story, related in *Jesus Freaks*, pp.162-165, is probably from the Book of Martyrs by John Foxe.
[25] *The Ante-Nicene Fathers*, Vol. VII, p. 353.
[26] In *Documents of the Christian Church*, edited by Henry Bettenson, p. 28. Also, McBirnie, p. 116, citing Eusebius.
[27] In *The Other Gospels*, edited by Ron Cameron, pp. 133-162.
[28] The work opens with the mention of Cerinthus and Simon, two opponents of John. It includes miracles and gospel elements that are also in the Gospel of John.
[29] Jerome, *The Nicene and Post Nicene Fathers*, p. 364-5; McBirnie, p. 117. The Reverend "The lives of the Holy Apostles and Evangelists," In The Holy Bible; Rockford, Illinois; Chandler brothers, 1881. Another significant discrepancy, possibly consistent, is that in the three gospels, Jesus prays in the Garden of Gethsemane that the cup pass from him if possible from him, nevertheless, not as I will, but as thou wilt" while in the Gospel of John he says, "shall I not drink the cup which the Father has given me." (Matt 26:39; Mark 14:36 "all things are possible for thee"; Luke 22:42: "if thou art willing... not my will but thine be done," another distinction between the Father and son; John 18:11).
[30] *Consummation of the Apostle Thomas,* in *The Ante-Nicene Fathers*, ed. Roberts and Donaldson, Volume VII, pp. 550-552.
[31] Pliny the Younger, in Bettenson, Henry, ed. *Documents of the Christian Church*, pp. 3-4.
[32] Eusebius, *History of the Church*, III. xxiii.
[33] Eusebius, *History of the Church*, III, xxiii. 1, 4; III, xxxi. 3; Irenaeus, *On Heresies*, III.
[34] The first saying of the "Gnostic" Gospel of Thomas may also indicate a connection between "*anignoskon*" and blessing.
[35] An example of such a reading is that assumed in a recent article when it is written: "Texts like Luke-Acts (Acts 1:6-8) show us that some Christians chose to delay the end indefinitely by creating a lengthy period of the church and its ministry before the end would be able to come..." April D. De Conick, "What's up with the Gospel of Thomas? in *Biblical Archeology Review,* Vol. 36 no. 1, 2010, p. 84.

Notes

[36] Stories of modern martyrs are collected in the book *Jesus Freaks*, credited to dc Talk and the Voice of the Martyrs.

[37] Maimonides, "Laws of Kings and their Wars," in *The Days of the Messiah*, p. 173.

[38] The peculiar character of twentieth century tyranny– whether it is of the left or the right– appears inseparable from the revolt of the modern mind against the medieval imagination. Surprisingly, these extreme opposites, communism and fascism, have a number of characteristics in common, in addition to the total power held by the ruling element, from which their common name is derived. Both arose out of the German philosophy of the nineteenth century– though the direct connection is clearer in the case of Marx. Both involve the rule of an idea or theory, which outlives any particular tyrant. Both begin in atheism, following the enlightened modern rejection of the medieval world. Both are *historicist*, rejecting the idea of a permanent human nature while understanding man to be a product of historical processes (and so both reject the idea of natural rights that are unalienable). Both are reductionist, reducing political science to biological or economic science, and both focus on one thing, whether race or class, as the most important of the human things. Both replace common sense ethics and ancient tradition with a new ethical principle, based on class or race. Both are "utopian," looking to a future condition considered to be a perfection, occurring at the end of history for the Marxists, or lasting for 1000 years, for Hitler. Finally, both are universal, or aim at world rule. Finally, both tyrannies killed millions of their own subjects in a genocide, aimed at racial purity, or a "classicide," aimed at eliminating the economic class of the bourgeois. These two things, the future condition and the killing of vast numbers of certain kinds of persons, are theoretically related in both these ideologies. That is, Marxist communism is not about holding hands and sharing things, especially with the "bourgeois." Marx calls the violence of the revolution "philosophy in action," ("A Contribution to the Critique of Hegel," in Tucker, *The Marx and Engels Reader*, 59-60), a "spiritual" violence, and describes this as an inversion of religion 53-54). It is as if an inverse religious sacrifice were projected into the political realm, as the means for the attainment of the promised utopia. This future condition betrays the outline of an inversion of the Christian vision of the Kingdom, whether it is imagined as one of racial purity of the fascists or of the return of the alienated human essence, its contemplation in the products of labor, and the universal communist condition. The inversion of the imagination in the course of modernity– culminating in the political result of German philosophy– reveals, more than anything else, the character of the diabolic or the anti-Christian. That this should occur in our age is another of the astonishing convergences that lead some to think that the time is indeed for us very near.

[39] Pereq Heleq, in *The Days of the Messiah*, p. 168.

On the Revelation

[40] Ibid, p.166. Maimonides states the Jewish position most clearly when he writes that Jesus was prophesied about by Daniel, not as the son of man who comes with the Ancient of Days (at 7:13), but rather where it is said that "outlaws of your people shall rise up in fulfillment of vision, but shall fail" (11:14). He does not suggest, for example, that Jesus is the one who tried to change the times and the law. Maimonides writes that as Rabbi Akiba was wrong about ben Koziba, in the early second century rebellion, when "all the wise men of his generation imagined him to be the messianic king...When he was slain, it became clear that he was not." "All the prophets declared that the Messiah will redeem Israel, save them, gather their disbursed, and strengthen their obedience to the commandments. But he caused Israel to perish by the sword and to have their remnant scattered and degraded. He replaced the Torah and led astray most of the world to serve a God besides the Lord" (pp.172-173). We think that when the Messiah appears at the Second Advent, the Jews will look on him who they have pierced, and then there will be agreement.

[41] How would the Magi know by seeing his star in the East that a king of the Jews had been born? The priests told Herod about Micah 5:2 identifying Bethlehem as the city, and this allows Herod to slay the innocents. The wise men, then, are not wise to tell a tyrant about the Messiah. Jesus escapes when an angel warns them to flee, and they go into Egypt, or perhaps to the Jewish community in Ethiopia.

[42] David R. Reagan, "What Year is it?" p. 10 cites Mitchell First, *Jewish History in Conflict: A Study of the Major Discrepancy between Rabbinic and Conventional Chronology*, pp. 135-137.

[43] Watchtower, *Revelation*, p. 179-180. Van Impe writes: "Some cultists declare that He came in 1914 or 1918 as an invisible spirit. Nonsense! The Bible declares that he shall return as he left" (1987, p. 8). The teaching was changed to say He would return within the lives of those alive in 1914, and then something was to happen in 1975. Something, though, did happen in 1914: the beginning of what might be a series of three world wars. Many things may be calculated. The key is to understand the meaning, and we do not. The Fatima vision occurred in 1917.

[44] R. H. Charles, *The Book of Enoch*, 1966 p. xvi. The Sadducees counted by a solar year, Enoch presents a 364 day year, divisible by sevens or weeks, though still off by a day and a quarter. The 52 weeks in a year are near to 7x7+1/2 week.

[45] Sir Francis Bacon, *Atlantis*, 93.

[46] *Daily Mail*, Oct. 7, 1998; BBC News, Oct. 21, 1998; *Washington Post*, Feb 10, 1999.

[47] *The Prophecies of St. Malachy*, Edited by Peter Bander.

[48] The Mayan calendar ends on December 12, 2012. Their astronomy knew that on that date, the rising sun on the winter solstice would align with the black hole in the center of the Milky Way galaxy. The Hopi prophecy includes the "gourd of ashes," developed near their land in Arizona. The prophecy

seems to indicate that this coincides with a reversal of the magnetic field around the earth, and a possible pole shift or switch of North and South. See Thomas E. Mails, *The Hopi Survival Kit, pp. 207-219.*

[49] Alvarez, Leo Paul S. de, University of Dallas.

[50] In C. G. Jung, *Civilization in Transition*, Collected Works Volume X.

[51] Damocles was a courtier at Syracuse under Dionysius, who spoke so much of the happiness of being a king or tyrant that Dionysius had him seated for a meal beneath a sword that hung by a hair.

[52] Jung frequently explains this principle, for example: "I do not regard the symbol as an allegory or sign, but take it in its proper sense as the best possible way of describing and formulating an object that is not completely knowable. It is in this sense that the *credo* is called a symbolum" (*Aion*, p. 73).

[53] Al Farabi, "The Political Regime." In *Medieval Political Philosophy*, p. 35. Modern psychology cannot distinguish between genius and madness, nor does it even try.

[54] Al Farabi, "On Plato's Laws" in *Medieval Political Philosophy*, pp. 84-85.

[55] Cited in *Biblical Archeology Review*, Vol. 36 no. 1, 2010, p. 85.

[56] David Aune, *Revelation*, vol. 1, pp. 3-4.

[57] Eusebius II, xxiii.

[58] Ibid. III, v.3.

[59] Macarthur, Jack, *Revelation*, Eugene, Oregon: Vernon L. Iverson Co., 1973, p. 13.

[60] Bauckham, Richard, "Revelation," in *The Oxford Bible Commentary*, pp. 1287-1306.

[61] The Beast is not called *Antichrist* in the Revelation, and the word does not occur in scripture except in the letter of John: "Children, it is the last hour; and as you have heard that antichrist is coming, so now many antichrists have come; therefore we know it is the last hour" (1 John 1:18). John seems to be wrong about this, unless the last hour covers thousands of years. John seems to have extended the idea to include the teachers of the Jerusalem heresy that Jesus was not divine: "Who is the liar but he who denies that Jesus is the Christ? (1 John 2:22; 4:2-3; 2 John 7). This is the Antichrist, he who denies the father and the son." John seems to use the word to describe heretical Christians, rather even than false Christs (pseudochristoi, Matthew 24:24). These are plural, whereas the Beast is singular or dual. One wonders whether John had yet seen the days of Nero when he wrote this letter. He must have heard of Caligula.

[62] Plato, *Republic* (497b). Not one city was then worthy of philosophic kingship.

[63] Ibid, (473a-b).The lines drawn on a baseball diamond, for example, between any two objects, such as home and first, are close enough, but not exactly straight. This imperfection, however, can be measured, and so implies the existence of mathematical truths in space. Is it not the same for virtue and the good?

On the Revelation

⁶⁴ *The Gospel of Thomas*, in *The Nag Hammadi Library*, p. 130; 118. The *Gospel of Thomas* may itself be, or be derived from, the postulated source of the above saying and other sayings common to both Matthew and Luke, called Q by the scholars who reasoned that it must have existed (Helmut Koester, Introduction to the Gospel of Thomas, in *The Nag Hammadi Library in English*, p. 117).

⁶⁵ As Eden is thought to be a condition of harmony that only man comes out of, so the Kingdom exists and is found when man reenters the harmony.

⁶⁶ Yarbro Collins, Adela. "The Apocalypse," in *The New Jerome Bible Commentary*, p. 1000.

⁶⁷Jack Van Impe, from the television show *Jack Van Impe Presents*. Dr. Van Impe is one of the foremost readers of the Revelation and Daniel together. His television show is a distillation of over fifty years of reading and preaching on the Revelation in relation to the political events of the present time. His understanding of the prophesied alliances and alignments of the nations seems to me unsurpassed. Many of the suggestions in his teaching seem most probable, and we will have occasion to follow his account at various points below. A flaw appears to be the failure to separate the visible and invisible things, where these two might, or should be separate. An example is in his identification of the heavens with the visible cosmos, and hence the spirits of the air with physical extraterrestrial beings. He generally does not comment on Fatima, and does not understand the significance, for his topic, of the history of philosophy, or the most fundamental thought of man on man. The fundamentals of his teaching are: 1) the prophesied time is that of the end of the *age* (*aion*) and not the end of the world, but rather, scripture teaches a "world without end," even as we say in the mass; 2) the five sections of the image are five world empires, preceded by the Egyptian and Assyrian and beginning with the Babylon of Nebuchadnezzar. From the head that is Babylon, the image continues through the Medo-Persian, Greek, and Roman Empires, through the division of the Eastern and Western empires, and the ten toes of a revived Roman Empire; 3) the European Union is the revived Roman Empire prophesied in the image of the second chapter of Daniel. 4) The church was in error to follow Augustine against the millennialists, in teaching that there would not be a thousand year reign of the saints; 5) there will be a literal rapture of the Christians before the tribulation; 6) the return of the Jews to Israel in 1948 and their taking of Jerusalem in 1967 are the fulfillment of the prophecy of the return of the Jews from worldwide dispersion and the beginning of the generation of the end times as prophesied by Isaiah and Ezekiel, and Daniel; And finally, 7) that the time of the Antichrist is ushered in with a three wave assault outlined in Ezekiel 38 and 39, leading to the battle of Armageddon.

⁶⁸ Oxford note to Revelation 1:9-20; Hebrews 4:12 reads: "For the word of God is living and active, sharper than any two-edged sword, piercing to the division of soul and spirit, of joints and marrow, and discerning the thoughts and intentions of the heart." The word taken in makes active a division in the

soul which is penance, and spiritually painful. This division can lead to forgiveness or mercy which bridges or even cures the more fundamental division, as that between that in us which follows law and that which follows sin.

[69] Most dreams consist of the dreamer themselves in this or that circumstance, while not recognizing that they are dreaming. A rarer sort of dream is like a vision of a symbol, without the dreamer being personally involved in the circumstance that is seen. Famously, it is written that the dream is 1/60th of prophecy (Guide, II.36).

[70] *The Gospel of Thomas,* in *The Nag Hammadi Library in English,* pp. 118-130. Jesus says the same thing in the Gospel of John: "he who hears my word and believes him who sent me, has eternal life; he does not come into judgment, but has passed from death into life."

[71] Adela Yarbro Collins, "The Apocalypse (Revelation)," in *The New Jerome Bible Commentary,* pp. 996-1016.

[72] The reference is to the women who, by the counsel of Balaam, enticed the men of Israel into the worship of Baal (Numbers 31:16; 25: 1-5). In the Book of Numbers, Balaam is a non-Israelite diviner called on by the Moabite Balak to curse Israel. The Lord refuses to allow the curse, because the Israelites are blessed. Balaam delivers an oracle to Balak about "What this people will do to your people in the latter days." The Oracle of Balaam is said to be one of four places in the Pentateuch or first five books where the end of days is addressed (Drosnin, Michael, *The Bible Code,* pp. 85. The four places are Genesis 49:1-2; Numbers 24:14-17; Deuteronomy 4:30; Deuteronomy 31:29). The Oracle of Balaam to Balak includes the statement: I see him now; I behold him, but not nigh: a star shall come forth out of Jacob, and a scepter shall rise out of Israel; It shall crush the forehead of Moab, and shall break down all the sons of Seth. Edom shall be dispossessed, Seir also, his enemies, shall be dispossessed, while Israel shall do valiantly. By Jacob shall dominion be exercised." The Oxford note suggests that the prophecy was fulfilled in the time of David, referring to 2 Samuel (8:2, 13-14). The connection between the Balaam and Balak of the Book of Numbers and the Balaam and Balak of the Revelation is not clear. The Oxford text explains the difference between the diviner sympathetic to Israel and the diviner guilty of treachery against Israel, and the Oxford notes suggest a difference between an early and a priestly tradition (note to Numbers 31:8).

[73] Bauckham, Richard, "Revelation," in *The Oxford Bible Commentary,* pp. 1287-1306.

[74] Victorianus, *"Commentary on the Apocalypse of the Blessed John"* Roberts, A., and Donaldson, J. *The Ante-Nicene Fathers* Grand Rapids; Eerdmans, 1985-1987. (Vol. VI, pp. 341--360).

[75] This line is often read as an indication of Christian anti-Semitism, and has an incorrect ring to us, who have seen the Holocaust of the twentieth century. I once met a man at a coffee shop counter who cited this line as justification for

his zealous anti-Semitism. The next day I brought him a paper with every reference to the Jews in the New Testament, which I had looked up from a concordance. Being the nation that gave birth to the Messiah and the nationality of all the apostles and the early saints among the women, Christian anti-Semitism seems strangely forgetful or unreflective. It is as though some dark cloud of ignorance were spread over mankind, until the Holocaust. For if there is such a thing as ethnic or national or cultural superiority, the Jews would be among the first to consider, perhaps along with the Greeks. And yet here, this line of scripture, is a place where the recovery of the memory of the historical context makes the text appear in a different light. The Temple– under the influence of the Romans, even in the reign of Augustus, where Herod is king of the Jews– is deeply corrupt. From the slaughter of the innocents to the murder of John the Baptist, through the Crucifixion and the stoning of Stephen to James the Just, right before the destruction of the temple, the Jewish polity, in both the rule of the Jewish Kingdom and the temple, to say the least, contains grave difficulties. The Essenes and many of the more spiritual Jews had left Jerusalem for the desert. Still, the persecution of the Christians by a faction of the temple, as a heretical sect that ought to be stomped out, had a deep historical impact and should not be forgotten. The disappearance of Christian Jews who follow the Law of Moses seems to have been one result. Although the Gentiles need not convert to Judaism in order to become Christians, the Jews who become Christian need not set aside Mosaic Law. There are certain details of the severity of law, where one might be persuaded by Jesus, like the command to stone the adulteress (John 8:3-11). No nation is immune to the evils of persecution.

[76] Watchtower, *Revelation: Its Grand Climax at Hand*, p. 66.

[77] *Authoritative Teaching*, translated by George W. MacRae, in *The Nag Hammadi* Library in *English*, pp. 278-283.

[78] Van Impe interprets this "Come up hither" as synonymous with the rapture and the twenty four elders as representing all believers (*Revelation Revealed*, 53-54, 155). He reads the events of the tribulation as occurring entirely after the church has been evacuated. This reading is questionable, and is given without reasoning, and yet a great deal of his reading may depend upon it. The reading carries on an American Protestant tradition. If this is the rapture, why is John the only one to ascend, or why should no clearer mention be made of the twenty-four elders ascending at this time? One would think that so central a part of the end times and apparently of the message of Jesus for the church or the servants of God would be described more clearly, as perhaps it later is. But the vision seems to occur in the present tense, first at a time when no one was found that could open the scroll, then when one was found who had conquered. So now the scroll can be opened or revealed to John. Again it would be strange if he were one of the elders, as it is that he is one of the apostles and foundations.

[79] On reading the Revelation, a friend once asked something like "What is with all the farm animals" in the images. One is reminded of the allegory through

Notes

animals of Enoch (86-90). Human things are described in terms of animals, one or two levels lower in being, so that invisible things can be described in visible terms. Joseph Mede identifies the four as the emblems on the 4 standards of Judah (lion), Reuben (man), Ephraim (ox) and Dan (eagle), arranged around the Levites and the tabernacle in Numbers 2, as reported in oral teaching (*A Key to the Apocalypse*, p. 41; Newton, II, ii, p. 311). These are then similar to the angels of the 7 churches, the heads of groups of men. Mede's synchronisms begin the Protestant reading of the Revelation.

[80] *Lives of Saints*, ed. Joseph Vann, 473-479.

[81] *Final Mysteries Unsealed*, x, 99, 124, 151, 166: "It is only within the last centuries that God has been unsealing the mysteries of this book and Daniel's dream" (124). "Daniel was ordered to preserve the message in written form so that future generations would be able to make sense of the events when they transpired (151)."

[82] Hal Lindsey, *There's a New World Coming*, p. 21.

[83] The Witnesses, and other groups as well, assume that the 144,000 is a group of their own correct sect, the "John Class." Like the assertion that Jesus began his invisible rule in 1914 (1988, p. 19), no reason is given for these assumptions. They are taken as first principles, and not questioned, and there are clearly other possibilities. The hypothesis of the sects are where each *must* be questioned, for while they say and do many true things, they are each based on an assumption that something in scripture corresponds to something in our world, and these assumptions are notoriously difficult, various, and often mistaken. Why should we assume that the 144,000 are followers of Mr. Russell? Why assume that our group must be given authority over our minds? It is right here, we think, that Christians should sacrifice the attachment to our own things, rather than raising their own flags to salute themselves, transporting political sectarianism into the ministry. Without hypothesis taken as first principles, neither the sects nor the ancient churches could exist as they do, and the divisions within Christendom would be more like the differences between the orders following the various saints, such as Francis or Dominick.

[84] This line connects the storm in Shakespeare's *King Lear* (III, iv, 9-11) with the Apocalyptic storm.

[85] The book called 4 Esdras, appended to the Catholic Bible, is thought to have been written in part (Chapters 3-14) by a Palestinian Jew that was a contemporary of John late in the first century. Whether the writer knew or did not know the Apocalypse of John, the work is remarkable for the account and interpretation of various points regarding the end times. In addition to the appearance on Mount Zion, some of these are: the explanation of "out of the sea; "when the number of those like yourself is completed;" That it comes by necessity, as travail in labor; that very little time remains; the Messiah is presented as a lion; the sea and land beasts are compared to Leviathan and Behemoth; the mountain carved without human hands; the seventy esoteric books; the scarcity of man in the tribulation, and the testing of the elect. The accounts sometimes seem at slight variance, as in that of those who meet him

On the Revelation

on Mount Zion, though 144,000 could also appear as a vast unnumbered multitude. He takes up the question of intercession, collecting the examples, as when Abraham petitioned the Lord for Sodom (2 Esdras 7). The work does not seem to know of Jesus of Nazareth as either the false or true messiah, but looks to the second coming, as do the Jews who are not Christians. Certain points seem curiously reversed, and might support the deception that the Beast is the messiah, such as on "out of the sea," or on the drying up of the Euphrates.

[86] The R. E. M. song "It's the End of the World as You Know It" begins: "That's great, it starts with an earthquake…"

[87] Bauckham writes: "…the two prophets are modeled on Moses and Elijah (both on both, not one on each; c. f. 2 Kings 1:10-12; 1 Kings 17:1; Ex 7:14-24).

[88] Melchizedek is very mysterious. He does the sacrament of bread and wine at Jerusalem in the time of Abraham, before Jerusalem was even a city (Genesis 14:17-20). There is a very interesting argument that he might have been Shem, the son of Noah, whose dates do overlap with Abraham. He spoke, and may have introduced, the name *Most High*.

[89] It is not said that the Ark of the Covenant was brought to Babylon. This omission is a clue, since it implies that the Ark was hidden or taken somewhere for its protection. According to Jeremiah, as reported in 2 Maccabees, the Ark was sealed in a cave near the tomb of Moses, visible from the place at Mt. Nebo where Moses surveyed the Holy Land. There it is written: "The place shall be unknown until God shows his mercy. And then the Lord will disclose these things, and the glory of the Lord and the cloud will appear… (2 Mac. 2:4-8).

[90] Isaac Newton, 1704 Letter; Stephen D. Snobelen, *Statement on the Date 2060*. One ominous coincidence is that of the sixth period of 360 years from the incarnation, also 2060 if the prediction is lunar and the dating solar. Again the beginning date of 800 A.D. is based upon hypothesis. But the Seven periods might then correspond to the seven seals.

[91] *Treatise on Christ and Antichrist*, in *The Ante-Nicene Fathers*, Vol. VII, p. 213.

[92] In addition to the assumption of the literal reading of Chapters 2 and 3 of Genesis, the line thought to contradict Darwin is "each after its kind" in the creation of plants and animals in Chapter 1. So it is thought, one species cannot give rise to another. But Genesis does not describe *how* each is created according to its kind. It addresses the *formal* rather than the *efficient* cause. Darwin does not address the formal causes or the kinds, but rather assumes them, and shows that the temporal manifestations of the tree of life are changing, and emerging, rather than permanent. The Bible does not address extinction or evolution of kinds, except in the order of plants, sea creatures, birds and mammals and man, which again is amazingly in accord with Darwinian zoology. The opposition to Darwin comes to the Christians by

accident: Those conservative opposed the new theories of Darwin and Mendel, and these also happen to be the readers of the Bible. The same occurred regarding Copernicus, until the thought became undeniable. The Bible, though, does not teach the opinions dethroned in these revolutions in thought.

[93] Carl Jung writes: "In the Roman liturgy, the font is designated the 'uterus ecclesiae,' the womb of the Church" (Collected Works, Vol. 9; *The Portable Jung*, p. 63).

[94] The metaphysical foundation of Jung is a sort of subjectivism, in which it is not clear that he distinguishes between the collective unconscious and Being, or between the archetypes and the light or forms. We hold that the archetypes of the human collective unconscious are knowledge, knowledge *of* the fundamental being or beings, in an "objectivist" metaphysics. The subjectivist metaphysics is like failing to distinguish between the Bride and God, which is ironically similar to what has been done traditionally by the churches.

[95] Jack Van Impe traces the revolution in the contemporary Protestant reading to a Dr. Gaebelein, who in 1890 began to teach that a revived Roman Empire would come into play during the time of the end (*Final Mysteries Unsealed*, p. 218). Victorinus (p. 358) presents an attempt to read the seven heads as seven successive Roman Emperors, but this does not quite work. Nero is the fifth emperor, Vespasian the ninth, Domitian, Nerva and Trajan the eleventh, twelfth and thirteenth. While Scofield and Lindsey do not include this teaching of the seven heads as seven successive empires, with two prior to Daniel's Babylon, the Catholic Gibbons or Baltimore Bible of 1899 contains the teaching (p. 289).

[96] Because of this aping, or similarity of pattern, it is possible from a Jewish perspective to consider whether Jesus is not this one who will be worshiped as divine and think to change the times and the law. This has never been what is thought. The basic Jewish understanding is that Jesus is deceived because the divine does not change shape or enter into the world, nor does the son of God become flesh. It is agreed that Jesus brought the world to recognize the God of the Jews, as was foretold. Christianity is an idolatry, violating the command not to worship other gods. One is tempted to say that if it appears as an idol, by all means do not believe the idol.

[97] C. G. Jung, "After the Catastrophe," paragraph 412, Collected Works Volume 10, p. 200.

[98] Daniel 8:5. The he goat, thought to be Alexander, comes "from the west across the face of the whole earth without touching the ground." This is strange, and not like what Alexander did, but more like something that could occur now.

[99] The Japanese power plant at Fukishima required that the electricity be kept on in order to avoid a meltdown. The backup generators were ruined by the flood, after the power went out in the earthquake. One wonders how many years the electricity must continue to be held on, and how many of these we have, even on the San Adreas Fault. Finally, one wonders whether mankind is

not simply too stupid to wield these powers. We do not know that fracturing the earth will not cause an earthquake.

[100] Leo Paul; S. de Alvarez writes: Is not a fortress an attempt to fix an order? Fortresses are used by those who believe in an unchanging fundamental order to things...The modes of ordering arms to which he wholly gives himself would seem to be the true fortresses (*The Machiavellian Enterprise*, p. 108). Machiavelli does not cite this line of Daniel.

[101] The Baptists follow this concern in avoiding the ecumenical councils, which attempt to restore the unity of Christendom. Putting Humpty-Dumpty back together again seems to be the project, though as we have suggested elsewhere, the unity of the church already *is*, and is not something humans are now to establish or reestablish. That the denominations are not better neighbors is an embarrassment.

[102] *City of God*, XVIII, 41, p. 650: "...such a city has not amiss received the title of the mystic Babylon...." Yet Augustine calls the Devil its king, and as we shall argue, this is not quite true, or is an oversimplification.

[103] The projection of the shadow, or of our own baseness and sin, onto others is a Jungian thought (*Aion*, pp. 8-10, etc) that coheres with the teaching of Jesus about the log in the eye and the splinter seen in the eye of another (Matthew 7:1-5).

[104] This, then, is the background of the Bob Dylan song *All along the Watchtower*, applied as the Witnesses apply the image of the Watchtower, to a modern fall of Babylon that allows for the return.

[105] Ibid, p. 7.

[106] Elaine Pagels, *The Revelation*, p. 132. Are the modern words, *nature* and *person*, used in the original?

[107] Our Fourth Amendment forbids this practice, familiar to us from George Orwell's prophetic 1984. Despite being illegal, contrary to our fundamental law, our governments ignored the wisdom of the founders and set it in place anyway, the tech companies too having corrupted congress with their campaign contributions and our FBI believing sincerely that there ought to be no limit to their powers to enter each persons home. James Otis addressed this principle in 1774, and his opposition to the British entry into each home of the colonists to be sure they were obeying the tax laws of the English King. The problem at its root is of course that human government is not wise, and unlimited powers are quickly abused, making the reason for their introduction appear a small advantage gained by giving up the whole, which at the time did not appear, since humans generally are incapable of fundamental thought and foresight. The majority maintain a schizophrenia regarding this, both denying it exists and then saying they have nothing to hide, so that they do not mind being spied upon. Those insisting upon the Bill of Rights are called mad, then when it is demonstrated to be occurring, slandered and ignored. Anyone doing anything political is targeted and interfered with, while those who keep their nose to the earth, concerned with the animal things, are otherwise not affected.

Notes

All political action can then be countered and controlled quite conveniently, ending free elections and political liberty.

[108] Scofield (p.1063) explains, from Daniel 2: 28, "not necessarily possessing the inhabited earth, but divinely authorized to do so."

[109] Scofield lists seven mentions of desolation in Daniel, of the sanctuary, by Antiochus (8:13); in Daniel's time of exile (9:17); of the land (9:18); of the sanctuary in 70 A.D.; and of the sanctuary by the Beast, (9:27, 11:31, and 12:11). The last three are due to the abomination.

[110] One is reminded of the question from *A Fiddler on the Roof*: "Could you not choose someone else, sometimes?" Similarly, Scripture is not only flattering to Israel, as a civil religion might be.

[111] Bloom, Alan. *Plato's Republic*. Interpretive Essay, p. 407.

[112] In the *Declaration*, Jefferson assumes that the attacking of noncombatants in war is barbarism. But for the Romans, the slaughter of whole villages was sometimes done according to the advantage of war. To the Greeks, the Romans are barbarous.

[113] Increase Mather wrote a book that helped to end the Salem witch hunt. In it he argued that the "very operation of hunting for witches might be the work of the Devil" (Paul Johnson, *A History of the American People*, p. 82-83). One sees in this a concrete example of the argument that the diabolical, while lacking the imagined mythic and temporal existence, might *become* real through the humans who somehow fall into it or become as if possessed by it, though it *is* not. The formula is: *"was, is not"* and *"is to ascend* from the bottomless pit and go to perdition" (17:8). The harm is real, done by the humans, as for example in the killings of their own people when there was not even a civil war, in Germany and Russia, in the tyrannies of the twentieth century. The numbers for the Nazi killing of Jews in about four years is over six million, and over seventy years the communist tyrannies combined killed over one hundred million.

[114] There is no indication that Jesus has any regard for animals, though St. Francis seems to begin this movement. Jesus mentions the birds of the air, and their life without toil, but is not squeamish at fishing, as we are. The Jews do not practice sport hunting, but would do animal sacrifice, which we find abhorrent and unnecessary. In a prophecy of the Kingdom, where "they shall not hurt or destroy," Isaiah 66:3 reads "Him who slaughters an ox will be like him who kills a man..." In a prophecy of the marriage of the Lord and Israel, Hosea foresees: "And I will make for you a covenant on that day with the beasts of the field, the birds of the air, and the creeping things of the ground; And I will abolish the sword of war from the land" (2:18). The kindness of man toward animals seems to us to be an outward manifestation of the harmony within, and cruelty, of faction and inner division. The harmony of man and animals, or our more providential dominion, may be a hint of the millennium. How do we hope the Lord will be merciful to us, when we do not have mercy on a dog? In the first chapter of Genesis, the animals are not given to man for food, but rather, the plants are given to man and the animals.

On the Revelation

[115] We have come to call this a "waste of Jesus," when preachers use the ministry to uphold every convention of morality, and by this miss the life and the opportunity. An example is the attempt to make the scriptures teach temperance or complete abstinence from alcohol. The life animates even common morality, but not by being confused with it.

[116] Leo Strauss, "Jerusalem or Athens?" In *Studies in Platonic Political Philosophy*, p. 152.

[117] The *Book of Enoch*, called 1 Enoch, is amazing in a number of ways. It is pre-Christian, and John and Jesus seem to have read it along with the prophets. A fragment was found among the Essenes at Qumran by the Dead Sea. In addition to the teaching of the revelation and the judgment, one is surprised to find many teachings familiar from the gospels, such as that the meek shall inherit the earth, the forgiveness of sins (*Enoch* 5), and the things regarding the Messiah and the new heaven and new earth (*Enoch* 45-47, 50-51). "He shall be the light of the Gentiles" (48) is another, though this is also found in the prophets.

[118] Islam does not realize its natural antipathy to atheistic communism and fascism, being like Christendom preoccupied with fraternal quarrels, as with the Jews and Christians. This is necessary because Islam does not understand the development of thought which has occurred in the history of the West. One wonders whether the one who brought the God of Abraham to the Arabs, Persians and others might not also bring the work of a careful, thoughtful reading of the Old and New Testaments, said to be taken as scripture along with the Koran.

[119] A partial solution to the problem of Israel would be to settle single plots for those who agree to allow Israel to exist– even linking them one by one, into a Palestinian state. This could be governed provisionally as a protectorate of the United Nations until the state attained maturity, so the people there are not policed by Israel. The division might be healed in one to three generations. The other part of the solution would be for the Palestinians to adopt the principles of non-violent opposition, following King and Gandhi. Israel is at war with those who vow to destroy her and act upon it, and there is little that can be done about this, except to beat them at war. We cannot always choose when we will go to war.

[120] Jack Van Impe cites Rabbi Akiva, Eleazar and Jacob and many other Jewish and Christian readers prior to Augustine.

[121] Easter Island is an example of what occurs to human civilization without foresight. Stuck on an island, this people seems to have consumed all the trees and flightless birds, rather than husbanding resources and discovering stewardship. Unless the last people sailed away, they seem to have died off in a civil war amid the building of the statues that mark their island for the ships at sea.

[122] 2 Esdras; *Epistula Apostolorum*.

[123] *Final Mysteries Unsealed*, p. 168.

Notes

[124] This is the section of the *Didache* supposedly added by an editor to his mid second century conflation of two earlier sources (*The Early Christian Fathers*, p. 165). The *Didache*, assumed to be Syrian and Alexandrian, does not refer to any writings at all of John. This would be either because John had not yet written, at some time in the nineties, or because there was a gulf between the eastern churches and the churches at Antioch and Alexandria.

[125] The musician James Taylor writes: "There's a song that they sing about a place in the clouds.../ You can believe it if it helps you to sleep / But singing works just fine for me."

[126] Saint Augustine, in his essay "On the Immortality of the Soul," argues wholly on the basis of the participation of the soul in knowledge.

[127] Aune, pp. 1117.

[128] Ibid, 1166.

[129] *The Narrative of Joseph*, in Roberts and Donaldson, *The Ante-Nicene Fathers*, Vol. VII, p. 468-471.

[130] The first two secrets are printed from *The Third Secret of Fatima*, Brother Michael of the Holy Trinity, pp. 48-49. The third is from the Vatican website: http://www.vatican.va/roman_curi.../rc_con_cfaith_doc_2000626_message-fatima_en.htm 06/28/2000.

www.ingramcontent.com/pod-product-compliance
Lightning Source LLC
Chambersburg PA
CBHW051534230426
43669CB00015B/2594